EZRA-NEHEMIAH

Smyth & Helwys Bible Commentary: Ezra-Nehemiah

Publication Staff

Publisher & Executive Vice President
Keith Gammons

Book Editor
Leslie Andres

Graphic Designers
Daniel Emerson
Dave Jones

Assistant Editors
Katie Brookins
Kelley F. Land

Smyth & Helwys Publishing, Inc.
6316 Peake Road
Macon, Georgia 31210-3960
1-800-747-3016

Library of Congress Cataloging-in-Publication Data

Redditt, Paul L.
Ezra-Nehemiah / by Paul L. Redditt.
pages cm. -- (The Smyth & Helwys Bible commentary ; Vol. 9B)
Includes bibliographical references.
1. Bible. Ezra--Commentaries. 2. Bible. Nehemiah--Commentaries. I. Title.
BS1355.53.R43 2014
222'.707--dc23

2014031671

SMYTH & HELWYS BIBLE COMMENTARY

EZRA-NEHEMIAH

PAUL L. REDDITT

SMYTH&HELWYS
PUBLISHING INCORPORATED • MACON GEORGIA

ADVANCE PRAISE

Truly an illuminating commentary from the mature pen of a faithful exegete, providing accurate insights into the ancient world and text of Ezra-Nehemiah along with provocative connections to and reflections on twenty-first century realities.

Mark J. Boda
Professor of Old Testament
McMaster Divinity College

Well known as one of the international pioneers in the study of post-exilic literature and especially the Book of the Twelve, Paul Redditt has contributed a commentary especially fitting for the uniqueness of the Smyth & Helwys series. Redditt goes beyond commenting on the text; he enters the text of Ezra/Nehemiah into dialogue with similarly dated texts such as Isaiah 55–66, Chronicles, Ecclesiastes, Job, the Passion Narrative, and the Book of the Twelve. He asks forcefully, what happens when "the life of faith . . . collides with a world that does not follow the rules" and a Bible that does not always identify errant positions as errant. Readers may have to "think about what they read and maybe even choose among biblical perspectives."

Trent C. Butler
Editorial Director, Retired
Holman Bible Publishers

In this commentary, Paul Redditt gives the reader a helpful guide to the oft-confusing literary and historical problems that plague the Ezra-Nehemiah texts. Writing from a critical standpoint, the author examines textual inconsistencies, theological conundrums, and historical and political issues that arise from a careful reading of the texts in order to aid the reader in understanding and appreciating these ancient writings.

Moreover, Redditt's insightful theological and ethical readings of the texts demonstrate that at times faithfulness to God may require a questioning and even rejection of some of the ideas expressed in these canonical works.

Mitchell G. Reddish
O. L. Walker Professor of Christian Studies
Stetson University

DEDICATION

In memory of

Dr. Donald L. Williams

CONTENTS

ABBREVIATIONS USED IN THIS COMMENTARY

Books of the Old Testament, Apocrypha, and New Testament are generally abbreviated in the Sidebars, parenthetical references, and notes according to the following system.

The Old Testament

Genesis	Gen
Exodus	Exod
Leviticus	Lev
Numbers	Num
Deuteronomy	Deut
Joshua	Josh
Judges	Judg
Ruth	Ruth
1–2 Samuel	1–2 Sam
1–2 Kings	1–2 Kgs
1–2 Chronicles	1–2 Chr
Ezra	Ezra
Nehemiah	Neh
Esther	Esth
Job	Job
Psalm (Psalms)	Ps (Pss)
Proverbs	Prov
Ecclesiastes	Eccl
or Qoheleth	Qoh
Song of Solomon	Song
or Song of Songs	Song
or Canticles	Cant
Isaiah	Isa
Jeremiah	Jer
Lamentations	Lam
Ezekiel	Ezek
Daniel	Dan
Hosea	Hos
Joel	Joel
Amos	Amos
Obadiah	Obad
Jonah	Jonah
Micah	Mic

Nahum	Nah
Habakkuk	Hab
Zephaniah	Zeph
Haggai	Hag
Zechariah	Zech
Malachi	Mal

The Apocrypha

1–2 Esdras	1–2 Esdr
Tobit	Tob
Judith	Jdt
Additions to Esther	Add Esth
Wisdom of Solomon	Wis
Ecclesiasticus or the Wisdom of Jesus Son of Sirach	Sir
Baruch	Bar
Epistle (or Letter) of Jeremiah	Ep Jer
Prayer of Azariah and the Song of the Three	Pr Azar
Daniel and Susanna	Sus
Daniel, Bel, and the Dragon	Bel
Prayer of Manasseh	Pr Man
1–4 Maccabees	1–4 Macc

The New Testament

Matthew	Matt
Mark	Mark
Luke	Luke
John	John
Acts	Acts
Romans	Rom
1–2 Corinthians	1–2 Cor
Galatians	Gal
Ephesians	Eph
Philippians	Phil
Colossians	Col
1–2 Thessalonians	1–2 Thess
1–2 Timothy	1–2 Tim
Titus	Titus
Philemon	Phlm
Hebrews	Heb
James	Jas
1–2 Peter	1–2 Pet
1–2–3 John	1–2–3 John
Jude	Jude
Revelation	Rev

Other commonly used abbreviations include:

AD	*Anno Domini* ("in the year of the Lord") (also commonly referred to as CE = the Common Era)
BC	Before Christ (also commonly referred to as BCE = Before the Common Era)
C.	century
c.	*circa* (around "that time")
cf.	*confer* (compare)
ch.	chapter
chs.	chapters
d.	died
ed.	edition or edited by or editor
eds.	editors
e.g.	*exempli gratia* (for example)
et al.	*et alii* (and others)
f./ff.	and the following one(s)
gen. ed.	general editor
Gk.	Greek
Heb.	Hebrew
ibid.	*ibidem* (in the same place)
i.e.	*id est* (that is)
LCL	Loeb Classical Library
lit.	literally
n.d.	no date
r.	reigned
rev. and exp. ed.	revised and expanded edition
sg.	singular
trans.	translated by or translator(s)
vol(s).	volume(s)
v.	verse
vv.	verses

Selected additional written works cited by abbreviations include the following. A complete listing of abbreviations can be referenced in *The SBL Handbook of Style* (Peabody MA: Hendrickson, 1999):

AB	Anchor Bible
ABD	*Anchor Bible Dictionary*
ACCS	Ancient Christian Commentary on Scripture
ANF	*Ante-Nicene Fathers*
ANTC	Abingdon New Testament Commentaries
BA	*Biblical Archaeologist*
BAR	*Biblical Archaeology Review*
CBQ	*Catholic Biblical Quarterly*

HTR	*Harvard Theological Review*
HUCA	*Hebrew Union College Annual*
ICC	International Critical Commentary
IDB	*Interpreters Dictionary of the Bible*
JBL	*Journal of Biblical Literature*
JSJ	*Journal for the Study of Judaism in the Persian, Hellenistic, and Roman Periods*
JSNT	*Journal for the Study of the New Testament*
JSOT	*Journal for the Study of the Old Testament*
KJV	King James Version
LXX	Septuagint = Greek Translation of Hebrew Bible
MDB	*Mercer Dictionary of the Bible*
MT	Masoretic Text
NASB	New American Standard Bible
NEB	New English Bible
NICNT	New International Commentary on the New Testament
NIV	New International Version
NovT	*Novum Testamentum*
NRSV	New Revised Standard Version
NTS	*New Testament Studies*
OGIS	*Orientis graeci inscriptiones selectae*
OTL	Old Testament Library
PRSt	*Perspectives in Religious Studies*
RevExp	*Review and Expositor*
RSV	Revised Standard Version
SBLSP	*Society of Biblical Literature Seminar Papers*
SP	Sacra pagina
TDNT	*Theological Dictionary of the New Testament*
TEV	Today's English Version
WBC	Word Biblical Commentary

AUTHOR'S PREFACE

The books of Ezra and Nehemiah do not immediately present themselves as devotional or sermonic reading. Indeed, a quick consultation of one set of three-year readings of the Revised Common Lectionary did not reveal one text from them for reading in worship, and a consultation of one year's daily readings, at least one of which is from the Old Testament, reveals not a single reading from Ezra-Nehemiah either. Other lectionaries or series of readings might reflect an occasional passage from one or the other, but only infrequently. At least one reason for such absence is the vindictive nature of some of the discourse; a second is the focus on buildings and rituals; and a third is the preponderance of lists. The most conspicuous of those lists is the so-called "List of Returnees" that appears in whole in Ezra 2 // Nehemiah 7, and in part in Nehemiah 12.

Those lists are lengthy and repetitive, and, furthermore, scholars who research such matters often insist that they presuppose a Jerusalem from a time far later than Ezra and Nehemiah, who lived in the fifth century BCE. Those scholars date the lists in the second century BCE. My own study of these lists and scholarly discussion thereof led me first to the conclusion that they belong to the latest strata of Ezra-Nehemiah. Indeed, part of this commentary was written under the conviction that the book(s) arose in toto during the fifth or fourth century, in any case prior to the end of the Persian Period in 331 BCE. The lists themselves, with the large totals of priests and Levites and emphasis on them, drove me to revise that view in favor of the scholarly position that the lists date from the second century BCE. Thus the books as we have them discuss events between 539 BCE and the end of the career of Nehemiah in roughly 445/4–433/2, but the writing of the books themselves stretched down to the Maccabean Period, i.e., the mid-second century BCE.

Obviously I do not hold to the traditional confessional view that the books of the Bible were all written by the persons whose names they bear, but that view, ancient as it may be, is not scriptural and should not be allowed to dictate how one reads the Bible. Genesis says what Genesis says regardless of who wrote it, and the Gospels say what they say regardless of the accuracy of the later traditions about their authorship. As they stand in the New Testament, all four are anonymous. Tradition supplies their names. Even the attribution of sayings or a whole work of the Bible to a great man (e.g., Moses or

John) does not prove he wrote it, and admitting as much today does not turn ancient writings, ancient sayings, or even biblical books into "frauds." In writing this commentary I also came to see as clearly, if not more clearly than I ever have before, that sometimes readers need to put biblical texts in dialogue with one another and to dialogue with those texts personally as well. The biblical writers often searched for God in a world that did not seem to be behaving as it should (see, for example, the books of Job and the accounts of the crucifixion of Jesus), and their solutions sometimes were not complete and satisfactory (see particularly the book of Ecclesiastes). The life of faith often collides with a world that does not follow the rules and a Bible that does not always identify errant positions as errant! Readers may well have to think about what they read and maybe even choose among biblical perspectives.

I would style this commentary, therefore, both a scholarly and a Christian commentary on Ezra-Nehemiah. What makes it a scholarly commentary is that I apply the methods of biblical scholarship to Ezra-Nehemiah. What makes it a Christian reading of the text is not that I find Jesus hidden in either Ezra or Nehemiah, whether by prediction, allusion, or "type," and not that I think Ezra and Nehemiah were "Christians before Christ," but that I measure the theology of the books and their heroes by the Christian gospel that God loved (and loves) all the people of the world, not just those who returned to Jerusalem from the exile with Ezra and Nehemiah, not just Jews, and—for that matter—not just Christians either. I find that theology already articulated in the message of Isaiah 56:3-7, who wrote so beautifully the following words.

> Do not let the foreigner joined to the LORD say,
> "The LORD will surely separate me from his people,"
> and do not let the eunuch say, "I am just a dry tree."
> For thus says the LORD:
> "To the eunuchs who keep my Sabbaths,
> who choose the things that please me and hold fast my covenant,
> I will give, in my house and within my walls,
> a monument and a name better than sons and daughters;
> I will give them an everlasting name that shall not be cut off.
> And to the foreigners who join themselves to the LORD,
> to minister to him, to love the name of the LORD, and to be his servants,
> all who keep the Sabbath, and do not profane it, and hold fast my covenant—
> these I will bring to my holy mountain, and make them joyful in my house of prayer;

their burnt offerings and their sacrifices will be acceptable on my
altar;
for my house shall be called a house of prayer for all peoples."
(NRSV)

When Ezra and Nehemiah do not measure up, I say so not
angrily but sadly and wistfully. I too do not measure up.
Whomever God loves and saves thereby is saved by God's grace,
and God does not need my permission to save anyone, though
God does call on me to spread the gospel of God's love.

Much of my previous academic publishing has dealt with
prophetic books in general and with Isaiah 24–27, Daniel, Joel,
Haggai, Zechariah, and Malachi in particular. All six are
exilic/post-exilic works that belong to the time frame of Ezra and
Nehemiah and later. A move from those works to Ezra and
Nehemiah, therefore, has been almost a "no brainer." My pro-
fessor/mentor at the Southern Baptist Theological Seminary in the
mid-1960s, Dr. Donald L. Williams, told us that Old Testament
studies in the ensuing decades would focus more and more on the
post-exilic period. He was certainly correct.

My special thanks go to Dr. Greg Earwood, my former pastor at
Faith Baptist Church in Georgetown, Kentucky, and the founding
president of the Baptist Seminary of Kentucky, for reading the
Hebrew text of Ezra-Nehemiah with me. Also I thank my colleagues in the data center at Georgetown College, Georgetown,
Kentucky, and the members of the library staff at Georgetown and
at Asbury Theological Seminary in Wilmore, Kentucky, for their
kind assistance. Further, I wish to thank the editorial board of the
Smyth & Helwys Commentary series for inviting me to join
that board and to write this commentary, and I especially want to
thank Old Testament general editor Sam Balentine and area editor
Mark E. Biddle for their work on it, and the editors and staff at
Smyth & Helwys, especially editor Leslie Andres. Finally, I am
grateful for the support and the assistance of my wife, who tolerates
lovingly my exclamations and ramblings over tedious points.

—*Paul L. Redditt*
Georgetown, Kentucky
October 2014

SERIES PREFACE

The *Smyth & Helwys Bible Commentary* is a visually stimulating and user-friendly series that is as close to multimedia in print as possible. Written by accomplished scholars with all students of Scripture in mind, the primary goal of the *Smyth & Helwys Bible Commentary* is to make available serious, credible biblical scholarship in an accessible and less intimidating format.

Far too many Bible commentaries fall short of bridging the gap between the insights of biblical scholars and the needs of students of God's written word. In an unprecedented way, the *Smyth & Helwys Bible Commentary* brings insightful commentary to bear on the lives of contemporary Christians. Using a multimedia format, the volumes employ a stunning array of art, photographs, maps, and drawings to illustrate the truths of the Bible for a visual generation of believers.

The *Smyth & Helwys Bible Commentary* is built upon the idea that meaningful Bible study can occur when the insights of contemporary biblical scholars blend with sensitivity to the needs of lifelong students of Scripture. Some persons within local faith communities, however, struggle with potentially informative biblical scholarship for several reasons. Oftentimes, such scholarship is cast in technical language easily grasped by other scholars, but not by the general reader. For example, lengthy, technical discussions on every detail of a particular scriptural text can hinder the quest for a clear grasp of the whole. Also, the format for presenting scholarly insights has often been confusing to the general reader, rendering the work less than helpful. Unfortunately, responses to the hurdles of reading extensive commentaries have led some publishers to produce works for a general readership that merely skim the surface of the rich resources of biblical scholarship. This commentary series incorporates works of fine art in an accurate and scholarly manner, yet the format remains "user-friendly." An important facet is the presentation and explanation of images of art, which interpret the biblical material or illustrate how the biblical material has been understood and interpreted in the past. A visual generation of believers deserves a commentary series that contains not only the all-important textual commentary on Scripture, but images, photographs, maps, works of fine art, and drawings that bring the text to life.

The *Smyth & Helwys Bible Commentary* makes serious, credible biblical scholarship more accessible to a wider audience. Writers and editors alike present information in ways that encourage readers to gain a better understanding of the Bible. The editorial board has worked to develop a format that is useful and usable, informative and pleasing to the eye. Our writers are reputable scholars who participate in the community of faith and sense a calling to communicate the results of their scholarship to their faith community.

The *Smyth & Helwys Bible Commentary* addresses Christians and the larger church. While both respect for and sensitivity to the needs and contributions of other faith communities are reflected in the work of the series authors, the authors speak primarily to Christians. Thus the reader can note a confessional tone throughout the volumes. No particular "confession of faith" guides the authors, and diverse perspectives are observed in the various volumes. Each writer, though, brings to the biblical text the best scholarly tools available and expresses the results of their studies in commentary and visuals that assist readers seeking a word from the Lord for the church.

To accomplish this goal, writers in this series have drawn from numerous streams in the rich tradition of biblical interpretation. The basic focus is the biblical text itself, and considerable attention is given to the wording and structure of texts. Each particular text, however, is also considered in the light of the entire canon of Christian Scriptures. Beyond this, attention is given to the cultural context of the biblical writings. Information from archaeology, ancient history, geography, comparative literature, history of religions, politics, sociology, and even economics is used to illuminate the culture of the people who produced the Bible. In addition, the writers have drawn from the history of interpretation, not only as it is found in traditional commentary on the Bible but also in literature, theater, church history, and the visual arts. Finally, the *Commentary* on Scripture is joined with *Connections* to the world of the contemporary church. Here again, the writers draw on scholarship in many fields as well as relevant issues in the popular culture.

This wealth of information might easily overwhelm a reader if not presented in a "user-friendly" format. Thus the heavier discussions of detail and the treatments of other helpful topics are presented in special-interest boxes, or Sidebars, clearly connected to the passages under discussion so as not to interrupt the flow of the basic interpretation. The result is a commentary on Scripture that focuses on the theological significance of a text while also offering the reader a rich array of additional information related to the text and its interpretation.

Combining credible biblical scholarship, user-friendly study features, and sensitivity to the needs of a visually oriented generation of believers creates a unique and unprecedented type of commentary series. With insight from many of today's finest biblical scholars and a stunning visual format, it is our hope that the *Smyth & Helwys Bible Commentary* will be a welcome addition to the personal libraries of all students of Scripture.

The Editors

HOW TO USE
THIS COMMENTARY

The *Smyth & Helwys Bible Commentary* is written by accomplished biblical scholars with a wide array of readers in mind. Whether engaged in the study of Scripture in a church setting or in a college or seminary classroom, all students of the Bible will find a number of useful features throughout the commentary that are helpful for interpreting the Bible.

Basic Design of the Volumes

Each volume features an Introduction to a particular book of the Bible, providing a brief guide to information that is necessary for reading and interpreting the text: the historical setting, literary design, and theological significance. Each Introduction also includes a comprehensive outline of the particular book under study.

Each chapter of the commentary investigates the text according to logical divisions in a particular book of the Bible. Sometimes these divisions follow the traditional chapter segmentation, while at other times the textual units consist of sections of chapters or portions of more than one chapter. The divisions reflect the literary structure of a book and offer a guide for selecting passages that are useful in preaching and teaching.

Commentary and Connections

As each chapter explores a textual unit, the discussion centers around two basic sections: *Commentary* and *Connections*. The analysis of a passage, including the details of its language, the history reflected in the text, and the literary forms found in the text, are the main focus of the *Commentary* section. The primary concern of the *Commentary* section is to explore the theological issues presented by the Scripture passage. *Connections* presents potential applications of the insights provided in the *Commentary* section. The *Connections* portion of each chapter considers what issues are relevant for teaching and suggests useful methods and resources. *Connections* also identifies themes suitable for sermon planning and suggests helpful approaches for preaching on the Scripture text.

Sidebars

The *Smyth & Helwys Bible Commentary* provides a unique hyperlink format that quickly guides the reader to additional insights. Since other more technical or supplementary information is vital for understanding a text and its implications, the volumes feature distinctive Sidebars, or special-interest boxes, that provide a wealth of information on such matters as:

• Historical information (such as chronological charts, lists of kings or rulers, maps, descriptions of monetary systems, descriptions of special groups, descriptions of archaeological sites or geographical settings).

• Graphic outlines of literary structure (including such items as poetry, chiasm, repetition, epistolary form).

• Definition or brief discussions of technical or theological terms and issues.

• Insightful quotations that are not integrated into the running text but are relevant to the passage under discussion.

• Notes on the history of interpretation (Augustine on the Good Samaritan, Luther on James, Stendahl on Romans, etc.).

• Line drawings, photographs, and other illustrations relevant for understanding the historical context or interpretive significance of the text.

• Presentation and discussion of works of fine art that have interpreted a Scripture passage.

Each Sidebar is referenced at the appropriate place in the *Commentary* or *Connections* section with a coded title that directs the reader to the relevant Sidebar. In addition, helpful icons appear in the Sidebars, which provide the reader with visual cues to the type of material that is explained in each Sidebar. Throughout the commentary, these four distinct hyperlinks provide useful links in an easily recognizable design.

Alpha & Omega Language

This icon identifies the information as a language-based tool that offers further exploration of the Scripture selection. This could include syntactical information, word studies, popular or additional uses of the word(s) in question, additional contexts in which the term appears, and the history of the term's translation. All non-English terms are transliterated into the appropriate English characters.

Culture/Context

This icon introduces further comment on contextual or cultural details that shed light on the Scripture selection. Describing the place and time to which a Scripture passage refers is often vital to the task of biblical interpretation. Sidebar items introduced with this icon could include geographical, historical, political, social, topographical, or economic information. Here, the reader may find an excerpt of an ancient text or inscription that sheds light on the text. Or one may find a description of some element of ancient religion such as Baalism in Canaan or the Hero cult in the Mystery Religions of the Greco-Roman world.

Interpretation

Sidebars that appear under this icon serve a general interpretive function in terms of both historical and contemporary renderings. Under this heading, the reader might find a selection from classic or contemporary literature that illuminates the Scripture text or a significant quotation from a famous sermon that addresses the passage. Insights are drawn from various sources, including literature, worship, theater, church history, and sociology.

Additional Resources Study

Here, the reader finds a convenient list of useful resources for further investigation of the selected Scripture text, including books, journals, websites, special collections, organizations, and societies. Specialized discussions of works not often associated with biblical studies may also appear here.

Additional Features

Each volume also includes a basic Bibliography on the biblical book under study. Other bibliographies on selected issues are often included that point the reader to other helpful resources.

Notes at the end of each chapter provide full documentation of sources used and contain additional discussions of related matters.

Abbreviations used in each volume are explained in a list of abbreviations found after the Table of Contents.

Readers of the *Smyth & Helwys Bible Commentary* can regularly visit the Internet support site for news, information, updates, and enhancements to the series at **www.helwys.com/commentary**.

Several thorough indexes enable the reader to locate information quickly. These indexes include:

• An *Index of Sidebars* groups content from the special-interest boxes by category (maps, fine art, photographs, drawings, etc.).

• An *Index of Scriptures* lists citations to particular biblical texts.

• An *Index of Topics* lists alphabetically the major subjects, names, topics, and locations referenced or discussed in the volume.

• An *Index of Modern Authors* organizes contemporary authors whose works are cited in the volume.

INTRODUCTION TO
EZRA-NEHEMIAH

Tragedy struck the small kingdom of Judah in the opening years of the sixth century BCE, when the Babylonian Empire under Nebuchadnezzar attacked it several times. The first attack (c. 600) came in response to Judah's withholding tribute, after which Nebuchadnezzar incited Judah's neighbors to raid the land. During one of those raids, King Jehoiakim died (in late 598), and Jehoiachin, his eighteen-year-old son, succeeded him. Shortly thereafter, Nebuchadnezzar himself invaded Judah, forcing Jehoiachin from the throne after only three months as king in 597, and took him and numerous other Judeans (nobles and persons with usable skills) to Babylon as captives. [Captives/Exiles] He installed Zedekiah, Jehoiachin's uncle, as his new puppet ruler. Unfortunately for Judah, Zedekiah allied himself with Egypt when Pharaoh Apries (called Hophra in Jer 44:30) planned an armed invasion of Mesopotamia (588). Nebuchadnezzar responded at once by invading Judah and besieging Jerusalem. Simply stated, the destruction of Jerusalem by Babylon was an incidence of raw imperial power leveled against the tiny state of Judah and its religious institutions.

Here is what may have happened. The Babylonian army probably lived off local farmers/shepherds during the siege. When Babylonian

---

Captives/Exiles

The old question "What's in a name?" is important in Ezra-Nehemiah. Technically, people carried from their homeland to another place are "captives." They live in captivity. "Exiles" are people "from" somewhere specific. P. R. Davies notes that the word "exiles" in the context of post-exilic Yehud (that is, the post-exilic area around Jerusalem that formed the Persian province) is already an interpretation of the events of the sixth century BCE with respect to the Judeans taken captive to Babylon. It already interprets the "exiles" as belonging to a piece of land from which they have been uprooted. Ezra 1:11, thus, stakes the claim for the biblical book Ezra-Nehemiah that the Judeans taken into captivity in Babylon actually "belong" in Yehud. Hence, when some of them "return" under Persian authority a generation

or two later, they return with an agenda to rebuild supported by a claim. The claim is that they, the returnees, are the rightful "Judah," the descendants of people forced from their land and forced to remain outside it; anyone else living there has no legitimate claim to the land. While there is some justification in making such a claim (they had been removed and were returning "home"), those not exiled also had a claim to the land (as Judeans still in the land), and Samaria seems to have been functioning in some sense as its capital. If readers of the Bible kept these distinctions in mind, they would read the objections of those Judeans and of Samaritan officials with more understanding and perhaps even more sympathy.

P. R. Davies. "Exile? What Exile? Whose Exile?" *Leading Captivity Captive: "The Exile" as History and Ideology* (ed. L. L. Grabe; JSOTSup 278; Sheffield: Sheffield Academic Press, 2011) 128–38; esp. 133–34.

soldiers breeched the wall by means of battering rams, scaling devices, and other instruments of war, Babylonian soldiers poured into the city. The weakened Judean army inside probably quickly lost the will to fight and melted into the general population of the city. The temple mount and the king's palace were looted and burned. Throughout the city, any gold, jewels, or other such valuables were taken as well, and some buildings were set on fire. The king and the most important persons were taken to Babylon. The numbers of exiles given in Jeremiah 52:28-30 (namely 3,023 in 597, 822 in 586, and 745 after the death of Gedaliah) look like actual counts, as opposed to the figure 10,000 that 2 Kings 24:16 says were carried away in 597. One suspects that even Jeremiah's numbers may have included people either killed or who simply disappeared.

L. L. Grabbe has recently suggested, however, that not all members of the upper classes in Jerusalem and Judah were carried into exile, and cites the Tobiad family mentioned in Nehemiah 2 and 6. Grabbe certainly seems to be correct about them, although the Bible takes no note of them. Readers will please note that past sentence. Such people will become important in Ezra-Nehemiah. Of the 10,000 2 Kings 24:14 says Nebuchadnezzar carried away in 597, v. 16 says he took 8,000 to Babylon, implying perhaps that the other 2,000 were left elsewhere. Then 2 Kings 25:11 says that Nebuchadnezzar carried away into exile "the rest of the people who were left in the city and deserters who had defected to the king" in 586, so the city was emptied of its populace.

Jeremiah 52:29, however, gives lower numbers. It says 3,032 were exiled in 597, 832 in 586, and 745 more went in 582. Given their precision, those numbers may constitute the actual count of exiles taken to Babylon. Second Chronicles 36 says simply that Nebuchadnezzar exiled all those who had not died in the siege, but does not say he took them all to Babylon. In any case, the elimination of those people would have left Jerusalem and Judah with a scarcity of experienced leadership and little possibility of fomenting additional rebellion. Some people from surrounding areas probably moved into the city and its environs. The city perhaps even came under the jurisdiction of Samaria.

The fall of Babylon to Persia in 539, however, awakened the possibility of a new day, and the rocky relationship between Jerusalem and Samaria is part of the tension in Ezra and Nehemiah. The city's inhabitants mourned their loss (see the book of Lamentations), and the deportees grieved their relocation to Babylon and even seethed in anger at their treatment there (see Ps 137). When King Cyrus revolted against his Median rulers (553–550) and eventually conquered the Babylonians as well (539), he made it possible for Judeans to return to their homeland *if they wished*. Jeremiah 51:24-58 even celebrates that event. That chapter appears to have grown over time from a prediction of the fall of Babylon into a celebration of its fall at the hands of Cyrus. (For the prediction/discussion of the Mede Cyrus's capture of the city itself, see Jer 51:28-32.) The book of Ezra opens on the happy note of the grace of Cyrus toward Jerusalem.

The books of Ezra and Nehemiah, along with Haggai, Zechariah, and Malachi, are the only books in the OT that deal *overtly* with the community in Palestine after the period of the captivity (587–539).[1] Further, only Ezra and Nehemiah actually narrate events from that period, describing as they do the return of several groups from Babylon, the rebuilding of the temple and walls of Jerusalem, and relating episodes from the careers of the two men after whom the books are named. To be sure, Haggai and Zechariah 1–8 presuppose the actions of the Davidic prince Zerubbabel and the high priest Jeshua, and Malachi seems to address the issue of mixed marriages dealt with by Ezra and Nehemiah, but the prophetic books do not actually narrate any events surrounding those issues. Hence, Ezra and Nehemiah alone carry into the Persian Period the *narrative* of Israel's life, whose earlier years were surveyed in the Pentateuch, Joshua through 2 Kings, and eventually 1 and 2 Chronicles.

The two books form one book in the Hebrew Bible, and there is good reason to see them as one. Ezra-Nehemiah discusses three pivotal periods in the history of post-exilic Yehud. (This commentary will use the name Yehud for the post-exilic area around Jerusalem that formed the Persian province because its boundaries are not the same as those of pre-exilic Judah. Yehud included only the northern half or so of old Judah and also parts of old Benjamin.) Those periods were (1) the return of exiles in 538 (see Ezra 1–6), (2) the career of the priest Ezra in 458 (a date sometimes debated by scholars) together with its concomitant reassertion of the perquisites of the returnees from the Babylonian Empire (see Ezra 7–10 + Neh 7:73b–8:18), and the work of Nehemiah (see Neh 1:1–7:73a + 9–13) in building the wall to enclose the "holy" city of Jerusalem (see Neh 11:1, 18). The repeated use of similar lists and the placement of the last Ezra narrative within the narrative about Nehemiah accomplish that agenda. That last comment is meant not to deny that the men were contemporaries but to underscore that the narratives about them were secondarily intertwined.

A. The Scope and Subject Matter of Ezra-Nehemiah

The MT treats Ezra and Nehemiah as one book, and the Masoretic scribes who copied it in the tenth century CE gave a verse total only at the end of Nehemiah and marked Nehemiah 3:32 as its midpoint. Indeed, the division into two books can be traced no further back than the second/third-century Christian theologian Origen, and in Hebrew Bibles only to 1488.[2] In addition, the appearance of the same list of returnees in Ezra 2 and Nehemiah 7 plus the existence of an account of work by Ezra in Nehemiah 7:73b–8:18 indicate deliberate redactional (i.e., editorial) shaping of Ezra-Nehemiah as a single volume. Hence, it is appropriate to treat both in one commentary as one edited volume.

The narrative opens in Babylon, among the Judeans taken there by Nebuchadnezzar in 597, 586, and 581 (see 2 Kgs 24:1-16 and 25:1-21; Jer 52:30). The Persian Empire under Cyrus defeated the Babylonian Empire in 539. [Kings of the Persian Empire] His successors Cambyses and Darius I pushed the reach of the Persian Empire east to the Indus River in modern-day Pakistan, south into Egypt and Lydia, and west to the Hellespont, but could not capture Greece itself. Cyrus issued an edict that year allowing the captives—for the most part people born in Babylon—to return to Yehud to rebuild the temple in Jerusalem (Ezra 1:1-4; see the shorter version in 2 Chr 36:22-23), an offer accepted by some of them, the first group apparently under a man named Sheshbazzar, and another

---

Kings of the Persian Empire

Name of King	Dates Reigned	Importance
Cyrus	549–529	Established Persian Empire; allowed captives to return to their homelands
Cambyses	529–522	Extended empire into Egypt; struggle for the crown upon his death
Darius	521–486	Reorganized empire into 20 satrapies; built roads to improve travel and communications; Jerusalem temple completed during his reign
Xerxes (biblical Ahasuerus)	486–465	Cruel to Egypt and Babylon; defeated by Greece; retained Asia Minor
Artaxerxes I Longimanus	465–424	Ruler (probably) when Ezra and Nehemiah returned to Palestine
Darius II Nothos	423–404	Reign illuminated in Egypt by the Elephantine Papyri; Bagoas was governor of Yehud
Artaxerxes II Mnemon	404–358	Egypt regained freedom (401); rebellions in Persia
Artaxerxes III Ochos	358–338	Reasserted Persian control into Egypt; poisoned to death
Arses	338–336	Poisoned as his father had been
Darius III Codomanus	336–331	Last Persian king; defeated by Alexander the Great

This chart reflects an initial burst of power and victory under Cyrus, organization and expansion under Darius, periods of altercation with Greece through the reign of Artaxerxes III Ochos, then chaos at home and eventual defeat by Alexander.

Based on data from John Bright, *A History of Israel* (3rd ed.; Philadelphia: Westminster, 1959) 472–73; and R. E. Hayden, "Persia," ISBE, 3.776–80.

The Extent of the Persian Empire

A Persian king overlooks a defeated city by the sea.

William Spencer Bagdatopoulos (1888–1965). *Greco-Persian Wars (499–449 BC), Battle of Salamis (480 BC)*. Signed W. S. Bylityilis. (Credit: Album/Art Resource, NY)

under Zerubbabel (a Davidic prince) and Jeshua (the high priest), probably in 521. [The Edict of Cyrus] (Readers should note that Hag 1:2, 14 and 2:21 call Zerubbabel the "governor of Judah"; the book of Ezra ascribes him no governing title or role.) The next year the prophets Haggai and Zechariah urged the people of Yehud to complete the rebuilding of the temple, which they did, finishing in 516.

The text of Ezra then skips forward to the actions of its namesake, the priest Ezra, who came to Jerusalem in the seventh year of King Artaxerxes I to establish the law. [Artaxerxes I or II?] The book of

The Edict of Cyrus

On this cylinder, Cyrus recounts his capture of Babylon and says of the peoples of the Babylonian Empire that he had resettled them and their gods in their former territories. While the edict says nothing about Yehud, its sentiments resemble the words ascribed to Cyrus in Ezra 1:2-4 and Ezra 6:3-12. In the biblical text, Cyrus mentions giving the survivors vessels of silver and gold to take with them. Michael D. Coogan sees in that claim an allusion to Exod 12:35-36, which says that the Egyptians gave the Israelites silver and gold jewelry and clothing to take with them on their trip to Canaan.

M. D. Coogan, *The Old Testament; A Historical and Literary Introduction to the Hebrew Scriptures* (2d ed.; New York, Oxford: Oxford University Press, 2011) 401–402.

James B. Pritchard, *The Ancient Near East* (Princeton and Oxford: Oxford University Press, 2011) 282–84.

The Edict of Cyrus mentioned in Ezra 1:2-4 is dated to the first year after Cyrus captured Babylon in 539. It is similar to an edict issued by Cyrus that was found inscribed on a clay cylinder. The cylinder measured about nine inches in length and circumference. It was designed to print copies of Cyrus's proclamation.

Front of the Cyrus Cylinder. c. 539–538 BC. Baked clay. Discovered in Mesopotamia in 1879. British Museum, London, England. (Credit: Prioryman, Wikimedia Commons, CC-by-SA-3.0)

Nehemiah also recounts the coming of its namesake, a cupbearer of Artaxerxes, to rebuild the walls of Jerusalem. He succeeded despite opposition from (presumably Persia-oriented) officials in Samaria. The book of Nehemiah also contains an account of Ezra's reading "the book of the Law of Moses" to the people of Yehud gathered in Jerusalem (Neh 7:73b–9:37), as well as notes about repopulating Jerusalem and Nehemiah's confrontations with various members of Jerusalem and Samaria. Thus two movements that reinforced one another during those years are crucial to the narratives in Ezra-Nehemiah: building the temple and its surrounding area and shaping the canon. Moreover, the narrated activities of those two, later namesake heroes "parallel the earlier work of Jeshua and

Zerubbabel, and in doing so . . . balance the work structurally, and give full expression to the author's conception of the ideal community of God as a union of the sacred and secular life of the people in a . . . theocracy established by God through the agency of the Persian kings."[3]

Together Ezra and Nehemiah, therefore, relate a carefully redacted narrative of the return of the "true "Israel" from Babylon to Jerusalem. Five lists anchor this case. (1) Ezra 2:1-70a shows a huge party of returnees coming to reclaim their land and to rebuild the temple acting on the direct command of King Cyrus (Ezra 1:1–6:22). (2) Ezra 7–8 details the journey of a second group of returnees under the priest Ezra acting on the direct command of King Artaxerxes (I), and the list of returnees in Ezra 8:1-14 ties Ezra 7–8 to the original group of returnees. (3) Ezra 9–10 shows the necessity of purging members of the original company of returnees who had removed themselves from the "true"

Artaxerxes I or II?

Ezra 7:1 and Neh 2:1 say that a king named "Artaxerxes" granted permission for Ezra and Nehemiah respectively to carry out missions in Yehud. The question is, however, which Artaxerxes granted permission? Artaxerxes I Longimanus ruled Persia from 465–424 BCE. He was succeeded by Xerxes II (423), Darius II (423–404), and then Artaxerxes II Mnemon (404–358). Artaxerxes III Ochus ruled from 358–338, but he ruled much too late to be the king in question in Ezra-Nehemiah. Traditionally, readers of the Bible have assumed that Artaxerxes I was the king during whose reign both Ezra and Nehemiah served. If, however, Ezra served under Artaxerxes II (404–359), his career would have followed Nehemiah's, a thesis advocated especially by the German scholar Albin Van Hoonaker between 1890 and 1924. Some scholars (e.g., Geo Widegren) think that sequence would solve certain issues in the text, but it would create a serious issue with the chronology of Ezra-Nehemiah. Even more firm in his rejection of this hypothesis, Carl G. Tuland raises eleven objections, concluding that the "theory of reversing the Ezra-Nehemiah sequence has been repudiated and should be eliminated." While certainty is not possible, this commentary will work with the traditional and majority view that both men served under Antiochus I.

Carl G. Tuland, "Ezra-Nehemiah or Nehemiah-Ezra?" *AUSS* 12 (1974): 47–62.

Geo Widengren, "IX The Persian Period," pp. 489–538 in *Israelite and Judean History* (ed. John H. Hayes and J. Maxwell Miller; Philadelphia: Westminster, 1977) here pp. 506–509.

---

community by marrying local Judean women. Ezra 10:18-44 anchors that narrative. (4) Nehemiah 7:5-73a, which employs (apart from transmission errors) the same list as Ezra 2:1-70a, shows the continued viability of that community, guaranteed now by the reconstruction of the wall around the city. Finally, Nehemiah 12:1-26 repeats some names from that list and describes one final purging of the community by Nehemiah, assuring readers that those in charge in Jerusalem were all persons or descendants of persons who had returned from Babylon to Judah.

Ezra-Nehemiah also provides insight into the history of the rise of the Hebrew canon. Ezra 1:1-2 knows and quotes the end of the book of 2 Chronicles. It mentions the prophet Jeremiah, although it does not quote him. Ezra 5:1-2 knows of and mentions the prophets Haggai and Zechariah, although again it does not quote them. The denunciation of mixed marriages in Ezra 9 draws on the list of traditional enemies of Israel known from Deuteronomy 7:1-4. The use in that same chapter of "sayings of Moses" from Deuteronomy (e.g. Deut 7:1 and 18:9, but also Lev 18:24-30), plus calling him a "prophet" (see Deut 18:15 and 34:10), provides further evidence of the knowledge of the Pentateuch as a whole and the acceptance of some prophets alongside it. The prayer reciting the "history of salvation" in Nehemiah 9:7-31 shows not just awareness of but also acceptance of the sweep of the narrative of the Pentateuch, Joshua, Judges, and several prophets. The failure to mention the kings probably owes less to not knowing Samuel-Kings than to a desire to avoid the issue of Israel's past monarchy since the returnees lived under the Persians. While there is no evidence that the author used the books of Isaiah, Jeremiah, Ezekiel, or others in the Twelve than Haggai and Zechariah, it appears likely that he was aware of some of them at a minimum (Jeremiah certainly; see Ezra 1:1), although he did not seem to treat them with the same respect as the Law. Still, the notion of the "Law *and* the Prophets" appears in a nascent form.

B. Literary Genres in Ezra-Nehemiah

Unlike Haggai and Zechariah 1–8, which are prophetic books, Ezra-Nehemiah presents itself as a narrative account of events that occurred in Jerusalem during the early and the middle years of the Persian Empire. Like a historian, the author supplied a chronology, assigning actions to the reigns of various Persian kings. Like a historian, he utilized sources, sometimes earlier texts from the Bible, including the Pentateuch, Haggai, Zechariah, and material that is also found in 1 and 2 Chronicles. Apparently, he also utilized narratives, official decrees, and lists from the world around him, presumably to buttress his case. [Possible Documents Employed in Ezra-Nehemiah] It also appears, however, as though he felt comfortable modifying those materials to suit his literary or theological needs. Also, like a historian, he was selective in his choice of materials, focusing on events and details he deemed important for his study.

His chronology in particular has not gone unchallenged, especially Ezra 4:6-23, where he reports on the fifth century BCE kings Ahasuerus (Xerxes I, r. 486–465) and Artaxerxes (r. 465–423) in connection with his discussion of actions that occurred early in the reign of Darius (r. 522/1–486). The placement of this material, however, probably has to do with the redactor's intention of making the first return in 539, the return of Ezra, and the mission of Nehemiah all part of one overall plan of God to repopulate the Persian province of Yehud with a godly people. Also the sequence of Ezra followed by Nehemiah has been debated, although not resolved. (See again [Artaxerxes I or II?].) Where the redactor's sources

Possible Documents Employed in Ezra-Nehemiah

In Ezra

Narratives
1:5-8. Captives preparing to leave Babylon for Yehud
3:1–4:3. First efforts at rebuilding the temple
5:1-5; 6:1-5, 13-18. An Aramaic account of building the temple
7:6-11 and 10:1-17. An Ezra "Biography"
8:15–9:5 (or 15). Ezra's "Memoirs" [N.B. The term "Memoirs" is used here only for convenience, and indicates simply that the point of view of these verses is the first person singular. Its use should not be taken to certify that Ezra actually wrote this material.]

Decrees and Other Sayings
1:2-4. The Edict of Cyrus (see 2 Chr 36:22-23)
4:8-23. Aramaic letters between Rehum and Artaxerxes (I)
5:6-17. Aramaic Letter of Tattenai to Darius
6:6-12. Aramaic Decree of Darius
9:6-15. A prayer

Lists
1:9-11a. A list of vessels from the house of God
2:3-67. A list of repatriates (see also Neh 7:7-73a)
7:1b-5. Ezra's genealogy
7:12-26. An Aramaic list of families
8:1-14. A list of names within Ezra's biography
10:18-44a. A list of priests who married foreign women

In Nehemiah

Narratives
1:1b-2:20; 3:33[Engl. 4:1]–7:3; 12:27-42; 13:4-31. Nehemiah's "Memoirs" (See the disclaimer above about the designation Ezra's "Memoirs.")
7:73b–8:19. An Ezra "Biography"
9:1-5. A service of confession
11:1-2. A draft to repopulate Jerusalem [It is not uncommon to see Neh 7:73b–10:40 (Engl. 10:39) listed as part of "Ezra's Memoirs," but those chapters are composite in nature. This analysis reflects the various documents underlying them.]

Decrees and Other Sayings
9:6-37. A prayer of confession
10:29-40 [Engl. 10:28-39]. A covenant

Lists
3:1-32. Work groups
7:6-73a. A list of repatriates (see also Ezra 2:3-67)
9:38–10:27 (MT 10:1-28). Names on a document
11:3-24. Heads of families in Jerusalem
11:25-36. Inhabitants of villages
12:1-26a. A list of repatriates (see also Ezra 2:3-67, Neh 7:6-73a)

Based considerably on D. J. A. Clines, *Ezra, Nehemiah, Esther* (NCB; London: Marshall, Morgan & Scott; Grand Rapids: Eerdmans, 1984) 4–9.

conflicted, he did not always eliminate the tension completely.[4] [Historical Tension in Ezra-Nehemiah] His choice of details did not always answer the questions modern historians are interested in: e.g., who was Sheshbazzar (Ezra 1:8, 11; 5:14, 16)? What was his relationship to Zerubbabel? Of course, his readers may well have known. Unlike a modern historian, he also concerned himself from beginning to end with God's role in the events he discussed (Ezra 1:1; Neh 13:31b). Hence, the work Ezra-Nehemiah would not qualify as "history writing" in the modern sense, but probably does qualify as a good effort for an ancient writer. That last statement does not mean that everything he said was necessarily correct, but it does mean that his narrative of Israel's story was not spun from thin air. It was neither historicized fiction nor fictionalized history, terms too modern to fit this ancient work. Probably it would be best simply to call it a "theologized narrative."

Historical Tension in Ezra-Nehemiah

In addition to the questions raised by the placement of Ezra 4:6-23, some other passages in Ezra-Nehemiah can be read as historically suspect because they conflict with each other. Ezra 3:10, for example, says Jeshua and his sons were in charge of building the temple, while Ezra 5:16 clearly says in a letter from Tattenai, the Babylonian governor of the province, that Sheshbazzar initiated the building project. Scholars sometimes resolve the difficulty by suggesting that Sheshbazzar began the project after his arrival in Jerusalem in 539/8, but that the work came to a halt and was restarted under the Davidide Zerubbabel and the priest Joshua (Hag 1:1-15). That resolution appears correct, but the text itself does not resolve the issue. Neh 2:1 mentions Artaxerxes without saying where he was, although the implication from Neh 1 is

Susa. Susa was the winter capital of Persia, but the other four were Persepolis, Babylon, Ecbatana, and Pasargadae. Problems with dates and other issues also appear in Ezra-Nehemiah. In response to them, A. H. J. Gunneweg argues that such passages show Ezra-Nehemiah not to be "exactly-dated history," but a narrative driven by a "historical/theological conception" of the early Persian Period. A good reading strategy, then, would be to follow the logic of the plot without trying to make it fit what moderns know (or think they know!) about post-exilic Judean history. All writers can move materials around to suit their development of their themes.

A. H. J. Gunneweg, "Zur Interpretation der Bücher Esra-Nehemia," *Congress Volume: Vienna 1980* (VTSup 32; ed. J. A. Emerton: Leiden: Brill, 1981) 146–61, here 159.

C. The Historical Reliability of Ezra-Nehemiah

A primary issue in the modern study of Ezra-Nehemiah, therefore, has been its historical reliability. Some scholars have maintained that the book of Nehemiah "certainly incorporated . . . some personal memoirs of Nehemiah," which were "written for the most part soon after the close of his first administration" (the thirty-second year of Artaxerxes; see Neh 13:6), "and which ranked as a historical document among the very best in the Hebrew Bible."[5] The assumption in this statement seems to be that proximity to the events reported assured historical accuracy. Others speak of the "Memoirs of Ezra" equally confidently. By contrast, however, C. C. Torrey considered the man Ezra a figment of the imagination of the Chronicler, the author of 1 and 2 Chronicles whom Torrey thought also wrote Ezra-Nehemiah,[6] and J. Becker argued that the so-called "Memoirs" of Ezra and Nehemiah alike were composed for their place in the book and exhibited the same compositional, linguistic, and theological characteristics as 1 and 2 Chronicles. He concluded that the first person accounts in both books constituted a theological narrative, or fictive memoirs, not eyewitness reports.[7] As such, neither would have any more (or less) claim to historical reliability than anything else in 1 and 2 Chronicles or Ezra-Nehemiah. [Historiography]

Even if Becker were to turn out to be correct that both sets of "Memoirs" were fictive—to use his word again, one still would not be required to conclude that Ezra-Nehemiah contained no historically reliable information, but only to recognize that its author(s) was (were) more interested in theology. Likewise, even if the traditional authors wrote the "Memoirs," they were still theologically

Historiography

The term "historiography" designates the writing of history. It includes both the process of writing a record of the past and the assumptions and procedures by which the past is examined and recorded. As a modern discipline, it has developed procedures and assumptions foreign to ancient ways of thinking/writing. Three in particular affect how historians acting as historians might read the Bible. First, modern historians work critically. That is, they do not accept conflicting accounts of the same event. If primary sources disagree, historians will assume that one if not both are false, and question both or seek a means to ameliorate their difficulties. Second, modern historians operate on the basis of the so-called "principle of analogy." Simply put, this principle holds that if a reported incident cannot happen now, it did not happen in the past. Third, historians seek human or other natural causes, not divine ones.

The Bible, of course, knows nothing of those principles. It places back to back diverging accounts of the same event. See, for example, the accounts of the death of Saul in 1 Sam 31 and 2 Sam 1. Did Saul's armor bearer kill him and then commit suicide, or did a passerby find him leaning on his sword, kill him, and take Saul's spear and armlet to David? Perhaps those accounts can be resolved, but the biblical text does not do so. Moreover, the Bible reports all kinds of events that are not repeatable, including the birth of Jesus to a virgin and the resurrection of Jesus. Likewise, it often attributes events like the occurrence of storms and the outcomes of battles to divine causality. Historians, thinking as Christians, might decide personally to accept those events just mentioned as divine acts, but they would do so on grounds other than the principles of historiography.

laced. The concerns of modern historians are not the same as the concerns of the ancient writers.

In any case, Becker did not prove his case beyond reasonable doubt. In the first place, the similarities in style between some of the narratives in Ezra-Nehemiah on the one hand and 1 and 2 Chronicles on the other may be due simply to an official-sounding style common to a body of trained scribes.[8] Those similarities do not prove common authorship in the modern sense of the term. In addition, several authors have challenged the conclusion that Ezra-Nehemiah stemmed from the Chronicler.[9] Second, the author of Ezra-Nehemiah appears to have used a number of other sources as well, thus reducing the amount of writing from the author himself available for comparison.[10] (See [Possible Documents Employed in Ezra-Nehemiah].) Further, it is sometimes a judgment call whether a given passage is from the biblical author or from some other source, making stylistic judgments like Becker's all the more risky. Modern readers may still evaluate the historicity of those documents, but they should judge each one on its own merits. Thus, E. S. Gerstenberger's comment is appropriate: "The main topics [of Ezra-Nehemiah]—building the temple, setting up the province of Yehud, constituting YHWH's community around YHWH's law, and carrying through a strict order (observance of the Sabbath, prohibition of mixed marriages, etc.)—have a certain plausibility about themselves."[11] He continues, however, "The ancient valuation of historical facts and individuals is situated in another system of coordinates. Individual events refer to the basic theological concern: the mission of Ezra and Nehemiah; Samaria's resistance against the building of the temple; the willingness of the returnees to complete enormous constructions; the gifts of the [Babylonian] neighbors for the temple; the return of the ancient, sacred utensils."[12] Several specific issues, moreover, draw scholarly attention concerning the historical accuracy of Ezra-Nehemiah. Four will be addressed here.

1. The Number of Returnees and the Import of that List for the Date of the Completion of Ezra-Nehemiah. One serious historical issue is the number of people who returned to Persian Period Yehud. Ezra 2:64-67 // Nehemiah 7:66-69 sets that number at 42,360 full citizens, plus 7,337 servants, and 200 (Ezra) or 245 (Nehemiah) male and female "singers" or "entertainers."[13] Those numbers are problematic. In the first place, Jeremiah 52:28-30 lists a total of 4,600 deportees: 3,023 in 597, 832 in 586, and 745 in 581, although 2 Kings offers a vague 10,000 carried away. Ezra-Nehemiah reports almost 50,000 people returning in 539 (or 520), over ten times the number Jeremiah reported as deported. In the second place, 2 Kings 24:14 says Nebuchadnezzar carried away 10,000 inhabitants from Jerusalem in 597, of whom apparently only 8,000 reached Babylon (2 Kgs 24:16). The narrative continues (2 Kgs 25:11) that in 586 Nebuchadnezzar carried away "the rest of the people who were left in the city and the deserters who had defected to the king of Babylon." Verse 12 does concede, however, that the Babylonians left behind "some of the poorest people of the land to be vinedressers and tillers of the soil." Fifty thousand returnees would be five times that number.

Such varying and conflicting numbers provide no reliable basis for determining the number of captives taken to Babylon. It might have been twice or more as large as the precise numbers given in Jeremiah, or even that prophet's number might have been too high. Regardless, to accept the figure of circa 50,000 in Ezra 2:64-67 // Nehemiah 7:66-69, one would have to assume that in 538/521, at least five or ten times more captives returned from Babylon than were carried away between 597 and 581. Not only that, Ezra 1:3 tacitly recognizes that some captives remained in Babylon, an admission reinforced by the accounts of the heroes Ezra and Nehemiah. Perhaps the majority of exiles remained in Babylon. In any case, the Jewish community in Babylon itself continued until the eleventh century CE and played a crucial role in the survival of Judaism itself after the destruction of Jerusalem in 70 CE. On the surface, moreover, it seems unlikely that the people in captivity would have increased appreciably in number, and certainly not as much as five- to tenfold and more. What, then, can one say about the numbers?

D. J. A. Clines attempts to salvage the accuracy of the numbers in Ezra 2 // Nehemiah 7 by accepting the suggestion of others that it contained the names of all those who returned to Jerusalem between 539 and 521, and not just one group.[14] Still, as just shown above, it is difficult to imagine such a large group of people descending on and surviving in an impoverished area, decimated by Babylon and inhabited by a remnant of Judeans and any other people who might have moved in from surrounding areas. (The supposition by Bible readers through the years that during the exile Judah lay devoid of inhabitants is only that: a supposition. Artifactual remains in Judah from the sixth century prove otherwise.) A number of modern scholars, therefore, have argued that the lists might represent later census figures. J. Blenkinsopp suggests a time near Nehemiah's ministry,[15] while others prefer a date for these chapters from the end of the Persian Period or even later.

Thus, if one accepts the list that appears in both Ezra 2 and Nehemiah 7 as representing some kind of actual tabulation of citizens, it is difficult to date the list any earlier than near the end of the Persian Period, i.e., at some time in the mid to late fourth century, just before the coming of Alexander the Great in 331. [Dates in the Career of Alexander the Great] C. E. Carter, however, arrived at population estimates for *all* of Yehud at the lower figures of 13,350 by 450 BCE and 20,650 (i.e., less than half the number listed in

---

Dates in the Career of Alexander the Great

 356 Born in Macedonia, the son of Philip II and Olympias

342–340 Tutored by the Greek philosopher Aristotle

340–336 Regent for Philip, who was assassinated in 336

336 Succeeded Philip, with the help of Antipater and Parmenion

335 Secured northern frontier of Macedonia against uprisings

334–333 Captured most of Asia Minor, organized a navy to protect Greece from Persia

332 Besieged Tyre for seven months, Gaza for two months, and took Egypt

331 Departed from Egypt to attack Persia, passing through Yehud

330 Defeated Darius III

330–327 Subdued eastern part of the Persian Empire

327–325 Attacked modern-day Pakistan and India, with mixed results

324 Returned to Greece and experienced troubles there

323 Died in Babylon in June

R. D. Milns, "Alexander the Great," *AB*, 1.146–50.

Alexander the Great on horseback. Detail from the Alexander battle. Mosaic from the Casa del Fauno, Pompeii. Museo Archeologico Nazionale, Naples, Italy. (Credit: Erich Lessing/Art Resource, NY)

Ezra 2 // Neh 7) by 331.[16] Thus, while the issue is unsettled concerning the date of the list, it is fairly clear that no horde of people circa 50,000 strong moved from Babylon to Jerusalem and Yehud in the late sixth century, and that they certainly did not move into a place devoid of human inhabitants.[17] There would have been insufficient roads, cities, houses, etc. to accommodate tens of thousands of new settlers, and that figure seems to exceed the upper limit of the likely *total population of Yehud* by even the end of the Persian Period. Where did the list come from, then?

Recent scholars have argued that parts of Nehemiah especially might be dated during the early Greek period[18] or even down to the time of the Maccabean Revolt (168–165 or 167–164 BCE), which was about the time when many scholars think Daniel also was written. J. L. Wright summarizes the evidence for that latter conclusion as follows. Jerusalem itself was sparsely populated before the Hasmoneans expanded it in the mid-second century, culminating a lengthy process that began under Nehemiah but took centuries to complete.[19] Even a casual reader will acknowledge that Nehemiah 3:1-22 describes a large city with ten different gates: Sheep (3:1, 22), Fish (3:3), Old (3:6), Valley (3:13), Dung (3:13), Fountain (3:15), Water (3:26), Horse (3:28), East (3:29), and Muster (3:32). This description, however, presupposes a city similar in size to Jerusalem in the seventh century or the second. D. Ussishkin agrees with this conclusion and argues that the whole sixth-century wall was restored by Nehemiah, but says that most of the city remained unoccupied, just as Nehemiah 7:4 reports.[20] That particular part of the issue will be left unresolved in this commentary. If, however, that description of the city and the numbers in the lists in Ezra 2 and Nehemiah 7 presuppose a city the size of Jerusalem in the second century, they give no hint of the dismay of Daniel itself over the fourth kingdom of Daniel 2 and 7, namely Greece. The tyranny of Antiochus Epiphanes (Greek ruler 175–163 BCE) described at great length in the visions of Daniel does not appear in Ezra. The Persian kings had been pliable in the hands of God, and the Greek kings had not yet destroyed the perspective of Ezra-Nehemiah that a Yehud obedient to YHWH could flourish through faith and obedience under a mighty foreign government.

Regardless, however, if the settled area of Jerusalem in the fifth and fourth centuries was limited to the city of David and the temple mount, one may conclude that the rebuilding of the city wall began under Nehemiah, but its population apparently did not reach the proportions presupposed in the book of Nehemiah until nearly as late as the Maccabean period. In that case, the text of

Ezra-Nehemiah did not reach its final form until centuries later than the time in which it is set literarily, 539–432. An additional indicator of a lengthy time of origination is that Nehemiah 7:1–13:3 contains words and phrases that occur elsewhere only in latter texts like Esther and Daniel. The second century works the Wisdom of Jesus ben Sira, 2 Maccabees, 1 Esdras (5:1-46), and *1 Enoch*, however, know and employ those chapters of Nehemiah, establishing a date before which time Nehemiah must have been completed.[21] What, then, can be hypothesized about the list in Ezra 2 // Nehemiah 7? Of what

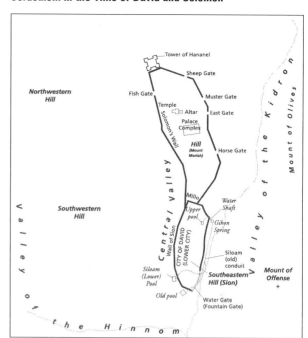

Jerusalem in the Time of David and Solomon

did it consist? It listed the leading families in Jerusalem, beginning with priests and Levites, from a time perhaps as late as the second century BCE. The book as a whole, however, from its beginning, sought to defend the claim of returnees from the exile as the community's legitimate leadership. As such, the three-fold insertion of the list was the last stage in the compilation of Ezra-Nehemiah.

This hypothesized reconstruction of the rise of the text may seem surprising, maybe even shocking, to some readers of this commentary. It is not intended, however, to be shocking. It is intended as a report of the serious investigation of the biblical text as it stands, an attempt to understand its difficulties. All that is required to accept it is two intellectual moves. One is to agree that the tradition that Ezra-Nehemiah was written by the two men whose name it bears is simply that—a tradition, and not a claim that the texts actually make for themselves. The other requisite is a willingness to try to see where the internal evidence of the texts themselves *might* lead. It might make sense to conceive of the production of Ezra-Nehemiah as a lengthy process beginning with the memoirs of Nehemiah and perhaps even memoirs of Ezra from the second half of the fifth century, plus later, secondary accounts of both men, combined and introduced by a narrative recounting the event of 539–520 (i.e., Ezra 1–6) that was written later still, supplemented by various materials like the list of high priests in Nehemiah 12:26 that names the high priests down to the end of the Persian Period

(323 BCE or even the early Greek period (down to the reign of Antiochus Epiphanes, 175–163). The numbers of the inhabitants of returnees given in Ezra 2 and Nehemiah 7 may have been among the latest additions in the second century BCE.

2. Rebuilding Jerusalem's Wall. The most obvious building narrative in Ezra-Nehemiah, besides the one concerning the rebuilding of the temple, reports the repairing of the wall around Jerusalem (Neh 2:11–3:32 + 4:16-23, MT 2:11–3:32 + 4:10-17). The completion of this event after fifty-two days of labor has been dated as October 2, 445 BCE,[22] although that date might be too precise. Josephus (*Ant.* 11.5.179), for example, said the repairing of the wall required two years and four months, but his statement may well have depended on a corrupt text of Nehemiah. Regardless, the project is described as plagued with problems, and the earliest restoration can hardly have amounted to more than repairing holes in an older wall and replacing doors in the gateways. Which wall Nehemiah repaired, and how much of the area inside was populated, then, is a major issue. Archaeological investigations thus far have found early Persian Period resettlement of Jerusalem only in the old city captured by David, in the area of the temple, and in the area between the two, an area called Ophel. That information would suggest a city much smaller in settled area and in number of inhabitants than the one destroyed by the Babylonians and much smaller than the one presupposed in the book of Nehemiah as it stands.

3. The Population of Jerusalem. The next issue concerning the historical accuracy of Ezra-Nehemiah is that of the population of Persian-era Jerusalem itself (see Neh 3:1–7:3 + 11:1-21). Nehemiah 11:1-2 says that the leadership of the people constituting one-tenth of the returnees volunteered to move into the still empty city. Verses 3-21 list those leaders by group and supply their number: a total of 3,044 persons in Nehemiah's time. That number is relatively modest, but recent estimates of the population of post-exilic Jerusalem run no higher than about 1,500 as late as the end of the Persian Period and even fewer in the fifth century.[23] Regardless, within Jerusalem's population some might have been Persian officials, or Judeans hired by the Persians. Some, quite likely, would have been priests, as Nehemiah reports. At least some members of the Davidic family who returned might well have lived there too. They and others may have also had servants who lived in the city. Perhaps not coincidentally, Zechariah 12:1–13:6 excoriates Davidides, Levites, and prophets in Jerusalem it considered false. Were they the primary residents of Jerusalem when those verses were penned?

At any rate, in writing a commentary like this, an author has to make a basic decision. The options appear to be three. (1) One could take Ezra-Nehemiah at face value and claim that it constitutes a precise, factual account of what went on during the time frame of 539 to 432. Unfortunately, one would then have to argue that the latest and possibly the best archaeological investigations and investigators are simply wrong. (2) One could take the option advocated by some scholars today that Ezra-Nehemiah is basically a religious narrative told to educate readers, and that archaeology and historical accuracy, therefore, are irrelevant. Or (3) one could accept the evidence adduced by archaeologists and a careful reading of the text and try to interpret Ezra-Nehemiah in light of that evidence. This author chose the third option. All three of the issues discussed here thus far, therefore, are interrelated and will be treated consistently.

4. The Reason(s) for Persian Permission to Rebuild Jerusalem. It is also instructive for readers of the Bible to ask why the Persians would have allowed the city wall to be rebuilt by Nehemiah (which project this commentary does *not* dispute). After the destruction of Jerusalem by the Babylonians in 586, Mizpah (located NNW of Jerusalem on the border between OT Israel and Judah) replaced Jerusalem as the functioning capital (2 Kgs 25:22-26; Jer 40:7–41:18). Ezra 4:1 mentions *local* resistance to the decision to rebuild the temple (i.e., the "adversaries" of Judah and Benjamin, i.e., post-exilic Yehud), which involved persons from the former Israel and others from Judah who had not been taken to Babylon. It is possible, maybe even likely, that they thought the leaders of Jerusalem and Judah deserved what the Babylonians had done to them. It is also possible that they were displeased at the Persian decision to allow those who so desired to return from Babylon to Jerusalem. The actions (in Ezra 5 and 6) of Tattenai, the Persian governor over

Map of Post-exilic Yehud

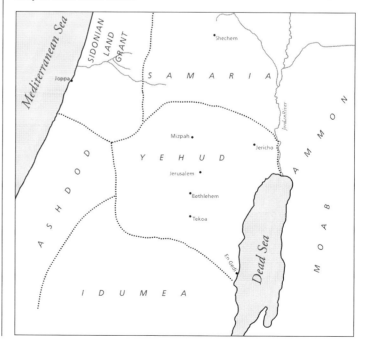

the empire's holdings from the Euphrates River to Egypt, seem plausible as efforts to find out specifically what kinds of building had been authorized in Jerusalem.

The desire on the part of returnees to rebuild the temple was understandable on religious grounds. What about the desire of Nehemiah and others to repair a wall around Jerusalem? That desire suggests that they may have wanted to reestablish it as a political center as well, and apparently they did so *with Persian permission*. Why, however, would the Persians agree? One suggestion is that their decision to allow Jerusalem's wall to be rebuilt was made in order to provide an inland defense center for Persia's own interests.[24] Continuing, the argument runs, the Persians very likely intended the building project "to create a web of economic and social relationships that would tie the community more completely into the imperial system. . . . [T]he careers of Ezra and Nehemiah were an effort [by Persia] to compel loyalty to the imperial system by tying the community's self-interest to the goals of the empire."[25] O. Lipschits, however, questions whether fortifying tiny Jerusalem would give Persia any kind of strategic advantage in a conflict with Egypt, but argues that a walled Jerusalem would serve Persia's purposes "as a center for gathering taxes and carrying out other important fiscal tasks."[26] Either way, the opposition of Sanballat and others in Samaria (Neh 2, 4, 6, and 13) is understandable as an expression of their wish to retain their limited control over Judah. In any case, Ezra-Nehemiah focuses on Jerusalem as the locus of the temple, not as a political center.

D. Languages, Text, and Place in the Hebrew Bible Canon

Note should be taken of an unusual feature of Ezra-Nehemiah, namely that it was written in two languages. Although written for the most part in Hebrew, two passages, Ezra 4:7–6:18 and Ezra 7:12-26, were written in Aramaic. The subject matter of both sections was the contents of official documents, which would have been written in Aramaic, the language of the empire. The use of Aramaic does not prove the authenticity of the letters, but it does lend an official air to them.

J. M. Myers judges the Hebrew of Ezra to be "late post-exilic" (i.e., dated around 400 BCE), and the Aramaic resembles that of the Elephantine Papyri (dated mostly in the fifth century).[27] Other considerations to be discussed above suggest a fourth- to second-century date for the book, however. The text of Ezra-Nehemiah as a whole seems to have been well transmitted, although occasional difficulties do appear.

The place of Ezra-Nehemiah differs in the Christian and Jewish canons. In the Christian Bible, it appears as two books near the end of the "books of history," i.e., between 1 and 2 Chronicles and Esther. In the Septuagint (Codex Vaticanus, anyway) it appears as Esdras A and Esdras B after Chronicles, but before Psalms. In the Hebrew Bible, by contrast, it appears in the third section, the *Kĕtûbîm*, just before the last book, (1 and 2) Chronicles. [The Order of Books in the Hebrew Bible] One should remember, however, that Hebrew Scriptures were copied on individual scrolls, not bound in a single book. The words attributed to Isaiah or of 1 and 2 Chronicles together would fill a scroll about as long as could be unrolled and handled conveniently. Books, by contrast, were printed on individual leaves, which, when bound together, could be turned easily, so length was much less of a problem. Books replaced scrolls for Christian Scriptures much earlier than for Jewish texts.

The inclusion of Ezra-Nehemiah among the holy books of the Jews seems to go back as far as Jesus ben Sira (late third, early second century BCE), whose grandson published ben Sira's teachings around 132. He included Nehemiah, but not Ezra, in his

---

The Order of Books in the Hebrew Bible

The order of books in the Hebrew Bible is quite different from that of the English Bible.

The Hebrew Bible has three, not five, divisions. They are *Tôrâ* (Law), *Nĕb'îm* (Prophets), and *Kĕtûbîm* (Writings). The *Tôrâ* is identical to the Christian Pentateuch: Genesis, Exodus, Leviticus, Numbers, and Deuteronomy. The *Nĕb'îm* are divided into two groups: the Former Prophets Joshua, Judges, Samuel, and Kings; and the Latter Prophets Isaiah, Jeremiah, Ezekiel, and the Book of the Twelve (the Minor Prophets in the same sequence as in the Christian order). The *Kĕtûbîm* follow this order: Psalms, Job, Proverbs, Ruth, Song of Songs, Ecclesiastes, Lamentations, Esther, Daniel, Ezra-Nehemiah, and Chronicles.

The time and process of the selection and arrangement of the contents of the Hebrew are lost. Scholars often speak of a "Council of Jamnia," a title/council hypothesized as the source of the Hebrew Bible, but there is no record of any such conference. Even if one did occur, it perhaps only validated the texts read in most synagogues. Josephus reflects that same list in his work *Against Apion* I, 37–43, where he speaks of twenty-two books, naming the ones listed in the previous paragraph, although counted in a manner that seems more consistent with the books of the Hebrew Bible.

Five of them belong to Moses, which contain his laws and the traditions of the origin of mankind till his death. This interval of time was a little short of three thousand years. But as to the

time of the death of Moses till the reign of Artaxerxes, king of Persia, who reigned after Xerxes [i.e., in 465 BCE], the prophets, who came after Moses, wrote down the history of their times in thirteen books [i.e., Joshua, Judges, Samuel, Kings, Chronicles, Ezra, Nehemiah, Esther, Isaiah, Jeremiah, Ezekiel, Lamentations, Daniel]. The remaining four books contain hymns to God [Psalms] and precepts for the conduct of human life [Proverbs, Job, Ecclesiastes].

The Christian order (which follows the order of the Greek Old Testament, the Septuagint) uses a sequential arrangement: i.e., past (Pentateuch and books of history); present (song and wisdom books); and future (Major and Minor Prophets). Probably not coincidentally, the New Testament follows that same order: past (the Gospels and Acts); the present (the letters); and the future (Revelation). The Hebrew order, however, uses the model of concentric circles. It starts with the holiest books, the *Tôrâ*, in the center. *Tôrâ* is surrounded and protected by the (theoretically) later *Nĕb'îm*, which can build on and interpret, but not contradict, the *Tôrâ*. The *Kĕtûbîm* form the outer circle and can build on and interpret, but not contradict, either the *Tôrâ* or the *Nĕb'îm*.

Josephus quotation from Lawrence H. Schiffman, *Texts and Traditions: A Source Reader for the Study of Second Temple and Rabbinic Judaism* (Hoboken, J.J.: KTAV, 1998) 117. Amplifications in brackets added by Paul L. Redditt.

hymn in honor of great ancestors in Sirach 44:1–50:21. The hymn includes in this order the Patriarchs, Moses, Aaron, Phineas, Joshua, and Caleb; the Judges, Nathan, David, Solomon, Rehoboam, and Jeroboam; Elijah, Elisha, Hezekiah, Isaiah, Josiah, Jeremiah, Job, the Twelve Prophets, Zerubbabel, Jeshua, and Nehemiah, as well as a priest named Simon, who served from 219–196 BCE. The hymn appears to have had in view a canon that included the *Tôrâ,* the *Nĕbîm,* and Nehemiah at least, and *might* also have included Psalms (attributed to David) and Proverbs (attributed to Solomon). It is possible though not certain that the mention of Nehemiah was intended to apply to the unified collection Ezra-Nehemiah, although not necessarily in its final form. In his Prologue to ben Sira's work (after 132 BCE), the grandson spoke of the Law and the Prophets "and the rest of the books," which he did not name. Christopher Begg suggests plausibly that Sirach 49:11-13 did not include Ezra the priest because its author was discussing the rebuilding of the temple and the wall of Jerusalem, and, unlike Zerubbabel, Jeshua, and Nehemiah, Ezra had nothing to do with those projects.[28]

E. The Relationship of Ezra-Nehemiah to 1 and 2 Chronicles

The idea that Ezra-Nehemiah and Chronicles share a common author has been widely held since L. Zunz in 1832 and F. C. Movers in 1834 made that case. Modern scholars would add that the "author" might well have been a "school," i.e., a group of trained scribes working over a period of years, rather than a single individual. S. Japhet in 1969 and H. G. M. Williamson in 1977 and 1986 contested the view of common authorship and argued that the traditions arose separately.[29] The issue is complicated by the fact that both Chronicles and Ezra-Nehemiah borrow extensively. Readers of this commentary are probably aware that Chronicles essentially rewrites Samuel/Kings from the death of Saul to the fall of Jerusalem, skipping certain information like the adultery of David and Bathsheba and the careers of Elijah as recorded in 1 Kings 17–19; 21 and 2 Kings 1–2 and Elisha as recorded in 2 Kings 2–9; 13. Thus, when one takes into account the large percentage of the books that consists of borrowed material, it is somewhat difficult to make stylistic determinations.

Still, Blenkinsopp ventures seven parallels between Chronicles and Ezra-Nehemiah that underscore religious interests and ideology shared by the works.

1. Preparation for building the first and second temple are described similarly: see Ezra 3:7 with 1 Chronicles 22:2, 4, 15 and 2 Chronicles 2:9, 15-16.

2. The altar is set up before the temple is built: see Ezra 3:2 with 1 Chronicles 21:18–22:1. (Of course, simple expediency would lead one to expect that sequence. The altar was essential; the building was not.)

3. Heads of ancestral houses endowed both temples in Ezra 2:69; 1 Chronicles 26:26, while 2 Kings 12:18 mentions only an endowment by Jehoash that included treasures from himself and three royal ancestors.

4. Both show great interest in the sacred vessels (Ezra 1:7; 7:19; 8:25-30, 33-34; see 1 Chr 28:13-19; 2 Chr 5:1). Second Kings 24:13, however, says the Babylonians destroyed those vessels.

5. The order of sacrifices (Ezra 3:4-6; see 2 Chr 2:3; 8:13) and the enumeration of sacrificial materials (Ezra 6:9, 17; 7:22; 7:17-18; 18:35-36; see also 1 Chr 29:21, 32) are nearly identical.

6. The descriptions of liturgical music and of musical instruments and indications of who plays them correspond closely (Ezra 3:10; Neh 12:35; see 1 Chr 15:19; 16:5-6; 25:1, 6; 2 Chr 5:12-13).

7. A liturgical saying from Chronicles appears in Ezra 3:11; the blessing in Ezra 7:27-28 is paralleled in 1 Chronicles 29:10-19 and elsewhere.[30]

This list is not exhaustive, so it would appear that Ezra-Nehemiah agrees too often with Chronicles for the similarities to be coincidental.

Which way did the borrowing go between Chronicles and Ezra-Nehemiah? Scholars have mounted arguments on both sides of the debate. As noted above, the scholarly consensus for over a century had been that Ezra-Nehemiah drew on Chronicles, although recently that consensus has been challenged.[31] Recent debate focused on four issues: (1) the fact that 2 Chronicles ends and Ezra begins with an extensive, shared text; (2) the fact that 1 Esdras begins with 2 Chronicles 35–36, continues through Ezra, and then jumps to and ends with Nehemiah 7:73b(MT 7:72b)–8:12, the narrative about Ezra's reading the law to the people of Israel; (3) the conclusion that Chronicles and Ezra-Nehemiah share a common literary style; and (4) the conclusion that they also share a common theology. Of these issues, the first will perhaps help solve the issue about the direction of borrowing.

The mention of the so-called Edict of Cyrus appears at the end of 2 Chronicles (36:22-23) and the beginning of Ezra (1:1-3a), and it runs fifty-four Hebrew words with only four minor differences. First, 2 Chronicles 36:22 has a final Hebrew letter *waw* or "w," with a vowel point making the letter the vowel "u" at the end of the name "Jeremiah" (the typical spelling in the book of Jeremiah), whereas Ezra 1:1 omits the "waw" (as do Jer 28:5, 6, 11, 12, 15; 29:1, and Dan 9:2). Second, 2 Chronicles 36:23 uses the divine name *YHWH*, while Ezra 1:3 contains the verb *yhy* (which the NRSV renders "may he be"). Third, 2 Chronicles 36:22 reads" by the mouth of" (*bpw*), while Ezra 1:1 reads "from the mouth of" (*mpw*). Finally, 2 Chronicles 36:22-23 spells the name Cyrus with a written first vowel, while Ezra 1:1-2 spells it with vowel points only.

Blenkinsopp's work will serve to illustrate those who think the Chronicler wrote Ezra-Nehemiah, using this text as part of his proof. He argues that the Chronicler intended from the beginning "to write the history from the First to the Second Temple, the latter anticipated in the final paragraph of Chronicles and narrated fully in Ezra 1–6."[32] Williamson will serve to illustrate the other side of the debate. He argues that the Chronicler borrowed the passage from the already existing Ezra 1 and added it for liturgical reasons.[33]

One telling issue here has typically been overlooked, and that is that the rest of the Hebrew Bible rarely ever mentions a canonical prophet. Here, however, two books back to back mention Jeremiah in a lengthy shared passage. To determine which came first, one might ask whether 2 Chronicles or Ezra-Nehemiah mentions Jeremiah elsewhere. The answer is "Yes, 2 Chronicles does." It mentions him three more times in its discussion of the fall of Jerusalem: in 2 Chronicles 35:27 and 36:12 and 21. The parallel passage in 2 Kings, however, does not mention Jeremiah. Nor is Jeremiah mentioned anywhere else in Ezra-Nehemiah. In fact, the only other place in the Hebrew Bible where Jeremiah is mentioned is Daniel 9:2. It is fair to conclude, therefore, (1) that the reference to Jeremiah was uniquely at home in the discussion of the fall of Jerusalem in 2 Chronicles and (2) that Ezra 1 borrowed the passage with its reference to Jeremiah from it.[34] An examination of other texts bears similar results. The list of the ancestors of Ezra in Ezra 7:1-5 contains no name not found in 2 Chronicles 6, not even the father or other post-exilic ancestors of Ezra. His latest mentioned ancestor was the priest Seriah, who was taken into exile in 586.

One text that appears to be an exception to the direction of borrowing is 1 Chronicles 9:2-34, which many scholars claim was borrowed from Nehemiah 11:2-34. The two passages differ markedly, however. Only a handful of names overlap: the Benjaminite Sallu (v. 7); the *priests* Azariah/Seriah, son of Hilkiah (brothers?), and Adaiah, son of Jeroham; the *Levites* Shemiah, son of Hasshub, and Mattaniah, son of Mica; and the *gatekeepers* Akkub and Talmon. Both lists have many other names, and 1 Chronicles 9 is much longer. This overlap is scant evidence, therefore, for literary dependence. In Chronicles, those verses stand outside the genealogical lists of 1 Chronicles 1–8, which serve to introduce the people of Israel as God's chosen people among all the peoples of the earth and to set up the rise of the Davidic monarchy. Moreover, they interrupt the connection between the genealogy of the Benjaminites and of the Benjaminite Saul, the discussion of whose family appears in 1 Chronicles 9:35-44. Thus, 1 Chronicles 8:1-40 introduces Saul's family as great warriors; 9:35-44 gives his genealogy; and 10:1-14 describes the death of Saul on the battlefield without so much as a whisper about his founding the monarchy. The Chronicler thereby recognized the existence of Saul, but never calls him "king."

What, then, was the function of 1 Chronicles 9:2-34? Perhaps better phrased, the question should be this: when would it make sense to incorporate a group of names from the post-exilic period into 1 and 2 Chronicles? One good time would be when 1 and 2 Chronicles and Ezra-Nehemiah were placed back to back in their transmission history. In that case, 1 Chronicles 9:2-34 would have constituted an interlocking device tying 1 and 2 Chronicles to Ezra-Nehemiah.

Where is one left concerning this issue? It seems best to start with the observation that 1 and 2 Chronicles narrate the life of the first temple, from its construction under David to its destruction by the Babylonians. Ezra-Nehemiah narrates the rebuilding of the temple, the community of returnees, and the wall around the city, with the insistence that only returnees belonged to the true Israel. It appears, further, that Ezra-Nehemiah knew and drew on 2 Chronicles and that the volumes were joined redactionally by means of 1 Chronicles 9:2-34 and Ezra 1:2-4.

F. The Relationship of Ezra-Nehemiah to 1 Esdras

A related question concerns the relationship of Ezra-Nehemiah to the later, apocryphal work called 1 Esdras or 3 Ezra. It begins with 2 Chronicles 35:1 (i.e., with Josiah's observance of the Passover) and continues through the fall of Jerusalem and many of the events reported in Ezra and one event in Nehemiah. These parallels are more easily grasped if seen in a chart. [2 Chronicles 35–36 and Ezra-Nehemiah Compared with 1 Esdras] The following observations can be made from that data. First, 1 Esdras may be said to eliminate the awkward ending of 2 Chronicles "Let him go up!"—an improvement sometimes cited as proof that 1 Esdras is both better and older than the present text of Ezra-Nehemiah. If one turns to the end of 1 Esdras, however, one finds that it ends with just such a truncated sentence: "and they came together." In Nehemiah 8:1, those words introduce the final appearance by Ezra himself. Thus, all one may actually say is that 1 Esdras differs from Ezra-Nehemiah in those two places; it is not necessarily better or primary. Second, one should note that 1 Esdras 8:8-24, like Ezra 4:7-23, mentions an appeal to Artaxerxes (presumably Artaxerxes I, r. 465–424) as part of the narrative of rebuilding the temple (520–515). If one wants to argue that there were other reasons for interjecting later traditions into this account, then those reasons apply to Ezra as well as to 1 Esdras. That latter work includes, moreover, a lengthy narrative (1 Esd 3:1–4:63) about a contest in the court of Darius won by the Davidic descendant Zerubbabel (see Hag 1:15b–2:9). Its purpose was almost surely to introduce properly the man Zerubbabel, who appears without introduction in Ezra 5:2.

2 Chronicles 35–36 and Ezra-Nehemiah Compared with 1 Esdras

2 Chr/Ezra/Neh	1 Esd	Subject
2 Chr 35:1-27	1:1-33	King Josiah celebrates Passover, is killed in battle by Pharaoh
2 Chr 36:1-21	1:34-38	Reigns of Jehoahaz, Jehoiakim, Jehoiachin, and Zedekiah
2 Chr 36:22-24 and Ezra 1:1-11	2:1-15	Edict of Cyrus and preparation to return to Jerusalem
Lacking	3:1–5:6	1 Esd adds 3:1–4:63, the narrative of a contest in the court of Darius that Zerubbabel wins, and transitions (5:1-6) back to the list of numbers of returnees
Ezra 2:1-70	5:7-46	Some captives return from Babylon to Jerusalem
Ezra 3:1-13	5:47-65	Altar set up in Jerusalem for sacrifices
Ezra 4:1-5	5:66-73	"Adversaries" offer to help rebuild the temple
Ezra 4:7-24	2:16-30	Letter to King Artaxerxes about rebuilding Jerusalem and finishing its walls
Ezra 5:1-17	6:1-22	Haggai and Zechariah urge restoration; Tattenai opposes
Ezra 6:1-12	6:23-34	Darius finds Cyrus's document permitting the return and funding the rebuilding of
Ezra 6:13-22	7:1-15	the temple
		Temple completed
Ezra 7:1-28	8:1-27	Ezra travels to Jerusalem carrying letter from Artaxerxes
Ezra 8:1-36	8:28-67	People who traveled with Ezra; gifts for temple they brought
Ezra 9:1-15	8:68-90	Issue of "mixed marriages"; Ezra's prayer
Ezra 10:1-5	8.91-96	People promise to divorce foreign wives
Ezra 10:6-44	9:1-36	People assemble in Jerusalem, foreign wives sent away
Neh 7:73b–8:13	9:37-55	Reading of the Law of Moses; 1 Esdras ends abruptly

This chart is derived from one by L. S. Fried, "Esdras, First Book of," *NIDB*, 2.308–309.

Since the beginning of the twentieth century, some scholars have argued that 1 Esdras reflected an earlier, more reliable Hebrew *Vorlage* (i.e., an earlier text) than the Masoretic Text.[35] In support of that view, they cite places where 1 Esdras has correct totals reported in error in the book of Ezra. One example must suffice. Ezra 1:5-11 lists a number of items handed over to Sheshbazzar and the Jews who were about to return Yehud. The list included 30 gold basins, 1,000 silver basins, 29 knives, 30 gold bowls, 410 silver bowls, and 1,000 other implements. Ezra gave the total, however, as 5,400 implements, which is more than twice the total of the numbers listed: 2,499. First Esdras 2:13-15 also supplied a list of those vessels: 1,000 gold cups, 1,000 silver cups, 29 censers, 30 gold bowls, 2,410 silver bowls, and 1,000 other vessels, an exact total of 5,469 implements. At first it might appear that 1 Esdras had a more original text than Ezra, but one could also understand the numbers in 1 Esdras as a correction by a careful scribe.

The conclusion that 1 Esdras relied on a better Hebrew *Vorlage* in fact seems unwarranted for several reasons. First, scholars holding that view typically have assumed that 1 Esdras is a fragment of a hypothetical text in which the account of Ezra's reading the law (Neh 7:32-8:12) followed directly on the end of the book of Ezra. It might be pointed out, however, that the episode of reading the law would fit better elsewhere, e.g., after his arrival in Jerusalem (Ezra 8) but before his reprimanding people for having broken the law by marrying foreigners (Ezra 9). Perhaps the narrative of Ezra's reading the law did belong with the rest of the Ezra narratives at some point in the history of their transmission. It does not follow from that concession, however, that the Hebrew *Vorlage* of 1 Esdras necessarily represented that text.

Second, 1 Esdras exhibited some of the same historical problems as the canonical Ezra. For example, despite variations in 1 Esdras 5 from the list of repatriates given in Ezra 2 and Nehemiah 7, the totals in all three lists were the same: 42,360 members of the congregation and 7,337 servants. (The lists do not agree, however, about the number of singers among those 7,337 servants: 1 Esdras 5 says the number was 265, while Ezra 2 sets it at 200 and Nehemiah 7 says 245.) Their total of nearly 50,000, however, is far larger than the total one obtains if one adds together the numbers given family by family in the lists themselves. It is difficult to argue from these data, therefore, that 1 Esdras has better information based on an earlier text.

Third, the author of 1 Esdras 3:1–4:57 created his own historical problem. He employed a narrative from the ancient Middle East and not in the book of Ezra to introduce Zerubbabel. At the end of the account, he said that Darius himself gave Zerubbabel permission to rebuild the temple before he ever left Babylon. The account also says that Darius contributed toward that reconstruction, exempted priests in Jerusalem from certain taxes, and provided a cavalry of one thousand to escort Zerubbabel back to Yehud (1 Esd 4:47-5:6). Later, however, while following the book of Ezra again, the author of 1 Esdras had opponents report that repatriates were rebuilding the temple on the basis of permission granted by Cyrus (1 Esd 6:8-22). That author then says that Darius consulted the records and learned that Cyrus had given such permission (1 Esd 6:23-26) and commanded the opponents to cease their opposition (1 Esd 6:27-34). Why, however, would Darius have had to search the archives at all if he had already searched the records and authorized and financed the rebuilding as 1 Esdras 4:47–5:6 claims? The answer, of course, is that no search would have been necessary. When the author of 1 Esdras interpolated 3:1–5:6, he created a problem with his inherited narrative. In addition, he contradicted himself in a couple of places. One example must suffice. In narrating the events of Ezra 1, he reported what Ezra 1:8 said: Cyrus delivered to Sheshbazzar the vessels Nebuchadnezzar had taken from the temple (1 Esd 2:12), but in the retelling of that event he added the name Zerubbabel (1 Esd 6:18), thereby anticipating Ezra 2:2.

In light of these considerations, it is doubtful that 1 Esdras rested on an earlier, better Hebrew *Vorlage* than did the MT. Grabbe offers a different reconstruction. He argues that the Ezra materials (found in 1 Esd 2 + 5–9) arose separately from the other traditions. Then the compiler of Ezra-Nehemiah picked them up and developed them his own way (in Ezra 6–9 + Neh 8:1–9:37). Later, someone else developed them by prefixing the description of celebration of Passover under Josiah (1 Esd 1:1-33 from 2 Chr 35:1-27), the narrative of the fall of Jerusalem (1 Esd 1:34-58 from 2 Chr 36:1-21), and the narrative about the contest among the guards at the Persian Court (1 Esd 3:1–5:6).[36] There is less to contest in this version of the growth of the materials. Clearly, many of the Ezra traditions were earlier than the compilation of Ezra-Nehemiah. Still, Grabbe's original core is no longer extant as a separate text. Thus the differences he saw between Ezra and 1 Esdras may be accounted for either from the *Vorlage* or from his hypothesized latter development. Either way, 1 Esdras does not necessarily offer a better, independent text. For purposes of this commentary, then, 1 Esdras will be treated as secondary.

G. The Authorship and Unity of Ezra-Nehemiah

Traditionally, Ezra and Nehemiah were considered the authors of the books that bear their names, a tradition defended by some modern scholars.[37] With the near-universal scholarly consensus that the Chronicler wrote Ezra-Nehemiah coming under challenge beginning in 1969, J. C. VanderKam raised the next question: was Ezra-Nehemiah originally one book or two? He listed three major types of evidence in favor of the latter view. First, lists designed to show that the Chronicler wrote both actually show surprising differences between them. For example, E. L. Curtis and A. A. Madsen listed 136 stylistic peculiarities of the Chronicler, of which 58 show no examples in Ezra or Nehemiah, and the remaining 78 show disagreement between Ezra and Nehemiah as well.[38] If, however, one limits comparisons to verses likely to have been written by the editor, there is little left for such comparative purposes, although some minor differences remain. Second, the books employed their sources differently. For example, Ezra quoted extensively from "official documents" (e.g., the so-called "Edict of Cyrus" in Ezra 1:2-4), but Nehemiah did not. Further, the material common to Ezra 2 and Nehemiah 7 contained not simply a list of returnees but a reference to the "seventh month." VanderKam noted that ninety years passed between the verses, without the author's seeming awareness.[39]

L. S. Fried offered a different theory of two authors, arguing that the real break in Ezra-Nehemiah comes after Ezra 6. (About that point she is correct.) Ezra 7 through Nehemiah 13 do interweave their narratives but are easily distinguished from the opening chapters (Ezra 1–6). Fried then subjected those seventeen chapters to study and determined that they arose from a disciple of Ezekiel.

> The story of Ezra 7–Nehemiah 13 seems to have been written by a follower of Ezekiel who saw in the return of the legitimate population of Israel, in the inauguration of its legitimate priesthood, in the work of Ezra and Nehemiah, and in the recommitment of the people to a covenant with YHWH, the instantiation of Ezekiel's visions of a restored Jerusalem. He modeled it after the most important story he knew, the story of Moses and the Covenant at Sinai. A later author prefaced it with the story of the temple's building and dedication ceremony.[40]

Fried is perhaps correct that the redactionally interlocked narratives of Ezra and Nehemiah appear to have been written first, but (1) other scholars have argued the same point, and (2) the particulars of the temple vision in Ezekiel 40–48 do not appear in the Ezra-Nehemiah narrative.

The focus in these remarks, however, is on Ezra-Nehemiah in its entirety. One can build the case that Ezra-Nehemiah came from one author/editor working well after the careers of both men. The first piece of evidence is the unusual degree to which the work in its entirety utilized earlier written sources. The Hebrew Bible contains no other book with such frequent appeals to written records.[41] Second, Grabbe has noted three series of extensive parallels between various parts of Ezra and Nehemiah. [Parallels between Ezra and Nehemiah] Third, these lists include several long-recognized pieces of evidence for the unity of the two that now take on new force. The evidence includes the use of the list of returnees with Zerubbabel and Jeshua, not just twice but three times (Ezra 2, Nehemiah 7 and 12, although this last list has limited overlap). One should also note the placement of the narrative of Ezra's reading of the law outside its most natural place somewhere in the book of Ezra to a place past the middle of Nehemiah (8–9). That relocation of the text is also part of the editor's program of making the two men contemporaries. These arguments suggest that at a minimum, the same editor (whether one person or a group) had traditions about Ezra in hand when he compiled Nehemiah and made the compilation using the same patterns. Perhaps one might concede that Nehemiah could have been a second volume of Ezra written slightly later (compare Luke-Acts in the New Testament), but not significantly later. The more likely conclusion, however, is that Ezra-Nehemiah in its entirety was composed as a single volume sometime well after the careers of the two men. For purposes of this commentary, then, Ezra-Nehemiah will be treated as a single volume.

The idea of authorship here does not involve the view that one person wrote Ezra-Nehemiah from scratch, or even that Ezra wrote the ten chapters that bear his name and Nehemiah the rest. Rather, the "author" of the Ezra-Nehemiah complex seems to have been a person or group that was the repository of or had access to a number of traditions, some of which concerned Ezra and Nehemiah. Those traditions included first person accounts that may have derived from the namesakes of the book. Concerning Ezra, see Ezra 8:1-34 (not vv. 35-36) and 9:1-15. The account of Ezra's reading of the law in Nehemiah 8:1-17 is a third person account, and the mention of Ezra in Nehemiah 9:6 (NRSV) is missing from the Hebrew text altogether and is supplied from the LXX. Several passages narrate episodes from the career of Nehemiah in the first person singular or plural: Nehemiah

Parallels between Ezra and Nehemiah

L. L. Grabbe offered three lists of parallels between Ezra and Nehemiah. The first was a set of parallels between Ezra 1–10 and Neh 1–10.

Ezra 1–10	Neh 1–10
1: royal commission (Cyrus edict)	1:1–2:9: royal commission (Artaxerxes)
3: task of rebuilding (altar, temple)	2–3: task of rebuilding (repair of wall)
4–6: hindrance by "enemies"	4 & 6: hindrance by "enemies"
6: work completed with God's help	6: work completed with God's help
7–8: Ezra and the law	8: Ezra and the law
9–10: resolution by public pledge	9–10: resolution by public pledge

Such lists are inevitably based on selectivity and generalizations, and in this case the generalization concerning "Ezra and the law" is a stretch. In Ezra 7–8, Ezra is called a scribe of the law, but there is no action like his reading of the law in Neh 8. Aside from that, Grabbe's first list may be allowed to stand.

Grabbe's second list was a set of parallels within the book of Nehemiah. They included parallels that he said do not fit his first scheme.

Neh 1–6 + 9–10	Neh 7 + 11–13
2: list of returnees	7: list of returnees
2: list of returnees	11:1–12:26 list of returnees
6:16-17: dedication of temple	12:27-43: dedication of the wall
6:18: organization of priests/Levites	12:44-47: organization of priestly/Levitical dues
9–10: mixed marriages/threats from "foreigners"/"peoples of the land"	13: mixed marriages/threats from "foreigners"/"peoples of the land"

Grabbe's final list charted parallels between the first part of Ezra (the "Joshua-Zerubbabel" narrative as Grabbe called it) and the second part (the Ezra narrative).

Ezra 1–6	Ezra 7–10
1: decree of Cyrus	7: decree of Artaxerxes
1: delivery of wealth/temple vessels	8: delivery of wealth/temple vessels
2: list of immigrants	8: list of immigrants
3: sacrifices offered	8: sacrifices offered
4: foreigners raise opposition	9: problem because of foreigners
6: opposition overcome	10: problem resolved
6: temple completed	Neh 8: mission completed (law read)
6: Tabernacles celebrated	Neh 8: Tabernacles celebrated

L. L. Grabbe, *Ezra-Nehemiah* (Old Testament Readings; London, New York: Routledge, 1998) 119–20.

1:1–2:20; 4:1–7:5 (of which 7:5 looks redactional); and 13:4-31. There is, apparently, no better explanation for the books to switch to the first person in places than that those two men wrote the chapters. As the above sentences make clear, however, those first person passages were scattered around and constitute only about seven of the twenty-three chapters. Ezra-Nehemiah also includes some third person accounts of the two men, and a wealth of other documents. In other words, Ezra and Nehemiah were two of the heroes of the books that bear their names, but no more than one-third of the chapters of the books should be ascribed to their heroes. As the books stand, they are the product of a later writer who had access to a number of documents, including (perhaps) some from Ezra and Nehemiah.

What justifies one's speaking of the "unity" of Ezra-Nehemiah is the common use of several features. For one thing, they share an appreciation for written documents and refer to them over and over, reciting them to good effect. Second, they both consciously use the same list of returnees from Babylon, which list, however, appears to be one of the latest-dated parts of the work. Third, part of the Ezra narrative appears in the book of Nehemiah, making the two men's careers seem to overlap whether they did or not. Fourth, the narratives share similar views about the primacy of repatriated Babylonian captives and about the temple and Jerusalem, views that set apart the repatriates as the true people of God. It appears that in the end a single, overarching perspective was imposed on the whole narrative. It carefully employs traditions from the beginning of the Persian Period (the rebuilding of the temple) and from the middle of that period (the rebuilding of the wall) to write one story about who constituted the true Israel. Finally, as K. Min argues, Nehemiah is simply incomplete and cannot stand without Ezra. A couple of simple examples must suffice. One is the mention of Ezra in Nehemiah 7:73b–8:18 with no introduction, which would leave unexplained his prominence in the ceremony described there. A second is the mention in Nehemiah 8:17 of someone named "Jeshua" (*Yēšûaʿ*), a name never used of the early hero Joshua in the Hebrew Bible.[42] (Nor, one might add, is that priest called Jeshua in Haggai or Zechariah, where the name is *Yĕhôšuaʿ*.) The reference, then, is to the "Jeshua" of the book of Ezra 2:2 and 36: 3:8, 9; 4:3; and 5:2.

H. The Date of Ezra-Nehemiah

The date of Ezra-Nehemiah has been addressed above in various places, and may be summarized here. Although the book draws on the biblical sources of Haggai and Zechariah (see Ezra 5:1), the unified book cannot date earlier than the career of its hero Nehemiah, who worked in Jerusalem between the twentieth and thirty-second years of Artaxerxes I, i.e., 445–433.[43] Nehemiah 13:6 says Nehemiah returned to the court of Artaxerxes, although the verse does not say he went to Susa (one of the capitals of Persia), where Nehemiah 1:1 situates him. (See again [Historical Tension in Ezra-Nehemiah]). "After some time" he returned to Jerusalem, but neither the exact date nor the length of his second stay is mentioned anywhere. The actions taken by Nehemiah during that second term (Neh 13:7-31) need not have taken very long. Even if the whole of Nehemiah 11–13 is placed in the second term of Nehemiah (as is sometimes argued), this basic conclusion still stands.

Scholars suggest a variety of later, more specific dates. H. G. M. Williamson, for example, thinks Ezra-Nehemiah arose after Chronicles and drew on it. Based on the absence of Greek influence on the book of Chronicles, Williamson dates that work about the middle of the fourth century, before Alexander the Great took over Palestine in 332/1, followed by a priestly revision dated somewhat later.[44] With regard to Ezra-Nehemiah, he thinks Ezra 1–6 was the latest material assembled for Ezra-Nehemiah. He dates those chapters (and thus Ezra-Nehemiah as it exists today) about 300, although he dates the Ezra and Nehemiah narratives themselves as early as 400.[45] M. Noth arrived at a similar date for Ezra-Nehemiah, namely the turn from the fourth to the third century based on the lengthy Aramaic description of the building of the temple (Ezra 4:8–6:18). He noted chronological discrepancies concerning Cyrus, Artaxerxes, and Darius, and he argued that the Aramaic section (Ezra 4:8–6:18), which discusses them, must have been written well after the reign not only of Darius I (522–486) but also of Darius II (423–404), and he suggested the late Persian Period or early Greek period, preferably 300.[46] Loring W. Batten thinks that Ezra flourished during the career of Artaxerxes II (404–358), but that a later editor, working after 300, mistakenly placed him first.[47] He then moves his comments on Ezra 7–10 to the end of his book. P. R. Davies offers an even later date. Starting with the absence of any mention of Ezra outside of the book until the second century BCE, he suggests that era as the point of origin of Ezra-Nehemiah as it now exists.[48] A growing number of scholars join him. Still, the absence of evidence does not, cannot, prove the nonexistence of something, so *logically speaking* Davies's evidence does not support his conclusion. Even so, the large numbers of people listed in Ezra 2 // Nehemiah 7 point to a date no earlier than near the end of the Persian Period, i.e., close to 321 BCE and more likely as late as the mid-second century BCE. *If,* moreover, the parallels between Ezra-Nehemiah and second century works cited above in "(C) The Historical Reliability of Ezra-Nehemiah" are valid, the date of final completion of the book falls about the middle of the second century. In summary, then, the date of Ezra-Nehemiah falls sometime after 433 (the last date mentioned), with a second recension perhaps in the fourth century, and a completion *possibly* as late as the second.

Readers encounter in Ezra-Nehemiah, therefore, the written composition of a series of editors who had in hand (1) traditions about two or more returns from Babylon to Jerusalem, (2) narratives about rebuilding the altar and temple in Jerusalem, (3) narratives about the work of Ezra and Nehemiah in the first person singular, (4) third-person traditions about the careers of both men, (5) lists of workers and their work, (6) the biblical book of Haggai, and quite likely Zechariah 1–8, and (7) various other materials. The redactors who arranged all those materials also had an exclusionist perspective that they superimposed over the whole of Ezra-Nehemiah, regardless of whether those traditions originally embraced that agenda. Only in the case of Haggai and Zechariah do readers have direct access to their sources, and Haggai and Zechariah do not articulate that agenda. Readers of this commentary will encounter, therefore, a deliberate attempt to read Ezra-Nehemiah straight through as a redacted piece. There will be no attempt to rearrange the various segments into an "earlier" or "better" version or to relocate some chapters as earlier commentators sometimes did. The arrangement of the materials, including anticipatory hints, the repetition and the displacement of traditions, and other issues will factor in the reading and interpreting the material. Confessionally, one can say that the final version is biblical; methodologically, one can say that the final version is one its final author/editor gave it and the one to be accounted for and interpreted. Earlier possible locations and meanings are not irrelevant, but the text as edited will be the focus of this commentary.

I. Groups in Persian Period Yehud

Even a cursory reading of Ezra-Nehemiah reveals a Jerusalemite/Judean community at odds within itself. John Kessler has described that community sociologically, and his work will be appropriated and summarized here. The post-exilic community reflected in Ezra-Nehemiah was anything but a homogenous community. As already mentioned above, the city of Mizpah apparently had replaced Jerusalem as the capital, a conclusion that Kessler notes but does not endorse. It is clear, however, that Yehud was *not* devoid of inhabitants, nor was Samaria, in 539 or 521. Nor were Yehud, Samaria, and Babylon the only places where worshipers of Yahweh dwelt. Others lived in Egypt, Mesopotamia (notably Elam and Babylonia), and elsewhere (Galilee, Gaza, Ashdod, and Idumea).

Kessler describes the role of the returnees by means of their similarities to and differences from a Charter Group, i.e., an elite group of people that moves into a geographical region, establishes a power base, and creates a sociological structure distinct from what was already in place. As Kessler describes it, a Charter Group typically is an ethnically defined, nonindigenous, enfranchised elite with a double allegiance: both to its old and its new lands. It creates a sociopolitical structure distinct from the one that already existed in the new land. The situation in post-exilic Yehud was, therefore, somewhat unlike that of a typical Charter Group in that people already in Yehud were culturally and religiously much *like* the members of the Charter Group. For both, therefore, the issue of who was inside and who was outside of the real Judah were especially acute. In particular, could non-returnees (e.g., "foreign" wives of returnees or people from northern Israel) belong to the community? The returnees also differed from a Charter Group in that they returned as a "re-founding" group, one that claimed to be the sole legitimate heirs of the land to which they returned. Hence, their relationship to Judeans who had remained behind was difficult. They also differed from a Charter Group in that they understood themselves to have been enfranchised not by one but by two power groups: the Persian government and those who remained in Babylon. What is more, the returnees could not claim to speak for or represent ex-Judeans who lived outside of Babylon, and the returnees' interest was less economic than it was spiritual: an attempt at ethnic, cultural, and religious identification with the site most deeply rooted in its historical and religious heritage. (One may ask, however, whether economics was not also a part of their agenda.)

The returnees would have had one clear advantage: their direct experience of Persian rule, which was moving westward toward Greece and also toward Egypt. Taking Ezra-Nehemiah at face value, the returnees came not only with personnel and finances from the Persian government but also with the authorization to control Yahwism in Jerusalem and Yehud. While Kessler does not say this, a reading of Haggai and Zechariah might suggest that the first returnees harbored hopes for a local Davidic king that the Persians were not prepared to allow. Kessler notes that the returnees' self-designation "those who had escaped from the captivity" (see Ezra 2:1; Neh 1:2; 8:17) testifies to their recognition of their dispossessed status. Their loyalty to Persia was counterbalanced apparently by hopes for national restoration, and those competing agendas play out in Ezra-Nehemiah. Control of the rebuilt temple in Jerusalem was their first accomplishment, and the rebuilding of the wall around it to set it off as holy was their second.

In Ezra-Nehemiah, therefore, three key elements demarcated the returnees from other groups in Yehud: genealogical/ethnic roots in the former kingdom of Judah, the experience of the captivity, and attachment to and acceptance of a specific form of Yahwism formulated by the returnees themselves. Two opposing movements arose among the returnees. The first was a movement to *include* some groups outside the returnees based on (1) a need for laborers, (2) the desire to increase the community's economic and demographic clout by involving people with disposable wealth, (3) kinship ties, and (4) the desire to rebuild the temple. The second was a movement to *exclude* other people, especially Yahwists from northern Israel who might have competed for positions of leadership. For the returnees, adherence to the Law of Moses could be measured by conformity to the returnees' definition of endogamy and rules of Sabbath observance (Neh 13; Ezra 10). Their reaction against foreign wives can be seen as their attempt to prevent the transfer of land outside of the Charter Group.

Whatever successes the returnees had in achieving their agenda, they did not ultimately win. As Kessler states matters, their ideas gave way to a more inclusive stance as seen, for example, in Ruth and Judith. One might well add Third or Trito Isaiah (Isa 56–66) and Jonah too, if one dates Jonah in the third century BCE. Still, those who determined the canon of Judaism saw fit to include Ezra-Nehemiah, perhaps as a testimony to faith during difficult days and to the providence of God.[49] [A "Bürger—Tempel—Gemeinde"?]

J. The Purposes of Ezra-Nehemiah

Ezra-Nehemiah is composed in three parts, each with its own purpose. Ezra 1–6 was designed to legitimate the returnees as the proper religious and local political leaders of Yehud. They came back under the commission and with the assistance of the Persian emperor Cyrus. As far as the redactor of Ezra-Nehemiah was concerned, the temple was for their exclusive use. Ezra 7–10 skips ahead a couple of generations, but it too was written to defend the prerogatives of the returnees over against any claims that the people who had remained behind in Yehud might claim or desire for themselves. Ezra returned with another small group of returnees to assure the ethical purity of worshipers there, a purity guaranteed by their descent from the original exiles held captive in Babylon. That claim had political ramifications, which is why Ezra 1–6, 7–10 and the narrative of Nehemiah place so much emphasis on their appointment by the Persians and their careful compliance with the

A "Bürger—Tempel—Gemeinde"?

A proposed model for understanding post-exilic Yehud is that of the "Bürger—Tempel—Gemeinde" proposed by Joel P. Weinberger, a Latvian scholar who articulated it during the 1970s. He thought that post-exilic Yehud should be understood as an ethnically based economic community centered on the temple. According to Charles E. Carter, Weinberger proposed two basic groups in such economies: temple personnel and the land they controlled and the non-priestly citizens of the ruling class, arranged by extended families of "father's houses." Control of such economies could lay with either group. Weinberger proposed that post-exilic Yehud contained three such communities, located in Jerusalem, the Jordan Valley, and the coastal plain. His reading of Ezra-Nehemiah supported his view.

While this model is helpful, it does not actually fit the description of Yehud in Ezra-Nehemiah according to many scholars. The model was not designed with Judean society in view, and it does not take into account the lengthy timespan during which Ezra-Nehemiah came into existence. Instead Weinberger takes the time of action of book of Ezra (539–458/7) as definitive for the time of the book's origin. Weinberger rejects views that Ezra-Nehemiah borrowed from other biblical texts, and he posits a population for the returnees of 150,000 by the time of Ezra. Carter thinks that Weinberger's estimates would yield a population for all of that area plus the Negeb, the Judean highlands, the coastal plain, and the Judean desert somewhere between 250,000 and 300,000 and calls that figure "impossibly high." (That is, they left no such an archaeological trail.)

American scholars, therefore, may well tip their hats to Weinberger for offering a provocative theory, but generally modify it at least. This commentary will develop a view of the return of the exiles and the nature of the society they wished/hoped to rebuild, based on the biblical texts themselves and reports of archaeological digs. Simply put, people are messy and leave remains. Careful archaeologists (and this writer is not one) can reconstruct much about their numbers, occupations, burial practices, diet, and religion from artifacts, *though* all that date must be *interpreted*. Moreover, the returnees left their own records, which were carefully shaped by *later* redactors to support the redactors' perspectives. This commentary will present Ezra-Nehemiah as the perspective of the returnees from Babylon as funneled through their successors in Jerusalem and Yehud. Ezra-Nehemiah presents the returnees as a determined if exclusivistic group convinced that God was leading them from exile in Babylon (as God had led Moses and the people of Israel from Egypt) to take back their rightful place at the head of society in and around Jerusalem and to restore worship in the temple for themselves.

Charles E. Carter, *The Emergence of Yehud in the Persian Period: A Social and Demograhic Study* (JSOTSup 294; Sheffield: Sheffield Academic Press, 1999) 46–48, 294–98, and 300–307.

Persians. Finally, the book of Nehemiah was written to defend the ongoing rights and perks of the returnees over against those of the Samaritans and those in Yehud who cooperated or at least sympathized with the Samaritans. It described the rebuilding of the walls of Jerusalem by the descendants of returnees only, making the city a holy zone/area around the temple, thus protecting it from ritual and ethical contamination. Overall as well perhaps, Ezra-Nehemiah was written to legitimate the claims of the returnees in the eyes of the captives still in Babylon and gain their agreement with and approval of the actions the returnees had taken. Isaiah 56:3-8, by contrast, articulated its author's view that God intended the temple to be used by all peoples, including foreigners and even people like eunuchs (v. 4), who were barred in Deuteronomy 23:1, 3 (see Lev 21:18-20) from worshiping in a holy place dedicated to God. This understanding of the overall trajectory of Ezra-Nehemiah will guide this commentary. The restoration of the exiled community to what the authors/redactors of the work considered the community's rightful position as the punished and liberated people of God unfolded in three distinct phases each prompted and guided by the return of a group of exiles. [The Three Phases of Restoration in Ezra-Nehemiah]

Matthew Levering sees these events as essential parts of salvation history. In doing so he is quite correct, but in defending his case he goes too far. In describing of the roles of Ezra and others, he asks, "Without Ezra the Scribe's reclamation of the Torah, could the Sermon on the Mount be imagined? . . . Without Zerubbabel and Joshua, Haggai and Zechariah, could Jesus have enacted the return of Yhwh to Zion?"[50] One may counter first that Ezra-Nehemiah exhibits an exclusivism foreign to the Sermon on the Mount and second that had those people failed, God could have used other people to accomplish the divine purpose of restoring Jerusalem, perhaps even in a different way. Readers probably should not suppose that the way God accomplishes God's purpose is the only means at God's disposal. It is one thing to say that God prompted those men (and perhaps others), that they responded, and consequently that God worked through them. Had they been unwilling or unable to act, however, God could and presumably would have inspired others to do God's will. It would also seem obvious that God worked through other people in the period of 539 to the late fifth century to accomplish God's will, people who are not named in the biblical record. Modern Christians would do well to remember that neither they nor ancient Jews are/were powerful enough to stop God's work by their disobedience, failure to act, or simple failure to understand what God wanted of them.

The Three Phases of Restoration in Ezra-Nehemiah

1. Restoring the Yehudite Community through Rebuilding the Temple, Ezra 1–6
2. Restoring the Yehudite Community through Reaffirming the Law, Ezra 7–10
3. Restoring the Yehudite Community through Rebuilding Jerusalem's Wall, Nehemiah 1–13

CONNECTIONS

1. A modern issue that resembles the relationship between Persia and the peoples of the Fertile Crescent is the morality of great nations in their relationships with underdeveloped nations. In the case of Persia, the conqueror was willing to return captives to their home and to cede a degree of local government to them. In contrast with the savagery of the Babylonians depicted in 2 Kings 24:10-16 and 25:1-21 and in 2 Chronicles 36:15-20, the Persians seem enlightened to modern readers. Indeed, Hebrew Bible scholars of even the recent past have accepted the depiction of the Persians as evidence of a kinder and gentler ruling power. Even if

true, however, any foreign power that controls its surrounding neighbors and uses them for its own foreign and domestic benefit must be seen for what it is. The various sectors of post-exilic Yehud saw things quite differently than the Persians did. The Persian officials perhaps thought of themselves as "liberators," but expected compliance by the "liberated." As difficult as it sometimes is to cut through such scenarios, it is much easier to see when that nation is one other than one's own. As the old saying goes, there is often "my side, your side, and the real side." The returnees seem to have seen themselves as the "true" Judah/Israel, while those who had remained in Yehud (and Samaria) perhaps saw them as the sinful upper class who had received what they deserved in captivity. Those who remained behind may have seen themselves as the rightful inhabitants of Yehud and Jerusalem. Their leaders apparently saw themselves as the real leaders, especially in Samaria. It is not necessary for modern readers to settle that dispute for them. Rather, readers are to learn from that situation.

One lesson moderns might learn is that there are multiple sides to national and international issues, both in the Bible and in modern times. One line of argument will perhaps make this point clearer. World War II was horrendous in its destructiveness, and it left many people and nations of the world struggling for survival. After the war, one institution designed by the United States, Great Britain, and other western powers to help them was the World Bank, traditionally headed by an American. At first, it had limited funds to loan, and granted loans under the most fiscally conservative rules it could design and still help struggling countries. France was the first country to receive aid, while Poland and Chile were rejected. The Marshall Fund was designed to help too, but it loaned mostly to European countries. In 1968, the World Bank changed and began loaning money to developing countries. Moreover, loans could be used to build schools, hospitals, and other such institutions. Third world nations that borrowed money for such causes incurred heavy debt loads to repay. In response to criticism, the World Bank changed some of its policies to aid poorer countries, but it was already held in disdain by many third world nations. [World Bank Protestor]

Some people would question whether morality is even an issue for nations (or corporations!), arguing that ethical conduct is a matter for individuals only. The Bible does, of course, hold individuals to correct standards of conduct, but prophetic texts such as Hosea 9:1-9; Joel 3:1-8; Amos 1:3-4, 6-8, 9-12, 13-14; Habakkuk 3:6-11; Zephaniah 2:1-15; Isaiah 14:24–17:16;

Jeremiah 4:1-10; 46:1–51:58; and Ezekiel 16:1-52; 25:1–27:36 predict national punishment on Israel/Judah and the nearby countries for the actions of people those political entities and their heads. Those texts (and others) all recognize that kings make decisions and individuals fight and otherwise act on behalf of nations and peoples, and the texts hold entire groups/peoples responsible for the actions carried out in their names or on their behalf. One must read the Bible very selectively to use it to buttress the idea that fair play and even generosity are individual matters only.

World Bank Protestor

This 2004 image perhaps catches the frustration of those living in third-world countries as they try to plot their own course of improvement and hit obstacles from the very people charged with and trying to help them.

World Bank Protestor, Jakarta, Indonesia. (Credit: Jonathan McIntosh, Wikimedia Commons, CCA 2.0)

2. Ezra and Nehemiah also show religion as a divisive force in Persian Period society in Yehud. It is quite clear that people who had not been in exile were viewed as suspect and that returnees wanted full and complete control of everything that went on in the temple. Some people from outside Jerusalem in pre-exilic Judah continued living in northern Israel and in Yehud in the Persian Period, and they disagreed with the returnees over who had rights with regard to the temple in Jerusalem after it was rebuilt. In support of its religio-political agenda, Nehemiah 10:30 reports a pledge of the returnees not to intermarry with local worshipers of God, an ugly incidence of religious prejudice generated out of the desire to rule Yehud and the temple. The books of Ezra and Nehemiah also depict the action of their heroes that must be termed cruel, namely of forcing divorces in cases even where the "offending" couple had children (Ezra 9–10; Neh 13:1-3, 23-31). Nehemiah 10:30 also shows the people pledging to avoid such conduct in the future lest the temple be polluted.

Ethical and religious purity, however, does not require such heartless legislation and action. Perhaps that heartless legalism is what caused Martin Luther to ignore Ezra and Nehemiah. In his collected works, he does not quote Ezra at all and he quotes Nehemiah only about four times. He refers to Ezra and Nehemiah by name about eight times, and briefly discusses the rebuilding of the wall in Nehemiah 3–6.[51] In contrast with this exclusivism, however, Zechariah 14:16-21 envisions a future for Jerusalem in which *all the peoples* who survive an anticipated war would come to Jerusalem to worship God at the autumnal feast of booths. The place would be so overrun with pilgrims that they would cook their sacred meals all over Jerusalem and in surrounding Judah. The whole area would become a place of common worship. It is incumbent upon readers of Ezra-Nehemiah, therefore, to seek specific reasons for some of the actions and interpretations of Hebrew Bible laws and not just assume that those rules were necessarily universal and that they held for the whole Hebrew Bible *or even* that they were necessarily moral. Readers might want to challenge such views as unfortunate or even as immoral applications of God's law. Just because an action is reported in the Bible as moral and as God's will does not necessitate that readers share that opinion, especially an action directly countermanded elsewhere as is true of this issue in Ezra-Nehemiah. Readers might also think carefully about their own views of other nations, in particular about nations with an overwhelming Muslim, Hindu, or Buddhist population. Are nations with a Christian majority or at least a Christian heritage favored by God? Regardless, should the predominant religion in another country dictate American policy toward that nation, positively or negatively?

3. Other literature in the Hebrew Bible as well (e.g., census lists, Ecclesiastes, and the Song of Songs) raises the issue of what it means to call a work "Bible" or "Holy Literature." Do/must books in the Bible address problems moderns confront and articulate a scientific worldview—or even a nonscientific worldview to which science must be expected to conform? Is the New Testament's witness to Jesus dependent on whether Genesis is scientifically correct? Must readers choose between the Bible and Charles Darwin or modern geologists? Modern readers often put biblical authors in impossible straights when moderns demand that under divine inspiration the authors wrote infallible solutions to intractable problems, which not only correctly addressed their own situations but also ours as well. Even if the books of the Bible "infallibly" addressed their own situation, is it not too much to demand that they address ours too? Is it not simply lazy and arrogant to expect such "timeless" truth from God on a platter? Integrity grows out of struggle and development—and even error—not through avoiding such things.

Charles Darwin

Charles Darwin (1809–1882). Portrait by Maull and Fox, c. 1854. (Credit: Wikimedia Commons, CC-PD-Mark)

Darwin was criticized by church people and clergy, but earlier in his life he had begun preparing to become an Anglican minister. Instead, he laid the foundation for modern biology with his theory of evolution. Religious opponents attacked his views, but there is nothing necessarily antagonistic between the theory of evolution and the Bible.

The Bible points to problems in human nature and culture, but it does not so much tell its readers, ancient or modern, what the solution is for each problem as to advocate an honest, if in some ways fallible and incomplete solution. But even in cases where it might seem to have advocated a particular solution, is there any reason to suppose that that solution is applicable in any and all other situations? In cases like those that the returnees faced as a handful of refugees arriving back home, is there any reason to suppose that solutions they thought God had directed to them are applicable to persons alive today? Even if Ezra's and Nehemiah's solutions were correct for their times and communities (and this commentary will investigate that question), readers—under God—still have to find solutions to their own, different problems. If this line of thinking seems forced and negative, readers should recall that in the past believers used the Bible to prove, for example, that the earth revolves around the sun (Eccl 1:5) and that slavery was ordained by God (Gen 9:25).

NOTES

1. The book of Esther also is set in the Persian Period, but not in Palestine. In addition, much of the Hebrew Bible reached its final form during the Persian Period, but yields only indirect evidence about the period.

2. Otto Eissfeldt, *The Old Testament: An Introduction* (New York: Harper and Row, 1965) 542.

3. Judson R. Shaver, "Ezra and Nehemiah: On the Theological Significance of Making them Contemporaries," in *Priests, Prophets and Scribes: Essays on the Formation and Heritage of Second temple Judaism in Honor of Joseph Blenkinsopp* (ed. Eugene Ulrich, John W. Wright, Robert P. Carroll, and Philip R. Davies; JSOT Sup 149; Sheffield: Sheffield Academic Press, 1992) 76–86, here 86.

4. Ezra 3:10, for example, says the priest Jeshua and his sons were in charge of building the temple, while Ezra 5:16 says in a letter from Tattenai, the Babylonian governor of the province, that Sheshbazzar initiated the building project. Hag 1:14-15 insists that Zerubbabel and Joshua (Jeshua in Ezra-Nehemiah) "came and worked on the house of the LORD of hosts their God on the twenty-fourth day of the six month" of 520.

5. L. W. Batten, *The Books of Ezra and Nehemiah* (ICC; Edinburgh: Clark, 1913) 14. This line of scholars includes numerous others, such as C. I. Keil in C. I. Kiel and

F. Delitzsch, *Biblical Commentary on the Old Testament: The Books of Ezra, Nehemiah, and Esther* (Grand Rapids MI: Eerdmans, 1950).

6. C. C. Torrey, *Ezra Studies* (Chicago: University of Chicago Press, 1910) 238–48. Roddy L. Braun ("Chronicles, Ezra, and Nehemiah," in *Studies in the Historical Book of the Old Testament* [VTSup XXX; ed. J. A. Emerton; Leiden, Brill, 1979] 52–63) argues that the author of Chronicles is not responsible for at least a significant part of Ezra-Nehemiah.

7. J. Becker, *Der Ich-Bericht des Nehemiabuches als chronistische Gestaltung* (Forschung zur Bibel 87; Würzburg: Echter, 1998) 6–7, 19–22. See A. S. Kapelrud, *The Question of Authorship in the Ezra Narrative* (Oslo: Dybwad, 1942) 95–96. C. C. Torrey, *Ezra Studies* (Chicago: University of Chicago Press, 1910) 240–42; M. Noth, *The Chronicler's History* (JSOTSup 50; Sheffield: Sheffield Academic Press, 1987) 62–65; original ed.: *Überlieferungsgeschichtliche Studien* (Halle: Niemeyer, 1943) 146. Peter R. Ackroyd ("The Chronicler as Exegete," *JSOT* 2 [1977]: 2–32, particularly14–20) also accepts the Chronicler as the overall author of Ezra-Nehemiah, but he carefully details differences in style between sources employed within Ezra-Nehemiah and that of the redactor, whom he also considers the Chronicler.

8. See Joseph Blenkinsopp, *Ezra-Nehemiah* (OTL; Philadelphia: Westminster, 1988) 48.

9. See Sara Japhet, "The Supposed Common Authorship of Chronicles and Ezra-Nehemiah Investigated Anew," *VT* 18 (1968): 330–71, and H. G. M. Williamson, *Ezra, Nehemiah* (WBC 16; Waco: Word, 1985) xxii, xxxiii–xxxv. Tamara C. Eskenazi scarcely mentions the Chronicler in her review article, "Current Perspectives on Ezra-Nehemiah and the Persian Period," *CR:BS* 1 (1993): 59–86. Becker (*Der Ich-Bericht*, 7), however, thinks his (i.e., Becker's) views on their fictive character would hold regardless of whether the verses stemmed from the Chronicler.

10. Blenkinsopp (*Ezra-Nehemiah*, 49) estimates that 70 percent of the book derives from sources.

11. E. S. Gerstenberger, *Israel in the Persian Period; The Fifth and Fourth Centuries BCE.* (Biblical Encyclopedia; trans. S. G. Schatzmann; Atlanta: Society of Biblical Literature, 2011) 30.

12. Ibid., 31.

13. Batten (*Ezra and Nehemiah*, 98) suggested the translation "entertainers." Whoever these people were, they were not temple singers. Temple singers had already been mentioned in Ezra 2:41 // Neh 7:44, and they would have all been men in any case.

14. D. J. Clines, *Ezra, Nehemiah, Esther* (NCB; Basingtoke: Marshall Morgan & Scott; Grand Rapids MI: Eerdmans, 1984) 44. See W. Rudolph (*Esra und Nehemiah* [HAT 20; Tübingen: Mohr Siebeck, 1949] xxiii and 11–15), who dates the list to 537 (xxiii).

15. Blenkinsopp, *Ezra-Nehemiah*, 83. Blenkinsopp offers a brief historical reconstruction of the rise of "Judaism" that has been challenged for positing such a self-understanding centuries too early. See the review by Joshua Schwartz in *Review of Biblical Literature*, 2011 (ed. Jan G. van der Watt; Atlanta: Society of Biblical Literature, 2011) 237–42. In this commentary, Blenkinsopp's exegetical insights will be duly noted and often accepted. The question of when "Judaism" per se arose is, however, more an issue of the history of religion than of exegesis, and as such will be left to the side.

16. C. E. Carter, *The Emergence of Yehud in the Persian Period: A Social and Demographic Study* (JSOTSup 294; Sheffield: Sheffield Academic Press, 1999) 201–202.

17. O. Lipschits, "Archaemenid Imperial Policy and the Status of Jerusalem," in *Judah and Judeans in the Persian Period* (ed. O. Lipschits and M. Oeming; Winona Lake IN.: Eisenbrauns, 2006) 32.

18. See, for example, Klaus-Dietrich Schunck, *Nehemiah* (BKAT xxiii/26; Neukirchen: Neukirchener Verlag, 2009) XV.

19. J. L. Wright, "A New Model for the Composition of Ezra-Nehemiah," in *Judah and the Judeans in the Fourth Century BCE* (ed. Oded Lipschits, Gary N. Knoppers, and Rainer Albertz; Winona Lake IN: Eisenbrauns, 2007) 347.

20. David Ussishkin, "The Borders and De Facto Size of Jerusalem in the Persian Period," in *Judah and the Judeans in the Persian Period* (ed. Oded Lipschits and Manfred Oeming; Winona Lake IN: Eisenbrauns, 2006) 147–66.

21. Wright, "A New Model," 347–48.

22. See Williamson, *Ezra, Nehemiah*, 260, who cites R. A. Parker and W. H. Dubberstein, *Babylonian Chronology 626 BCE–CE 75* (Brown University Studies 19; Providence: Brown University Press, 1956).

23. Oded Lipschits "Persian Period Finds from Jerusalem: Facts and Interpretations," *Journal of Hebraic Studies* 9, article 20, p. 21, http://www.jhsonline .org and http://purl.org/jhs. See more fully Lipschits, "Archaemenid Imperial Policy, Settlement Processes in Palestine, and the Status of Jerusalem in the Middle of the Fifth century BCE," *Judah and the Judeans in the Persian Period* (ed. Oded Lipschits and Manfred Oeming; Winona Lake IN: Eisenbrauns, 2006) 19–52.

24. K. G. Hogland, *Achaemenid Imperial Administration in Syria-Palestine and the Missions of Ezra and Nehemiah* (SBLDS 125; Atlanta: Scholars Press, 1992) 243.

25. Ibid., 244.

26. Lipschits, "Archaemenid Imperial Policy and the Status of Jerusalem," 39.

27. J. M. Myers, *Ezra-Nehemiah*, lxiii.

28. Christopher Begg, "Ben Sirach's Non-mention of Ezra," *BN* 42 (1988): 14–18, here 17–18.

29. Sara Japhet, *I & II Chronicles* (OTL; Louisville: Westminster/John Knox, 1993) 3–7, and Williamson, Ezra, Nehemiah, xxii, xxxiii–xxxv.

30. Blenkinsopp, *Ezra-Nehemiah*, 53.

31. See, for example, Schunck, *Nehemiah*, XII.

32. Bleninsopp, *Ezra-Nehemiah*, 51. See also Myers, *II Chronicles*, xxxi.

33. H. G. M. Williamson, *1 and 2 Chronicles* (NCB; London: Marshall, Morgan & Scott; Grand Rapids MI: Eerdmans, 1982) 419.

34. P. L. Redditt, "The Dependence of Ezra-Nehemiah on 1 and 2 Chronicles," in *Unity and Disunity in Ezra-Nehemiah: Redaction, Rhetoric, and Reader* (ed. M. J. Boda and P. L. Redditt; Hebrew Bible Monographs 17; Sheffield: Sheffield Phoenix Press, 2008) 229–33. The article argues that Ezra-Nehemiah borrowed from additional passages in Chronicles. See the article for examples and details.

35. See O. Eissfeldt, *The Old Testament; An Introduction* (trans. P. R. Ackroyd; Oxford: Blackwell, 1965) 574–75. See Blenkinsopp, *Ezra-Nehemiah*, 70–72 for a good overview of the issue.

36. L. L. Grabbe, *Ezra-Nehemiah* (Old Testament Readings; London, New York; Routledge, 1998) 121. Recently Lisbeth S. Fried edited a volume dedicated to the issue of the relationship between Ezra-Nehemiah and First Esdras: *Was 1 Esdras First? An Investigation into the Priority and Nature of 1 Esdras* (SBLAIE 7; Atlanta: Society of Biblical Literature, 2011). Three of the essays argued for the priority of 1 Esdras, seven for the priority of Ezra-Nehemiah, and six studied the nature of 1 Esdras. To be sure, defenders of the priority of 1 Esdras include Gary Knoppers and Lester L. Grabbe, heavyweights in the debate. Still, the preponderance of scholars argues the other way, and the issue is important but not crucial for this commentary.

37. J. C. VanderKam, "Ezra-Nehemiah or Ezra and Nehemiah," in *Priests, Prophets and Scribes: Essays on the Formation and Heritage of Second Temple Judaism in Honour of Joseph Blenkinsopp* (ed. E. Ulrich, J. W. Wright, R. P. Carroll, P. R. Davies; JSOTSup 149; Sheffield: Sheffield Academic Press, 1992) 62–63. The list is from E. L. Curtis and A. A. Madsen, *A Critical and Exegetical Commentary on the Books of Chronicles* (ICC; New York: Scribner's, 1910) 2–5.

38. VanderKam ("Ezra-Nehemiah or Ezra and Nehemiah?" 67) admits that the explanation for this difference may simply be a difference in what sources were available.

39. Ibid., 67–68. That ninety years depends on a scholar's dating scheme for Ezra-Nehemiah, but even assuming a date of 520 for the action in Ezra 4:1-5 and 458 as the date for Nehemiah's journey to Jerusalem, there is still a gap of over sixty years. J. Pakala ("The Disunity of Ezra—Nehemiah," in *Unity and Disunity in Ezra-Nehemiah* [ed. Mark J, Boda and Paul L. Redditt; Hebrew Bible Monographs 17; Sheffield: Sheffield Phoenix Press, 2008] 204–15) also challenges the unity of Ezra-Nehemiah, based on his analysis of Ezra 3:4-5, 4:1-24, 6:16-22, 7:6b, 7:8, 8:15-20, Neh 8:1, 2, 9 (MT) 9:6, and 13:16. In these passages, he finds evidence of *dis*juncture between Ezra and Nehemiah.

40. L. S. Fried, "Who Wrote Ezra-Nehemiah—and Why Did They?" *Unity and Disunity in Ezra-Nehemiah; Redaction, Rhetoric, and Reader* (ed. Mark J. Boda and Paul L. Redditt; Hebrew Bible Monographs 17; Sheffield: Sheffield Phoenix Press, 2008) 97.

41. T. C. Eskenazi, "Ezra-Nehemiah: From Text to Actuality," in *Signs and Wonders: Biblical Texts in Literary Focus* (ed. J. C. Exum; SBLSS; Atlanta: Society of Biblical Literature, 1989) 165–94.

42. K. Min, "Nehemiah without Ezra?" in *Unity and Disunity in Ezra-Nehemiah; Redaction, Rhetoric, and Reader* (ed. Mark J. Boda and Paul L. Redditt; Hebrew Bible Monographs 17; Sheffield: Sheffield Phoenix Press, 2008) 169.

43. Richard J. Saley, "The Date of Nehemiah Reconsidered," in Gary A. Tuttle, ed., *Biblical and Near Eastern Studies; Essays in Honor of William Sanford LaSor* (Grand Rapids MI: Eerdmans, 1978) 151–65, here 163.

44. Williamson, *1 and 2 Chronicles*, 16.

45. Williamson, *Ezra, Nehemiah*, xxxv–xxxvi.

46. Noth, *The Chronicler's History*, 72–73. See also A. S. van der Woude, *The World of the Old Testament* (trans. Sierd Woudstra; Grand Rapids MI: Eerdmans, 1989) 224.

47. Loring W. Batten, *The Books of Ezra and Nehemiah* (ICC; Edinburgh: T. & T. Clark, 1913) 2–3.

48. P. R. Davies, *On the Origins of Judaism* (London, Oakville: Equinox, 2011) 16–19.

49. See J. Kessler, "Persia's Loyal Yahwists: Power Identity and Ethnicity in Archaemenid Yehud," in *Judah and the Judeans in the Persian Period* (ed. O. Lipschits and M. Oeming; Winona Lake IN: Eisenbrauns, 2006) 91–121.

50. Matthew Levering, *Ezra & Nehemiah* (Brazos Theological Commentary on the Bible; Grand Rapids MI: Brazos, 2007).

51. See *Luther's Works, Lectures on the Minor Prophet, III. Zechariah* (ed. Hilton C. Oswald; St. Louis: Concordia, 1973) vol. 20, p. 26. See also vol. 16, p. 221; vol. 17, pp. 124, 126, 130; and vol. 47, pp. 204 and 249.

INTRODUCTION TO EZRA

The name Ezra looms large in rabbinic tradition, and the man himself receives considerable attention in Ezra-Nehemiah. He is, of course, the namesake of the first part of the work Ezra-Nehemiah and a giant perhaps second only to Moses in rabbinic literature. (The attribution of authorship of Ezra-Nehemiah and the date of its compilation are discussed in the Introduction to Ezra-Nehemiah, in "G. The Authorship and Unity of Ezra-Nehemiah," and in "H. The Date of Ezra-Nehemiah.") This brief introduction will first treat the person of Ezra, followed by brief comments about the structure and message of the book itself.

A. Ezra in the Hebrew Bible

Despite the fact that the book was named for Ezra, a priest and scribe, he does not appear until chapter 7. The first six chapters deal with the return of exiles to rebuild the temple. Suffice it to say, the repatriates had other concerns as well, not the least of which were (re)claiming their ancestral land (Ezra 2:70), building houses (Hag 1:2-6), finding wives (Ezra 9–10; Neh 13), and earning a living. The book opens with Cyrus's edict granting permission to the exiles to return to Yehud under a man named Sheshbazzar (539), and continues with a list of repatriates who returned under Jeshua the high priest and Zerubbabel, a descendant of David (Ezra 2), before it relates the rebuilding of the temple in the face of opposition between the years 520 and 515 (Ezra 3–6). Next, it

The Prophet Ezra

Pedro Berruguete (1450–1504). *The Prophet Ezra.* S. Eulalia, Paredes de Nava, Spain. (Credit: Scala/Art Resource, NY)

Though the artist calls Ezra a "prophet," he was actually a priest who led the Returnees from Babylon to adopt severe rules of purity that excluded many people living in Yehud from the temple.

introduces Ezra, who in the seventh year of Artaxerxes I (458) gathers another group of exiles and brings them to Yehud (Ezra 7–8). It concludes with Ezra's efforts to prohibit intermarriage (Ezra 9–10). One other narrative about Ezra, one of his reading the law in Jerusalem, stands separate from the other Ezra traditions in Nehemiah 7:73–8:18 or 9:37. There he summons the returnees to obey the law. He is mentioned nowhere else in the Hebrew Bible. (The LXX gives Ezra's name in Neh 9:6 as the one who offered the prayer that follows, but the name is missing in the MT and apparently was added after the book was translated. The NRSV and some other translations follow the LXX and add Ezra's name.) [Was Ezra a High Priest in Jerusalem?]

Was Ezra a High Priest in Jerusalem?

Although Ezra is never called the "High Priest" in Ezra-Nehemiah, many scholars have argued that he was. The German scholar Klaus Koch gave this issue particular attention, advancing and defending three theses.

1. "Ezra's march from Babylon to Jerusalem was [presented as] a cultic procession which [the author of] Ezra understood as a second Exodus and a partial fulfillment of prophetic expectations" (p. 184). In response one might agree that motifs from the exodus do appear. For example, the host nation pays the Jews as they leave, but that motif in much clearer in Ezra 1–2. Also here as in Ezra 1–2 the Persian king is portrayed as a benefactor, although not first as a tyrant like the Egyptian pharaoh. The more important issue is that no one is called "high priest" in the Ezra passages, not even Ezra. Koch's argument is one from silence. By contrast, Eliashib is called the high priest in Nehemiah 3:1 and 13:28. The issue in those passages had changed.

2. "Ezra came to Jerusalem as the real high priest of the family of Aaron. His purpose was to change his people into a 'holy seed' around the holy place, which God had given as a tent-peg and source of life during the times of political servitude" (p. 190). He is quite correct that Ezra 7:1-5 traces part of Ezra's lineage from Aaron to Jehozadak, the last high priest before the exile. That Ezra descended from that priest, however, does not prove or even intimate that Ezra was the high priest. It only shows that Ezra's priestly credentials were beyond reproach. It is anyone's guess how many other postexilic priests also descended from Jehozadak. In connection with this point Koch also hypothesizes that Ezra deposed Meremoth from office, about which alleged event the book of Ezra is totally silent. Koch also surmises that "Ezra must have had his office in the temple" (p. 191). He also appeals to 3 Esdras as proof, which does call him "high priest" (1 Esdras 9:39, 40, 49), but the date of 3 Esdras is probably later. Scholars do often suggest that it preserves a better text than the MT in places, but Koch makes no argument for its higher validity than the MT at this point.

3. "Ezra was sent to all his 'people beyond the river' including the Samaritans. His aim was to establish one Israel out of all 12 tribes, which explains the later acceptance of the Pentateuch by the Samaritans" (p. 193). Koch is quite correct that "Samaritans" were not yet despised as "Samaritans" in the book of Ezra. The break in the community came later. It is also irrelevant to the issue of whether Ezra was the "high priest."

What can one say in opposition to the thesis that Ezra was the high priest? (1) Ezra is never called "high priest" in the book that bears his name; in fact, no one is. (2) There was already a high priest in Jerusalem when the temple was rebuilt: Joshua ben Jehozadak. (3) Ezra 8:37 names Meremoth as the priest who received the money from King Artaxerxes I. His authority at the temple was thus recognized, although the title was not used (as Koch admits). The author of Ezra 7–10, however, seems reluctant to recognize his authority, since Ezra was going to oppose him. This statement is not meant to suggest that Ezra desired that office; there is no way to know. The point of the Ezra narratives is, however, that Ezra was a *reformer*, not a part of the temple power structure.

Klaus Koch, "Ezra and the Origins of Judaism," *JSS* 19 (1974): 173–93.

B. Ezra after the Hebrew Bible

The New Testament nowhere mentions Ezra, not even in the book of James where the law plays such a prominent role. In Jewish legend, however, he is quite prominent. Ezra 7 mentions his journey to Palestine, and legend addresses the comparative paucity of returnees at that time (about 1,500 males; see Ezra 8:1-14) as compared with those who are said to have returned with Zerubbabel and Joshua (over 49,000; see Ezra 2:3-65 // Neh 7:8-67). According to the legend, Ezra had been forced to remain in Babylon to care for his old teacher Baruch. When he finally was able to travel to Jerusalem, he was unable to persuade many of the other exiles in Babylon to return with him. Consequently, no prophets appeared in Jerusalem after Haggai, Zechariah, and Malachi, all of whom returned early according to legend. A different tradition holds that despite Ezra's spiritual superiority, God *commanded* Ezra to remain in Babylon as long as Joshua the son of Jehozadak was alive and serving as high priest after the rebuilding of the temple, because God did not want to see the chain of high priests broken.[1] Ezra hoped to preserve the purity of the Jewish exiles in Babylon, and as a start he carefully worked out his own pedigree. Then he took with him all Jews of mixed pedigree to Jerusalem!

That last-mentioned motif points to the tension between exiles and those left behind and reflects consternation over the intermingling of returnees with those who had remained behind in Yehud. It also, however, lumps the returnees together as being as sinful as those who had remained behind during the exile. For the Babylonian tradition, the only "pure" Judeans were those who had remained in Babylon! It goes beyond the biblical books of Ezra-Nehemiah, wherein the returnees who kept themselves apart from all people living in Judah at the time of the return constituted the true Israel and those who remained in Babylon were simply ignored.

Again according to rabbinic tradition, Ezra performed two tasks on his mission to Jerusalem. First, he preached against intermarriage between returnees and locals in Yehud (see Neh 7:73b–8:12). Second, he was zealous to spread the Torah and observance of it. He was so zealous in spreading Torah that the traditions claimed, "If Moses had not anticipated Ezra, Ezra would have received the Torah."[2] In legend, however, Ezra did originate his own Decalogue, the so-called "ten regulations of Ezra." [The Ten Regulations of Ezra] He was also credited with dividing Torah into sections to be read Sabbath by Sabbath so that it was read in its entirety annually and

The Ten Regulations of Ezra

1. Readings from the Torah on Sabbath Afternoon
2. Readings from the Torah on Mondays and Thursdays
3. Holding sessions of the court on Mondays and Thursdays
4. Doing laundry work on Thursdays, not Fridays
5. Eating garlic on Friday as an aphrodisiac for Sabbath evening
6. Baking bread early in the morning to have some ready in case the poor came begging
7. Covering the lower part of women's bodies in modesty
8. Combing the hair before taking a ritual bath
9. Bathing of those who are ritually unclean before offering a prayer or studying Torah
10. Permitting peddlers to sell cosmetics to women

Though these regulations do not carry the same moral weight as the Ethical Decalogue (Exod 20:1-17 // Deut 5:6-21), they nevertheless give practical instructions for living a decent life in a believing community.

L. Ginzberg, *The Legends of the Jews* (Philadelphia: The Jewish Publication Society of America, 1968 edition) 4.356.

with ordering its copying in the Hebrew square script (the kind of script used in writing Hebrew today).[3]

The apocryphal book called "IV Ezra" or "Second Esdras" (and known only in translations in Latin, Syriac, Ethiopic, Arabic, Georgian, and Armenian) is a Jewish apocalypse written a generation after the destruction of the second temple in Jerusalem by Rome in BCE 587.[4] It ends with Ezra praying for divine inspiration to restore the Scriptures of the Jews. God agrees and directs Ezra to return the next day bringing five men with him. Meanwhile, they were to prepare "many" writing tablets (4 Ezra 14:19-26). As directed, Ezra and the five returned to the field. Then on the third day God gave Ezra the contents of ninety-four books, the twenty-four of the Jewish canon[5] plus seventy more secret books. Ezra was to make the twenty-four public but hide the other seventy for the "wise people among the Jews" (4 Ezra 14:27-47).

Another Jewish tradition speaks of Ezra's role in transmitting the Hebrew Bible. According to it "Moses received the Torah from Sinai and delivered it to Joshua, and Joshua to the elders,[6] and the elders to the prophets, and the prophets delivered it to the men of the Great Synagogue."[7] The "Great Synagogue" is an imprecise term, but it traditionally included Ezra, Mordecai, Zerubbabel, Nehemiah, the high priest Joshua, and even Daniel's three companions Hananiah, Mishael, and Azariah. They are said to have introduced the threefold division of the Jewish Scriptures Torah, Nebiim, and Kethubim.[8] Such traditions attest the high esteem in which Ezra was held, but were the creations of later generations based on their reading of Hebrew Bible texts? For the purposes of this commentary, their main importance is the attention they draw to Ezra.

C. The Structure of the Book of Ezra

The structure of the book of Ezra is twofold. The first part, Ezra 1–6, describes the returnees' efforts against great odds to rebuild the temple in Jerusalem (520–515 BCE). The second part, Ezra

7–10, jumps ahead almost six decades (to c. 458 BCE) to discuss the career of Ezra (see [Was Ezra a High Priest in Jerusalem?]), and gives a more detailed overview of the book's contents. [Outline of Ezra]

D. The Plot of the Book of Ezra

In the analysis of narratives, people often speak of a four-fold structure: opening or setting (time and place), complications, climax, and denouement. Viewed from that perspective, the book of Ezra has a double plot. In the opening of the first plot (Ezra 1), the setting or place is Babylon, the time is the first year of Cyrus (539), king of Persia, and the characters are a mass of approximately 50,000 people, led by Sheshbazzar under the control of Cyrus, King of Persia. The first "complication," the alteration in their conditions, is Cyrus's permission for all returnees who wished to return home to Jerusalem and the Persian province called Yehud. The second stage of the plot is the restoration of the altar of sacrifice (Ezra 3) and the rebuilding of the temple (Ezra 4–6). The rebuilding project ended with the celebration of Passover. As it turns out, however, the temple and its community came under the influence of

Outline of Ezra

Part One: Rebuilding the Temple, 1:1–6:22
    Judean Exiles Return Home, 1:1-11
  The Setting: Babylon in 539, 1:1
  Royal Commission: Cyrus, 1:2-4
  The Return with Sheshbazzar, 1:5-11
 Census of Returnees, 2:1-70
  People Who Led the Return, 2:1-2a
  The Tally of Returnees by Fathers' Houses, 2:2b-67
  Totals of Gifts by the Heads of Some Families, 2:68-69
  Settlement in Jerusalem and its Environs, 2:70
 Resumption of Worship in Jerusalem, 3:1-13
  Keeping the Feast of Tabernacles, 3:1-6a
  Founding the New Temple, 3:6b-13
 Opposition to Building the Temple, 4:1-24
  The Adversaries of Yehud, 4:1-5
  Written Objections to the Rebuilding of Jerusalem, 4:6-10
  The Letter to King Artaxerxes, 4:11-16
  The Reply from King Artaxerxes, 4:17-22
  Cessation of the Work in Jerusalem, 4:23-24
 Resumption of Work of the Temple, 5:1-17
  Encouragement by Haggai and Zechariah, 5:1-2
  Tattenai Writes to King Darius, 5:3-5
  Contents of the Letter of inquiry, 5:6-17
 Completion of Temple Repairs, 6:1-22
  Resolution by Darius, 6:1-12
  Completion of Repairs, 6:13-15
  Dedication of the Temple, 6:16-18
  Keeping the Feast of Passover, 6:19-22

Part Two: Rebuilding the Temple Community, 7:1–10:44
 Preparation in Babylon, 7:1-28
  Narrator's Introduction of Ezra and his Task, 7:1-10
  Letter of Artaxerxes to Ezra in Aramaic, 7:11-26
  Ezra's Praise of God in Response, 7:27-28
 Return of Exiles with Ezra, 8:1-36
  Tally of Returnees by Fathers' Houses, 8:1-14
  Assembly and Recruiting the Levites, 8:15-20
  Further Preparations: Sanctification, 8:21-30
  Journey to Jerusalem and Arrival, 8:31-32
  Offerings for the Temple, 8:33-34
  Worship at the Temple and the Delivery of Artaxerxes' Gift, 8:35-36
 Conflict Concerning the Purity of the Community, 9:1-15
  Report about Mixed Marriages, 9:1-2
  Ezra's Reaction: Mourning and Prayer, 9:5-15
 Resolution of the Problem by Public Divorce, 10:1-17
  Ezra's Action and Communal Reaction, 10:1-6
  Communal Assembly to bring about Separation, 10:7-17
  List of People Involved, 10:18-43
  Concluding Summary, 10:44

The outline of Ezra 7–10 draws from but is not identical to Tamara Cohn Eskenazi, *In an Age of Prose* (SBLMS 36; Atlanta: Scholars Press, 1988) 60–61.

local Judeans who had not been in exile but had intermarried with returnees. This complication required a second exodus with more priests and Levites needed. Ezra led that group (Ezra 7–8). The climax came in Ezra 9 in the scene where Ezra forced the issue of marrying those who had not been in exile, and the denouement (the banishment of returnees who had married local women) came in Ezra 10.

E. The Message of the Book of Ezra

The book of Ezra sometimes lays out directives about how to live, though other lessons—perhaps even crucial ones—may need to be teased out of the narrative of the mangled aftermath of choices made in trying to follow God's law. As is usual in much of the Bible, the book of Ezra does not always say that a given choice is an inappropriate enactment of a decision to follow God. The reader may need to "read between the lines" and make moral judgments—always a delicate task fraught with the possibility of error.

1. The opening chapter addresses the fundamental question associated with the exile: did that awful experience mark the turn of God's back on the people of pre-exilic Judah? The thoroughness of the Babylonian destruction of Jerusalem, its temple, the Davidic monarchy, and any semblance of national independence suggested that the answer to this first question was a resounding "YES!" The book of Lamentations concluded its contemplations on that event with the question of whether God had utterly rejected Jerusalem and its people. In the midst of the exile, however, God began to work anew, and God did so through the most unlikely of champions—the Persian conqueror Cyrus. God even spared Babylon instead of destroying it, and allowed a limited amount of self-government throughout the burgeoning Persian Empire. Perhaps, practically speaking, Cyrus thought he had made a calculated choice about how to govern his empire, but the author of Ezra 1 saw YHWH, the God of Israel, at work in the policies of Cyrus. His policy of allowing exiles to return home, coming after almost seventy years of exile, opened the possibility of a new chance at living lawfully at home in Jerusalem and Yehud.

2. The whole book shows that God directs and judges human conduct, appearances to the contrary notwithstanding. How, though, could anything good come out of the destruction of Jerusalem? In answering this question, one must concede that nothing good came to those who died in the warfare, who starved afterward, or who lost their identity when taken to Babylon. Still,

some of the poorest people of the land were allowed to remain in Judah to be vinedressers and farmers (Jer 52:16). *Possibly* the lot of some of them was better after the fall of Jerusalem than before, although the majority would have been worse off in the tiny little country of Judah. If the exiles in Babylon had plenty of time to repent of how they had treated people back home in Judah, the Bible does not say that they did so. Ezekiel did his best to remind his fellow exiles of their past infidelity to God (see Ezek 8–11, 16, 20), and for centuries previously, various prophets had warned both northern Israel and its southern neighbor Judah that God demanded righteousness (see Hos 1–3, Amos 7:1-9, and Mic 2:2-7 concerning Israel; and Isa 5:1-7 and 22:1-25 as well as Zeph 1:2–2:3 concerning Judah). Nevertheless, God working through Cyrus made it possible for the exiles to return to Yehud. It should be noted, however, that not all exiles chose to return. Perhaps an intact Babylon looked more appealing to them than did a ruined Jerusalem.

3. The book of Ezra also teaches that the worship of God is "a" or even "the" primary concern of human life. Beginning with the "Edict of Cyrus," Ezra 1 emphasizes the obligation of the returnees to rebuild the temple. To be sure, they also rebuilt houses to live in, and Haggai criticized them for their tardiness in completing the temple (Hag 1:4-6). Still, when they were able to turn their attention to the project, the returnees rebuilt the building between 520 (Hag 1:1; 2:1) and 515 (Ezra 6:15). The book of Ezra details some of the opposition to its restoration, and concludes its first part (chs. 1–6) with a description of the observance of the feast of Passover in Jerusalem (Ezra 6:19-22).

4. Religious observance and the worship of God got caught up in the larger political world in which those practices took place. What would the Persians allow? Who would govern Yehud, and with what constraints? These were matters beyond the ability of the returnees to determine for themselves. Persia called the shots. The perspective of Ezra 4–6, however, was that God called the shots and used Persia to accomplish the divine will.

5. Religious observance and practice in the fifth century BCE (as they often are now) were caught up in politics, and not always with positive results. Ezra 7 portrays Ezra as a priest and scribe sent by King Artaxerxes[9] "to make inquiries about Jerusalem and Judah according to the law of your God, . . . and also to convey the silver and gold that the king and his counselors have freely offered to the God of Israel, whose dwelling is in Jerusalem . . ." (Ezra 7:14-15). As benign as those verses sound, they nevertheless disclose a foreign king sending money for the temple through a priest responsible to

that king for how the money was used and thus for how worship was conducted. Even if the Persian monarchs were benign despots, they were despots nonetheless, and modern readers of Ezra-Nehemiah should never forget that.

6. Among whom God's people live and whom they marry do matter: to God, to religious authorities, and to civil authorities. In the book of Ezra, Judean religious and civil authorities seem largely to be the same people, though that is not so in the case of the man Nehemiah. Ezra 9 and 10 record forced divorces and apparent great anguish and hardship in the name of an interpretation of marriage laws found nowhere else in the Hebrew Bible. Perhaps, one might argue, extreme circumstances require extreme measures. Do they, however, require broken marriages, displaced children, and similar actions?

CONNECTIONS

1. Remarkably, the book of Ezra contains not one word of recrimination against the Persians. Perhaps that omission grew out of respect for and satisfaction with the new Persian overlords and their willingness to allow exiles all over their newly conquered empire to return home. Their action possibly earned them favorable sentiments on the part of the exiles. Isaiah 45:1 goes so far as to call Cyrus God's new "messiah" or "anointed one," and Isaiah 45:2-7 depicts God as fighting Cyrus's enemies in a new "holy" war. It appears as though some exiles returned almost immediately with the Davidide Sheshbazzar (Ezra 1), and another group came perhaps in 521 or so with Zerubbabel the Davidic prince and Jeshua the high priest (see the comments on Ezra 1 and 2 for a fuller discussion).

Perhaps, however, the silence about the Persians was the result of knowing what not to say. The Persians were fierce warriors, people not to be messed with. It was, therefore, necessary for the writer(s) and editor(s) behind Ezra to speak carefully about their overlords. These observations suggest that Ezra-Nehemiah was written both to inspire the returnees and to paint the Persians in as positive a light as possible. Behind that paint job, however, stood a determination on the part of the returnees to pursue their own objectives.

Modern Westerns seldom see themselves as foreign oppressors. Westerners want oil especially, but other minerals, raw products, and cheap manufactured goods as well from the so-called "Third

World." Americans in particular think of themselves as beneficent and wonder why third world countries, even those they call their "partners," resent them. Readers would do well to approach Ezra-Nehemiah as a carefully worded document written by a struggling people and meaningful to the struggling peoples of the world trying to earn a decent living in a world run by a giant power. To be sure, Persian power was relatively benefi-cent to some peoples, but it supported a huge army and navy almost relentlessly at war against Egypt or Greece.

Such warfare took its toll in taxes, defenses, and troop movements throughout the Persian Empire. Readers of this commentary might ponder what effects, negative and positive, American interests have on struggling peoples else-where. How much does the presence or absence of petroleum and other things westerns need/crave dominate American politics? How much does American diplomacy depend on American military might as opposed to principles like justice?

Xerxes, the King of Persia, Watches the Battle of Salamis

Xerxes I (c. 519–465 BCE), King of Persia, watches the Battle of Salamis from Mount Aegaleos. (Credit: NGS Image Collection/The Art Archive at Art Resource, NY)

2. The narrative in Ezra 9–10 describing the denunciation of mixed marriages and forced divorced shows the significance of religious regulations for everyday living. A Jewish saying runs something to the effect that "A God who does not tell people what to do with their pots and pans and with their genitals is not very useful." The saying has a point. Religion is intimately bound up with how people live, eat, and procreate. The problem, of course, is that laws and regula-tions can also become means to subjugate people or at least to hold them at arm's length. An example of such misuse of a narrative, moreover, is the use that American Christians made of the narrative of Noah's cursing Canaan, apparently for inappropriate sexual behavior toward his father (see Gen 9:20-27, esp. v. 25). In the hands of slavery-era ministers and other believers, however, that narrative became a biblical warrant for owning African slaves. Africans' slavery was held to be God's curse upon them. At least as late as my own childhood, white people I knew continued to use

Dr. Martin Luther King, Jr.

Rowland Scherman, photographer. Civil Rights March on Washington, DC, August 28, 1963. Pictured: Dr. Martin Luther King, Jr., President of the Southern Christian Leadership Conference, and Mathew Ahmann, Executive Director of the National Catholic Conference for Interracial Justice, in a crowd. (Credit: National Archives and Records Administration)

that interpretation as the biblical basis for laws and customs relegating African Americans to second-class citizenship and for the custom of racial segregation even in churches. The simple truth is, of course, that in the Bible Canaan was the progenitor of the olive-skinned Canaanites, and the narrative constitutes an explanation for Canaan's subservience to Israel. The text had nothing at all to do with black people, although it was an example of religious-based segregation and subjugation. Since the second half of the twentieth century, however, this country has made discernible though insufficient progress in racial relations, led sometimes by ministers, both black and white, in those developments.

NOTES

1. L. Ginzberg, *The Legends of the Jews* (Philadelphia: The Jewish Publication Society of America, 1968 edition) 6.441.

2. Ibid., 4.355.

3. Ibid., 4.356.

4. M. E. Stone, "Esdras, Second Book of," *ABD*, 2:611–614, here 611.

5. See [The Order of Books in the Hebrew Bible].

6. Josh 24:31, where they are mentioned.

7. Ginzberg, *Legends*, 6.447.

8. Ibid., 6.448.

9. The king presumably was Artaxerxes the First, who ruled 465–424 BCE; see the discussion in the Introduction to Ezra-Nehemiah.

PART ONE:
REBUILDING THE TEMPLE,
1:1–6:22

JUDEAN EXILES
RETURN HOME

Ezra 1

COMMENTARY

The book of Ezra describes events from two different times. Ezra 1–6 discusses the return in the late sixth century of exiles from Babylon and the building of the altar and temple in Jerusalem. [Outline of Ezra-Nehemiah] Inserted within those chapters is a description (Ezra 4:6-23) of contention over the building of the wall around Jerusalem, a project from the time of Nehemiah. Among other purposes, the location of that narrative helps to bond the subject matter of Ezra-Nehemiah.

Outline of Ezra-Nehemiah

Restoring the Yehudite Community through Rebuilding the Temple, Ezra 1–6
Restoring the Yehudite Community through Reaffirming the Law, Ezra 7–10
Restoring the Yehudite Community through Rebuilding the Wall, Nehemiah 1–13

Following the account of the return of exiles under Sheshbazzar (Ezra 1–2) and that of the rebuilding of the temple (Ezra 3–6) comes a narrative about the return of the book's namesake (in Ezra 7–10) with a large number of priests and Levites and Ezra's efforts to maintain the biological and spiritual integrity of all persons associated with the temple.

The Introduction to Ezra-Nehemiah includes the following statement about Ezra-Nehemiah. Ezra-Nehemiah is composed in three parts, each with its own purpose. Ezra 1–6 was designed to legitimate the returnees as the proper religious and local political leaders of Yehud. They came back under the commission and with the assistance of the Persian emperor Cyrus. As far as the *redactor of Ezra-Nehemiah* was concerned, the temple was for their exclusive use. Ezra 7–10 skips ahead a couple of generations, but it too was written to defend the prerogatives of the returnees over against any claims that the people who had remained behind in Yehud might assert or desire for themselves. Ezra returned with another small group of returnees to assure the ethical purity of worshipers there, a purity guaranteed by descent from the original returnees. That claim had political ramifications, which is why Ezra 1–6, 7–10, and the narrative of Nehemiah place so much emphasis on their appointment by the Persians and their careful compliance with the Persians. Finally, the book of Nehemiah was written to defend the ongoing rights and perks of the returnees over against those of the Samaritans and those in Yehud who cooperated or at least sympathized with the Samaritans. It described the rebuilding of the walls of Jerusalem by the descendants of returnees only, making the city a holy zone/area around the temple, thus protecting it from ritual and ethical contamination. Overall, Ezra-Nehemiah was written to legitimate the claims of the returnees in the eyes of the captives still in Babylon and (perhaps) to gain their agreement with and approval of the actions the returnees had taken. *It was written also to stake the returnees' claim to the temple in Jerusalem.* Isaiah 56:3-8, by contrast, articulated its author's view that God intended the temple to be used by all peoples, including foreigners and even people like eunuchs (v. 4) who were barred in Deuteronomy 23:1, 3 (see also Lev 21:18-20) from worshiping there.

Ezra 1 introduces this grand drama in terms of the time (the second year of Cyrus the Great), the issue (the rebuilding of the temple in Jerusalem), and the characters responsible for that task (members of the exiled community in Babylon who wished to return to Jerusalem). The narrative begins on a positive note: Cyrus, the king of Persia and the conqueror of Babylonia, granted permission to the exiles in Babylonia to return to Jerusalem and Yehud and to rebuild the temple in Jerusalem. In fact, according to v. 4, Cyrus commanded other residents living near them to aid the exiles with gifts when they left. Cyrus himself returned to the exiles items taken from the temple by the Babylonian army, and the returning exiles were to be led by an exile named Sheshbazzar, "the prince (or leader) of Judah." Whatever claim Sheshbazzar might have had to royalty or leadership in the exilic community, his role here is that of delivery person for Cyrus. Cyrus is not merely the hero of Ezra 1, but in the succeeding five chapters he and the third Persian ruler Artaxerxes I support the efforts of the returnees in their rebuilding efforts against the questions of local officials about the aims of the returnees. Readers might note, however, that Persian rulers could be viewed as tyrants. The book of Esther draws its suspense from the unlimited power of the Persian king Xerxes I (r. 486–465 and died at the hands of an assassin) to treat wives and other couriers and subjects as he chose, and Daniel 7:5 caricatures Persia as a savage bear with the bones of its prey protruding from its mouth. [Outline of Ezra 1]

The Setting of Ezra 1

The places where Ezra 1 is set are basically two. As Johanna W. H. van Wijk-Bos states, the destroyed city of Jerusalem "stands in the center of the story that is told here. It is the point to which Babylon is the counterpoint."[1] The opening words of the book of Ezra provide the date for this narrative. The time was the "first year of King Cyrus," which would have been 539 BCE. Cyrus had actually come to power in Elam beginning in 559, but it took twenty years for him to capture Babylon in what appears to have been a bloodless takeover following a decisive battle at a place called Opis. The first year of Cyrus's rulership over Babylon is in view here. While his residence was possibly Ecbatana (see Ezra 6:2), the place of the action in Ezra 1 was the city of Babylon, where plunder from Jerusalem had been stored in the house of Nebuchadnezzar's temple. Verse 7 says that Cyrus personally rescued those items and turned them over to "Sheshbazzar, the prince (or leader) of Judah." His name perhaps parodied the name Šamaš-ab-ussur, Shamash the protector, and it resembles the Babylonian name Sin-ab-usur, which means something like Sin (the moon god), protect the father.[2] He is unknown outside of Ezra 1 and 5, but there is no reason to question his existence.

According to Jeremiah 52:28-30, a total of 4,600 Judeans had been taken to Babylon by the Babylonians in three separate deportations, although 2 Kings 24:14-16 mentions only two and gives the number of only those exiled in 597 as 7,000 men of valor and 1,000 artisans for a total of 8,000. (See Introduction to Ezra-Nehemiah for a full discussion.) Jewish names (especially famous names like Yeshua/Joshua and names compounded with "Yah" like Nehemiah and Seraiah in Ezra 1 and 2) appear in Babylonian records discovered by archaeologists, although names like Zerubbabel ("seed of Babylon") show that a number of the exiles took on Babylonian names. Ezra 1 does not say where the exiles lived, but Ezekiel 1:1 and seven other verses in that book mention "the exiles by the river Chebar." Actually, the Chebar was a canal that branched off the Euphrates River north of Babylon and flowed about sixty miles southeast past the city of Nippur and then rejoined the Euphrates south of modern Warka (biblical Erich).[3] Apparently, that region was the center of the exilic community.

The verse also alludes to the book of Jeremiah, where two verses predict that the Babylonian captivity would last seventy years. Jeremiah 25:11 says, "This whole land shall become a ruin and a

---

Outline of Ezra 1

The Setting of Ezra, 1:1
The Royal Commission by Cyrus, 1:2-4
The Return with Sheshbazzar, 1:5-11
  Aid for the Journey by Neighbors, 1:5-6
  Temple Vessels Entrusted to Sheshbazzar, 1:7-11a
  The Return under Sheshbazzar, 1:11b

Jeremiah and the Destruction of Jerusalem under Nebuchadnezzar

Eduard Bendemann (1811–1889). *Jeremiah and the Fall of Jerusalem*. (Credit: Foto Marburg/Art Resource, NY)

The artist imaginatively depicts Jeremiah at the destruction of Jerusalem.

waste, and these nations will serve the king of Babylon seventy years." Jeremiah 29:10 reads, "For thus says the LORD: only when Babylon's seventy years are completed will I visit you, and I will fulfill to you my promise and bring you back to this place." Those verses perhaps simply signified that the exiles would not live to return to Yehud. Ezekiel 29:11-13 puts the exile's duration at forty years, and it probably means the same thing.

The primary point of Ezra 1:1, however, was that the liberation of the exiles was not really the work of Cyrus, but of YHWH, who used Cyrus to fulfill God's promise. Deutero Isaiah anticipated this verse by having YHWH say that he chose Cyrus for that task (Isa 44:27-45:4) and that he stirred Cyrus to victory (Isa 45:13). Likewise, the Cyrus Inscription quotes Cyrus as saying that the gods of Babylon, Marduk in particular, chose him to liberate the Babylonians. A Judean exile in Babylon would not credit the Babylonian gods with any such power, so Deutero Isaiah made the daring claim that YHWH had chosen Cyrus for the special task of liberating the exiles. Second Kings 21:10-15 made it clear that the fall of Jerusalem and the beginning of the exile was the work of YHWH, who used Nebuchadnezzar as God's instrument. Likewise, Ezra 1:1 explained that the end of the exile also was God's work, in which God used Cyrus as God's instrument. Thus, this verse offered an interesting contrast to the use of the verb "stirred" in passages where God stirred the spirit of other kings or nations to punish Israel: Babylon (Jer 51:11); Pul (or Tiglath-Pileser), king of Assyria (1 Chr 5:26); and the Philistines and Arabs (2 Chr 21:16).

Cyrus the Great

Guiart des Moulins. *La Bible Historiale*, 1350–1355. Manuscript illumination on parchment. Illustration for the First Book of Esdras: The reconstruction of the Temple in Jerusalem ordered by Persian King Cyrus. Volume 1, fol. 207 verso. Russian National Library, St. Petersburg, Russia. (Credit: Erich Lessing/Art Resource, NY)

One should also note that Ezra 1:1 reads the same as 2 Chronicles 36:22: "In the first year of King Cyrus of Persia, in fulfillment of the word of the LORD spoken by Jeremiah, the LORD stirred up the spirit of King Cyrus of Persia so that he sent a herald throughout all his kingdom and also declared in a written edict: . . ." (NRSV). The word spoken by Jeremiah may well have been that reported in Jeremiah 51:1, where Jeremiah reports God as promising to send a destructive "wind" or "spirit" against Babylon, and v. 11, a prose addition, which reports that God had sent the kings of the Medes to destroy Babylon for having destroyed Jerusalem. The prophet Jeremiah is never mentioned again in Ezra-Nehemiah, but he is mentioned three other times in the previous twenty-four verses of 2 Chronicles. This observation supports the view that the author of Ezra-Nehemiah borrowed Ezra 1:1-3a from 2 Chronicles and not the reverse as is often argued by scholars today.[4] Moreover, 2 Chronicles 36:22 // Ezra 1:1 echoes superscriptions that appear frequently in the Latter prophets, in which a prophet's activity is situated within the context of a foreign power; see Isaiah 1:1; Hosea 1:1; Amos 1:1; Micah 1:1; Zephaniah 1:1; Haggai 1:1; 2:1, 10, 20; and Zechariah 1:1, 7; 7:1.

Cyrus reversed the Babylonian policy of exile and allowed Babylonian captives from various places to return home. The so-called "Cyrus Cylinder," perhaps written by a Babylonian scribe although containing statements purportedly by Cyrus, lists a number of places to which Cyrus allowed exiles to return, but it does not mention Yehud. (See the photo and discussion of the Cylinder in the Introduction to Ezra-Nehemiah.) Ezra 1, however, reports a similar edict pertaining to the Judeans settled in Babylon. The same edict is reported in two other places in the Hebrew Bible, and a look at it will be instructive. [The Wording of the Cyrus Cylinder]

The edict permitted the exiles to return to Yehud if they wished, and authorized the rebuilding of the house of God in Jerusalem, which T. C. Eskenazi argues was one objective for the whole book of Ezra-Nehemiah, not just Ezra 1–6.[5] The same edict also closed 2 Chronicles. It also reappeared in Ezra 6:3, 5, and Josephus paraphrased it (*Ant.* 11.3-4).[6] [The Threefold Use of the Edict of Cyrus in 2 Chronicles and Ezra] The divine figure behind this building project was none other than YHWH, here recognized by Cyrus himself. The human instrument behind the rebuilding was that same Persian king. His authorization of its construction was a continuing theme in Ezra 1–6, which emphasizes the participation of Cyrus, Darius, and even Artaxerxes I (see Ezra 4:3; 5:13; 17; 6:3-5, 6-12, 14).

The Wording of the Cyrus Cylinder

 The so-called "Cyrus Cylinder," which was displayed in five museums in the United States in 2013, recounts Cyrus's victory over Babylon and his treatment of the temples of their gods. Relevant excerpts from that document follow.

I am Cyrus, king of the world, great king, legitimate king, king of Babylon, king of Sumer and Akkad, king of the four rims [of the earth], ...
    Furthermore, I resettled upon the command of Marduk, the great lord, all the gods of Sumer and Akkad whom Nabonidus has brought into Babylon . . . to the anger of the lord of the gods, unharmed, in their (former) chapels, the places which make them happy.

While Cyrus may have built temples in various places to local gods, archaeologists have uncovered no edict authorizing/commanding a temple for YHWH in Jerusalem. One can say, however, that such behavior was characteristic of Cyrus elsewhere.

J. B. Pritchard, ed. *ANET*, 282–84.

Cyrus II called Cyrus the Great, 559–529 BCE. Founder of the Persian Empire. 18th-century engraving. (Credit: Scala/White Images/Art Resource, NY)

The Threefold Use of the Edict of Cyrus in 2 Chronicles and Ezra

2 Chronicles 36:23	Ezra 1:2-3, 7	Ezra 6:3, 5
		[3]In the first year of Cyrus the king, **Cyrus the king** issued a decree:
"Thus says Cyrus, King of Persia: 'YHWH the God of heaven gave to me all the kingdoms of the earth, and he appointed me to build for him a house in Jerusalem, which is in Judah. Whoever among you from his people, YHWH his God [is]* with him and let him go up.'"	[2]**"Thus says Cyrus, king of Persia: 'YHWH, the God of heaven, gave to me all the kingdoms of the earth, and he appointed me to build for him a house in Jerusalem, which is in Judah.** [3] **Whoever among you is from his people,** may **his God** be **with him, and let him go up** to Jerusalem which is in Judah; and let him build the house of YHWH, God of Israel; he is the God who is in Jerusalem.'" . . . [7] And King Cyrus released **the vessels of the house of God, which Nebuchadnezzar took from Jerusalem**, and he donated them to the house of God."	"[Concerning] **the house** of God **in Jerusalem**, let the place where they continually offer sacrifices by fire be rebuilt; . . . [5] **Also the vessels of the house of God**, which are of gold and silver, **which Nebuchadnezzar took from** the temple which is in **Jerusalem** and brought to Babylon, let them be restored and brought back to the temple which is in Jerusalem."

* There is no verb in 2 Chronicles 36:23 corresponding to *yĕhî* (may . . . be) in Ezra 1:3.
Stylization and modifications by P. L. Redditt.

The recovered Cyrus Cylinder recorded Cyrus's version of the capture of Babylon and his kindness toward people the Babylonians had exiled earlier. Statements from his message relevant to this discussion include the following: (1) Marduk, the chief Babylonian god, had made Cyrus king; (2) Cyrus would allow kings of conquered people to go home; (3) he would allow their subjects to return home too; and (4) he was returning images of foreign gods to their temples.[7] Ezra 1:(1)2-4 made similar claims. (1) Its author claimed that YHWH, the God of Israel, used Cyrus to fulfill God's word given by Jeremiah the prophet (Jer 1:1), a statement that also echoes if not quotes Isaiah 45:1. (2) Cyrus sent Sheshbazzar, the "prince (or leader) of Judah," back to Jerusalem (Ezra 1:8). (3) Cyrus decreed that any exile who so wished could return to Jerusalem (Ezra 1:3-4). There being no images of YHWH to return, Ezra 1:7-11 had Cyrus give the vessels from the temple in Jerusalem to Sheshbazzar to take to Jerusalem.

The Royal Commission by Cyrus, 1:2-4

The version of Cyrus's edict in Ezra 1:2-4 is longer than the version in 2 Chronicles 36:23, expanding it by repeating the authorization and adding that King Cyrus released "the vessels of the house of God, which Nebuchadnezzar took from Jerusalem." That statement was unnecessary in 2 Chronicles 36, which had just finished describing Nebuchadnezzar's plundering of the temple and taking things to Babylon. In the passage's secondary setting in Ezra 1, the note contained in addition the authorization for the exiles to rebuild the temple. That authorization, in and of itself *historically* likely, was *polemically* necessary to the aims of Ezra-Nehemiah. In it, the returnees, acting under Persian authority, not those who had remained in Yehud, were the only ones authorized to build the temple. In light of the struggles in Yehud between the returnees and those who remained in Judah over the control and even worship at the new temple, the twofold divine authorization (i.e., of both Cyrus and the returnees) was crucial. [Worship at the Temple and Elsewhere during the Exile] It showed that the returnees and they alone, not those who had remained behind in Judah during the exile, constituted the "true" Judah/Israel.

King Cyrus's edict also calls upon the people among whom the exiles lived in Babylon to assist the exiles' return to Yehud by giving them "silver and gold, [along] with goods and animals, besides freewill offerings for the house of God in Jerusalem." Such a directive is possible, although readers of the biblical text must decide

Worship at the Temple and Elsewhere during the Exile

It is worth noting that the temple area apparently had not gone unused in the years following the destruction of the building by the army of Nebuchadnezzar. Jer 41:4-5 narrates an event shortly after the fall of Jerusalem when a group of 80 men from Shechem, Shiloh, and Samaria came to Judah to present grain and incense offerings at the site of the temple in Jerusalem. Unfortunately for them, they were caught up in the bloodbath surrounding the assassination of Gedaliah (see also 2 Kings 26:22-26) sometime after the fall of Jerusalem, but their worship suggests that the destruction of the temple did not terminate the use of the site for all kinds of sacrifices. Moreover, its destruction became a matter of sorrow and the anniversary of its destruction seems to have been mourned in nearby Bethel, a little over ten miles to Jerusalem's north. Zech 7:1-3 reports a question from the people of Bethel asking whether after the reconstruction of the temple they should continue to mourn its destruction by Nebuchadnezzar. Zechariah's answer in Zech 8:18-19 was that those months and others should be observed in the future as times of celebration. Finally, sacrifice to YHWH was carried out elsewhere in the former northern state of Israel. Ezra 4:1-5 relates an incident when certain "adversaries" of the returnees came to them with the request that they be allowed to help rebuild the temple on the grounds that they worshiped the same God and had been offering sacrifices to God since the Assyrian king Esarhaddon (r. 681–669) had brought them to settle in Israel.

how probable either the command or obedience to it might have been. It is instructive, however, to note the similar directive God gave the Egyptian people at the time of the Exodus. [Similarities between Ezra 1:4, Exodus 12:35-36, and Pilgrimage Narratives]

The third version (in Ezra 6:1-5) of the edict differs significantly from the other two. First, it deals only with Cyrus's permission to rebuild the temple; it says nothing about the Judeans' returning home. Second, it was written in Aramaic, the official language of the Persian Empire, while the other two were written in Hebrew. Third, it gives instructions concerning the size, cost, and materials of the building, items mentioned later in Ezra 1 but not in the edict itself. The differences have led some scholars to doubt the veracity of the Hebrew versions. E. J. Bickerman pointed out, however, that the Aramaic version served a different function from the other two. The Aramaic version purported to be an official document kept for the king, whereas the Hebrew versions appear to have been variants of a document meant to be read and posted among the exiles.[8] This suggestion has merit. The Cyrus Inscription contained the idea that Cyrus had resettled "the gods" of the Babylonians and other people in their sacred cities, which perhaps meant that Cyrus had returned images of gods to the places from which they were taken and authorized temples to be rebuilt to house the images. Since the worship of YHWH was or was supposed to be imageless, returning the "gods" was impossible. His role could only be to order the work done and perhaps underwrite some (or all) of the costs.

Verses 2-4 also shed light on the role of the written word in Ezra-Nehemiah. As noted, they cite Cyrus's edict (appealed to again in 4:3). Ezra 1 forms an inclusio with Ezra 6:12 (which cites it again) and the action in Ezra 6:13-22 to bring the temple to completion. Indeed, Ezra 1:1-3 and Ezra 6:12, 22, and 26 form an inclusio around Ezra 1–6.[9] However, where one might expect to find an appeal to the edict (i.e., in 4:6-16), one does not. Instead, one finds

---

Similarities between Ezra 1:4, Exodus 12:35-36, and Pilgrimage Narratives

A comparison of Ezra 1:4 with Exodus 12:35-36 shows a similarity of theme. Israel was about to leave a foreign country, and their "hosts" aided them in leaving in Ezra 1:4 and paid them to leave in Exod 12:35. The passages also exhibit contrasts, however. In Ezra 1:4, it was Cyrus who ordered the Babylonians to share, whereas in Exod 12:33-35, the people themselves, not Pharaoh, chose to give the Israelites gifts and then urged them to leave. Also, in Exod 12:35 the "generosity" of the Egyptians was motivated by their fear of God, and the transfer of goods was expressly called "plunder." No such explanations for giving appear in Ezra 1. If Ezra 1:4 borrowed from Exod 12:33-35, the borrowed material was given its own twist.

Ezra 1:4	**Exodus 12:35-36**
. . . and let all survivors, in whatever place they reside, be assisted by the people of their place with silver and gold, with goods and animals, besides freewill offerings for the house of God in Jerusalem.	[35]The Israelites had done as Moses had told them; they had asked the Egyptians for jewelry of silver and gold, and for clothing, [36]and the LORD had given the people favor in the sight of the Egyptians so that they let them have what they asked.

M. D. Knowles points out that Ezra 1–2, 7–8 as well also employ "pilgrimage imagery." She argues that the "motif of pilgrimage may be a more comprehensive heuristic device [than simply noting parallels with the book of Exodus] by which to interpret the accounts. The return narratives in Ezra emphasize Jerusalem as the destination of the journey (and not the larger geographic region of the promised land); they are explicitly cultic (with priests, sacrifice, and cultic vessels specifically highlighted); and they involve several journeys of the nation (not one constitutive trip made by the people together)" (57). On the one hand, the exodus narrative speaks of "an oppressed group which leaves a place of bondage as a single group and enters into a land of freedom." On the other hand, a pilgrimage narrative describes a journey whose purpose is to worship God. A reader will note the emphasis on priests in Ezra 2. The narrative also uses the vocabulary of pilgrimage (e.g., "to go up"). Third, the travelers on a pilgrimage "return home." To be sure, the parallel here is not perfect. In Ezra 1–2, 7–8 the "home" of the worshipers is Jerusalem, not Babylon whence they came. Still, in Ezra 1–2 the community is reborn as a worshiping community, and it is reborn yet again in Ezra 7–8, when Ezra's group returns "home" to Jerusalem. Knowles does not extend the comparison into the book of Nehemiah, where Nehemiah returns to Jerusalem to rebuild/repair the wall around the city.

M. D. Knowles, "Pilgrimage Imagery in the Returns in Ezra," *JBL* 123 (2004): 57–74.

---

an account about the rebuilding of Jerusalem's wall. J. L. Wright observes that when Artaxerxes, the king of Persia (r. 465–424), searches his records, he agrees with the opponents of the returnees that Jerusalem had been a rebellious city (Ezra 4:17-22) and orders work on the wall stopped (4:23).[10] In Ezra 4:24, however, the narrative returns to an account of the building of the temple (begun in 4:1-3), which does restart, but under the impetus of the prophets Haggai and Zechariah (5:1-2). The Babylonian governor Tattenai asks them who authorized the rebuilding of the temple (5:3-5), and the situation leads to his leading an envoy to King Darius, asking him to consult the Cyrus Edict (5:9-16). When he does he finds the relevant record in *Ecbatana*, not in *Babylon* where Cyrus issued it (5:17–6:2), and authorizes the resumption of the work (Ezra 6:6-12). This account, therefore, is designed to show full *Persian* support for the temple, as expressed in writing by both Cyrus and Darius, regardless of what the *Babylonians* may have done or recorded.[11] This verse, by the way, also constitutes one of the bases for commentators of an older era to see Cyrus as a "type" of Christ.[12]

Wright further notes that the narratives ". . . illustrate the point that Judah does not require a monarchy of its own. The construction project progressed and succeeded not because of a Judean king and the prophet whom he consults for the 'word of God,' but . . . by virtue of an authority mediated through texts."[13] Even David and Solomon are "mere incumbents on a throne that also can be occupied by foreign rulers who likewise engage in Temple-construction."[14] To dismiss the Davidic monarchy so lightly might well be too strong a reading, but Wright clearly articulates the author's point for the future: the temple would flourish with Persian permission. Wright also comments on the larger function of the Cyrus Edict, namely that it was not "a static entity, but . . . a rich source which requires interpretation to reveal its full message."[15]

Judah and Benjamin

Ezra 1:5 specifically mentions families from Benjamin and Judah, a combination of tribes that needs discussing since Benjamin had been part of the northern kingdom of Israel during the days of the divided kingdom. In the early Persian Period, however, the Persian province of Yehud seems to have included Jerusalem, the nearby hill country (excluding the Shephelah), and Benjamin, plus the Judean desert bordering the Dead Sea (perhaps including Jericho and Ein Gedi). In the north it included the cities of Bethel and Jericho, and in the south the city of Hebron. Bethlehem was near its geographic center, Jerusalem just to its north. The total size was about 1,900 square kilometers (680 square miles), making it about half the size of Rhode Island. Since a number of populated sites were in former Benjaminite territory, references to Benjamin as well as Judah are to be expected.

The two areas are mentioned together in the same verse 18 times in the Hebrew Bible. Outside of Chronicles, Ezra, and Nehemiah, they appear only at the beginning of the Jephthah narrative (Judg 10:9) and in connection with the secession of the north from Rehoboam (1 Kgs 12:23; 2 Chr 11:1, 3). In Chronicles, Benjaminites, Ephramites, and Judeans joined up with David's band before he was elected king of Judah at Hebron (1 Chr 12:17). They are said to have heard the message of the prophet Azariah to Asa (2 Chr 15:2, 8, and 9), and soldiers from both tribes joined Amaziah in his war against Edom (2 Chr 25:5). Hezekiah had the high places and altars in Judah, Benjamin, Ephraim, and Manasseh destroyed (2 Chr 31:1), and Levites collected money from those same four tribes for the restoration of the temple under Josiah (2 Chr 31:1). Texts in Ezra-Nehemiah treat the two as a religio-political unity (Ezra 1:5, 4:1 and 10:9, Neh 11:36).

Information taken from C. E. Carter, *The Emergence of Yehud in the Persian Period: A Social and Demographic Study* (JSOTSup 294; Sheffield: Sheffield Academic Press, 1999) 88, 102–107. Also see pp. 84–87, figures 1–4 and p. 210, figure 18.

The Return with Sheshbazzar, 1:5-11

The chapter continues with a brief narrative (Ezra 1:5-6), which Eskenazi called a "Proleptic Summary."[16] It reports plans to carry out the king's commands, thus anticipating the rest of the plot of Ezra 1–6. The heads of the families of Judah and Benjamin [Judah and Benjamin], i.e., tribes with members among the exiles, along with the priests and the Levites, prepared to leave. The author mentioned these two groups separately from the laity and from each other for emphasis, to make sure that the reader understood that the returnees included both. The author includes another phrase, however: "everyone whose spirit God had stirred." That statement perhaps implied that every

Jew in Babylon obeyed the order, but that clearly was not so. Perhaps instead it was a claim that those whom God stirred prepared to leave. Clearly the sentence as it stands in the texts is already looking forward to the lengthy list of returnees in Ezra 2:2b-58 // Nehemiah 7:7-67. Let readers of this commentary take note: Ezra-Nehemiah is a narrative about the returnees, and not really about those who had remained behind in Jerusalem and Judah after Babylon destroyed them.

The chapter closes with a discussion of the transfer of goods from Cyrus to the returnees. It contains an inventory of items Cyrus supplied for the temple. In particular it says that "King Cyrus himself brought out the vessels of the house of the LORD that Nebuchadnezzar had carried away and placed in the house of his gods" (v. 7). Once again the redactor of Ezra-Nehemiah drew upon Chronicles, this time on 2 Chronicles 36:18 (see 2 Kgs 25:13-17), where the mention of things taken is comfortably at home in the discussion of actions taken by Nebuchadnezzar during the fall of Jerusalem. The emphatic claim that Cyrus himself delivered the same items to "Sheshbazzar, the prince (or leader) of Judah," is meant to show that Cyrus granted permission for the return of the objects to Jerusalem while he was still in Babylon. (See here too the Cyrus Cylinder, which speaks of his granting permission immediately for exiles in Babylon to return to their homes.)

The twofold mention of "King Cyrus" by name also emphasizes his direct permission to rebuild the temple. Verse 7 by itself makes the point: Cyrus rescued the vessels that Nebuchadnezzar had placed "in the house of his gods." [The House of His Gods] Then Cyrus had them "released into the charge of Mithredath the treasurer, who counted them and turned them over to the Sheshbazzar (v. 8). This action constituted a transfer from royalty to royalty, handled through an official mediator. If the Babylonian people paid personal reparations to the individual returning exiles, Cyrus himself paid religious reparations to a descendent of David by returning everything taken from the temple in Jerusalem. The source for this verse, and possibly Ezra 7:11b too, is probably the Aramaic account in Ezra 4:8–6:18, specifically 5:14. [The Source for Ezra 1:7, 11b] It does not seem to be the creation of the author of Ezra 1.

The House of His Gods

The comment about the "house" of Nebuchadnezzar's gods is vague, since Babylon contained many temples and Babylonians were notorious polytheists. At the head of their pantheon were three gods: Anu, the high god with whom people had little contact; Marduk, the chief god of Babylon; and Ea, the god of water and wisdom. Next in rank came three more: Shamash (the sun god), Sin (the moon god), and Ishtar (the goddess of war, sexual love, and procreation). The remaining gods ranked beneath these six. More to the point here is that each temple would have been dedicated to one deity. The distinction being drawn here is between the one God of Judah and the numerous gods of Babylon, presumably each with his own individual "house."

The Source for Ezra 1:7, 11b

The source for Ezra 1:7, 11b was probably the account in the Aramaic language in Ezra 4:8–6:18, specifically 5:14, which insists that Cyrus delivered the vessels from the temple directly to Sheshbazzar, although a second source may well have been 2 Chr 36:7-8, 18. L. L. Grabbe considers the letter from Tattenai in Ezra 5:7-17 the document most likely to be authentic in the whole of Ezra 1–6, but one ought to be careful about taking all of it at face value. The loss of the vessels of the temple was important enough to be mentioned in two other biblical books (2 Kgs 24:13; 25:14-15; 2 Chr 36:10, 18). Neither contained a list as extensive as the one that followed in Ezra 1, so neither provides a check on that chapter. Nor did the Chronicler's list of vessels made by David for the temple (1 Chr 28:14-17) serve that purpose. That the Babylonian army stole everything that was worth stealing is surely a safe conclusion, but 2 Kings 24:13 says Nebuchadnezzar cut to pieces all the vessels of gold in the temple of the Lord, which Solomon of Israel had made. How much of the booty from the temple and its environs survived for Cyrus to return thus is impossible to calculate. The redactor emphasizes that Cyrus returned the vessels taken by Nebuchadnezzar because the redactor was concerned to show continuity between the old temple and the new. The Cyrus Inscription mentioned that Cyrus returned images of gods to temples looted by the Babylonians but made no mention of other implements.

L. L. Grabbe, "'The Exile' under the Theodolite: Historiography as Triangulation," *Leading Captivity Captive: The "The Exile" as History and Ideology* (ed. Lester L. Grabbe; JSOTSup 278; Sheffield: Sheffield Academic Press, 1998) 94.

The inventory of temple items returned to Sheshbazzar included 30 gold basins, 1,000 silver basins, 29 knives (for slaughtering animals),[17] 30 gold bowls, 410 silver bowls, and 1,000 other vessels, for a total of 2,499. Verse 11, however, gives the total number of vessels as 5,400. Second Chronicles 36:18 lists the number of gold basins as 1,000, the number of silver bowls as 2,410, and the grand total as 5,460 vessels, all emendations made on the basis of the text behind 1 Esdras 2:13-14. The MT text clearly has been disturbed, and the figures from 1 Esdras present either an earlier and better or a later and corrected set. Regardless, the claim that Cyrus returned gold vessels seems to contradict 2 Kings 25:13, which says Nebuchadnezzar cut to pieces all implements of gold and silver. The author of Ezra 1 had conflicting information. Perhaps some of the vessels of gold and silver escaped, despite the sweeping generalization in 2 Kings 25:13.

Ezra 1:11b provides a transition to Ezra 2, which credits Sheshbazzar with leading the exiles back to Yehud. He is mentioned again only in Ezra 5, which reports that Cyrus delivered the vessels of the temple to him (5:14), and that he "founded" the temple (5:16). Zechariah 4:8, however, ascribes this last-mentioned act to a man named Zerubbabel. Since "founding" a temple seems to have been a ceremonial act, as opposed to actually building the temple, it is possible that both men performed this act, although Zerubbabel's connection with the event seems unassailable in light of Haggai and Zechariah, contemporaries of the event. If it was done only once, it was done by Zerubbabel.

A concluding observation is pertinent here. The earthly hero of this chapter was King Cyrus of Persia, not Sheshbazzar the Davidide, who is little more than a deliveryman. His role was to bear the temple treasures from Babylon to Jerusalem. Ezra 5:14 and 16 mention him again in the same role, but the emphasis of the narrative is on Cyrus and the credit goes to him in Ezra 1 and 5.

Whatever success, if any, Sheshbazzar may have had in rebuilding the temple is simply ignored. Indeed, the text does not even say he actually began the project. Credit for that action went to Zerubbabel, another Davidide in Babylon, who is mentioned in Ezra 2:2, 8 (// Neh 7:7 and 12:1) as returning with thousands of returnees, in Ezra 4:2-3 in connection with rebuilding the altar, and in Ezra 5:2 in connection with beginning to rebuild the temple. Otherwise only Nehemiah 12:47 mentions Zerubbabel in a note concerning paying singers in the temple. There is no hint of hope that Sheshbazzar or Zerubbabel would rule the country as a son of David (contra Hag 2:20-23, which names Zerubbabel as God's signet ring). The only royal figures in Ezra are Persian.

Signet Ring

Signet of Toutankhamon. Egyptian Antiquities of the Louvre Museum, Paris, France. (Credit: Guillaume Blanchard, Wikimedia Commons, CCA-SA 1.0)

Becking summarizes the message of Ezra 1 under three points, summarized and partly restated here. (1) The return is presented as a fulfillment of prophecies by Jeremiah (Jer 25:12, 29:10, and/or 30–31). This use of the earlier prophet suggests that the author was presenting the returnees as the continuation of pre-exilic Yahwism. (2) The motif that "we all returned as one," whether historically correct or not, was theologically crucial to the group behind the Ezra narratives as a safeguard for the idea of continuity with the past. (3) The portrait of Cyrus (and subsequent Persian kings) as friendly toward the Israelites in exile and supportive of their return indicated that they construed themselves as the legitimate inhabitants of Yehud.[18]

CONNECTIONS

1. One way that early Christians made texts like Ezra 1 applicable to Christian living was by employing typological exegesis. The Venerable Bede will serve as an excellent example of that way to read the Bible in the following comments on Ezra 1.

Therefore the LORD made Cyrus similar to [God's] only-begotten Son, our Lord Jesus Christ. Just as Cyrus . . . freed the people of God, and sent them back to their homeland and ordered them to rebuild the temple, . . . so [Jesus] the mediator between God and humanity,

The Venerable Bede

J. W. Cook, *The Venerable Bede*. 19th C. Engraving. (Credit: Private Collection/Ken Welsh/Bridgeman Images)

after destroying all over the world the kingdom of the devil, called back from that tyranny his elect, who had been scattered, and now gathers them in his church.[19]

Such studies had a long and useful history both among Jews and Christians, and they could make relevant even mundane writings. This particular example has the further merit of taking the text of Ezra 1 at face value, a merit not always found in typological exegesis. Still, the parallels are forced and contribute little to the understanding of the biblical text under discussion. Meaningful Bible study cannot remain rooted in the past, of course, but it needs to take seriously and try to discern what the text might have meant to its original audience. In other words, the first issue in studying a text in Ezra-Nehemiah is what it said and what it might have meant to its first audience(s). Second, it is fair to ask what it might have meant to later readers, including contemporary readers. Uncovering some of those meanings will be the task of these efforts at showing "connections" between Ezra-Nehemiah and modern readers.

2. One important point that was somewhat obscured by Bede's handling of Ezra 1 was God's use of a pagan to carry out God's will. If it was an act of courage for many of the prophets of the Hebrew Bible to predict God's punishment of God's own people and be rejected by those people—their people—it may also have been an act of courage on the part of prophets like the so-called Second Isaiah and the author of Ezra-Nehemiah to point to the new conquerors, the Persians, as instruments God was using to restore the exiles to their homeland. The authors of Ezra-Nehemiah themselves said what Bede saw: God was at work through other people who worshiped other gods to accomplish God's work. Perhaps one of our questions today needs to be, "How is God using Muslims to carry out God's work?" Perhaps another is, "How is what we are doing, as individuals and as a nation, contributing to that work?" Do we naturally assume that if Muslims are for something, we should be against it? We might be hesitant, perhaps rightfully so, to see God at work in all wars. Yet the military successes of Cyrus

formed the background, perhaps better said the opportunity, for God to work in exiled Judah's favor for improvement.

Would the peoples of the old world have been better off if old empire builders had not aggressively attacked and subjugated their neighbors? Surely the answer is affirmative. When modern nations go to war, or at least take advantage of their neighbors, can Christians and Christian nations do a peaceful work under God to correct abuses? One would hope so.

NOTES

1. Johanna W. H. van Wijk-Bos, *Ezra, Nehemiah, and Esther* (Westminster Bible Companion; Louisville: Westminster John Knox, 1998) 7.

2. See E. S. Gerstenberger, *Israel in the Persian Period* (trans. S. S. Schatzmann; Biblical Encyclopedia 8; Atlanta: Society of Biblical Literature, 2011) 100, and Isaac Kalimi, "Sheshbazzar," in *IDB*, 5.220–21.

3. H. O. Thompson, "Chebar," *ABD*, 1.893.

4. See P. L. Redditt, "The Dependence of Ezra-Nehemiah on 1 and 2 Chronicles," *Unity and Disunity in Ezra-Nehemiah* (ed. M. J. Boda and P. L. Redditt; Hebrew Bible Monographs 17; Sheffield: Sheffield Phoenix Press, 2008) 216–40, here 229–39.

5. T. C. Eskenazi (*In an Age of Prose* [SBLMS 36; Atlanta: Scholars Press, 1988] 41) argued the reverse, namely that the phrase "the house of God" included the whole city of Jerusalem, not simply the temple. That conclusion has not gained wide acceptance.

6. Josephus used as his source biblical materials, including the book of Isaiah, which he names. There is no reason to suppose he had other texts at his disposal here.

7. J. B. Pritchard, ed., *Ancient Near East: An Anthology of Texts and Pictures* (Princeton and Oxford: Princeton University Press, 2011) 282–84.

8. E. J. Bickerman, "The Edict of Cyrus in Ezra 1," *JBL* 65 (1946): 250–53.

9. See the list of occurrences of God's actions in the past in Mark McEntire, "Portraits of a Mature God: What Would a Theology of the Hebrew Scriptures Look Like If Ezra-Nehemiah Was at the Center of the Discussion?" *PSSt* 39 (2012): 113–24, here 117.

10. J. L. Wright, "Seeking, Finding, and Writing in Ezra-Nehemiah: Responses and Reflections," *Unity and Disunity in Ezra-Nehemiah* (ed. Mark J. Boda and Paul L. Redditt; Hebrew Bible Monographs 17; Sheffield: Sheffield Phoenix Press, 2008) 280.

11. Ibid., 277–80.

12. *Matthew Henry Commentary on the Whole Bible*, http://www.biblestudy-tools.com/commentaries/matthew-henry-complete/ezra/, on Ezra 1–4, 6 January 2014.

13. Wright, "Seeking, Finding, and Writing," 285.

14. Ibid., 286.

15. Ibid., 287.

16. Eskenazi, *In an Age of Prose*, 38, 41. The word "prolepsis" designates an early indicator of a later development.

17. The word for knives used here (*maḥălāpîm*) appears nowhere else in the Hebrew Bible, but a derivative term is the technical term in late Hebrew for the knife used in the ritual slaughter of animals. See Judah J. Slotki, *Daniel·* *Ezra·* *Nehemiah* (Soncino Books of the Bible; London, New York: Soncino Press, 1985) 114.

18. Bob Becking, "We All Returned as One!" *Judah and the Judeans in the Persian Period* (ed. Oded Lipschits and Manfred Oeming; Winona Lake IN: Eisenbrauns, 2006) 13.

19. Bede, *Patrilogiae cursus completes* (Series Latina, 221 vols.; Paris: Migne 1844–64), in *Ancient Christian Commentary on Scripture: Old Testament* (ed. Marco Conti; Downers Grove IL: InterVarsity, 2008) 5.304.

A CENSUS OF THE RETURNEES

Ezra 2

COMMENTARY

The Route of the Return

[Outline of Ezra 2] The returnees lived in Babylon, and the distance from Babylon to Jerusalem was 500+ miles almost due west. No one would have made the trip due west because it would have led straight through the Arabian Desert. Travelers instead would have followed the "Fertile Crescent," traveling northwest along the Euphrates River perhaps to Aleppo, where they could swing southwest to enter Judah from the north. A shorter, more southern but more difficult route went through Tadmor, right along the edge

Outline of Ezra 2

People who Led the Returns, 2:1-2a
A Tally by Fathers' Houses, 2:2b-58
People who Could Not Prove Their Ancestry, 2:59-63
Totals for the Entire Assembly, 2:64-67
Totals of Gifts by the Heads of Some Families, 2:68-69
Concluding Statement about Where People Settled, 2:70

Map of the Route of the Return

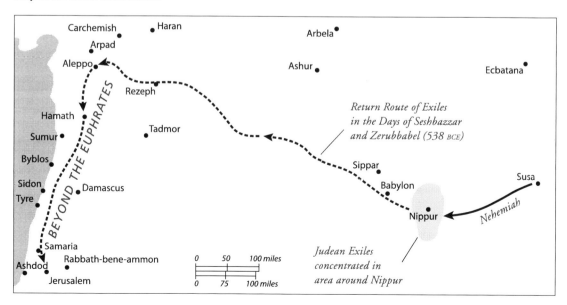

of the Arabian Desert. Regardless of the mode of transportation, the trip could be long and difficult.

A Census of the Returnees, 2:1-70

Ezra 2 appears to provide a list of repatriates who returned to Judah with Sheshbazzar. Historically speaking, however, that list can hardly be correct (see the discussion below on the census lists), and in fact the text does not explicitly make that claim. The chapter simply names people who led a return, gives a count of Judeans either by their "fathers' houses" or by their cities, and ends with totals of the people in the assembly, a number that far exceeded the totals of groups listed by fathers' houses and cities. The chapter also supplies totals of the gifts for the temple given by the heads of some of the families, and it concludes by noting that the people settled in their towns. Two issues stand out in the chapter and are better dealt with as a whole than verse by verse. These issues are the contents of the census list itself and the date of the return described in Ezra 2. The first issue is complicated by the fact that the same list with only minor differences appears again in Nehemiah 7:5, which makes explicit reference to the list in Ezra 2.

Census List

One of the most difficult issues in Ezra-Nehemiah is a proper understanding of the list in Ezra 2:1-70 + 3:1 and Nehemiah 7:6-73. Such an understanding depends first on analyzing them to determine what they actually contain. This task can be addressed first by analyzing the parallel lists, seeking seams in the lists. The analysis will show that the two chapters draw on several earlier lists, which the redactor/author of Ezra-Nehemiah (in Introduction to Ezra-Nehemiah, see "C. The Number of Returnees and the Import of that List for the Date of the Completion of Ezra-Nehemiah," and "G. The Authorship and Unity of Ezra-Nehemiah") "tweaked" in both chapters to make them fit their contexts and to suit his own purposes. [Components of the Lists in Ezra 2:1–3:1 and Nehemiah 7:6-73]

First, the redactor introduced both lists with the claim that they represented those who returned from Babylon to Judah with Zerubbabel, Jeshua, and other leaders. Several of those leaders are unknown outside these lists: Reeliah (Ezra 2:2) // Raamiah (Neh 7:7), Nahanani (Neh 7:7), Bilshan (Ezra 2:2 and Neh 7:7), Mispar (Ezra 2:2) // Mispareth (Neh 7:7; probably the same person), and Nehum (Neh 7:7, but probably the same person as Rehum in Ezra 2:2). Participation in those returns, and perhaps descent from those

---

Components of the Lists in Ezra 2:1–3:1 and Nehemiah 7:6-73

Ezra 2:1–3:1	**Nehemiah 7:6-73**
2:1-2a. These were the people . . . who came from . . . Babylon . . . with Zerubbabel, Jeshua, Nehemiah	7:6-7a. These were the people . . . who came from . . . Babylon . . . with Zerubbabel, Jeshua, Nehemiah . . . .
2:2b-58. Census numbers	7:7b-60. Census numbers
2:59-60. Laity who failed to prove that they belonged to Israel	7:61-62. Laity who failed to prove that they belonged to Israel
2:61-63. Priests who failed to prove they were priests	7:63-65. Priests who failed to prove they were priests
2:64-67. Totals in the census	7:66-69. Totals in the census
2:68-69. Gifts to help erect the temple	7:70-72. Gifts for the work on the wall
2:70. Priests, Levites, some of the people, singers, gate-keepers, all Israel lived in their towns	7:73a. Priests and all others lived in the towns
3:1. When the seventh month drew near, . . . the people assembled in Jerusalem (for the festival of booths)	7:73b. When the seventh month drew near, . . . all the people assembled (for the reading of the law by Ezra)

---

people, were necessary to any claim to participation in the temple. Perhaps others came, but the traditions and people behind Ezra-Nehemiah do not recognize the legitimacy of their worship in Jerusalem.

Some of those leaders appear elsewhere in Ezra-Nehemiah. The pair Seraiah (Ezra 2:2) and Azariah (Neh 7:7) are son and father, respectively (Ezra 7:1). Azariah appeared also in the list of those who helped repair the wall (Neh 3:23-24), but the name is also a variant for the name "Ezra." Baanah (Ezra 2:2 // Neh 7:7) appears elsewhere in the list of those who signed a covenant not to take foreign wives, but to tithe and otherwise to provide for the temple (Neh 10:27). It appears also in texts dealing with earlier periods, which presumably did not refer to the same man. Similarly, a man named Mordecai appears in both lists. The only other person with that name in the Hebrew Bible was the cousin of Esther, again apparently a different person since he had returned to Yehud.

Next, the name Rehum appears in the list in Ezra, but not in Nehemiah 7:7, where it is replaced by the name Nehum. Apparently the change to Nehum was simply an error, since the name Rehum appeared in the list of priests (Neh 12:3). In Nehemiah 10:25, he appeared as a person signing the covenant not to take foreign wives. The name Rehum also appears in the Aramaic narrative in Ezra as the name of a royal deputy located in Samaria (Ezra 4:8, 9, 17, 23) during the reign of Artaxerxes (I, r. 464–423). One might suppose, perhaps, that the two were different men with the same name who were contemporaries. Finally, Bigvai (Ezra 2:2 // Neh 7:7) also appeared in Ezra 2:14 // Nehemiah 7:19, in Ezra 8:14 in a genealogy, and in Nehemiah

10:16, among those signing the covenant. *If* he is the same man as Bagoas or Bagohi who appears in the Elephantine Papyri as is sometimes said, he was the governor of Judah in 407 to whom the Jews in Elephantine addressed their letter requesting help in rebuilding their temple.[1]

The significant point about all of these names except those of Zerubbabel and Joshua is that *they belonged to the period of Nehemiah.* Hence, the name "Nehemiah" that was listed third in both books almost surely was Nehemiah son of Hacaliah, and the man named "Azariah" listed fourth in Nehemiah 7:7 was possibly Ezra.[2] Hence, the introductory lists themselves point to a time of origination *during or after* the career of Nehemiah. Indeed, as argued in the Introduction to Ezra-Nehemiah, *the lists themselves* (though not the surrounding narratives) point to a time possibly as late as the second century BCE. Blenkinsopp notes that this list exhibits the common practice in ancient literature of anticipating later stages or developments in a community's growth by introducing them into their point of origin.[3] It is also important to note for understanding Ezra-Nehemiah that the list enfranchises only returnees to take part in the building and claims that they did it. The larger number perhaps is meant to include all returnees who had participated in building, keeping up, and worshiping there from the late sixth century on. In any case, the real Judah did not contain any locals that had remained in Jerusalem during the exile or their descendants.

This list, as it turns out in a consecutive reading of Ezra-Nehemiah, made its appearance here for only the first time. It or something like it will reappear in Nehemiah, and similar lists will appear several other places. Together Ezra and Nehemiah relate a carefully redacted narrative of the return of the "true "Israel" from Babylon to Jerusalem. Ezra 7–8 details the journey of a second group of returnees under the priest Ezra acting on the direct command of "Artaxerxes," and the list of returnees in Ezra 8:1-14 ties Ezra 7–8 to the original group of returnees. Ezra 9–10 shows the necessity of purging members of the original company of returnees who had removed themselves from the "true" community by marrying local Judean women, and Ezra 10:18-44 anchors that narrative. Nehemiah 7:5-73a then employs the same list (apart from transmission errors) as the one in Ezra 2:1-70a, and it shows the continued viability of that community, guaranteed now by the reconstruction of the wall around the city. Finally, Nehemiah 12:1-26 repeats a couple of names from that list, and Nehemiah

12:27-47 assures readers that the descendants, i.e., the readers' "group," were the ones who repopulated Jerusalem.

Second, the names in the census list given in the two books (Ezra 2:2b-58 // Neh 7:7b-60) do not add up to the total given later in the accounts: 42,360 plus 7,337 servants (Ezra 2:64-65 // Neh 7:66-67). That total is the same in both Ezra and Nehemiah even though the number by houses is 1,417 higher in Nehemiah than in Ezra. Moreover, the number of servants in both chapters is listed at 7,337, even though Nehemiah 7:67 included "245 singing men and singing women," while Ezra 2:65 included only "200 singing men and singing women." The number 245 was probably original in both, with the Hebrew words for "forty" and "five" getting lost.

The import of the differences, however, is that the verses supplying the total probably came from a different hand than the one that compiled the list of fathers' houses. The hand supplying the total was most likely that of the redactor, and the total number was *perhaps* from the latest redactor's own time. If modern estimates of the population of Persian Judah are correct, the numbers are higher than the maximum for any point during the Persian Period. [Estimates of the Population of Yehud] Indeed, it was probably the tally for a census or other official use as late as the second century BCE, rather than the time of Nehemiah.[4]

In addition, despite the totals at the end of each list, those within the list said to have returned from the exile actually add up to only 29,818 in Ezra and 31,099 in Nehemiah. Of them, 652 people

Estimates of the Population of Yehud

The number 42,360 plus 7,337 servants is too high as the number of repatriates. Albertz has calculated the number of exiles taken to Babylon at 20,000, a number higher than many would accept. (2 Kgs 24:14 gives 10,000 as the number of captives in 597; Jer 52:28 says 3,023 Judeans.) 2 Kgs 25:11 says the Babylonians took "all the rest of the population" in 586. Jer 52:28 says they took 823 from Jerusalem plus another 745 after the death of Gedaliah. Between 597/586 and 520, the exilic population is not likely to have grown from any of these numbers to 50,000. Besides, it is quite clear that some or many exiles chose not to return, but remained in Babylon. For the period immediately after the exile, many scholars accept a population estimate for Judah of only 20,000 (see Bright), and for the time of Nehemiah less than 50,000 (see Wright). Even Wright's estimate may have been based on the numbers in Ezra 2 and Neh 7, however. Others assume the number in this list included heads of households only and calculate a population of four or five times that figure. Ezra 2:64 and Neh 7:66, however, seem to have offered a total for the whole returning community, specifying that the numbers of servants and singers included men and women. The list in Ezra 8:1-14, by contrast, specifies males only, employing the term *zĕkarîm*. If the number 50,000 is difficult to accept, 250,000 is impossible. On the opposite extreme, Carter set the entire population of Judah at approximately 13,350 in Persian Period I (538–450) and 20,650 in Persian II (450–332). Working with those numbers, Becking looked at archaeological reports of sites (re)started in Yehud in the sixth century, and taking into consideration that some returnees may have chosen to live in occupied towns he estimated the number of returnees during the first half of the Persian Period as 4,000. Regardless of who—Bright/Wright or Carter/Becking—is closer to correct, it is clear that the returnees to Judah did not number 50,000+ people. Indeed, one can scarcely imagine the stress on the land, roads, villages, economy, etc. an infusion of that many immigrants would cause to a small, poor area like Yehud.

R. Albertz, *Die Exilszeit: 6. Jahrhundert v. Chr.* (Biblische Enzyklopädie 7; Berlin, Cologne: Kohlhammer, 2001) 80.

B. Becking, "'We All Returned as One,'" *Judah and Judeans in the Persian Period* (Winona Lake IN: Eisenbrauns, 2006) 9.

J. A. Bright, *A History of Israel* (3rd ed.; Philadelphia: Westminster, 1981) 365.

C. E. Carter, *The Emergence of Yehud in the Persian Period; A Social and Demographic Study* (JSOTSup 294; Sheffield: Sheffield Academic Press, 1999) 201.

G. E. Wright, *Biblical Archaeology* (rev. ed.; Philadelphia: Westminster, 1962) 202.

in Ezra 2:60 (642 in Neh 7:62) could not prove that they descended from Judeans. Wherever the lists came from, only 29,260 (Ezra) or 30,455 (Nehemiah), i.e., about 60 percent of the total numbers, represented what the redactor considered the *true* Israelites, including the *true* priesthood. The remaining 40 percent or so of the 42,360 people plus 7,337 servants apparently did not pass his test.

Those persons who were *not* part of the true Israel or the true priesthood seem to have constituted an issue of concern for the redactor, given the concern of Ezra-Nehemiah overall for the true Israel. The criterion for inclusion set forth by the redactor with respect to the laity in Ezra 2:59 // Nehemiah 7:61 seems to have been simply that one belonged to one of the fathers' houses that developed in the exile.[5] Here again the redactor seems to have differed from his source(s), which numbered laity either by their fathers' house (Ezra 2:2b-19 // Neh 7:8-24) or by their town (e.g., most of Ezra 2:20-35 // Neh 7:25-38). No such latitude was possible for priests, however, who had to have been included in genealogical records (Ezra 2:61-63 // Neh 7:63-65). J. E. Dyck thinks that for the redactor, even the people enumerated by village only were excluded from the "true Israel." If so, those included in the true Israel are reduced to about 40 percent (i.e., only 21,183 of 49,697 in Ezra, 22,415 of 49,697 in Nehemiah).[6]

Third, the redactor of Ezra-Nehemiah "tweaked" the accounts to fit them into their respective narratives. The context for the list in Ezra 2 is the redactor's narrative of the so-called "Edict of Cyrus" that allowed exiles to return home and rebuild the temple. In Nehemiah, however, the redactor said that Nehemiah "found" the book of the genealogy of those who were the first to return from Babylon (Neh 7:5). At the end of both lists, moreover, the redactor again shaped the narratives to fit their different contexts. In Ezra he reported that upon arrival some of the heads of the families made freewill offerings toward the erection of the temple (Ezra 2:68), whereas in Nehemiah he simply said they contributed "to the work" (Neh 7:70), presumably the work on the wall, the subject under discussion.

Also, the redactor incorporated in his Nehemiah account the notice (Neh 7:73a) that the people settled in their towns. The continuation of that narrative appears later (Neh 11:1-2), in an account of the drafting of additional population for Jerusalem. Finally, the redactor rounded off each narrative in similar words about what the people did "when the seventh month came," though in Ezra they observed the festival of booths (Ezra 3:1), while in Nehemiah Ezra read the Law of Moses to the people (Neh 8:1a). Even that verse shows seams, however. The original conclusion to it probably was the observance of the festival of booths recorded later (Neh 8:9-18). The intervening verses (Neh 8:1b-8) concerning Ezra's reading of the law actually prepared the reader not simply for the observance of the festival but also for the confession of sin that follows (Neh 9:1-37) and Nehemiah's second term as governor (Neh 13:4-31).

This analysis reveals, then, that the redactor used a census tally (Ezra 2:2b-58 // Neh 7:7b-60), information about laity and priests who did not pass muster as "true" Judeans or priests (Ezra 2:59-60, 61-63 // Neh 7:61-62, 63-65), and "totals" (Ezra 2:64-67 // Neh 7:66-69) of the entire post-exilic community. Even some of the repatriates did not belong to the "true Israel" or the "true priesthood" because they could not prove their descent from one of the fathers' houses. The redactor worked these materials into two different contexts, which he shaped to make his own points (Ezra 2:1-2a, 2:70 // Neh 7:5, 6-7a, 73a).

The Date of the Return

It should be clear that the date of the "return" discussed in Ezra 2 is problematic. The putative date (derived from Ezra 1) would seem to be 539 or shortly thereafter. Internal evidence within Ezra 2 just reviewed, however, has shown that the list of leaders of the return (Ezra 2:1-2a) presupposed the careers of Ezra and Nehemiah, so *as it stands* the whole list cannot be earlier than 445 (the date of Nehemiah's initial trip to Jerusalem) and appears to be several centuries later. The first two of those leaders, Zerubbabel and Jeshua, however, returned to Judah earlier than Ezra's or Nehemiah's career. They were already in Yehud by the second year of the reign of Darius, (i.e., 520; see Hag 1:1), and they were instrumental in the getting the reconstruction of the temple started then. (See the whole book of Haggai and Zechariah 4, especially 4:6b-10a.) Traditional and even some critical scholars have concluded that the list in Ezra 2 actually recorded those who returned with Zerubbabel and Jehsua,[7] but as seen above that is unlikely. Given the analysis of the census list offered there, it is clear that Ezra 2 did not provide specific information about any single return, certainly not one as early as 539 or 521. Rather, the chapter serves the redactional function of moving some of the exiles and the action of the book from Babylon to Jerusalem.

Did Sheshbazzar return to Jerusalem in 539? There is no reason to doubt that he did, and he perhaps began the work on the temple, work that seems to have ceased some time prior to the rise of Darius I in 521 (see Ezra 5:16-17). Possibly Zerubbabel and Jeshua also returned with Sheshbazzar, but it is also possible that they returned to Jerusalem later, maybe about the time of the rise of Darius I (521), possibly with his permission to continue rebuilding the temple, but with the intention to do so regardless. [Zerubbabel in Haggai and Zechariah] There is, of course, no scriptural warrant for that suggestion. It is simply an attempt to account for the presence in Ezra 2 of two key figures not mentioned in Ezra 1. Sheshbazzar himself is not mentioned again except in Ezra 5:16-17, where he is said to have to have "founded" or to have "laid the foundation" of the temple. Sometimes people wonder whether Zerubbabel and Sheshbazzar were the same person, but that is unlikely since both names are Babylonian and their work appears to have been completed during the reigns of two different Persian rulers: Sheshbazzar under Cyrus (Ezra 1:8) and Zerubbabel during the time of King Darius (r. 522–486), during whose reign the temple was actually built at the urging of Haggai and Zechariah. Later, Ezra is reported to have brought a group with him (Ezra 8:1-14, 16-20), and other groups may have come as well.

Zerubbabel in Haggai and Zechariah

The prophets Haggai and Zechariah flourished "in the second year of King Darius" (Hag 1:1; 2:1, 10, 20; Zech 1:1, 7) and "in the fourth year" (Zech 7:1). Both men speak of Zerubbabel, and Haggai anticipates God making Zerubbabel the new king. Haggai has God say that Zerubbabel will be "like a signet ring" (2:23). A signet ring, of course, was a ring with someone's signature mark on it. Kings in particular used them to "sign" or seal documents. Jer 22:24 quotes God as saying of King Jehoiachin of Judah, "Even if King Coniah [another name for the same man] were the signet ring on my right hand, from there I would tear you off and give you into the hands of those who seek your life, . . . even into the hands of King Nebuchadnezzar of Babylon and into the hands of the Chaldeans" (i.e., the Babylonians).

Hag 2:23 is a direct reversal of that prediction. After the punishment of the exile and the return of many Jews from exile, Haggai proclaims that God is about to make Zerubbabel "like" God's signature ring. Zerubbabel was already the "governor" of Judah (whatever the term translated "governor" might have meant exactly), and God was about to undo his act with regard to Jehoiachin, presumably by making Zerubbabel king. If that way of expressing the prediction

seems coded, it would also seem to have been necessary. It is not clear that the Persians ever intended to make a king of Zerubbabel—or anyone else in Yehud—but the hope for a new David seems to have run high during Zerubbabel's stay in Jerusalem. Zech 4, moreover, envisions two "anointed ones," usually considered to be the king and the high priest, standing by "the Lord of the whole earth" (Zech 4:14). Into that vision someone inserted (in Zech 4:6b-10a) a statement about Zerubbabel's "founding" the new temple, apparently seen as a kingly action.

What happened to Zerubbabel is anyone's guess. Sometimes scholars suggest that the Babylonians removed Zerubbabel from whatever "office" or station he might have held in light of thinking like that of Haggai and Zechariah. There is, however, no evidence to support the view that Zerubabbel himself even wanted to rule. One can, in fact, read his situation quite differently: namely that Zerubbabel was an exile with Davidic ancestry who was sent to Jerusalem by the Persians to see to the completion of the temple. While Haggai and Zechariah seem to have entertained political hopes for Zerubbabel, he may have preferred to return to Babylon, where, perhaps, he was more comfortable. In any case, he disappears from the Bible.

People Who Led the Return, 2:1-2a

Second Chronicles 36:21 alludes to texts where the book of Jeremiah predicts a seventy-year exile (e.g., Jer 25:11-12; 29:10), but the redactor of Ezra-Nehemiah omits that reference and focuses instead on the return of the exiles. Ezra 2 opens with a list of the leaders said to have brought the exiles back to Yehud. No date is supplied for Ezra 2, perhaps implying thereby that the return in question was the same one as in Ezra 1. (At any rate, that is the way the text is typically read.) As noted above, the reality seems to be instead that Zerubbabel and Jeshua returned later, perhaps in 521. The reference to the "province" is the area in which the returnees lived.[8]

The Tally of Returnees by Fathers' Houses, 2:2b-67

The tally is a composite put together by the redactor. The first section (Ezra 2:2b-58) is simply a tally of Judeans, including laity (24,144 in all), priests (4,289), Levites (74), singers (128), gatekeepers (139), and temple servants (392). They add up to 29,166 people, of whom just over 17 percent are temple personnel. If those numbers are accurate for any period, they reflect a laity burdened by support of temple personnel and their families, even if some of those temple employees had to earn a substantial part of their living by another occupation.

The repatriates are classified by their "fathers' houses" in vv. 3-20 and by towns in vv. 21-35. [Fathers' Houses] The phrases "the descendants of" and "the children of" appear to have been interchangeable (see Ezra 2:21 // Neh 7:26). Henry interestingly and perceptively notes the small number of returnees from Anathoth, and he directs his readers' attention to Jeremiah's predictions of its demise (see Jer 11:21-23).[9] One father's house mentioned in Nehemiah is missing from Ezra: the children of Hashum (Neh 7:22). Likewise, five fathers' houses (the children of Jorah in Ezra 2:18) and four cities (the children of Magbish in Ezra 2:30, of Akkub in Ezra 2:45, of Hagab in Ezra 2:46, and of Asnah in Ezra 2:50) are missing in Nehemiah. Two sets of names have been inverted in the lists: Jericho (Ezra 2:34 // Neh 7:36) and Lod, as well as Hadid and Ono (Ezra 2:33 // Neh 7:37). Otherwise minor differences in spelling and in the counts constitute the only discrepancies. It is not certain how to account for them.

Fathers' Houses

ΑΩ "Fathers' houses" is a term designating a real or fictive group of exiles organized in Babylon to sustain themselves in their own culture. The term signifies that the exiles organized themselves by families in order to remember and uphold the traditions of their homeland.

Rainer Albertz, *Die Exilszeit: 6. Jahrhundert v. Chr.* (Biblische Enzyklopädie 7; Stuttgart: Kohlhammer, 2001) 92.

J. P. Weinberg, "Das *Bēit 'abōt* im 6.-4. Jh. V. u. Z," *VT* 23 (1973): 400–14.

Map of Yehud

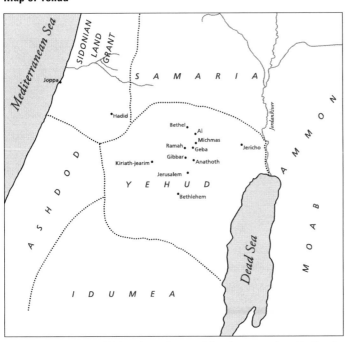

This map contains possible locations of many of the places mentioned in Ezra 2, but not all the locations of sites are known.

Perhaps the differences are attributable to nothing more than scribal slips, including omissions.

The list may well have been an authentic census tally from some time in Judean history. G. Hölscher makes that suggestion and assumes it represented a tax register, which would account for the laity in the list.[10] It seems too high for the years immediately after the exile, but it might well reflect an estimate of the population some time in the fourth or (even better) the second century. The numbers ascribed to inhabitants of specific villages may have included people who were not repatriates and/or did not belong to a house.

The laity, by fathers' houses, Ezra 2:2b-19. The people in this list are reported by fathers' houses only. Fourteen of these seventeen fathers' houses appear elsewhere: fourteen are represented among those who sign an agreement to support the temple (Neh 10:1-26; MT 10:2-28); eleven among those traveling to Judah with Ezra (Ezra 8); and six among those agreeing to divorce their wives (Ezra 10).[11]

The laity, by towns, Ezra 2:20-35. The people in the next part of this list were enumerated by town. Dyck thinks that the lack of known fathers' houses marked these people as outside the "true Israel" because of their inability to trace their linage, even though the list might imply that they knew their original hometown.[12] Consequently, the redactor of Ezra-Nehemiah may have deemed them outsiders. What is clear is the proximity of these towns to Jerusalem.

Gibbar (or Gibeon, Neh 7:25), an important site in the early monarchy especially, lay in Benjaminite territory about eight miles northwest of Jerusalem. *Bethlehem,* David's hometown, was five miles south. *Netophah* may have been near the spring 'Ain en-Natûf, three miles southeast of Bethlehem. *Anathoth,* the home of

Jeremiah, lay only three miles north of Jerusalem. *Azmaveh* was perhaps Hizmeh, five miles north of Jerusalem. *Kiriath-jearim,* the site where the Philistines stashed the ark of the covenant, lay on the boundary between Judah and Benjamin, perhaps nine miles west of Jerusalem. *Chephirah,* another Benjaminite town, lay five miles southwest of Gibeon. The site of *Beeroth* remains undetermined. Probably *Ramah* was situated five miles north of Jerusalem, *Geba* probably a mile further north. *Michmas* was about seven miles north of Jerusalem, *Bethel* and *Ai* about twelve miles north. The location of *Nebo,* not to be confused with the mountain in Transjordan from which Moses was said to have viewed Canaan, is uncertain, as is *Magbish.* The phrase "other Elam" may refer to the fathers' house of the same name (Ezra 2:7 // Neh 7:12; see also Ezra 8:7; 10:2, 26), in which case it was not a town and is out of place here. *Harim* (missing from Nehemiah) is a priest's name elsewhere, and this name may be out of place too. *Lod* (on the road between Jerusalem and Joppa), *Hadid,* and *Ono* (location not known exactly, but possibly about seven miles south of Joppa) were Benjaminite cities. *Jericho,* on the Jordan River, was the eastern-most city named. The word *Senaah* is unknown, but the large number given has caused scholars to speculate that it might mean something like "despised ones" and refer to a group and not a city.[13]

The priests, Ezra 2:36-39. This list includes only four groups of priests, in contrast with the twenty-four listed in 1 Chronicles 24:7-18, where interestingly Pashhur (listed in Ezra 2:36) is missing. H. G. M. Williamson suggests that the list in 1 Chronicles comes from a time late enough that his family had lost its priestly status.[14] A descendent of Pashhur is mentioned (as are Jedaiah and Meshillemitha, the latter a descendant of Immer) in the Chronicler's list of returning priests who settled in Jerusalem (1 Chr 9:10-13), but Harim is not. The most remarkable feature of the list, however, is the large number of priests: 4,289, or more than 10 percent of the total number of citizens (42,360, not counting servants) given in Ezra 2:64. One wonders how a small community could support such a large group of priests. In any case, the numbers for the priests and other temple workers show unmistakably that vv. 36-58 presuppose a functioning temple and a large, well-developed hierarchy of workers there.

The Levites, Ezra 2:40. By contrast with the priests, the number of Levites is much smaller: only 74. To be sure, Deuteronomistic theology made all Levites priests (Deut 18:1-2). Sooner or later the priesthood itself was limited to people who claimed descent from

Aaron, and the other Levites were assistants. That was the situation in Ezra-Nehemiah. The details of the development may be left open here.

The singers, Ezra 2:41. The singers are said to be the descendants of Asaph, a Levite held to have been one of David's chief musicians and who is said to have composed some of the psalms (viz. 50 and 73–83). Their number, which probably included various types of musicians, was greater than that of the Levites: 128.

The gatekeepers, Ezra 2:42. Porters were necessary at any temple. Nehemiah 12:25 adds that they guarded the storehouses. The list contains six names as heads of houses of the porters.

The temple servants, Ezra 2:43-54. The Hebrew word for this group was *hannĕtînĕm,* literally "the Nethanites" or "the ones given." J. M. Myers thinks they were slaves,[15] but the text does not say so. Rather, they appear to have been temple functionaries appointed by David to assist the Levites (Ezra 8:20). L. W. Batten thinks they performed the humblest functions at the sanctuary, and J. J. Slotki thinks they hewed wood.[16] Whether their group actually existed in David's time is not clear, but they appear to have functioned in the post-exilic temple.[17] Blenkinsopp thinks this group was non-Israelite in origin because of the appearance of foreign names (viz., Ziha, Rezin, Bezai, Meunim, Nephisium, Barkos, and Sisera).[18] Foreign names in the post-exilic period, however, do not prove that people were not Judean, as the Babylonian name Zerubbabel shows.

The descendants of Solomon's servants, Ezra 2:55-58. These people were mentioned as state slaves in connection with Solomon's reign (1 Kgs 9:20-21 // 2 Chr 8:7-8), including galley slaves (2 Chr 8:18). Here, however, their function is not mentioned. Blenkinsopp thinks that by the time of the writing of Ezra-Nehemiah, they may have merged with the temple servants.[19] That suggestion would explain the two being lumped together in the count: 392.

Laity not able to relate their fathers' house, Ezra 2:59-60. The town Tel-melah (salt-mound) is the only one of the five that has been tentatively located; it may be the city named "Thelma," located East of Babylon in salt flats near the Persian Gulf. The name Tel-harsha means forest mound.[20] Repatriates though they were, they could not trace their ancestry back to Judah. The result was that the redactor did not consider them "true Judeans." They numbered 652.

Priests not able to trace their descent, Ezra 2:61-63. Some priests also were unable to trace their descent. Hence, they were treated as ritually "unclean" (i.e., ritually contaminated in some way, with the result that they were prohibited from offering sacrifices). An official determined that they should not receive a share of the food for priests until their status could be cleared up by a priest using the Urim and Thummim. The Hebrew Bible does not describe these objects, but in pre-exilic texts the High Priest carried them in his breastplate (Exod 28:30; Lev 8:8). They were manipulated in such a way as to render a yes-or-no answer to a question. Their use may have died out in the pre-exilic period. If so, the governor's injunction would seem to have been permanent. [Governor]

The total supplied in 2:64-67 by the redactor (42,360 plus 7,337 servants) has been discussed above. The text also enumerates the horses, mules, camels, and donkeys (only the latter two animals in Nehemiah, a result probably of faulty transmission of the text) that arrived with the people. Blenkinsopp cogently suggests that they might have been added in view of the mention of animals in Ezra 1:4, 6.[21]

These verses conclude the narrative about the journey from Babylon to Jerusalem to rebuild the temple. The redactor has tweaked this conclusion to make it fit two different contexts. In Ezra 2 he wrote of gifts of the heads of the fathers' houses for the treasury. The gifts presumably were for the temple. In Nehemiah 7 he wrote of gifts to the work, which he then divided into gifts from the governor (unnamed) to the treasury, followed by the gifts of the heads of fathers' houses to the treasury of the work. Nehemiah 7 gives every appearance of having added these short lists to the one in Ezra 2, which it modified. The result is clumsy in its repetition of the phrase "some of the heads of the fathers' houses," but in its context in Nehemiah it provides a transition back to the events surrounding the building of the wall. More will be said about this list in comments on Nehemiah 7:73b–8:18 in connection with its use in and redaction of the book of Nehemiah.

Governor

AΩ The word in the Hebrew text, Tirshatha, is sometimes just transliterated (as in the Jewish TANAKH Translation) or is translated as "governor" (NRSV and REV) or "His Excellency" (NAB and NJB). Slotki thinks the word refers to Zerubbabel, but scholars have offered other suggestions, including the meaning "circumcised." The word remains unintelligible.

D. J. A. Clines, in a footnote to Ezra 2:63 in *The HarperCollins Study Bible* (New York: HarperCollins, 1993) 703.

Judah J. Slotki, *Daniel· • Ezra •·Nehemiah* (Soncino Books of the Bible; London, New York: Soncino, 1951) 123.

Wilhelm T. in der Smitten, "Der Tirschata in Esra-Nehemia," *VT* 21 (1971): 618–20.

Offerings for the Temple, 2:68-69

Based on the ending of Ezra 1, a reader would expect a report noting that when the repatriates arrived in Jerusalem, they took the treasures King Cyrus had given them directly to the house of God there. A comparison of these verses with Ezra 1:11 reveals immediately that the lists are different. The first list (Ezra 1:10-11) mentioned only vessels taken from Jerusalem by Nebuchadnezzar. The gifts (in Ezra 2:68-69) may be intended instead to show the disposition of the silver and gold given by those who did not return (see Ezra 1:4, 6). Nevertheless, it appears that the redactor drew upon an actual list of goods for the temple, including tunics for priests to wear (which had not been mentioned anywhere in Ezra 1). The two lists in Nehemiah 7 both mention tunics for the priests as well.

Settlement in Judah, 2:70

In contrast with Ezra 2:68-69, v. 70 would fit well with Ezra 1:11, closing that narrative with the note that the people settled in their various towns. That observation does not prove that v. 70 was the original culmination of Ezra 1, however. The verse just as easily could have been the creation of the redactor, who looked back to 1:11, just as in vv. 68-69 he looked back to 1:4, 6.

The NRSV emends v. 70 based on 1 Esdras 5:46, so that it reads, "The priests, the Levites, and some of the people *lived in Jerusalem and its vicinity;* and the singers, the gatekeepers, and the temple servants lived in their towns, and all Israel in their towns." The italicized words are not in the Hebrew text. The emendation depends on the acceptance of the view that 1 Esdras offers a text earlier and superior to the Hebrew. The sequence of groups named differs between the two texts, and both verses seem repetitious, perhaps developed in the course of transmission. The differences, in any case, do not justify emending either text in light of the other. Thus, the reading in the MT underscores the reality of early post-exilic Jerusalem: it had been destroyed substantially. How much was still livable or had been rebuilt during the exile, *if any*, is unknown, and likely there had been little. The text in 1 Esdras may better reflect the conditions at the time Ezra-Nehemiah was written than the conditions of 539 or even 520.

If a list of towns seems merely geographical or even pedestrian, it has not always been so read. Bede commented on the allegorical meaning of various terms:

> Jerusalem signifies the universal state of the holy church, which is all over the world. The towns, which belong to Judah, signify each of the virtues of the faithful, in which they are defended from the temptations and attacks of the evil spirits as in a fortress made of different towns. . . . Finally the towns in which [the repatriated exiles lived]

may be interpreted as the different churches of Christ, by which together the one universal church is formed.[22]

More recently, Dyck has read the chapter from an ideological perspective. He argues that the list both "masks (intentionally or unintentionally) the problematic nature of Jewish identity in [the early post-exilic] period, but also reproduces the struggle for identity and control."[23]

A Second Exodus

S. Japhet calls attention to parallels between the exodus from Egypt and the return from Babylon. The Exodus is a well-known biblical concept, explicitly articulated also by Jeremiah (16:14-15 = 23:7-8) and Second Isaiah (48:20; 51:9-11; 52:4). Japhet also says that this analogy forms the foundational structure for the whole of Ezra-Nehemiah. The people of Israel, Ezra and other priests, and Nehemiah and his entourage follow this basic pattern of setting out on a journey directed by God and led by God's representatives. She thinks this pattern raises forcefully the issue of the historicity of the three narratives of Ezra-Nehemiah.[24] One might respond, however, that similar patterns do not prove that the events did not happen so much as they point to "hidden" patterns discerned within an ongoing tradition.

The Exodus

Julius Schnorr Von Carolsfeld (1794–1872). *Moses and the Crossing of the Red Sea*. Engraving for the Bible, Germany, 1860. (Credit: CCI/The Art Archive at Art Resource, NY)

Summary

Ezra 2 turns out to be the literary creation of the redactor of Ezra-Nehemiah, who combined a list of repatriates (2:1-58) with a narrative about repatriates who could not prove their ancestry (2:59-63) and totals from a census from his own time (2:64-67) into a narrative of a return of thousands of exiles prior to the rebuilding of the temple under Jeshua and Zerubbabel between 520 and 515, which he would describe in Ezra 4–6. This account is fictive in the sense that a return of such magnitude is unlikely. What is not fictive is that a number of exiles did return, presumably under Sheshbazzar (Ezra 1), Jeshua and Zerubbabel, Ezra, perhaps Nehemiah, and others as well.

CONNECTIONS

1. People count, so many nations count their people. Accordingly, the Constitution of the United States, Article 1, Section 2, in its first sentence provides for a census within three years of its adoption and every ten years thereafter. The underlying reason for the census was to maintain proportional representation among the states to the Congress. The persons presupposed by the lists in Ezra 2 // Nehemiah 7 also counted people. Their lists, however, were intended to enfranchise returnees from Babylon and also to exclude those who had remained behind, in whole or in part, from full participation in the governance of refounded Yehud. [Jonathan Edwards, Writing on Ezra 2] The lists also enfranchised certain priests and Levites for service in the rebuilt temple (vv. 36-38, 40), as well as singers, gatekeepers, and servants (vv. 41-58) for their lesser, hereditary duties. On the one hand, modern readers can understand displaced people wanting back their old positions when they were permitted to return. On the other hand, they can understand other people, those who had remained behind, resenting and rejecting those claims. Did their decades of living in or near Jerusalem and in Yehud give them no rights? Was it their fault that the returnees had lost their positions and perquisites? As far as that goes, why should people in Samaria, who had suffered their own reversals to the Assyrians and who had filled the power gap in Judah during the Babylonian exile, suddenly surrender power to the returnees? Bible readers need to remember that Ezra-Nehemiah offers the perspective of only one group. Others of their contemporaries could read the fall of Jerusalem as evidence of God's rejection of

Jonathan Edwards, Writing on Ezra 2

"Great numbers tarried behind [in Babylon], though they still retained the same religion with those that returned, so far as it could be practiced in a foreign land." Without a temple, worship without sacrifices prevailed. In the larger context of this remark, Edwards said that God used the shortcoming of the returnees to prepare the way for Christ. That might or might not be the case; the book of Ezra does not speak on that issue either way. The point in this commentary is only that many exiles did not return with Zerubbabel and company. The returnees constituted only part of the exiles. Ezra 7–8 will recount another return of exiles in 456 under Ezra, and the book of Nehemiah makes it clear that other exiles remained in Babylon as late as 444. Indeed, Babylon remained a center for Judeans until its destruction, and exiles remained in Babylonia for centuries. Indeed, there is a Babylonian version of the Jewish Talmud.

Jonathan Edwards, ed. Stephen J. Stein, *Notes on Scripture*, vol. 15 of The Works of Jonathan Edwards (New Haven: Yale University Press, 1998) 371.

Jerusalem and its leaders. In fact, had they wished, they could have pointed to the words of Jeremiah the prophet as proof.

The United States also has its disenfranchised people. They begin, of course, with Native Americans who were systematically attacked and disenfranchised by waves of new settlers from various places in Western Europe. Those settlers soon began to bring/allow in others as indentured servants. They also began to import African slaves, and later Chinese and other Orientals in work groups. The Statue of Liberty, in fact, implores, "Give me your poor and huddled masses." As those groups achieved or were granted freedom from service obligations, they too wanted to compete on level ground for the benefits of American culture. They perhaps did not have the claim to prior ownership that the Native Americans had, but they certainly had legitimate claims to free opportunity.

The point of these remarks is not so much to advocate for this or that ethnic, racial, or national group in the United States (although such advocacy seems warranted to this author), but to point out that there were competing claims to land ownership and the right to perquisites in post-exilic Yehud. It is easy for readers convinced of the correctness and holiness of the claims of the returnees or the original authors and audience of our national narratives to agree with them, but readers need to remember that other people had claims too. Readers may agree with the authors of Ezra-Nehemiah that God brought back the returnees without at the same time approving all of their claims and all the methods they employed to regain control. If the text rarely criticizes the returnees, silence never constitutes a logical proof for the correctness of a position.

2. In the twentieth century, a return similar to the one from Babylon to Yehud occurred in modern-day Israel. Jews who had been mostly driven from the Holy Land after the fall of Jerusalem to the Romans and been persecuted for hundreds of years by Christians in Europe wanted a land of their own where they could live freely. Who could quarrel with that? Originally, some Jewish thinkers thought of claiming basically unsettled land in Latin America, but the call of Zion was too strong.

Even before the beginning of the twentieth century, therefore, some Jews began returning to what was then the Muslim country of Palestine. During World War I, Britain promised Palestinians independence and Jews a "national home" in Palestine. Whether the British leaders realized the potential conflict between those promises is beside the point here, but during the years of its mandate (1922–1948), Britain denied Zionist claims that the

Palestine, 1945

LEBANON

Safad

● Acre　　　SYRIA

Hafia

Tiberias

Nazareth

Baysan

Jinin

Tulkarm

Nablus

Jaffa　　　TRANSJORDAN

Ramallah

al-Ramla

Jerusalem

Gaza

Hebron

Beersheba

EGYPT

This map shows the boundaries of the British protectorate at the end of World War II before the post-war rise in Jewish immigration.

whole area belonged to Jews. Events escalated out of their control after World War II, so in 1947 Britain turned the matter over to the United Nations to resolve. That organization proposed to partition the area. Palestinians perceived that action as an unwarranted and illegal attempt to take over and give away land that had been theirs for centuries. Granted, they said in effect, Palestine had been a Jewish land thousands of years ago, but the Romans had ended that state of affairs and most Jews had gone away. Palestinians argued then and still argue today that what is now Israel was and should have remained their land. Hence, rightly or wrongly (readers of these lines perhaps decided for themselves years ago), Palestinians overwhelmingly refuse to recognize the right of Israel to exist as a Jewish state. They live an uneasy and troubled life in or around the land where their ancestors lived for centuries, while the Jewish state prospers there through the hard work of its citizens and with significant western backing.

It remains to be seen what the new "return" of Jews will mean, if that term and analogy with the exile is appropriate. Many Christians turn to the book of Revelation and/or to other eschatological texts to discern the future of the Holy Land. Ezra-Nehemiah will be of little use in discerning that outcome, though it certainly might be used polemically.

NOTES

1. See *ANET* (2011), 450–51.

2. Joseph Blenkinsopp, *Ezra-Nehemiah* (OTL; Louisville: Westminster, 1988) 85. George Rawlinson (exposition of Ezra 2 in *The Pulpit Commentary* [New York, Toronto: Funk and Wagnals, n.d.]) disagrees strongly: "[I]t seems strange that such a theory should ever have been seriously maintained, since not only does Ezra declare the list to be a catalogue of those "which came with *Zerubbabel* (ver. 2), but Nehemiah himself warns that it is a register of the genealogy of them which came up the first" (Neh 7:5). To Rawlinson one can only reply, "Yes, that is what the text says, but it flies in the face of other considerations, both archaeological and textual."

3. Joseph Blenkinsopp, "The Development of Jewish Sectarianism from Nehemiah to the Hasidim," *Judah and the Judeans in the Fourth Century B.C.E.* (ed. Oded Lipschits, Gary N. Knoppers, and Rainer Albertz; Winona Lake IN.: Eisenbrauns, 2007) 395.

4. Philip R. Davies (*On the Origins of Judaism* [London, Oakville CT: Equinox, 2011] 91) says bluntly, "A sixth-century 'Return' is almost certainly the product of later invention, simplifying a more complicated and lengthier process of political and religious transformation and obliterating the memory of Neo-Babylonian Judah in favor of an exclusive attention to the Judean 'exiles,' descended from people taken largely from Jerusalem and its immediate environment." He too argues that people returned from Babylon over a long period, but the later description of that "return" was shortened for simplicity's sake and informed by polemical considerations from a later period.

5. A "father's house" was a real or fictive family group organized among exiles in Babylon to sustain themselves in their own culture. See R. Albertz, *Die Exilszeit; 6. Jahrhundert v. Chr.* (Biblische Enzyklopädie 7; Berlin, Cologne: Kohlhammer, 2001), 92. See also Joel P. Weinberg, "*Das Bēit Ābōt im* 6-4. JH. V. U. Z.," *VT* 23 (1973): 400–14. The word *zĕrah* in Ezra 2:59, translated "descent" in the NRSV, usually referred to one's offspring or "seed."

6. Jonathan E. Dyck ("Ezra 2 in Ideological Critical Perspective," *Rethinking Contexts, Rereading Texts* [ed. M. Daniel Carroll R.; JSOTSup 299; Sheffield: Sheffield Academic Press, 2000] 141). Further, Dyck (143–44) points to the significance of the "heads" of the fathers' houses in Ezra 1:5, 2:68-69, 3:12, 4:3, 8:1, 10:16 and Neh 10:1-27, 11:3-24 and 12:12-26.

7. This suggestion was put forward originally by Eduard Meyer, *Die Entstehung des Judentums* (Halle: Niemeyer, 1896) 190. It was endorsed lately by Geo Widengren, "The Persian Period," in *Israelite and Judean History* (ed. J. H. Hayes, J. M. Miller; Philadelphia: Westminster, 1977) 491.

8. F. C. Fensham, "Mêdînâ in Ezra and Nehemiah," *VT* 25 (1975): 795–97.

9. See *Matthew Henry Commentary on the Whole Bible*, http://www.biblestudy-tools.com/commentaries/matthew-henry-complete/ezra/2.html, on Ezra 2:23 (accessed 6 January 2014).

10. See Blenkinsopp, *Ezra-Nehemiah*, 86.

11. Ibid.

12. Dyck, "Ezra 2," 141–44.

13. Blenkinsopp, *Ezra-Nehemiah*, 86–87. Many of the site identifications and distances given above came from him.

14. H. G. M. Williamson, "The Origins of the Twenty-Four Priestly Courses," *VTSup* 30 (1979): 251–68.

15. J. M. Myers, *Ezra-Nehemiah* (AB 14; Garden City: Doubleday, 1965) 19

16. L. W. Batten, *The Books of Ezra and Nehemiah* (ICC; Edinburgh: T&T Clark, 1913) 87; J. J. Slotki, *Daniel· • Ezra· • Nehemiah* (London, New York: Soncino, 1985) 121.

17. H. G. M. Williamson, *Ezra, Nehemiah* (WBC 16; Waco: Word, 1985) 35.

18. Blenkinsopp, *Ezra-Nehemiah*, 90.

19. Ibid., 91.

20. Ibid., 92.

21. Blenkinsopp (*Ezra-Nehemiah*, 93) adds that one might hear an echo of the exodus narrative, specifically Exod 12:38.

22. Bede in J.-P. Migne, in *Ancient Christian Commentary on Scripture* (ed. Marco Conti; Downers Grove IL: Inter-Varsity, 2008) 5.306.

23. Dyck, "Ezra 2," 130, 145.

24. Sara Japhet, "Chronology and Ideology in Ezra-Nehemiah," *Judah and the Judeans in the Persian Period* (ed. O. Lipschits and M. Oeming; Winona Lake IN: Eisenbrauns, 2006) 504.

RESUMPTION OF WORSHIP
IN JERUSALEM

Ezra 3

COMMENTARY

[Outline of Ezra 3] The overarching subject of Ezra 1–6 is the restoration of the temple in Jerusalem. Introduced in Ezra 1 and mentioned in Ezra 2:68, that project became the chief focus of Ezra 3–6. The setting of the book had moved from Babylon to Jerusalem in Ezra 2. The date given in Ezra 3:1 was the "seventh month," Tishri, with no mention of the year. [Months in the Hebrew Calendar] In the flow of the narrative, the returnees left Babylon in 539, and Ezra 3:1 speaks

Outline of Ezra 3

Resumption of Worship in Jerusalem, 3:1-13
  Keeping the Feast of Tabernacles, 3:1-6a
  Founding the New Temple, 3:6b-13

Months in the Hebrew Calendar

Prior to the exile, the Jewish Bible generally just numbered months, beginning in the spring. Four months, however, retain Canaanite names: the month of Abib is the first month and is mentioned only in Exod 13:4; 23:15; and 34:18; the month of Zib is the second; the month of Ethnaim is the seventh; and the month of Bul is the eighth. During the exile, Yehudites adopted the Babylonian calendar. These months are Nisan, Iyyar, Sivan, Tammuz, Ab, Elul, Tishri, Marheshvan, Kislev, Tebeth, Shebat, and Adar. The first and seventh months were fixed by the equinoxes, but the lengths of the months were based on the phases of the moon. Months were thirty days in length, and extra days were added to keep the calendar in sync with the seasons. Obviously, adjustments had to be made from time to time with extra days inserted. The following table lists all three sets of names and their equivalents in modern western calendars.

Numerical	Canaanite	Babylonian	Modern Equivalents
First	Abib	Nisan	March/April
Second	Zib	Iyyar	April/May
Third		Sivan	May/June
Fourth		Tammuz	June/July
Fifth		Ab	July/August
Sixth		Elul	August/September
Seventh	Ethnanmim	Tishri	September/October
Eighth	Bul	Marheshvan	October/November
Ninth		Chislev	November/December
Tenth		Tebeth	December/January
Eleventh		Shebat	January/February
Twelfth		Adar	February/March

See D. F. Morgan, "Calendar," in vol. 1 of *ISBE*, 575–76.

Jerusalem in Ruins

Carl August Zscheckel (1824–1870). The Destruction of Jerusalem under Nebuchadnezzar in 586 BCE. Woodcut. (Credit: Art Resource, NY)

The Babylonians attacked Jerusalem twice, first in 598 (2 Kgs 24:13-16) and then again in 587, when they savagely destroyed it (see 2 Kgs 24:18-21 // 2 Chr 36:15-21), an act of political will and cruelty inflicted on the capital of a stubborn but weak and rebellious vassal. Not until 520–515 did the returnees rebuild the temple.

of "when the seventh month came," usually and plausibly taken to be in the year 538. The city, including the temple, lay in ruins from the Babylonian destruction. The author emphasized two persons mentioned in Ezra 3:2, Zerubbabel, the son of Shealtiel, and Joshua, the son of Jozadak, who together spearheaded the work of rebuilding the altar. Their work in urging the actual rebuilding of the temple itself, however, can be confidently ascribed not to 538 but to 520 BCE, based on the superscriptions in Haggai 1:1, 1:15b–2:1, 2:10 and Zechariah 1:1, 7. The first act of the returnees "in the seventh month" of 538, however, was very important in that the returnees restored the altar on its foundation (or platform) and observed the autumnal feast of booths or tabernacles (Ezra 3:3-6). Their second act was to initiate work on the temple itself the next year (i.e., 537 BCE) after their arrival in Jerusalem (Ezra 3:8-9). At the time that work began, the people held a ceremony celebrating their new beginning, but it met with a mixed reception (Ezra 3:10-13). Let the reader of this commentary note: Ezra portrays the temple as the house of God rebuilt by the exiles. As will be seen eventually, Nehemiah rebuilds the wall of Jerusalem to define the space within the wall as sacred space. Others in Jerusalem may well have had a broader perspective, but the redactor of Ezra-Nehemiah builds a careful case that both were built by returnees for themselves, the true people of God.

In his reconstruction of the events, the author of Ezra 3:1-13 relied heavily on Hebrew Bible intertexts, which he supplemented with descriptions of practices of his own day.[1] The only text he actually quoted was Psalm 118:1, the first verse of a song of thanksgiving, but he knew and alluded to laws, prophetic texts, and other narratives. Those texts included Haggai 1:15b–2:2 and also Numbers 29:12-38 (about observing the festival of booths mentioned in Ezra 3:4), Haggai 1:12–2:8 and 2:20-23, as well as Zechariah 3–4 concerning Zerubbabel and Joshua (see Ezra 3:8.). His use of information about the construction of Solomon's temple emphasized the continuity between the two temples and, thus, the legitimacy of the second. The tone of this narrative overall was positive, ignoring until the end of the chapter the dissent the work provoked within the community of Yehud (Ezra 3:12-13).

Three matters are of such importance in the narrative that they need to be addressed up front. The first is the relationship between Sheshbazzar and Zerubbabel. (See [Zerubbabel in Haggai and Zechariah].) According to the author/redactor, Sheshbazzar carried the temple vessels from Babylon to Jerusalem in the company of a group of returnees (Ezra 1:11b). The author/redactor also reported that Zerubbabel accompanied the repatriates to Jerusalem (Ezra 2:2-67). The reader is expected to think that the people assembled in Ezra 3:1 were the same as those said to have returned in Ezra 2, but that list is quite late—as noted in comments on Ezra 2—since it mentions Nehemiah and other fifth-century persons at the beginning. (It also reports vastly more returnees than were likely to have come to Yehud at one time; see the comments on Ezra 2.) Haggai 1:1, 2:1-2 and Zechariah 4:1-4, moreover, say that Zerubbabel did his work during the reign of Darius I, not that of Cyrus. How should readers understand the relationship between Sheshbazzar and Zerubbbael?

One might say, of course, that Sheshbazzar and Zerubbabel were two names for the same person. Both names were Mesopotamian in origin, however, so neither could be called his Hebrew name and the other a Babylonian name as in the case of Daniel/Belteshazzar (Dan 1:7). Nor did the Hebrew Bible anywhere say the two were the same. If the two were different men, as seems to have been the case, the date of Zerubbabel's return is unknown, except that it had to be prior to the work of Haggai and Zechariah in 520, who mention him. Ezra 2:2 to be sure places him among those who returned to Jerusalem in 539, but that list is chronologically difficult. (See the comments on it in connection with Ezra 2.) His Babylonian name and his descent from the exiled king Jehoiachin[2] point to his Babylonian connections, and his genealogy makes clear his descent from David. His work on the temple probably stemmed from his royal heritage. Still, he is portrayed as being among the first returnees, and there is no real reason to challenge

Tracing Zerubbabel's Lineage

Hag 1:1, 12, 14; 2:2, 23; Ezra 3:2, 8; 5:2; and Neh 12:1 call Zerubbabel "the son of Shealtiel," but 1 Chr 3:19 traces his genealogy back to Jehoiachin through Pedaiah. (Contrast the genealogy through Shealtiel to Jehoiachin in Matt 1:12. Luke 3:27, however, says Neri was the father of Shealtiel.) R. W. Klein speculates that Shealtiel died childless and Pedaiah fathered Zerubbabel for Shealtiel in a Levirate marriage. Both Peduah and Shealtiel, however, appear to have been exiles in Babylon. All that our sources say is that Zerubbabel, a Babylonian-born Judean, was a descendant of David. Since Haggai was a contemporary, his tracing of Zerubbabel's lineage is probably to be preferred.

R. K. Klein, "1 Chronicles," *The Harper-Collins Study Bible* (New York: HarperCollins, 1993) 611.

that view regardless of the problems with the list in Ezra 2. [Tracing Zerubbabel's Lineage]

Still there is a problem in that the Hebrew Bible appears to credit two different parties with responsibility for the work on the second temple: on the one hand the man Sheshbazzar in 538 (Ezra 5:16), who also is credited with bringing temple vessels back to Jerusalem from Babylon (Ezra 1:8-11), and on the other hand Zerubbabel and Jeshua (mentioned in Ezra 2:1) in 537 (Ezra 3:8). Haggai 2:1-9 and Zechariah 4:9 credit the last two with that work too, but in the second year of King Darius, i.e., 520. How does one account for these differences? One suggestion is the Persian document named Sheshbazzar, but Zerubbabel actually directed the work.[3] Ezra 3:8 seems to concur that Zerubbabel (along with the priest Jeshua) directed the work. Yet Ezra 5:16, in retrospect, explicitly credits Sheshbazzar with laying the foundation himself. How, then, might a reader understand what was going on in the texts?

The place to begin its resolution is with Ezra 1:8-11. There the person Cyrus made responsible for the work on the temple is Sheshbazzar, and Ezra 5:16 simply completes what the reader would have expected after Ezra 1:8-11, namely that Sheshbazzar began to rebuild the temple as soon as possible after he arrived in Jerusalem. Specifically, he "laid its foundation" or prepared the ground. Since, however, the redactor of Ezra also had in hand some version of Haggai/Zechariah 1–8, he knew that the temple was still unfinished in the second year of Darius, i.e., 520. What had happened? He seems to have reasoned that there must have been a work stoppage soon after Sheshbazzar began the project, one caused, he surmised, by dissension within tiny Yehud. (Actually, Hag 1:2-15a suggests that they had been busy building their houses, farming, and getting on with the business of resuming life in Yehud, although it also points to tension if not dissension.) Thus, the people set up the altar of the temple in the seventh month of 538, but only began to reconstruct the temple itself. The author also knew from Haggai 1:12–2:9 that in 520 Zerubbabel had (re)started the building project, which had languished under the hardships of early post-exilic Yehud. He had a framework, therefore, for Ezra 3–6, into which he could add his explanations for the delay.

His reconstruction was plausible. He first reported the work of rebuilding the altar "in the seventh month" (i.e., of the first year in Jerusalem or 538) and then the work of laying the temple's foundation in 537. Next he noted resistance to it in Ezra 4:1-4. Then he reviewed other difficulties (Ezra 4:5-23), leading up to complaints that read as if they belong during the time of Nehemiah—thereby linking the building of the temple and the building of the wall. (In the study of the book of Nehemiah, this commentary will argue that the wall is conceived as setting off Jerusalem as "holy" space [see Neh 11:1, 18], not as a defensive wall.) Then, in Ezra 4:24 the author returned to events of 537, simply noting that the work stopped. In Ezra 5:1 he jumped ahead to the work done during the time of Haggai and Zechariah in 520. In Ezra 6:1-12 he updated the decree of Cyrus with one of Darius, reauthorizing the temple in the process, and finally in Ezra 6:13-18 he described the rebuilding of the temple itself. In short, although Ezra 3–6 does not constitute a straightforward, chronological account, it does provide a coherent understanding of what was going on, and it ties those events to Nehemiah's work on the "holy" or sacred space/city.

Keeping the Feast of Tabernacles, 3:1-6a

The first section of Ezra 3 alludes to a number of Pentateuchal texts concerning the altar and sacrifices. The transition verses draw on the Chronicler's traditions about the building of the first temple. The mention of importing cedar from Lebanon (Ezra 3:7, see 1 Chr 22:4) appears to conflict with the instructions of the prophet Haggai that the people of "Judah" were to "go up to the hills and bring wood to build the house" (Hag 1:8). The book of Haggai makes it clear that the new temple was much plainer than the former, so much so that old people who had seen Solomon's temple were dismayed at its replacement (Hag 2:3). The author of Ezra-Nehemiah records that displeasure as well (Ezra 3:12) but mutes it. Perhaps by his time the second temple was more splendid than when it was built.

The opening phrase reads, "When the seventh month came." The date was vague, probably intentionally so. Ezra 1 had said that Cyrus issued his edict in his first year. No further date appeared in Ezra 2, so a reader might assume that the exiles listed there returned Cyrus's first year, although the text did not say that, and the comments on Ezra 2 showed the difficulties associated with reconstructing the history behind the chapter. After pausing to list the repatriates, the author resumed his narrative in Ezra 3. He knew (presumably from Hag 1:7-15a) that the people rebuilt the temple under the direction of Zerubbabel and Jeshua, whom, therefore, the author placed at the head of his list in Ezra 2:2. They report rebuilding efforts beginning in the second year of Darius (i.e., 520), on the twenty-fourth day of the sixth month (see Hag 1:15a). The author of Ezra, however, began by narrating the rebuilding of the altar, not the temple. In his version of the events, the returnees settled in their towns, then gathered "in Jerusalem" in the "seventh month" (presumably in the year 538) to restore the altar and make their sacrifices.

Excavated Altar at Dan

While the altar at Dan was anathema to authors of the Bible, its construction was similar to the one in Jerusalem. That altar has been excavated by archaeologists and gives moderns a good idea of what the altar in Jerusalem would have looked like.

Image courtesy of www.HolyLandPhotos.org.

[Excavated Altar at Dan] That restoration, however, was not attributed to Sheshbazzar, who is not mentioned again until Ezra 5:14, 16, but to Jeshua and to Zerubbabel. Each man will be discussed briefly.

Although identified only as a priest in this chapter, Jeshua was the high priest in Jerusalem when the temple was rebuilt (see Hag 1:1, 14; 2:2; Zech 3:1). In fact, he came from a line of high priests. Jeshua's grandfather Seraiah was the high priest under Zedekiah (r. 597–586), whom one of Nebuchadnezzar's officers took to Nebuchadnezzar's camp when the city fell, and Nebuchadnezzar had him executed (2 Kgs 25:18-21). Next, Jeshua's father Jozadek (also called Jehozadek) became chief priest, and he too was taken into exile (1 Chr 6:15). Jeshua either was taken there too or was born in or near Babylon. He returned to Jerusalem and inherited his father's office.

T. C. Eskenazi emphasizes the "democratization" of Ezra-Nehemiah, in that the author thought in terms of the work of the people, not just the "great men" associated with it.[4] An example of this "democratization" appeared in this narrative: the author added specifically that Jeshua's fellow priests also participated. Basil the Great (c. 333–379) also read this spreading of sponsorship from kings to priests as a democratic politic: "But, when the followers of Salathiel and Zerubbabel returned, they led the people more democratically, transferring the rule henceforth to the priesthood because of the intermingling of the priestly and royal tribes."[5] Even so, that "democratization" had its limits. The book of Ezra insists that only returning exiles did the work, not people who had remained behind (Ezra 3:12-13; see Hag 2:2-9). It also notes that Levites served as overseers (Ezra 3:8-9), which is quite possible and maybe even likely. Who would have been more able to supervise work on the temple?

Zerubbabel, the son of Shealtiel, had been an exile, presumably born in Babylon, as his name suggests. (It meant something like "shoot of Babylon" or "seed of Babylon.") It was not unusual for Judeans born outside Israel to have foreign names, and the book of Daniel points to the practice of giving Israelite captives a Babylonian name. Specifically, Daniel was given the name Belteshazzar and his friends the new names Shadrach, Meshach, and Abednego. Zerubbabel was the grandson of King Jehoiachin, who was taken to Babylon in the First Deportation in 597.

Jehoiachin's uncle, Zedekiah, followed him on the throne, but his reign ended with his defiance of the Babylonians. After their capture of Jerusalem, they blinded Zedekiah before making him an exile. The Hebrew Bible never mentions his death. The exilic community, at least the large group carried to Babylon in 597, probably considered Jehoiachin the real king of Judah anyway. [The Last Five Kings of Judah] Jehoiachin's elevation in exile by Evil-Merodach of Babylon in 562 was a high point in their dreary time in Babylon (2 Kgs 25:27-28). That elevation in status probably meant to the exiles that if they were ever allowed to return to Palestine, Jehoiachin could go with them.[6] He did not, apparently, live that long.

The Last Five Kings of Judah

The last five kings of Judah were Josiah (r. 640–609), Jehoahaz (r. 609), Jehoiakim (r. 609–597), Jehoiachin (r. 597), and Zedekiah (r. 597–586). In 609, Pharaoh Neco of Egypt decided to come to the aid of the Assyrians, who were at war against their rebellious Mesopotamian subjects, the Babylonians. Josiah attempted to block the Egyptian army, and let the Mesopotamian powers keep fighting. Neco killed Josiah at Megiddo (which lay strategically along the route to Mesopotamia), and then confined Jehoahaz his successor at Riblah, in Syria north of Israel and Damascus. Next, he installed Jehoiakim as king of Judah, and took Jehoahaz to Egypt with him. Jehoiakim switched his allegiance to the powerful new Babylonian king Nebuchadnezzar (r. 605–562) but revolted after three years. Nebuchadnezzar besieged the city, and Jehoiakim died during the siege. He was succeeded by his son Jehoiachin who ruled only three months, at which time he surrendered to Nebuchadnezzar. The Babylonian king replaced him with his uncle, Zedekiah, a younger brother of Jehoiakim. Judah revolted again, and Nebuchadnezzar destroyed the city and its temple, and he put an end to the Judean monarchy, the descendants of David.

The following diagram shows those five kings by generation and by sequence.

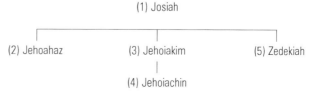

(1) Josiah
(2) Jehoahaz   (3) Jehoiakim   (5) Zedekiah
(4) Jehoiachin

S. Japhet points out that the author of Ezra-Nehemiah avoided mentioning Jehoiachin, upon whom Zerubbabel's right to the throne depended. She suggests that his omission was due to the author's acceptance of the Persian Empire. That omission, in turn, she saw as evidence that the author had little interest in the Davidic monarchy.[7] Japhet's argument is an argument from silence, although she may well be correct.

One should note that Ezra 3:2 mentions Jeshua the priest first, reversing the sequence of names from that in Haggai 1:1, 12, 14; 2:2, 4, as well as the sequence in Ezra 2:2; 4:3; and 5:2 (an Aramaic-language document), and in Nehemiah 7:7; 12:1. The reversal is perhaps due to the fact that in Ezra 3:2 alone the subject was the building of the altar, the place where priests functioned. Haggai 1:1 labeled Zerubbabel a *paḥat*), which official Babylonian records designated a "governor." The Hebrew Bible, however, used the term much more broadly, so its use by Haggai does not prove that Zerubbabel held official status as a governor, although that is possible. Regardless, he seems to have been a direct descendant of a Davidic ruler, and perhaps for that reason was expected by the people to participate in the rebuilding of the temple. Zechariah trumpeted Zerubbabel's founding the temple and predicted his completing it (Zech 4:9). The author/redactor of Ezra, however, mentioned the role of the people in the rebuilding project, including Zerubbabel's "brothers" or "kinsmen" in the project.

The Prophet Zechariah

The prophet Zechariah. Facade of Certosa, detail. Certosa di Pavia, Pavia, Italy. (Credit: Scala/Art Resource, NY)

That author/redactor further emphasized that the altar was built in conformity with the "Law of Moses," i.e., the Torah. The phrase "Moses the man of God" appeared elsewhere in the Hebrew Bible five times: Deuteronomy 33:1, Joshua 14:6, Psalm 90:1, 1 Chronicles 23:14, and 2 Chronicles 30:16. The phrase "as was written in the law" points to Deuteronomy 33:1 among these texts. Both Deuteronomy 27:6 and Exodus 20:25 required the use of unhewn stones in an altar (see also the allusion in 1 Macc 4:47). Thus, the author of Zechariah 3 signaled the nature of the stones to his readers, who perhaps were expected to understand their nature from the allusion. He also claimed thereby strict adherence to the law in that building project.

An interesting question in the study of Ezra-Nehemiah is the contents of the law read by Ezra (see Neh 8 and 9), and that issue will be discussed in the comments on Nehemiah. For the author of Ezra 3, however, the issue was settled. He thought in terms of the legal corpus from Exodus through Deuteronomy, as his frequent allusions show. What about Genesis, however? The author mentions only Abraham among the patriarchs, and then in a prayer that draws heavily on other Scriptures. (See also Neh 9:7.) Even so, the references to bringing Abram from Ur of the Chaldeans and to the covenant with Abraham point unmistakably to the author's familiarity with Genesis. Hence, it is fair to say that he may have included Genesis in that "law" as well. At least he trusted those traditions. Moreover, that late-fourth century author assumed that his readers were familiar with the law's provisions and stressed the compliance of the returning people of God with the law of God given through Moses.

The author says that the returnees built the altar on its fixed or established place (*mĕkônōtāyw*). Doing so assured maximum continuity with the past in worship and the legitimacy of the altar. Next, the author introduced a new motivation for rebuilding the altar: fear of their neighbors. J. Blenkinsopp compares their action with actions at the building of previous altars. David had built an altar at the threshing floor of a Jebusite named Ornan (the Chronicler's spelling of the name Araunah used in 2 Sam 24:16-24) to preclude danger from YHWH. Similarly the returnees avoided disaster from the surrounding peoples and YHWH by building an altar even before the temple was rebuilt (1 Chr 21:28–22:1). Blenkinsopp also says that accounts of repairs under Joash (2 Chr 24:14) and Hezekiah (2 Chr 29:27-29), both of which described repairing the altar, informed the author's thinking about rebuilding the altar in 538.[8]

The identity of the ominous neighbors is quite vague: "the peoples of the land." In its singular form "people of the land" (*ʿam haʾāreṣ*), this phrase at times had differing meanings. In pre-exilic times it often referred to land-owning, full citizens of the upper class (Gen 23:7; 2 Kgs 11:14, 18-20; 21:24; 23:30, 35; 25:19). With the fall of Jerusalem, the term was used to refer to those people who, along with the king and the priests, Jeremiah blamed as responsible for the plight of the nation (Jer 1:18; 34:19; 37:2; 44:21; see also Ezek 7:27; 12:19; 22:29). During the exile, the term still denoted that same class, but as full members of the congregation in exile (Ezek 45:22; 46:3, 9). In the post-exilic period, the term could be used in its old sense of Israelite landowners (Hag 2:2; Zech 7:5). In Ezra-Nehemiah, however, its plural form included all the other inhabitants of Yehud and the surrounding area except the deported and returned people of God, who were called "the exile" (*hagōlâ*).[9]

The people sacrificed "burnt offerings in the morning and in the evening." Late passages in the Pentateuch commanded twice daily animal offerings (Exod 29:38-42; Num 28:3-8). In the pre-exilic period, the evening offering was cereal (2 Kgs 16:15; see also Ezek 46:13-15, which directed that the cereal offering be given in the morning with the meat offering). The author clearly knew post-exilic practice and legislation supporting it.

The mention of daily offerings and of the seventh month led directly to a discussion of the autumnal feast, "Tabernacles." It was one of the three major festivals of ancient Israel, the other two being the Feast of Unleavened Bread (associated with Passover) and the Feast of Weeks (which fell seven weeks later at the end of the grain harvest and was associated with the giving of the Law on Mount Sinai). The Feast of Tabernacles came in October, after the harvest of summer crops. It was a pilgrimage festival, which meant that people traveled to a sanctuary to observe it. Its name derived from the practice of making little huts of interlaced leaves for privacy during the week of celebration. It also became associated with the wandering in the wilderness after the exodus (Lev 23:43). The nature of the festival had changed over time, and the author insisted that it was celebrated during the career of Ezra as it had not been since the days of Joshua, the hero of the conquest of Canaan (see also Neh 8:13-18.)

Even so, the author presumed that the reader would know the laws pertaining to the sacrifices to which he referred with his phrase "as it is written." The laws for sacrifice at the festival appear three places in the Pentateuch: Leviticus 23:34-36, 39-43; Numbers 29:12-39; and Deuteronomy 16:13-15. Of the three, the author seems to have had in mind the laws in Numbers, which specified how many of which kinds of animals were to be sacrificed day by day. He alluded to that feature of the legislation with his sentence, "They made offerings each day, according to its number." He thought that the people would have celebrated the festival in the seventh month as soon as they had repaired the altar, and he narrated the events based on the legislation he knew and assumed they followed.

Once the altar had been rebuilt, the people offered other sacrifices as well. They included the daily burnt offerings (morning and evening according to Ezra 3:3), offerings in observance of "new moons" (see also Num 28:9-15), and "freewill offerings" (sacrifices offered simply as an expression of love or dedication to God). Directions for freewill offerings could be lumped together with directions for votive offerings (sacrifices offered in fulfillment of a vow) in Pentateuchal legislation (see Lev 22:17-25; Deut 12:17). These offerings began "on the first day of the seventh month." This phrase not only repeated information from Ezra 3:3 but also formed an *inclusio* with v. 1, which began with the words, "when the seventh month drew near."

Work on the Temple Begun, 3:6b-13

Ezra 3:6b-13 discusses the first phase of the rebuilding of the temple. That work began with the laying of the foundation of the temple. The author envisioned a crowd of people in attendance, including Zerubbabel, Jeshua, Levites, and the remaining repatriates. In distinction from Zechariah 4:9, which said that Zerubbabel "founded" the temple (perhaps a celebratory act not unlike "laying the cornerstone" in modern America), the author of Ezra 3:6b seems to mean that the foundation itself had not been laid. The next verse says that Zerubbabel, Jeshua, the priests, the Levites, and the other returnees appointed the Levites to have "oversight of the work." Then the author lists Jeshua, Kadmiel (see Ezra 2:40 // Neh 7:43 and other narratives from the time of Nehemiah), and several sons of Henadad, including Binnui (a contemporary of Ezra and Nehemiah credited among other things with helping to repair the wall of Jerusalem), Hodaviah (see Ezra 2:40), and other sons. Since Zerubbabel is not mentioned after v. 8, it is not too much to say that the author deliberately downplayed whatever role he might have had in the restoration of the temple, as did the author of Zechariah 6:11b-13. [Deemphasizing Zerubbabel in Zechariah] In fact, what happened to him is a mystery.

Ezra 3:6b-7 forms the transition to the narrative of the laying of the foundation of the temple, which had not yet occurred. [The Translation of *yussād* (laid) in Ezra 3:6b] The returnees perhaps did not have the skill to do masonry. In any case, as reported of David and Solomon before them (1 Kgs 5:1-18; 2 Chr 2:1–5:2), they are said to have hired inhabitants of Tyre and Sidon to do the actual work.

Deemphasizing Zerubbabel in Zechariah

The book of Zechariah, during the course of its growth, seems to have deemphasized Zerubbabel as did Ezra. Zerubbabel was the hero of Zech 4, the one who would be a great mountain (i.e., king) beside Joshua, the high priest. His role in founding (or else laying the foundation of) the temple is made explicit by what appears to be an explanatory insertion (Zech 4:6b-10b). Zech 6:11b-13 also constitutes an insertion into an exhortation for Zechariah to make crowns as a memorial to be placed in the new temple (Zech 6:9-11a + 14-15). The verses almost surely originally named Zerubbabel as the one to receive the crown(s) and called him the Branch (a Messianic title) and the one who would build the temple (see Zech 4:9), with a priest (presumably Jeshua) at his side. As the text now stands, however, the name Zerubbabel does not appear in vv. 11b-13, although that of Jeshua does instead in 6:11. Accordingly, W. H. Rose mounts a book-long argument that the term/name Zemah (Branch) refers not to Zerubbabel but to a different, future royal figure (19–21). Part of Rose's argument is that the unnamed priest beside the throne in 6:13 is a future, shadowy, unnamed person, not the priest Joshua just named in Zech 6:11 (59–68). Even the name Joshua is surprising, however, since crowns are typically for kings. Thus, despite Rose's argument, it seems likely that the verse originally identified the Branch as Zerubbabel, but was later changed to name Joshua as the Branch in v. 11.

W. H. Rose, *Zemah and Zerubbabel: Messianic Expectations in the Early Post-exilic Period* (JSOTSup 304; Sheffield: Sheffield Academic Press, 2000).

The Translation of *yussād* (laid) in Ezra 3:6b

AΩ The translation of the sentence "the foundation of the temple of Y<small>HWH</small> had not been laid yet" needs explanation. At issue is the verb *yussād*, which is a pual (passive, intensive) verb. It has a variety of meanings, including "to be founded" or "to cause the laying of the foundation of." The first meaning denotes sponsorship or leadership, sometimes associated with a ceremony. The second meaning denotes the actual work of laying a foundation. In Zech 4:8 the first meaning was intended, but in Ezra 3:6 the second, the physical work of laying a foundation, was intended, as Ezra 3:10 makes clear. See the NRSV: "But the foundation of the temple of the L<small>ORD</small> was not yet laid."

Ezra 3:7 reported in general terms that the people paid the workers for their time and products. The list of workers and materials depended, however, on three verses in Chronicles, two of which named David's provisions for the first temple (1 Chr 22:2b, 4) and one that reported Solomon's promise of payment to King Huram of Tyre for timber and supplies (2 Chr 2:10; see also 2:15). Ezra's list stands in conflict with the book of Haggai, which reported that the prophet sent people into the nearby hills to secure wood for the temple (Hag 1:8), but in agreement with the expectations of Third Isaiah about its rebuilding:

> The glory of Lebanon shall come to you,
>> the cypress, the plane and the pine together,
> to beautify the place of my sanctuary;
>> and I will glorify the place for my feet. (NRSV, Isa 60:13)

The returnees began the rebuilding effort "In the second year . . . in the second month" (Ezra 3:8). A translation of this verse runs, "In the second year after they arrived at the house of God in Jerusalem, in the second month, Zerubbabel the son of Shealtiel, Jeshua the son of Jozadak, the rest of their brothers the priests and the Levites, and all the returnees from the captivity began [or made a beginning], and they appointed Levites twenty years old and upwards to superintend over the building of the house of Y<small>HWH</small>."

Eskenazi thought that the phrase "after their arrival at the house of God" (Ezra 3:8a) proved that the designation "house of God" referred to the whole city of Jerusalem on the grounds that the phrase indicated the returnees arrived at the house of God before the temple was founded.[10] The previous verses, however, had just discussed rebuilding the altar and not Jerusalem as a whole, so it is much more likely that the verse simply meant the returnees arrived at the site or ruins of the temple. Still, her inclination is correct. Nehemiah 11:1, 18 calls

Cedar Trees in Lebanon

Cedar of Lebanon on Mount Lebanon in the Bchareé region. (Credit: Mark Connally, HolyLandPhotos.org)

Though the mountains of Lebanon were once covered with magnificent cedar trees, very few are left today.

Jerusalem "holy" and conceives all of it as sacred space.

Williamson argues that the author was aware of a gap in time between Ezra 1 and 2.[11] That is probably so, but he obscures that gap in his narrative. The temple was not completed until the reign of Darius (see Ezra 6:13-15), but the redactor of Ezra 3 nevertheless had Zerubbabel, Jeshua, and their cohorts resume rebuilding the temple itself in the "second year," i.e., the second year after their return or 537. There was, though, no mention of Sheshbazzar in Ezra 3. He is mentioned again only in Ezra 5:14, 16, the latter of which verses ascribes the laying of the foundation to him. In Ezra 3:8 the author/redactor named Zerubbabel, Jeshua, and others as workers on the temple in the second year of reconstruction or 537, as he had in Ezra 2.

The narrative names Jeshua, his sons, and his relatives, as well as Kadmiel and his sons as Levites who had returned with Zerubbabel and the high priest Jeshua (see Ezra 2:40; Neh 7:43). The other names in Ezra 3:9 are a little challenging, but the NRSV and other translations draw upon Ezra 2:40 and Nehemiah 7:43 to read the names "Binnui" and "Hodavah."[12] [The Text and Translation of Ezra 3:9] They and the sons of Henadad took charge of the workers. The name "Henadad" did not appear in Ezra 2 or its parallel version in Nehemiah 7, but it did appear in connection with accounts of repairs (Neh 3:18, 24) and in a list of people who signed a

The Text and Translation of Ezra 3:9

AΩ The Hebrew text of Ezra 3:9 reads, "And joining them were Jeshua and his sons and his brothers; Kadmiel and *his sons*, (and) the sons of Judah as one(s) to oversee the one(s) doing the work on the house of God, [i.e.,] the sons of Henadad and their sons plus the Levites." Henadad is also mentioned in Neh 3:18, 24, and 10:9, where he is said to be the father of Binnui. Hence, the NRSV reads the italicized words (phrase in English) "his sons" (*bniu*) as *bnui*, i.e., the name "Binnui." The emendation is slight, involving only the reversal of two letters, and it brings the names in Ezra 3:9 in line with the three verses in Nehemiah.

covenant (Neh 10:9). Bowman suggests, therefore, that it was introduced secondarily from Nehemiah.[13] If so, the connection may have been simply the mention of workers. One should note, however, that the building project in Nehemiah concerned the city wall, not the temple. This connection with Nehemiah, which perhaps has the better text, shows again the dependence of the early chapters of Ezra on traditions from the time of Nehemiah or later.

The narrator of the account recognized the work of those other than the "great men" by means of the clause "the builders laid the foundation."[14] The prophet Zechariah, by contrast, emphasized the role of Zerubbabel (Zech 4:9). The author of Ezra had mentioned Zerubbabel earlier in the chapter (Ezra 3:2), but does not mention him here where "David the King" was mentioned in what is probably a phrase borrowed from the Psalter. In other words, the author acknowledged the great king of Jerusalem only as the one who wrote the instructions for instrumentalists accompanying the psalm sung in the next verse!

Exactly what work the builders did and how they performed it is not made clear, perhaps because the author did not know. The prophet Haggai only ordered the people to secure timber (Hag 1:8), suggesting that in 537/520 both the foundation and building stones remained on site from the first temple or else that Sheshbazzar had already made some progress on rebuilding the temple, so that the workers could continue with woodwork. Ezra 3:10, however, omits any reference to Zerubbabel, whom Zechariah celebrated for his role in the ceremonial founding of the temple (Zech 4:9). It says the priests played the trumpets, which were not the familiar ram's horns, but "long, straight, slender metal tube[s], with flaring end [s]."[15] The Levites played the cymbals, which were typically associated with the trumpets.[16]

One more problem appears in the phrase "the Levites, the sons of Asaph." The list of repatriates in Ezra 2 and Nehemiah 7 apparently distinguished the "sons of Asaph" (who were singers and musicians [see 1 Chr 16:7; 25:1, 2; 2 Chr 20:14; 29:13]) from the Levites, whereas the author of Ezra 3:10 considered them a branch of the Levites.[17] In doing so, the author betrayed a gap between his own time and that of the list of repatriates, a gap during which the sons of Asaph became recognized as Levites.

This celebration of worship is said to have been conducted "according to the directions of King David of Israel," possibly a reference to 1 Chronicles 16:37-42. The priests sang responsively, employing Psalm 118:1, which underwent a slight change when it came over into this narrative. The Psalter used the *hiphil* (or causative) second masculine plural imperative verb imploring the people to "give thanks" at the beginning of the hymn. The author of Ezra, by contrast, prefaced the quotation with the note that the priests "responded with praising," and he converted the imperative into an infinitive construct, resulting in a phrase that can be translated as follows: "giving thanks to YHWH, for he is good." [Two Types of Infinitive in Hebrew] He then quoted the rest of Psalm 118:1: "for his steadfast love endures perpetually," adding the phrase "toward Israel" at the end of the verse. [The Meaning of the Word *lĕʿôlām*] The Chronicler reported that the Levitical singers present when Solomon had the ark brought to the temple sang the same song (2 Chr 5:13), and the people in attendance at the dedication of Solomon's temple offered the verse as a prayer (2 Chr 7:3). The author of Ezra underscored the continuity between the two temples with his note that the Levites sang the same song when the foundation of the house was laid.

Two Types of Infinitive in Hebrew

AΩ In Hebrew there are two types of infinitives, the infinitive absolute that functions much like infinitives in English, and the infinitive construct that functions more like a participle. The infinitive used here was the second type.

The Meaning of the Word *lĕʿôlām*

AΩ The Hebrew word *lĕʿôlām* does not really mean "forever," as it is often translated, but something like "perpetually." BDB translates it "long duration, antiquity, futurity." Those meanings show that the time span could be in the past or future. So the word *ʿôlām* with the prefixed preposition *lĕ* should be translated as has been suggested here. The translation "forever" carries modern connotations (e.g., endless, eternal) foreign to the Hebrew word and worldview.

The song as sung in Ezra 3 also specified the recipient of God's mercy: Israel. To be sure, the people of Israel were called on to sing antiphonally with the priests in Psalm 118:1, but the author of Ezra made it explicit that God extended the divine mercy to Israel. That name probably had in view the repatriates only in Ezra 3. The word for mercy (*ḥesed*) also meant faithfulness, obligations to one's community, and acts flowing from corporate solidarity. Moreover, that mercy was ongoing. The exile had not ended it. God again was acting mercifully toward Israel because God had entered into a covenant with the people. Lest readers miss the point, the author reminded them once again of God's role in all that was happening.

According to v. 11b, "all the people responded with a great shout when they praised the LORD" (NRSV). The phrase about the sound of human shouting constituted a literary device used in various places in the Old Testament: Genesis 45:1-2; 1 Samuel 4:4-6a, 4:13-14a; 1 Kings 1:40; 2 Kings 11:12 // 2 Chronicles 23:11-12; 2 Chronicles 23:11-13; and here in Ezra 3:12. The device transitions a reader from one place or group to another. Here the sentence anticipates not only the action that follows, where sounds of joy intermix with sounds of grieving, but also the note in Ezra 4:1 that "the adversaries of Judah and Benjamin heard" that the returnees were building a temple.[18]

Despite the author's sweeping generalization, however, not everyone in attendance was happy with the planned new edifice, and the author was honest enough to admit the problem. The first temple had been splendid; this one apparently seemed inadequate in comparison. Many "who had seen the first house on its foundations" wept at the sight of the second. Possibly, those weeping had remained in Judah during the exile, since it is unlikely although not impossible that people old enough to remember the first temple (which was destroyed in 586) would have been strong enough to make the return trip to Yehud some forty-seven years later (in 539). Regardless, the author reports in v. 12 that the cries of the unhappy people were so loud that one could scarcely hear the singing of God's praises over their wailing. Was that wailing at least partly caused by their exclusion from membership in "Israel" by the people rebuilding the temple?

The prophet Haggai faced a similar issue about the temple in 520, when people complained that the new temple did not measure up to the splendor of Solomon's temple (Hag 2:3; see perhaps Zech 4:10). Haggai answered that the people's job was to rebuild the temple; God would make it splendid by sending treasures from the nations, with the result that "the latter splendor of this house shall be greater than the former" (Hag 2:9, NRSV). It appears as if the author of Ezra 3 drew upon that account in his discussion of the events of 538. He made further, explicit references to Haggai and Zechariah in Ezra 5:1-2 and Ezra 6:14.

In any case, the rebuilding of the temple was underway. The repatriates had rebuilt the altar in its old location and had laid the foundation for a new temple on the site of the first one. The wailing at the inadequacy of the second temple, however, was but the first negative reaction to the project. The next three chapters detail some of the difficulties the returnees had to face before they completed their restoration project.

CONNECTIONS

1. One aspect of the community of Yehud that has become obvious already is that it was badly divided. Before the exile, Jerusalem itself

had been the home of kings, priests, and perhaps other influential families, but also of some of their servants and other common citizens. The surrounding countryside had been populated largely by farmers/shepherds, a few better off than others. During the exile, various people changed social status as far as their meager fortunes and differing abilities would allow. Various sorts of non-Judean people lived there in 586, including refugees from the northern tribes who moved into Judah after the fall of Samaria in 722.

The surrounding major cultures influenced Yehud: those of Egypt, Assyria, Babylonia, and Persia. Minor cultures did as well: those of Philistia, Tyre, Lebanon, Aramea (from Damascus), Edom, and Moab, to name but the most obvious. When the Babylonian returnees arrived in Yehud, they found a "mixed" group of people living under Persian control, administered by Persian appointees. The returnees' ideas of being chosen by God and through God by the Persians to take over Jerusalem and Yehud were not shared by the peoples who had lived there themselves for decades (and their families perhaps for centuries). In short, the population of early post-exilic Yehud was divided by wealth, ethnicity, and claims of ownership.

In that respect, at least, the United States is divided by the same kinds of claims. The dominant Anglo-European culture has systematically subjugated Native Americans, eastern and some other Europeans, Africans, and Asians. Families who have emerged as dominant in American culture over the last four centuries believe that they have earned what they have by hard work, and many no doubt have worked hard. Other ethnic and racial groups may have worked hard too, but were often not in a position to command respect and pass on possessions.

What sorts of divisions affect us today? Several come to mind immediately. Throughout their society, Americans see divisions based on family wealth, education, race, the use of new technology, and in some cases criminal activity. [Population of the United States by Ethnicity/Race] United States Census Counts, for example, show a remarkable racial diversity, and they may well undercount the non-white population, which makes up 27.6 percent of the population. In a capitalist society, wealth (especially if combined with frugality and long hours of hard work) can beget wealth, maybe even vast wealth. When one

Population of the United States by Ethnicity/Race

Race/Ethnicity	Number	% of US Population
White	223,555,265	72.5
African American	38,929,319	12.6%
Asian American	14,679.254	4.8
American Indian/Alaskan	2,932,248	0.9
Hawaiian/Pacific Islander	540,013	0.2
Some Other Race	19,107,368	6.2
Two or More Races	9,009,073	2.9

European Cathedral

Notre Dame Cathedral, Paris, France. (Credit: Tristan Nitot, Wikimedia Commons CCA-SA 3.0)

does not need or choose to spend all one earns, wealth can replicate itself. Political races in twenty-first-century America often harden, even exacerbate those divisions. Will modern Americans be any more successful than Persian Period Yehudites in finding ways to get along and to share?

2. The division alluded to in Ezra 3:12-13 raises a different, although related question. Ezra 3 includes no mention of the vast amount of gold and silver mentioned in Ezra 2:69. In fact, Ezra 3 ignores the whole issue of splendor, and Haggai 2:2-9 makes it quite clear that the new temple lacked the splendor associated with the former one. Haggai's expectation was that God would fill the house with splendor to be made possible by the giving of the nations who came there.

Clearly, sincere worshipers want to build appropriate and, where possible, beautiful buildings to house worship. The great cathedrals of Europe and many beautiful churches in the United States and elsewhere give abiding testimony to the majesty of God and the gratefulness of worshipers who would finance such edifices. The same thing could be said also for the temples, mosques, and other worship centers of people of various religions. Still, worshipers would do well to remember that the finest and purest sanctuaries are the believing hearts of the people who worship.

NOTES

1. H. G. M. Williamson, *Ezra, Nehemiah* (WBC 16; Waco: Word, 1985) 44.

2. J. Blenkinsopp, *Ezra-Nehemiah* (OTL; Philadelphia: Westminster, 1988) 100. See E. W. Hamrick, "Ezra-Nehemiah," *The Broadman Bible Commentary* (Nashville: Broadman, 1970) 4.441.

3. D. J. A. Clines, exegetical note on Ezra 2:2a in *The HarperCollins Study Bible* (London: HarperCollins, 1993) 702.

4. T. C. Eskenazi, *In an Age of Prose* (SBLMS 36; Atlanta: Scholars Press, 1988) 48–53.

5. Basil the Great, "Letter 236.2," in *Fathers of the Church: A New Translation* (Washington, DC: Catholic University of America, 1947) 28:168–69.

6. See R. Albertz. *Die Exilszeit. 6. Jahrhundert v. Chr.* (Biblische Enzyklopädie 7; Stuttgart: Kohlhammer, 2001) 95.

7. S. Japhet, "Sheshbazzar and Zerubbabel—Against the Background of the Historical and Religious Tendencies of Ezra-Nehemiah," *ZAW* 94 (1982): 72–73.

8. Blenkinsopp, *Ezra-Nehemiah*, 97.

9. For a fuller discussion of this issue, see A. H. J. Gunneweg, "עם הארץ—A Semantic Revolution," *ZAW* 95 (1983): 437–40. The article is summarized here. M. McEntire ("Sacrifice in 2 Chronicles 36–Ezra 6," *Proceeding Eastern Great Lakes and Midwest Biblical Societies* 12 [1992]: 37) argues that the phrase referred to inhabitants in surrounding countries that the repatriates feared.

10. Eskenazi, *In an Age of Prose*, 54.

11. Williamson, *Ezra, Nehemiah*, 47.

12. See R. A. Bowman, "Ezra: Exegesis," *Interpreter's Bible* (ed. G. A. Buttrick; New York, Nashville: Abingdon, 1954) 3.593.

13. Ibid.

14. Eskenazi, *In an Age of Prose*, 23.

15. *Brown-Driver-Briggs*, 348.

16. L. W. Batten, *The Books of Ezra and Nehemiah* (ICC; Edinburgh: Clark, 1913) 121.

17. Following Williamson, *Ezra, Nehemiah*, 48. By contrast, Batten (*Ezra and Nehemiah*, 121) argued that the sons of Asaph should be understood as Levites here *and* in Ezra 2:40-41 as well. The sons of Asaph do follow the Levites in chapter 2, but they appear to be a separate group. The groups listed are priests, Levites, singers, gate-keepers, and temple servants.

18. Isaac Kalimi, "Human and Musical Sounds and Their Hearing Elsewhere as a Literary Device in Biblical Narratives," *VT* 60 (2010): 568.

CESSATION OF WORK
ON THE TEMPLE

Ezra 4

COMMENTARY

Cessation of the Work on the Temple

[Outline of Ezra 4] The joy felt by some or many of the people of Jerusalem over the new beginning of the work of rebuilding the temple (Ezra 3:11) soon ended. The second part of their task was yet to begin: the rebuilding of the altar. They immediately faced a complication. Unnamed "adversaries," i.e., inhabitants of the area who had not been in Babylon, volunteered to assist with the rebuilding of the temple in Jerusalem. When they were rebuffed, they reported to the Persians that the returnees were attempting to rebuild the walls of Jerusalem (an act of apparent rebellion). Persian authorities, therefore, ordered the work to stop until matters could be clarified. The work stopped until the second year of King Darius of Persia, i.e., 520. [What Do Archaeological Remains Suggest about Judean/Samaritan Relationships?]

Outline of Ezra 4

The Adversaries of Judah and the People of the Land, 4:1-5
Written Objections to the Rebuilding of Jerusalem, 4:6-10
The Letter to King Artaxerxes, 4:11-16
The Reply from King Artaxerxes, 4:17-22
Cessation of the Work on the Temple, 4:23-24

What Do Archaeological Remains Suggest about Judean/Samaritan Relationships?

While there is little reason to question the antipathy between the heroes of Ezra 4 and the leaders of Samaria, one should be careful about generalizing the friction between Yehud and Samaria. G. Knoppers examined literary and other archaeological remains pertaining to the relationship overall between inhabitants of the two areas in the early Persian Period. His conclusions were twofold: "On the one hand, the available evidence grants some credence to the claims in Ezra-Nehemiah that Samaria and its leadership were a force to be reckoned with. . . . On the other hand, the material evidence for cultural continuity between the two regions contrasts with the tensions and opposition found in Ezra-Nehemiah. Culturally speaking Samaria and Yehud shared much in common. . . . [The distinction that one properly may speak of is more] an administrative and political one and not so much a cultural one."

Gary Knoppers, "Revisiting the Samarian Question in the Persian Period," *Judah and the Judeans in the Persian Period* (ed. Oded Lipschits and Manfred Oeming; Winona Lake IN: Eisenbrauns, 2006) 279–80.

The Adversaries of Yehud, 4:1-5

The end of Ezra 3 reports that locals bewailed the planned new edifice, for reasons not specified. Likewise, Haggai 2:3 (dated in v. 1 in 520) notes that people in Yehud/Jerusalem deemed the planned temple "as nothing" in their sight, and the prophet promised that God would fill the uninspiring building with the "treasure of all nations" and with splendor (Hag 2:7) if the people would but build it. Apparently, however, the new temple when built was a small, plain building constructed by local people using locally available materials (see Hag 1:8), not a splendid edifice underwritten by and built for a king. Thus, the temple as built stood in marked contrast not only with the temple of Solomon but also with the description of it in Ezra 6:3-5, which speaks of an opulent temple ordered built by Cyrus, using the gold and silver taken from the First Temple by Nebuchadnezzar and returned by Cyrus for the Second. (See the comments on Ezra 6.)

The opening verses of Ezra 4 continue the narrative from the previous chapter about the rebuilding of the temple. The mention of the tribe of Benjamin along with Judah reflects the location of Jerusalem in the center of post-exilic Yehud, which included territory farther north than the old Judean border. (See [Map of Post-exilic Yehud] in the Introduction to Ezra-Nehemiah.) By this time as well, Idumea (old Edom) had taken over southern Judah. Blenkinsopp cautions, however, that calling the opponents "Samaritans" at that time would be anachronistic, since Samaritans did not yet comprise a separate *religious* community in the early Persian Period.[1] Besides, the opponents seem to have been residents of Yehud, not post-exilic Samaria. Indeed, v. 2 identifies them as persons relocated to Judah by the Assyrian king Esarhaddon. (In this connection, Terry Clark, a friend, colleague, and former student of mine whose doctoral dissertation dealt with aspects of the book of Ezekiel, called my attention to the vision in Ezek 8–11. It is set in 592, about six years before the fall of Jerusalem, and it constitutes a conspicuous example in that it anticipated and explained the downfall of Jerusalem as the consequence of its sinfulness. Still, it held out hope for the exiles in Babylon who would return home in God's good time. [See Ezek 11:14-21.]) To be sure, Samaria seems to have exercised administrative control over Yehud on behalf of Persia, but Ezra 4:2-3 had in view people who for over two centuries had lived in surrounding Judah.

Artifacts from the period suggest that Samaria and Yehud actually exhibited significant cultural similarities. Their differences were more administrative and political than anything else. It is also possible that some sort of temple also existed already on Mount Gerizim, which stood between the cities of Samaria and Jerusalem. That the two areas shared diplomatic and perhaps even fraternal relationships as late as the fifth century is shown by the joint letter written by Bagavahya, governor of Yehud, and Deliah, the son of Sanballat and governor of Samaria, urging Arsames, the satrap of Egypt, to rebuild the temple to YHWH that had stood there for years and had been destroyed by Egyptians.[2] [What's in a Name?]

The returnees, however, are portrayed as being in no mood to share leadership in political Yehud or the temple. Any power implied by the adversaries' reference to Esarhaddon of Assyria was quickly countered (in the book of Ezra, at any rate) by an appeal to the name of Cyrus, the Persian victor over the old Assyrian and Babylonian empires (died c. 531). Ezra 1:1 and 3:7 trace the initial permission for exiles to return from Babylon to Cyrus, though it is doubtful that nearly 50,000 exiles returned to Yehud during his reign (see the discussion of the population of Yehud on p. 35 of this volume) or the reigns of his successors.

Two titles of people considered opponents in Ezra 4:1-5 require explanation. The first is "adversaries" (v. 1). These people presented themselves to the returnees (led in these verses by Zerubbabel and the heads of the returning families) as descendants of people taken to Israel by the Assyrians under the direction of King Esarhaddon (r. 681–669) after the fall of the northern kingdom to Assyria under King Shalmaneser V (r. 727–722). (See 2 Kgs 17:6, which says that the Assyrians carried away the Israelites to Assyria.) In return, the Assyrians resettled people from other places in the cities of Samaria or northern Israel as a new ruling class.[3] Perhaps those new leaders simply added YHWH to the gods they already worshiped (2 Kgs 17:29-41), or perhaps they became devotees of God alone.

The request of the "adversaries" to assist with rebuilding the temple might seem today both appropriate and encouraging. The author/redactor of vv. 1-5, however, did not see the offer that way. He construed it as an attempt to intrude in temple matters by

What's in a Name?

Modern names are chosen for a number of reasons, often ranging from family tradition to whimsy. That was not always so. Names like Smith and Farmer seem to have arisen from an early ancestor's occupation, names like Jackson and Robertson from the name of a man's father, and other names for various reasons. My family name, for example, seems to have derived from a place in England: Reed Ditch to Redditt. Likewise, names in the Bible sometimes were compounded from an area. Zerubbabel means "seed of Babylon." Others were compounded using the name of a person's god. Sheshbazzar (mentioned in Ezra 1:8, 11; and 5:14, 16) employed the name of the god Shamash, and may have meant Shamash (the sun god) protects the son. The name Delaiah (Ezra 2:60 // Neh 6:10) is a compound using the short form of the name YHWH, the most frequently used name for God in the Hebrew Bible. Of course, his name gives no guarantee that he was a worshiper of YHWH, but more than likely he was. At any rate, those who named him more than likely were.

people who had no place in them. He reports the rejection of the offer by the leaders of the community: Zerubbabel, Jeshua, and the heads of the families of Israel. The use of the name "Israel" in connection with the returnees is probably intended at least partially to reserve for them only the right to build and to worship and to exclude the "adversaries" from the community.

Verses 4-5 speak of "the people of the land." They are probably the same people as the "adversaries" of vv. 1-3 since they are said to have made the returnees afraid to rebuild the temple. In that case, the distinction being drawn was simply that traditionally their families had not been part of the Diaspora. Verse 4 says they discouraged the "people of Judah" (another designation for the returnees), thereby frustrating their hopes to rebuild until the reign of Darius I. In addition, the author charges the "people of the land" with bribing Persian officials (v. 5), thereby delaying the work. Ferdinand Dexinger argues that those people were Samaritans, based on the allusion to 2 Kings 23:19 and the following narrative. That suggestion, however, involves naming people not otherwise mentioned or blamed in the text.[4] L. S. Fried instead identifies the "people of the land" not as the people of Judah as a whole nor as Samarians either, but as officials who administered the government of the satrap called "Beyond the River" on behalf of the Persians. They included people whose titles Fried translated as "the chancellor, the satrapal scribe, the judges, the investigators, and the rest of the colleagues, the Persian officials from Susa in Elam and from Uruk in Babylon . . . ."[5] Given their standing with Persia, it would not have been difficult for such "people of the land" to dissuade the "people of Judah and Jerusalem," i.e., the returnees. It is not clear, however, that the "people of the land" represent a new group introduced into the narrative. Rather, as said earlier, they appear to be the same people under discussion in vv. 1-3, i.e., descendants of people from surrounding small countries moved to Israel by Assyria, who wanted a part in the rebuilding of the temple.[6]

An Overview of Rebuilding the Temple in Ezra 3–6

Since the main topic of Ezra 3–6, the second major section of the book of Ezra, is the rebuilding of the temple, it will be useful to outline once more the passages dealing with that project.

3:1-7. Jeshua and Zerubbabel rebuild the altar.
3:8-13. They lay the foundation for the temple.
4:1-5. They resist participation by local adversaries.

5:1-2. Haggai and Zechariah urge the rebuilding of the temple; Jeshua and Zerubbabel lead the work.

5:3–6:12. Tattenai halts the rebuilding of the temple, but it is resumed on the basis of Cyrus's permission (see Ezra 1:2-4), researched on the order of Darius.

6:13-15. The returnees finish rebuilding the temple.

6:16-18. The returnees dedicate the temple with a massive sacrifice.

These four chapters highlight the work of Jeshua and Zerubbabel, supported by the prophets Haggai and Zechariah, whose books clearly represent one of the literary sources for the account in Ezra 3–6. In addition, the redactor had access to information about the Persian court, which he used to good advantage. Ezra 4:6-23, however, derives from yet a different source and describes events surrounding the rebuilding of the city wall, work carried out under Nehemiah, and work to be dated after 458 during the reign of Artaxerxes I, i.e., over half a century later. Verse 24 then returns to the subject of vv. 1-5.

Why, however, would the editor place these verses about rebuilding the wall of the larger city in the middle of an otherwise fairly consistent account of the rebuilding of the temple? The answer probably is that the verses are proleptic. That is, vv. 6-23 anticipate and introduce the second major building activity of the book Ezra-Nehemiah in connection with the first activity. To the editor of Ezra-Nehemiah, both projects were part of one grand action (the return of the people of God,

Artaxerxes

Gustave Doré (1832–1883). Artaxerxes I of Persia. King of the Persian Empire 465 BC–424 BC. Artaxerxes Granting Liberty to the Jews. Engraving by Ligny on an illustration from G. Dore for *The Bible in Images.* (Credit: www.creationism.org /images/DoreBibleIllus/)

i.e., the exiles, to Jerusalem, the building of the temple, and the rebuilding of the wall around Jerusalem) following one great plan. Consequently, he introduced the rebuilding of the wall in connection with the rebuilding of the temple. The two building projects were described similarly. Work began on the projects by returnees; work on both was opposed locally; work on both resumed with written permission of the Persian government; and work on both

The House of God and the City of Jerusalem

Tamara C. Eskenazi has argued that there is no distinction between the "house of God" mentioned in Ezra 4:3 and "Jerusalem," whose walls and foundations are the subject of the letter to Artaxerxes in Ezra 4:12-22. This theme, she argues, is but one of three primary themes in Ezra-Nehemiah. The other two are (1) a shift in focus from leaders to participating community and (2) the primacy of the written text as a source of authority over the spoken word. One may grant her those two developments, especially the second. Written texts do stand front and center in Ezra 4-6, 7:11-26; Neh 7:5-69 // Ezra 2:2b-58; Neh 7:73–8:12; 9:3; 9:38–10:39; and 12:1-26. Still, it is much harder to accept her argument that the concept of the house of God had morphed into the idea of the city.

Regardless, according to Oded Lipschits, early post-exilic Jerusalem was very small and narrow, perhaps running north/south approximately 300 meters in the northern part of the city of David. In addition, it seems to have included a trapezoidal area around the temple running 60 meters wide on the south side, 120 meters wide on the north side, and approximately 170 meters south to north. The city's population was perhaps as little as 1,500. D. Ussishkin, by contrast, thinks that Nehemiah restored a much larger portion of the city, but agrees that its population was small. In any case, the temple was its most important feature during the early post-exilic period, and Jerusalem had few inhabitants. Still, the city and the temple seem quite distinct. In connection with Ezra 4:1-3, one is better off simply to admit that the editor used a letter concerning the wall to support his case about the temple.

Tamara C. Eskenazi, *In an Age of Prose* (SBLMS 36; Atlanta: Scholars, 1988) 53–57.

Oded Lipschits, "Persian Period Finds from Jerusalem: Facts and Interpretations," http://www.jhsonline.org, *Journal of Hebrew Scriptures*, vol. 9, article 20, p. 21. See also "Achaemenid Imperial Policy, Settlement Processes in Palestine, and the Status of Jerusalem in the Middle of the Fifth Century BCE," *Judah and the Judeans in the Persian Period* (ed. Oded Lipschits and Manfred Oeming; Winona Lake IN: Eisenbrauns, 2006) 19–52; here 32.

D. Ussishkin, "The Borders and De Facto Size of Jerusalem in the Persian Period," *Judah and the Judeans in the Persian Period*, ed. Oded Lipschits and Manfred Oeming (Winona Lake IN: Eisenbrauns, 2006) 147–66.

---

was concluded successfully despite opposition from locals. It was all a single rebuilding project. (For a somewhat different interpretation of this topic, see [The House of God and the City of Jerusalem].) With this information in view, it is possible to turn to two other major issues concerned with the chapter.

Written Objections to Rebuilding, 4:6-23

As mentioned above, Ezra 4:6-23 is concerned with permission to rebuild the wall around Jerusalem, a task ascribed to Nehemiah in the book bearing his name. Of particular note, however, is the attention it pays to written correspondence concerning written records. Oral claims, apparently, were not trusted; they had to be reinforced by written records. This is a motif that will appear again and again in Ezra-Nehemiah, and it suggests a rise in the number of scribes, a group whose *raison d'etre* was the writing and preserving of records. (They were probably rare in Israel/Judah before the mid-eighth century, i.e., the time the "writing prophets" originated.[7]) References to letters, records, and reading will dot the entirety of Ezra-Nehemiah. One may ask how a writer in Yehud could have access to letters between their opponents and the Persian government. In answer readers may need to admit that some, maybe even most or all of them, were re-creations by the editor of Ezra-Nehemiah. Still, the letters dealt with public matters, and the contents of official proclamations would have been made known. Thus the letters may report the gist of correspondences even where there was no official copy available to the redactor.

The Use of Two Languages

A second special issue in Ezra 3:1–6:18 is the use of two languages: Hebrew in Ezra 3:1–4:7 + 6:19-22 and Aramaic in Ezra 4:8–6:18, representing two different sets of traditions. [What Is Aramaic?] It will be useful to revisit the whole of Ezra 3–6 once again, this time to sort out the traditions/records employed. Both sets report events surrounding the rebuilding of Jerusalem. The sequence in the Hebrew material goes as follows. In the seventh month (September-October of the Jewish lunar calendar) of their first year back, Jeshua and Zerubbabel "set the altar in its place" (Ezra 3:3), so that the people could celebrate the imminent Feast of Tabernacles (Ezra 3:1-6a). The

> **What Is Aramaic?**
>
> AΩ Aramaic is a Semitic language closely related to Hebrew, perhaps as close as Dutch or Danish is to German. It can be traced to people in northern Syria. When the Assyrians conquered the Arameans in the mid-eighth century BCE, Aramaic became an international language. It remained such until the fourth century, after which it was replaced by Greek. It was still spoken in Israel as late as the time of the New Testament, as shown by its use of the Aramaic words "talitha cumi" (little girl, arise" in Mark 5:41), maranatha ("our Lord, come" in 1 Cor 16:22), and Golgatha ("place of a skull" in Matt 27:33; Mark 15:22; and John 19:17).

people also gave money to buy cedar from Lebanon to rebuild the temple (Ezra 3:6b-7; for Solomon's temple see 1 Kgs 7:13-51 and 1 Chr 3:1–5:1). The next year, their second in Jerusalem, Zerubbabel and Jeshua led the people to begin rebuilding the temple itself (Ezra 3:8-9). A founding ceremony marked the start of the project, with mixed reactions by the people assembled (Ezra 3:10-13). Then a complication arose as local non-repatriates, descendants of foreigners sent to Israel in 676 BCE by Esarhaddon, king of Assyria, asked to participate (Ezra 4:1-3).

Local opposition is mentioned also in Ezra 4:4, where the opponents were called "the people of the land." Their obstruction continued from the days of Cyrus (r. 539–530) to those of Darius (520–486; Ezra 4:5). Ezra 4:6-7 is a redactional piece, serving to move the narrative forward in time. First, it mentions Ahasuerus (or Xerxes, r. 486–465), during whose reign locals filed a complaint against the leaders in Jerusalem with Persian officials. Then it mentions Artaxerxes, presumably Artaxerxes I (r. 465–424), to whom some opponents wrote a letter reported in the following verses. It seems safe to say, then, that Ezra 4:6-7 functioned to provide the transition to the Aramaic language materials in Ezra 4:8–6:18, which contained a narrative of opposition to the rebuilding of the *city wall* and an account of the rebuilding of the *temple*, i.e., two different events. The Hebrew narrative resumed in Ezra 6:19 with the account of the observance of the Feast of Passover "on the four-teenth day of the first month." The year was not stated. Given the placement of this passage in the book of Ezra following the Aramaic account, the author of Ezra probably intended for readers to think the celebration occurred in the spring of 515, just after the completion of the temple "on the third day of the month of Adar in the sixth year of the reign of King Darius," i.e., March 515 BCE. The Hebrew narrative of the Passover celebration itself that follows (Ezra 6:19-22) mentions that the "king of Assyria" aided the repatriates in their building project. Probably the author of Ezra-Nehemiah had in mind Darius, king of Persia, however, rather than an Assyrian monarch from centuries earlier. (Hmm. Help from a pagan Persian was allowable, but not help from local worshipers of YHWH!)

At any rate, Ezra 6:19-22 completes the account of rebuilding the temple with a narrative about worship there. Thus, the Hebrew narrative opens with the account of the celebration of the Feast of Booths (Ezra 3:1-7), moves to an account of the celebration connected with laying the foundation of the temple (Ezra 3:8-13), takes up the issue of resistance to building the temple (Ezra 4:1-5), and concludes with an account of the celebration of the feast of Passover (Ezra 6:19-22).

The interposed Aramaic section (Ezra 4:8–6:18) begins with an exchange of letters between Artaxerxes I and Rehum (Ezra 4:8-23). These letters never mention the temple, however. Instead, they are concerned with the rebuilding of the city of Jerusalem, particularly its walls. Chronologically they belong later, during the reign of Artaxerxes I (465–424), i.e., well after the completion of the temple, but before or during Nehemiah's career that began in the twentieth year of Artaxerxes' reign. Nevertheless, they *function* in Ezra 4:8-24 to flesh out the portrayal of opposition to rebuilding mentioned earlier in Ezra 4:1-3 and to foreshadow the later rebuilding of the walls under Nehemiah. Indeed, Ezra 4:6-23 constitutes a deliberate redactional link with the traditions about Nehemiah, showing that the return to Jerusalem, the rebuilding of the temple, and the rebuilding of the wall around it were three parts of one whole work of God. It is possible the final author of Ezra-Nehemiah knew that Darius did not follow Cyrus directly (though he might not have known that Cambyses did) and used the exchange of letters as a temporal connector between the two Persian kings. Regardless, at the end of the exchange of letters, the action in the Aramaic section reverts to the year 537 with the notice that work stopped on the temple until the second year of

King Darius, i.e., 520 (Ezra 4:24, a transitional and redactional verse).

The Aramaic narrative continues with an account of the prophets Haggai and Zechariah urging the people to build the temple (Ezra 5:1-2) and an account of opposition to the project by Tattenai, governor of the Persian province of which Yehud was a part (Ezra 5:3–6:13). That account, like Ezra 4:8-24, also contains an exchange of letters: one from Tattenai to Darius (Ezra 5:6-17) and one from Darius to Tattenai (Ezra 6:3-12). The first of those letters mentions Sheshbazzar, whose work on the temple was not mentioned in the Hebrew account of building the altar (Ezra 3:1-4:7; 6:19-22), but had been mentioned in Ezra 1:8, 11.[8] The Aramaic section closes with the notice that work on the temple began once more, and this time was completed (Ezra 6:13-15). It also reports that the people held a dedication celebration for the temple (Ezra 6:16-18).[9]

This analysis by language shows that Ezra 3–6 was deliberately constructed and edited

The Prophet Zechariah

Peter Paul Rubens (1577–1640). Study of Zacchariah (pencil & watercolor on paper), Victoria & Albert Museum, London, UK. (Credit: The Stapleton Collection/Bridgeman Images)

principally to offer a picture of the building of the altar and the temple in the sixth century. In doing so, it employed traditions in two languages, traditions that reported events covering a longer period, i.e., from the late sixth down to the middle of the fifth century. The entire four chapters were constructed to show the faithful, worshiping community overcoming all obstacles, local and international, to fulfill the task of rebuilding the temple and reestablishing worship in Jerusalem under proper priests and Levites (see Ezra 3:8-11; 6:16-18).

Written Opposition to the Rebuilding of Jerusalem, 4:6-10

The discussion in Ezra 4:6-10 of opposition to rebuilding the wall of Jerusalem begins by mentioning *written* objections to rebuilding

Hellenistic Rules of Rhetorical Historiography

Lisbeth S. Fried argues that Hellenistic rules of rhetoric illuminate the use of letters in Ezra 1–6. Greek rhetorical handbooks say that a text ought to consist of four parts: prologue, narrative, proof, and epilogue. The prologue should praise the character of the main person or cause, and the epilogue should induce sympathy for the person or cause being defended. In between come a narrative and the proof of the validity of the person/cause. In Ezra 1–6, chapters 1–3 constitute the prologue, Ezra 4:1–6:15 forms the body of the text (i.e., narrative and proof), and Ezra 6:16-22 constitutes the epilogue. The narrative and proofs in 4:1–6:15 also follow Hellenistic rules. The narrative accuses the "people of the land" of being the enemies of the returnees. Specifically, Ezra 4:6-7 accuses them of writing letters in an effort to convince the Persian king to forbid the rebuilding of Jerusalem's city wall. Fried further notes that the mention of rebuilding the wall in connection with rebuilding the temple conforms to Aristotle's advice that if one does not have direct evidence of malfeasance, one should offer evidence from another context that proves that the activities of accused people are the sort of objectionable action the accused are in the habit of doing. In other words, in the letters to the Persian kings, the proponents of rebuilding the temple are linked with the proponents of rebuilding the wall, and both rebuilding projects are presented as opposed to the best interests of Persia. In Ezra 6, of course, the rhetorical ploy is shown to have failed.

To be sure, the action in Ezra 1–6 was situated earlier than the Greek period, and its writing may well have occurred earlier too. One need not assume that Greek rhetoricians invented the methods they articulated and regularized.

Lisbeth S. Fried, "Ezra's Use of Documents in the Context of Hellenistic Rules of Rhetoric," in *New Perspectives on Ezra-Nehemiah* (ed. Isaac Kalimi; Winona Lake IN: Eisenbrauns, 2012) 11–26; esp. 16–17 and 25–26.

Jerusalem filed by the opponents of the returnees. The citation of such documents had a lengthy history in the ancient world. [Hellenistic Rules of Rhetorical Historiography] Taken at face value, the whole discussion is *anachronistic* in its context. Verse 6 says that opponents wrote during the reign of Ahasuerus, the Bible's name for the Persian king Xerxes I (r. 486–465), and v. 7 reports a complaint during the reign of Artaxerxes, presumably Artaxerxes I (r. 465–423). (See [Artaxerxes I or II?].) Verses 8-23 describe events dated during the reigns of King Artaxerxes I, as the text clearly says. Verse 24, however, concludes the action described in vv. 1-5, action taken circa 520 BCE. Why would the editor/author make such jumps back and forth in time? Presumably, he did so in order to show the link between rebuilding the temple and rebuilding the wall. O. Lipschits suggests, cogently, that vv. 8-23 originally described events from the reign of Artaxerxes I before the career of Nehemiah and calls them proleptic. That is, at the beginning of its description of the rebuilding process (the building of the temple), Ezra 4 looks ahead to the end of that effort, the rebuilding of the wall as described in the book of Nehemiah. This prolepsis points unmistakably to a common editor behind Ezra-Nehemiah in the form they appear in the Old Testament. (See the introductory comments on Nehemiah 4–5 for more on this issue.)

Two brief notes appear in Ezra 4:6-7, the second of which informs the reader that the following letter would be in Aramaic. (Actually, the next fifty-two verses, i.e., through Ezra 6:22, are in that language, not just the letter.) The redactor then composed vv. 8-10 as an introduction to an exchange of letters in Ezra 4:11-16 and 17-22. The "great and noble Osnapper" mentioned in v. 10 was Ashurbanipal (r. 669–c. 627), the last of the great Assyrian kings. (Indeed, in 605 Nebuchadnezzar of Babylon ended the

Assyrian Empire.) The exchange of letters was between the Persian king Artaxerxes I and two men named Rehum (the deputy) and Shimshai (the scribe). These latter two men said (v. 8) they were writing on behalf of "the people of the province Beyond the River."[10] The book of Ezra reproduces the Aramaic version of the letters for its readers.[11]

Whether the redactor really thought Xerxes and Artaxerxes reigned between Cyrus and Darius may be doubted. What is clear is that he placed the action described in Ezra 1:1–4:5 during the time of Cyrus, i.e., between 539 and 537. Then he dated the completion of the temple in Ezra 5:1–6:17 during the reign of Darius, which began in 521. Haggai 1:1–2:9, which urges the building of the temple and dates itself during the second year of the reign of Darius, further corroborates that date.

The Letter to King Artaxerxes, 4:11-16

The well-crafted letter attributed to Rehum and Shimshai begins with a brief, polite, and subservient greeting. Then it calls attention to an effort to rebuild the walls of Jerusalem, and charges the people of Jerusalem with plans to withhold tribute (money paid to Persia to honor it), customs (taxes imposed on items consumed), and tolls (money paid for passage on a journey). Such action would be treasonous in the eyes of the Persians. Next, the letter attempts to ingratiate its authors to the Persians by reminding them that the authors were employed by the Persians: they "shared the salt of the palace." Hence, they felt obliged to inform their masters of what was going on.

Continuing, the letter suggests that the king order a search of Persian records, where he would discover that Jerusalem was a "rebellious" city. In all likelihood, Persian records would reveal no such thing; the Babylonians had destroyed Jerusalem in 586, some forty-seven years before Persia conquered their capital city of Babylon in 539. Any "rebellion" and "sedition" that Jerusalem's inhabitants had committed had been in opposition to Babylonia and its king, Nebuchadnezzar. The letter to Artaxerxes even concedes that those actions had occurred "long ago." Still, the city's sedition was so serious, the letter informs the Persian king, that it had been "hurtful to kings and provinces"—so hurtful, in fact, that the city had been destroyed.

Finally, the letter warns Artaxerxes that if the city was rebuilt, Persia would lose its hold over the province "Beyond the River." The river referred to here is the Euphrates. The name "Beyond the

River" referred to a Persian satrapy between the Euphrates and the Mediterranean Sea, as it does also in Ezra 4:10, 16-17. The letter may be understood as alarmist propaganda articulated against the hopes and wishes of a tiny group of returnees in a tiny part of the province. From a modern perspective, one may doubt whether what happened in Jerusalem would have been felt any farther away than Samaria. To the extent that the letter reflects the fears of local officials in Yehud who represented Persian authority in Jerusalem, they may have been well founded. Any suggestion that the efforts to rebuild Jerusalem represented a danger to Persia itself was simply ill founded and forced.

The Reply from King Artaxerxes, 4:17-22

The king sent an answer addressed to Rehum, Shimshai, and their associates in Samaria. The author makes the point that the letter was translated from the Old Persian language. Does this pointed mentioning of translation constitute an erudite ridicule of the Persian monarch for not knowing the "universal" language of Aramaic? Regardless, Artaxerxes conceded that Jerusalem (under the Davidic dynasty) had ruled over the whole province of Beyond the River, an area much larger than the Old Testament otherwise claims for Israel or Israel/Judah after the division of the monarchy. One typical biblical depiction of the land of the Hebrews portrays their land as stretching from the city of Dan in the north to Beersheba in the south (see Judg 20:1; 1 Sam 3:10; 2 Sam 17:11; 2 Sam 24:2, 1 Kgs 10:29; 1 Chr 21:1). Another definition of boundaries is from the River to the Brook or River of Egypt (Gen 15:18; 2 Kgs 24:7; Mic 7:12), boundaries that extended from the Euphrates River in modern Syria to the Brook Zered in the Sinai. So far as is known from the Bible or archaeology, ancient Israel never ruled that much territory, though the hope to rule it did surface in those few texts. If that hope had been realized, Israel/Judah would have been the greatest power between Mesopotamia and Egypt.

An ancient people imputed to have ruled so vast an empire in the past were clearly—to Artaxerxes anyway—to be feared. More important to him, however, was the discovery that after coming under the sway of Assyria and Babylon, the land of Israel/Judah was the site of rebellion and sedition, i.e., revolt against those powers. A people with such a past was not to be trusted at first glance. The king demanded time to search the records to see if the charges were true.

Cessation of the Work in Jerusalem, 4:23-24

Verse 23 says that the letter from Artaxerxes was read to Rehum and Shemshai, who hurried to Jerusalem and made the people halt their work. Verse 24, however, makes an abrupt shift *back* in time to the subject under discussion in Ezra 3:1–4:5, the building of the temple. It says the work halted on the temple (i.e., in 537) until the second year of Darius, i.e., in 520. On one level, that second statement was simply historically correct; the temple was rebuilt during the reign of Darius, regardless of how much (or little) had been done earlier. On another level, a theological level, by means of vv. 8-24 the redactor of Ezra-Nehemiah turns the narrative of the two building projects (the wall and the temple) into a twofold program. Ezra 5 then resumes the narrative of the rebuilding of the temple. This narrative sequence ties the two projects together, but it gives meaning to the building of the wall. It makes it clear that the city wall surrounds the temple to guard it.[12] The temple represented Yehud's dependence on YHWH, while the wall surrounded the temple and marked off the holy area. Between the two projects, the work on the temple was more important for the redactor. Thus, he deliberately placed the two projects side by side and argued that rebuilding the altar and the temple was more important. [Bede on the Finishing of the Temple] The rebuilding of the altar and the temple were but the beginning efforts, however. Looking ahead to later chapters, J. L. Wright argues that "the holiness that was confined to the altar, priests and temple in Ezra 1–6 is transferred to the leadership in Ezra 8:28, to Israel in Ezra 9, and to the entire city in Nehemiah 3:1-32, 11:2, 12:27-47."[13]

Bede on the Finishing of the Temple

The Venerable Bede developed a different understanding of Ezra 4:17-24, based partly on his reading of John 2:20. In that verse, opponents of Jesus are depicted as quarreling with his saying in the previous verse: "Destroy this temple, and after three days I will raise it up." The opponents replied that the temple had been under construction forty-six years (during Herod's enlargement and beautification), so Jesus certainly could not rebuild it in three days. Bede completely ignored Herod's work, if he even knew of it, and tied the saying to Ezra's account. He claimed that forty-six years passed between the start of the rebuilding under Cyrus and its completion under the leadership of Zerubbabel and Joshua. He then crafted a typology: just as the form of the human body is completed in the first forty-six days of gestation, so also the formation of Jesus' body in the womb took forty-six days!

Bede, "Homilies on the Gospels," 2.1, in Marco Conti, ed., *Ancient Christian Commentary on Scripture: Old Testament. V; 1-2 Kings, 1-2 Chronicles, Ezra, Nehemiah, Esther* (Downers Grove IL: Intervarsity, 2008) 312–13.

CONNECTIONS

1. Why are holy places, like temples and churches, important? Can people not meet God anywhere? Of course they can. People meet God in good and bad times and places. Moreover, what makes a place or time "holy" or "sacred" is that something auspicious and even awe-inspiring takes place, namely a meeting between the

Jesus' Temptations

Ary Scheffer (1795–1858). *The Temptation of Christ*. 1851–1852. Oil on canvas. Louvre, Paris, France. (Credit: © RMN-Grand Palais/Art Resource, NY)

human and the divine. Still, some places seem to be more fitting for such meetings than others. Mountaintops seem particularly appropriate or suitable for such meetings. One need only recall that Moses met God on Mount Sinai (Exod 20 and the following chapters), and Jesus was transfigured on an isolated mountain (Mark 9:2; Matt 17:1). It may simply be that elevated places remind us of our finitude, impress us as being "closer" to God, and prepare us for close encounters with God. The loneliness of the wilderness was the setting for Jesus' temptation (Matt 4:1-11), though one of the temptations was for Jesus to throw himself from the highest point of the temple. Neither height nor seclusion, it would seem, guarantees worship. Indeed, many believers would count worship in large crowds among their most important spiritual times.

All genuine worship brings people face to face with God, whose perfection reveals to worshipers their sin. Public worship and public repentance makes worshipers more accountable to their family, friends, neighbors, and associates. It should make more compassionate citizens out of worshipers. The shared experience of the Holy not only transforms individuals but also transforms the relationships between humans. Private worship should lead to interpersonal transformations as well, but it can do so only after the worship.

2. Why was sacrifice so important in ancient Israel? The answer may be that an experience that costs nothing redeems little. Most readers will have had the experience of doing something wrong, saying "I'm sorry," and feeling as if no amends have been made. Often restitution is necessary. Thus, laws like Exodus 21:28–22:14 establish the necessity of compensation for doing damage. Still,

broken relationships are healed ultimately by forgiveness, not by material restitution. Sometimes, in fact, attempts at compensation seem trivial and/or insincere.

Regardless, the offering of a sacrifice recognized that even an act committed against another human was also an act against God. Sacrifice without repentance, moreover, was a sham. For some sins, e.g., blasphemy and murder, there was no sacrifice. Sinners could only throw themselves on the mercy of God. Ultimately in the Old Testament in connection with wrong deeds against God, it is the broken and sincere heart that God accepts (Ps 51:17).

Not all sacrifices, however, were sacrifices for sinful behavior. Some were offerings of thanksgiving to God for God's beneficence. Some were offerings for ritual offenses, and others were for incidents of omission or when one was rendered ritually unclean. Sacrifices were accompanied by prayers, reminding the worshiper of the divine presence in such contexts.

Perhaps the next question, then, is why the New Testament turned away from sacrifices. The main reason, of course, is that Jesus laid down his life as the perfect offering for sins, once for all time. Another reason perhaps is more practical. As long as people for the most part lived in rural communities and owned live animals and grew crops, sacrifices were quite possible. As cities grew and fewer people farmed, it became more difficult to transport live animals and fresh plants to a sanctuary. A third reason applied to Gentile Christians. They gave up their sacrifices to Gentile gods, but perhaps did not live close enough to Jerusalem to offer sacrifices there. Indeed, they may have seen no reason to do so. The final reason, however, affected not only Christians wanting to offer sacrifices at the temple in Jerusalem but also Jews. With the destruction of the temple by the Romans in 70 CE, the place for animal sacrifice was destroyed and even Jews had to reinvent their religion as one that did not sacrifice. The "broken and contrite heart" became the only sacrifice possible, and thus the only one necessary, for Jews as well.

Thus, the concept of sacrifice remains alive for Christians. All Christian living becomes a sacrifice. Christian worship may well include or end with Communion, a reminder of Jesus' atoning sacrifice. The Bible calls Christians to share financially, especially with the poor. People are at times compelled to risk their lives or their careers in sacrificial acts as varied as diving into water to save a person from drowning to befriending and helping someone destitute or discriminated against by society.

3. Ezra 4 offers a study of subgroups within a society. One might suppose that a country as small as Yehud and with a population as small as it had would be harmonious, but that seems not to have been the case. The returnees from Babylon faced Judeans and Samaritans who had never been exiled and who may well have thought of themselves as protected by God and deserving of leadership. In addition, the Samaritans may have been in control of Yehud officially. The returnees also met people of different ethnic backgrounds sent there by the Assyrians after the destruction of the northern kingdom of Israel and who wanted to have a role in rebuilding the temple. The returnees, however, wanted to rebuild the temple and preserve the leadership roles and even exclusive access for themselves. Modern readers may well need to read between the lines in Ezra 4 to discern God's will for the temple articulated in Isaiah 56:3-8 that God would welcome all peoples to the restored temple and make them joyful there: "For my house shall be called a house of prayer for all peoples," says the Lord (v. 7). Modern readers also will need to look to see the will of God with regard to other ethnicities and even other religions to determine how to relate to them with love, kindness, and integrity.

4. This episode is instructive in another way as well. J. Havea subjects Ezra-Nehemiah to an ideological reading in which he argues that Artaxerxes was concerned for the safety of his own kingdom (see Ezra 4:17-22), and well he might have been, we might say. He was, after all, king of Persia. Havea does not say so, but readers would do well to recall that this material about the wall was deliberately relocated historically to connect it with the rebuilding of the temple. The two were intimately and irrevocably connected in the mind of the redactor—and in Ezra 4. Havea emphasizes the psychological and spiritual connection between those two (re)building projects. For Artaxerxes, the wall signifies that the people of Yehud might spawn a rebellion from within the city and its sanctuary to its God. Havea writes, "In my reading the bar(rier) not only signifies where sacred ends but also the fear that rebellion will overflow from this sacred space." The two groups (returnees and Persians) "look upon the same bar(rier) from opposite sides, and they identify as profane the other side of the bar(rier)."[14]

5. If it seems remarkable to modern readers that an empire as powerful as that of ancient Persians would worry about possible resurgent behavior in tiny Yehud and its ruined capital Jerusalem,

those readers should simply look around their own world. In the 1980s, for example, Great Britain fought a war (April 2 to June 14, 1982) over the Falkland Islands (population just over 3,000), and the United States went to war (October 25 to December 15, 1983) against the tiny island of Grenada (population c. 100,000). To be sure, both nations offered their justifications. Britain claimed and still claims it owns the Falklands (located thousands of miles from its home islands, almost at the Arctic Circle), and its opponent, neighboring Argentina, attacked them. One could argue, however, and hear shrill denouncements for doing so, that neither country had the right to dominate those islands. Similarly, in Grenada, the United States feared a communist takeover of the island and the possible detention of American citizens studying medicine there. At least some of those students, however, reportedly felt no danger at all. The reason for mentioning these two incidents of armed intervention is

Grenada and the Falklands

that colonial and other powers generally act in their own interests, no matter what they say to justify those actions. The second reason follows naturally. The appearance of truth often is more important than the truth, if for no other reason than truth is often hard to substantiate. Even in tiny ancient Yehud, there were returnees, Persian officials, traditional Israelites and Judeans, people relocated to Yehud by earlier foreign powers, and people who had moved into Yehud from elsewhere after the fall of Jerusalem. It would take divine wisdom to sort through all the claims, and a will to cooperate after the sorting was done. Sadly, those requirements are almost always lacking where money, property, and livelihoods are at stake. In Ezra 4, our sympathies naturally lie with the returnees, who are telling the story. Readers should not forget, however, that the other players are God's children too. Neither should readers forget that their own opponents, at home and abroad, likewise are God's children.

NOTES

1. Joseph Blenkinsopp, *Ezra-Nehemiah* (OTL; Philadelphia: Westminster, 1988) 107. R. J. Coggins ("The Interpretation of Ezra 4:4," *JTS* 16 [1965]: 124–27) cites H. H. Rowley and John Bright as scholars who accept this view. It is based on Josephus's (*AJ* 11.4. 84) retelling of the Ezra account, which begins, "But when the Samaritans, who were still enemies to the tribes of Judah and Benjamin, heard the sound of the trumpets, they came running together, and desired to know what was the occasion of this tumult. . . ." Coggins, by contrast, argues correctly that the "people of the land" were the inhabitants of Judah still there when exiles started returning. The Samaritans themselves built their own temple at Samaria decades later in the mid-fifth century, according to an easily available report of archaeological finds at the site by Yitzhak Magen, "Bells, Pendants, Snakes and Stones, *BARev* 36/6 (2010): 26–33.

2. Gary N. Knoppers, "Revisiting the Samaritan Question in the Persian Period," *Judah and the Judeans in the Persian Period* (ed. O. Lipschits and M. Oeming; Winona Lake IN.: Eisenbrauns, 2006) 278–79.

3. See "From Annalistic Reports" of Sargon II, in *ANET* (2011), 266–68.

4. Ferdinand Dexinger, "Limits of Tolerance in Judaism: The Samaritan Example," *Jewish and Christian Self-Definition* (ed. E. P. Sanders, A. I. Baumgarten, and Alan Mendelson; Philadelphia: Fortress, 1981) 88–114; here 92–94.

5. L. S. Fried, "The *'am hā'āreṣ* in Ezra 4:4 and the Persian Imperial Administration," *Judah and the Judeans in the Persian Period* (ed. Oded Lipschits and Manfred Oeming; Winona Lake IN: Eisenbrauns, 2006) 141.

6. See David Bossman, "Ezra's Marriage Reform: Israel Redefined," *BTB* 9 (1979): 32–38.

7. K. Schmid, *Literaturgeschichte des Alten Testaments: Eine Einführung* (Darmstadt: Wissenschftliche Buchgesellschaft, 2008) 44.

8. Sheshbazzar was not mentioned in Haggai or Zech 1–8, either, and those books offer perspectives from the two prophets that Ezra 5:1-2 credits with spurring the people to build. Zech 4:9, in fact, insists that "the hands of Zerubbabel have founded this house; his hands shall also complete it." The Bible does not record the fate of either man.

9. A. H. J. Gunneweg ("Die aramäische und die hebräische Erzählung über die nachexilische Retauration—ein Vergleich," *ZAW* 94 [1982]: 301) well summarized one principal difference between the Hebrew and Aramaic sources: the Hebrew version narrated an interruption of work on the temple because of local opposition, while the Aramaic document narrated a stoppage of work on city walls because of arguments that were made in the Persian court.

10. See F. K. Wong, "Beyond the River," *NIDB*, 1.451. The name also appears in Ezra 5:3, 6; 6:6, 8, 13; 7:21, 25; 8:36; and Neh 2:7, 9; 3:7.

11. Anson F. Rainey and R. Steven Notley (*Carta's New Century Handbook and Bible Atlas* [Jerusalem: Carta, 2007] 166) argue that the allusion "must certainly be understood against the background of the Megayzus rebellion," and they posit a destruction of the fortress that was Jerusalem. Clearly, that is a different reconstruction of events than the one posited in this volume.

12. See J. L. Wright, "Seeking, Finding, and Writing in Ezra-Nehemiah," *Unity and Disunity in Ezra-Nehemiah* (ed. M. J. Boda and P. L. Redditt; Hebrew Bible Monographs 16; Sheffield: Sheffield University Press, 2008) 297.

13. Ibid., 300.

14. John Havea, "Shifting the Boundaries: House of God and the Politics of Reading," *Pacific Journal of Theology*, 2/15 (1996): 61–62.

RESUMPTION OF THE WORK ON THE TEMPLE

Ezra 5

COMMENTARY

[Outline of Ezra 5] If Ezra 4:1-5 discusses a local, late sixth-century squabble over rebuilding the temple, Ezra 4:6-23 jumps ahead to the fifth-century task of rebuilding Jerusalem's wall, and Ezra 4:24 recognizes that the work on the temple had stalled, then Ezra 5:1–6:18 turns to efforts to rebuild the temple and to questions from Persian officials about it. Ezra 5, part of the Aramaic narrative in Ezra 4:8–6:18, concerns itself with the roles of Haggai, Zechariah, Zerubbabel, Joshua, and others in restarting the project (Ezra 5:1-2) and with the inquiry of Tattenai (Ezra 5:3-5), the Persian governor of the province of which Yehud was a part. This inquiry too resulted in written correspondence with royalty in Persia (Ezra 5:6-17), but this time with King Darius I (r. 522–486). The result was recognition of the legitimacy of rebuilding the temple (Ezra 6:1-12), a project that came to a successful conclusion in March 515 BCE.

> **Outline of Ezra 5**
>
> 📖 Encouragement by Haggai and Zechariah, 5:1-2
> Tattenai Writes to King Darius, 5:3-5
> Contents of the Letter of Inquiry, 5:6-17

Darius on His Throne

Darius I the Great (550–486 BCE) giving audience. Detail of a relief in the Treasury of the Palace at Persepolis, 491–486 BCE. Persia, Achaemenid period. Persepolis, Iran. (Credit: SEF/Art Resource, NY)

Encouragement by Haggai and Zechariah, 5:1-2

Ezra 5:1-2 draws upon Haggai 1:2–2:9 and Zechariah 6:11-13, 8:1-9, which urged the rebuilding of the temple, with Jeshua and Zerubbabel leading the work. [The Roles of Jeshua and Zerubbabel] These two verses simply say that

The Roles of Jeshua and Zerubbabel

The prophet Haggai called on the high priest Jeshua (called Joshua in Haggai and Zechariah) and the royal prince Zerubbabel to lead the rebuilding of the temple (Hag 2:4-9), and Zech 4:9 says Zerubbabel did just that. Haggai also predicted that God would make Zerubbabel "like a signet ring" (Hag 2:23). That phrase not only has in mind but also reverses Jer 22:24. There, through Jeremiah, God announces to King Coniah (a.k.a. Jehoiachin, Zerubbabel's grandfather) that even though Coniah was God's signet ring, God would rip him from the divine finger and throw him away (i.e., send him into exile) for disobedience. Furthermore, Jeremiah says, no son (descendant) of Coniah/Jehoiachin would reign over Judah.

It is the second part of this threat with which Haggai disagrees. Readers would do well to recall, however, that God's threats and promises were often conditional. Proper behavior could change the future—why else bother to correct wayward people or warn and praise godly ones? Here is one such case, where (presumably in light of the sufferings and repentance of the people and perhaps even the Davidides) God had lifted the curse on the royal house. As it turned out, however, Zerubbabel disappeared from the pages of the Bible, and neither he nor any other descendant of David ever ruled Judah/Israel as king afterward. What happened to him is a mystery, but it is not out of the question that he did not wish to remain in Jerusalem/Yehud and simply returned to Babylon. Zech 4:5b-10a predicts that the prince Zerubbabel would complete the temple whose reconstruction he had begun. Zech 6:9-15, however, tacitly admits the disappearance of Zerubbabel by saying that Joshua (the priest), instead of Zerubbabel (the Davidide) would wear a crown (v. 11), build the temple (v. 12), and bear royal honor. Zech 9:9-10 predicts a future king, but does not say he would be a son of David. Still, following the talk about a Davidic king in Haggai and Zech 1–8, it is hard to believe that Zech 9:9-10 had in mind a non-Davidic king. That is especially so since the following chapters have much to say about the "house of David."

In view of this endorsement of returnees, readers may want to ask whether Haggai and Zechariah themselves were returnees. The books carrying their names do not say in the case of Haggai, but Neh 12:16, a verse in the third list of returnees under Zerubbabel (see also Ezra 2 and Neh 7), specifically mentions Zechariah. Haggai most likely should be considered a Returnee as well.

David Martin (1639–1721). "Jeshua and Zerubbabel" from *Historie des Ouden en Nieuwen Testaments: verrykt met meer dan vierhonderd printverbeeldingen in koper gesneeden.* (Credit: Pitts Theological Library)

This engraving depicts Jeshua, son of Jozadak, and Zerubbabel, son of Shealtiel, organizing the rebuilding of the Temple in Jerusalem. The artist painted a more elaborate temple than the returnees built.

the two men began to build, with the prophets Haggai and Zechariah supporting the project and unnamed others aiding. The reference to the "Jews who were in Judah and Jerusalem" is not an all-inclusive description but a carefully written delineation of the legitimate workers: returnees only. Ezra 5, moreover, like the rest of the book, does not call Zerubbabel a "prince" or "governor" (but see Hag 1:1 and 2:21) or Jeshua the "high priest" (but see Hag 1:12, Zech 3:1, and Zech 6:11). Indeed, even Sheshbazzar was called a "prince" (Heb. *nāśîʾ*) only in Ezra 1:8 and not in Ezra 5. In other words, the author of Ezra-Nehemiah went out of his way to avoid politicizing the rebuilding project.

Tattenai Writes to Governor Shethar-bozenai, 5:3-5

The project, nevertheless, caught the attention of Tattenai, the governor of the Persian province called "Beyond the River." [Who Was Tattenai?] (See [The Extent of the Persian Empire].) Tattenai, an assistant named Shethar-bozenai (otherwise unattested in the Old Testament), and other underlings came to Jerusalem to investigate the building project. Their question was twofold, and the first part was straightforward. The NRSV renders it, "Who gave you a decree to rebuild this structure?" The second part is more ambiguous. The NRSV reads, "and to finish this structure," understanding the word *ʾuššarnāʾ* (translated "structure") to refer to the "temple." That is perhaps the most plausible, but not the only possible reading. The phrase might refer to work inside the building. [The Meaning of *ʾuššarnāʾ*]

Another issue concerns the tone of the question. Frequently, readers see jealousy as an underlying motive. M. Henry, a commentator from an earlier century, attributes it to that emotion.[1] Williamson, however, contends that nothing in the text demands that Tattenai's inquiry be understood as hostile and that the question was posed in such a way that it suggests Tattenai anticipated legal justification for the building project.[2] Williamson is correct about the question, but Ezra 4:1-5 had deliberately politicized the rebuilding of the temple and had

Who Was Tattenai?

The identity of Tattenai was illuminated by the discovery of a Persian tablet, dated in 502 BCE, that refers to a slave owned by "Ta-at-tanni, governor of Ebir-nari" (A. T. Olmstead, "Tattenai, Governor of 'Across the River," *JNES* 3 [1944]: 46). He was the governor of the Persian province "Beyond the River," and was answerable to Ushtannu, the governor of "Beyond the River and Babylon." It would make sense for him to go to Babylon for answers to questions, even if the King of Persia was elsewhere. The book of Ezra, however, has Tattenai dealing directly with King Darius and not a governor.

The Meaning of *ʾuššarnāʾ*

The Aramaic word *ʾuššarnāʾ* is peculiar, and it raised questions in the early translations. Greek versions employ the translation *chorēgia* (supplies). Various modern scholars suggest "lumber," "building materials" or "supplies." Philip A. Noss and Kenneth J. Thomas, however, point to 1 Kgs 6:14-18, which speaks of paneling the temple inside with cedar boards. In their understanding, the term would refer to finishing work inside the building. Certainty is impossible.

Philip A Noss and Kenneth J. Thomas, *A Handbook on Ezra and Nehemiah* (UBS Handbook Series. New York: United Bible Societies, 2005) 135.

A Textual Issue in Ezra 5:4

AΩ Ezra 5:4 actually reads in Hebrew, "We also asked them this . . . ." That reading would turn v. 4 into a sentence attributed to Tattenai. The reading would make sense, in that Tattenai does ask the following question. The Septuagint and the Syriac Peshitta, however, employ the third person plural, thereby attributing the sentence to the narrator rather than to actors in the narrative. The NRSV and other modern translations accept the versions, which is done in the comments here as well.

connected it to the rebuilding of the wall, which was, obviously, a political action. It might be better to say that Ezra 5:3-5 does not narrate tension with Persia, but that it does form part of a three-chapters-long narrative about tension with locals. The polemical aim of the entirety of Ezra 1–6 was to show, on the one hand, that the rebuilding of the temple was done with Persian support as would be the rebuilding of the wall to be described in Nehemiah. On the other hand, the aim was to show that any trouble in connection with rebuilding was caused by local persons (who had not been exiles) acting in their own interests, not those of Persia or the returnees. [A Textual Issue in Ezra 5:4] Verse 5 points explicitly to the divine protection of the workers until the matter could be researched in Persia. The positive outcome of that inquiry, however, had already been anticipated in the discussion of the letter exchange about Nehemiah's wall in Ezra 4:6-23.

Contents of the Letter of Inquiry, 5:6-17

The rest of Ezra 5 discusses the contents of the letter from Tattenai to King Darius in Persia. Darius had been mentioned in Ezra 4:5, and the events of Ezra 5 occurred in 520, the second year of his reign. He had come to power through warfare. Specifically, upon the death of Cambyses in 522, the Persian Empire was thrust into a crisis. According to a pro-Darius account of the events, a man named Gautama, pretending to be Baryida (the younger brother of Cambyses), gained control of Persia. He, however, was opposed and defeated by Darius, who established himself as the new, legitimate king in 521. He claimed descent from the same family as Cyrus, though through a different line, a claim that seems suspect to modern scholars. He became king with the help of six other major families in Persia, and he had workers carve a relief and an inscription of his victory on the face of a cliff near the village of Behistun. Possibly the most powerful of the entire line of Persian kings, he was able to extend Persian power as far west as Marathon, Greece, where, however, he was defeated and his westward march stopped in 490.

Ezra 5:6-7a functions to move the action of the book from Jerusalem to the palace where Darius was staying. The name of the city in which that palace stood is not named though Ezra 6:2

The Cliff of Behistun

Behistun Inscription, describing conquests of Darius the Great in Old Persian, Elamite, and Babylonian languages. These reliefs and texts are engraved in a cliff on Mount Behistun (present Kermanshah Province, Iran). (Credit: Hara1603, Wikimedia Commons PD-self)

mentions Ecbatana, the capital of the province of Media. If Ezra 1 grounded the decision to allow Judeans to return home from Babylon in Cyrus's first year to rebuild the temple, Ezra 5–6 narrates the accomplishment of that goal during the early years of the reign of Darius. To do so, the chapters also introduce another letter, this one from Tattenai (identified as the governor of the province named Beyond the River), Shethar-bozenai (a companion, perhaps Tattenai's assistant), and their associates (i.e., lesser subordinates). It was addressed to King Darius.

The letter itself (Ezra 5:7b-17) takes the form of a report from Tattenai and his associates to Darius. They describe checking on the building project, inquiring from the builders on whose authority the work was being done, and the identity of the head builders. The letter summarized the answer of the workers in four points. (1) The builders were servants of "the God of heaven and earth" (i.e., everything), and they were rebuilding an ancient temple built originally by a great king (i.e., Solomon). [Solomon's Temple] (2) Their ancestors had angered their God by their

Solomon's Temple

Though Solomon's temple was small, 1 Kgs 6:1-38 and 2 Chronicles 3:1–5:2 describe it and its furnishings as splendid. Older residents of Yehud could remember that splendor of Solomon's temple. The new temple seemed ordinary, perhaps even shameful. According to Ezra 3:13, they cried rather than rejoiced at the site of it. Herod's temple in the New Testament itself was the same size but more ornate. In addition, Herod built a huge retaining wall to support a larger courtyard around the temple to accommodate larger crowds of worshipers. The "Wailing Wall" in Jerusalem today was part of that retaining wall. The picture below may resemble Herod's temple more than Zerubbabel's.

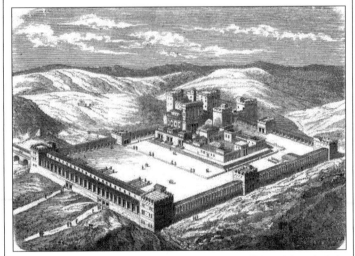

A 19th-century engraver's conception of the appearance of the temple of Solomon in its setting in the city of Jerusalem. (Credit: Art Resource, NY)

disobedience, so their God sent Nebuchadnezzar, king of Babylon, to destroy the original temple and to carry disobedient worshipers to exile in Babylon. (3) King Cyrus had decreed that the temple in Jerusalem should be rebuilt, and he sent back to Jerusalem the treasures that the Babylonian king Nebuchadnezzar had stolen from the temple (cf. Ezra 1:1-10). (4) Sheshbazzar had come to Jerusalem and laid the foundation of the house (i.e., in 539), which had not yet (i.e., in 520) been completely rebuilt.

The word rendered "structure" in both v. 3 and v. 9 by the NRSV may have meant "roof."[3] That is, the officials asked about finishing the building and roofing it. The comment in v. 8 that "It is being built of hewn stone, and timber is laid in the walls" may well refer to the building technique still seen today in the smaller mosque in the old city of Jerusalem, the Al-Aqsa Mosque, which stands at the south end of the temple mount (opposite the Dome of the Rock, which stands near or on the site of the temple). The Al-Aqsa Mosque is made of stone, and its builders used rows of timbers to tie the building together, to reinforce its stone walls lengthwise, and to support its roof.[4]

This letter is remarkable in that only the third and fourth points—exiles had returned to Yehud and were rebuilding the temple with permission from Cyrus—deal with the questions Tattenai asked (in Ezra 5:3-4). The first two points dealt with matters important to the readers of Ezra-Nehemiah.[5] The opening comment that they worshiped "the God of heaven and earth" implicitly claimed that the Persians too fell under God's universal control and had acted according to God's will (however unwittingly). The reference to the original building of the temple, however, looks back to the narrative of its construction, planned by David and carried out by Solomon, described in 1 Chronicles 10:1–2 Chronicles 7:22. The second point summarizes Israel's disobedience culminating in the destruction of Jerusalem by Babylon described in 2 Chronicles 8:1–36:21.

The rhetorical effect of presenting this entire summary as a report to Darius by Persian officials is significant. It establishes two points in the mind of the Darius of the narrative—and, more important, in the minds of the book's readers. It shows first that the temple was a building of long standing before its destruction by Babylon, indeed that its rebuilding had been authorized and at least partially funded by Cyrus. It shows second that loyal returnees from Babylon were the ones rebuilding the temple, not unknown persons or groups. To clinch their argument, they invited Darius to search Persia's own records to verify what they were saying. Of course, what appears in the book of Ezra is an account of things as seen by the returnees, but in its account the appeal is made to Persian records.

Erhard S. Gerstenberger makes a point about the function of the elders in Ezra 5. According to v. 5, it was they who determined to continue with the building project until Darius could hear their case and render his decision. They are also depicted in vv. 6-17 as speaking for the community to Tattenai and his associates. Gerstenberger concludes, "indeed, there is no other leadership personality available, either of noble or priestly origin."[6] If the Davidides and the priests exerted leadership over Yehud in the fifth century, which they seem to have done (see Zech 11–14), Ezra 1–6 does not show them doing so in the late sixth century. Sheshbazzar's function in laying the foundation for the temple and Zerubbabel's role in the rebuilding itself constitute the only mention of Davidides. The verses also show that the rebuilding project was only in its initial phase in 519.[7] The priests and the Levites also are ascribed work on the temple only. That will change in Ezra 7–10. In Ezra 7:25, King Artaxerxes is said to have granted Ezra the priest the authority to appoint magistrates and judges to govern and judge the people.

CONNECTIONS

1. This chapter reminds readers that governments can play a positive role in assuring that groups have the right to worship as they see fit. If on the one hand the Persian kings seemed bent on con-

quering surrounding kingdoms, on the other hand they were unusually generous in allowing their subject peoples in exile to return home and to worship their own gods. The religion of the Persian Empire was Zoroastrianism, an early monotheistic faith, but the Persians seem not to have been missionaries for its spread. (In fact, they may have preferred to keep a proper relationship to that sole god to themselves!) Since the Persians allowed the exiles to return to Yehud, modern scholars often portray them in an unwaveringly positive light. In doing so, they have possibly been too generous and have missed some of the tension lying behind the biblical text itself. That tension was between (1) worshipers of YHWH who had been in exile and worshipers who had not, and also (2) between people descended from residents of Judah and people descended from people who had migrated there after the fall of Israel in 722 or the fall of Judah in 586.

Similarly, Christians in the United States often miss the point of the religious freedom clause in the First Amendment to the United States Constitution and want to claim that the United States is a "Christian nation." For proof, they point to the Pilgrims who came on the *Mayflower*, to other important civic and religious figures, and to the first amendment to the Constitution of the United States.

Pilgrim Fathers Boarding the Mayflower

Anonymous. *Pilgrim Fathers boarding the Mayflower for their voyage to America.* After painting by Bernard Gribble. Ann Ronan Picture Library, London, Great Britain. (Credit: HIP/Art Resource, NY)

That amendment, however, reads in part, "Congress shall make no law respecting an establishment of religion, or prohibiting the free exercise thereof . . . ." It cuts two ways. (1) It prohibits the establishment of a state church. There would be nothing like the Church of England. That is, one did not need to be an Anglican or even a Christian, adhere to any particular set of religious beliefs, or follow any particular set of religious instructions or practice to enjoy full constitutional rights. (Alas, one did have to be a free male!) (2) There would be no restrictions of persons or groups in their exercise of religion.

The operative word is "religion." All religions, not just Christianity, are protected. Protestants in public schools would not wish to be forced to offer prayers through the Virgin Mary or to listen to readings from *The Book of Mormon*. Why, then, should Jewish, Muslim, Hindu, or atheistic children in public schools have to listen to prayers or to readings from the New Testament or to recite the Lord's Prayer?

2. However tolerant religiously the Persians may have been, they were also conquerors. They fought wars all around their land, from India to Greece to Egypt. They ruled subject peoples, no doubt, with an eye for what was in the Persians' own *self-interest*. Their religion, however, did not interfere with their politics, in particular with their war making, which is the most violent kind of political action.

Today the United States often enters wars against other peoples without being attacked as it was in World War II. It sends combat soldiers to various countries as "peace keepers" and conducts "police action" where it thinks its own interests or those of its allies are at stake. It is probably not coincidental that since the turn of the twenty-first century the United States has been engaged in battles in the area of the Persian Gulf, an area that holds perhaps as much as two-thirds of the world's proven petroleum reserves (not counting oil in shale). It may well be that the best interests of the United States and of the Gulf nations coincide, but years of warfare show that not everyone in the area agrees or at least not over how the profits from the sale of oil should be handled. It is too easy today for Americans to assume that they are always the victim or the potential victim and never the aggressor or the primary bene-factor.

3. Ezra 5 portrays Haggai and Zechariah as spokespersons for rebuilding the temple, not as the champions of morality moderns usually think of in connection with the prophets. Modern readers would do well, however, to recall the moral instructions of both books. The book of Haggai, to be sure, is quite short, but Haggai 2:22 anticipates God's overthrow of the powerful and brutal Babylonians for their sinfulness. Zechariah 1–8 is longer. It opens in Zechariah 1:2-6 with an explanation for the exile: it was God's punishment for the sinfulness of Judah. Next, it depicts the elimi-nation from Judah of thieves and liars (Zech 5:3) and the shipment of wickedness to Babylon (Zech 5:5-11). It reaches its ethical climax in Zechariah 7:9-10 with the commandments to "render true judgments, show kindness and mercy to one another . . . [and not to] oppress the widow, the orphan, the alien, or the poor, [and not to] devise evil in your heart against one another." Also perti-nent to this discussion is the picture in Zechariah 8:21-23 and Zechariah 14:16-21 of people from every nation coming to

Jerusalem to worship. Supporting the temple and demanding social justice, thus, were not mutually exclusive.

NOTES

1. *Matthew Henry Commentary on the Whole Bible*, http://www.biblestudytools .com/commentaries/matthew-henry-complete/ezra/5.html, on Ezra 5:3-17 (accessed 6 January 2014).

2. H. G. M. Williamson, *Ezra, Nehemiah* (WBC 16; Nashville: Thomas Nelson, 1987) 76.

3. Lester L. Grabbe ("'The Exile' under the Theodolite: Historiography as Triangulation," *Leading Captivity Captive; "The Exile" as History and Ideology* [ed. Lester L. Grabbe; JSOTSup 278; Sheffield: Sheffield Academic Press, 1998] 94) says that the letter from Tattenai is the document in the narrative most likely to be authentic. Even if the author did draw on such a letter (which is certainly possible), ancient historians did not adhere to modern standards of historiography. It seems clear that Ezra 5:11-12 draws from the Chronicler, and Ezra 5:13-16 repeats information from Ezra 1.

4. See the readable discussion by Peretz Reuven, "Wooden Beams from Herod's Temple Mount: Do They Still Exist?" *BARev* 39/3 (2013): 40–47, on this issue p. 44. The following article, "Cedars of Lebanon: Exploring the Roots," p. 52, shows a photo of an Egyptian depiction of cedars of Lebanon being shipped by sea to Egypt.

5. Sigmund Mowinckel, "אֻשַׁרְנָא Ezr. 5:3,9," *ST* 19 (1965): 130–35.

6. Erhard S. Gerstenberger, *Israel in the Persian Period: The Fifth and Fourth Centuries B.C.E.* (trans. Siegfried S. Schatzmann; Atlanta: Society of Biblical Literature, 2011) 102.

7. C. G. Tuland, "A Clarification of Terms, Date, and Text," *JNES* 17 (1956): 269–75, here 269.

COMPLETION OF
TEMPLE REPAIRS

Ezra 6

COMMENTARY

[Outline of Ezra 6] The letter from Tattenai (in Ezra 5:7-17) to King Darius I created the desired effect. The king ordered that the archives in Babylon be searched for the

Edict of Cyrus, since that is where (according to Ezra 1) the edict had been issued. It did not turn up there, however. Instead, a scroll with the inscription was found in Ecbatana, the capital of Media. (Cyrus had captured that city from an opponent named Astyages in 548 and used it as a power base.) As a consequence of reading the edict, Darius ordered that Tattenai permit the work on the temple to continue. Tattenai complied, and work resumed until the temple was completed on the third day of the month of Adar (the twelfth month of the year), in the sixth year of Darius (calculated often as March 12, 515 BCE). The people celebrated its completion with a dedication ceremony, and Passover was celebrated there on the fourteenth day of the new year (i.e., April 21, 515). With this event, the first complication in the plot of Ezra would be mastered.

The account of these events may be divided into four basic sections. The first, Ezra 6:1-12, describes the search for Cyrus's edict and its contents. Those contents come as no surprise to the reader of Ezra, since vv. 3-5 repeat Cyrus's orders in Ezra 1 concerning the building of the temple, and vv. 6-12 relate Darius's order to Tattenai that he permit the work to continue. The second section of the narrative, Ezra 6:13-15, summarizes the resulting work on the temple, leading to its completion. Third, Ezra 6:16-18 describes the ceremony of sacrifice dedicating the temple. Finally, Ezra 6:19-22 discusses the observance of the feast of Passover at the temple shortly thereafter.

Darius's Palace in Persepolis
This artist's reconstruction of Darius's palace in Persepolis captures its grandeur.

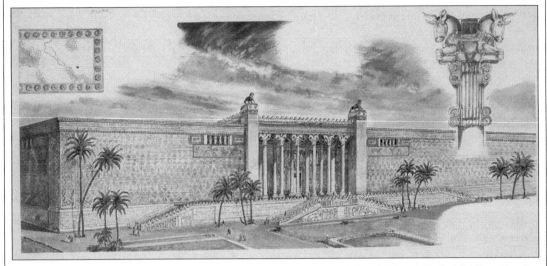

Reconstruction of Darius's Palace, called Apadana, in Persepolis with a map of Ancient Persia and detail of a capital. Artwork. (Credit: © DeA Picture Library/Art Resource, NY)

Resolution by Darius, 6:1-12

Ezra 5 ended (v. 17) with Tattenai's request that Darius verify the information given him by the leaders of Jerusalem by having the royal Persian archives in Babylon searched for a record of Cyrus's generosity to the returnees.[1] Apparently no such record was found there, but one was found on a scroll in Ecbatana. As reported in Ezra 6:3-5, Cyrus ordered that the temple be rebuilt, but these verses added dimensions not mentioned in Ezra 1. They also omitted the point in Ezra 1 that the Babylonians, like the Egyptians at the time of the exodus, gave the returnees gold and other valuables for their trip. He also ordered that the temple gold and other items taken from Jerusalem by Nebuchadnezzar be returned there and that the cost for rebuilding be borne by the Persian government.

The decree of King Darius in Ezra 6:3 called for a building sixty cubits tall and sixty cubits wide. [How Long Was a Cubit?] Although the length was not specified, one might *assume* sixty cubits again. In that case, the proposed building would have been a cube.[2] Its floor area, in any case, would have been three times the size of Solomon's temple in Jerusalem, which had measured only sixty by twenty cubits, and it stood only thirty cubits high (1 Kgs 6:2). The temple as rebuilt in Jerusalem under Zerubbabel, however, was a

How Long Was a Cubit?

The length of a cubit in ancient Israel was the length of a man's arm from the tip of the middle finger to the point of the elbow. The dimensions of buildings in Persepolis during the Persian Empire imply a length of 52 centimeters (i.e., about 20 inches).

Raz Kletter, "Weights and Measures," *NIDB*, 5.832–41, here 840.

plain building that drew ridicule or lamentation from some of the population of Jerusalem (Hag 2:3-9). The account in 2 Chronicles 3:2-3 of Solomon's building of the temple both informs and complicates the issue. There the nave (or main building) is said to have been sixty cubits long by twenty cubits wide. The height of the temple is not specified, but thirty cubits would be a good guess. Many scholars suppose simply that the numbers in the accounts were mangled in transmission and probably originally agreed with 2 Kings.[3] The vestibule in front of the nave, however, measured twenty feet across the entire front and one hundred twenty cubits tall (2 Chr 3:4)! In that case, the entryway would dominate and obscure the building itself. Readers should consult a commentary on Chronicles for help on that quandary.

What, then, might one conclude about the dimensions given in Ezra 6:3? They are said to have come from a decree from a Persian king. They might simply have been meant, therefore, to demonstrate the largess of that king, who had, after all, allowed the exiles to return.[4] The reality on the ground in Jerusalem in the early days and even at the time the redactor of Ezra-Nehemiah worked did not measure up in terms of size or grandeur. His resolution may have been that the Persian king authorized a grander building than the people of Yehud were able to build. The Chronicler, by contrast, conceived of Solomon's temple as the grandest temple ever built, a conception that may have caused him to overstate the temple's grandeur in order to emphasize to the post-exilic community to whom he wrote that Solomon had built a temple worthy of the great God worshiped in it.

In any case, Ezra 6 does not belabor the size of the new temple or suggest that it would be larger than Solomon's. Since the temple was a place for sacrifice (i.e., an outdoor activity), and since the population of early post-exilic Jerusalem and Yehud was quite small, there was no need for a larger building than the one that stood in Jerusalem in 586 when the city fell. Apparently, based on the reported description of the rebuilding of the temple and its plain appearance (see Hag 2:1-3), it was quite ordinary, if not actually embarrassing. Even if Darius did pay for its rebuilding, as he is said to have done in Ezra 6:8, the people commissioned to do the work were returnees, not necessarily craftsmen. Besides, who would want to insult the Persian king over the size of the temple he permitted and gave money to rebuild, especially since the king would never see it?

One other feature in the instructions for the temple merits attention: the phrase "three courses of hewn stones and one of timber"

(v. 4). Actually, the second phrase in the MT reads "a course of new," with the noun for "timber" perhaps implied, but such a reading seems unlikely. Who would use new, i.e., unseasoned, timber in a building? Consequently, the text is routinely understood to contain a defective spelling (one missing consonant) for the word "one." That solution is adopted here in the translation offered in the first sentence of the paragraph.[5]

Tattenai had observed (in Ezra 5:8) that "timber is laid in the walls." How, though, were the different "courses" (Ezra 6:4) constructed? Roland de Vaux reports that excavations in the Middle East show that timbers were used in stone and brick construction alike:

> Sometimes . . . wooden joists are found in a wall built entirely of stones; alternatively, the joist-framing sometimes begins above a stone footing and locks together a brick superstructure. . . . It may be, then, that the Temple had stone foundations, on top of which was a brick superstructure: the walls would have been paneled with cedar (1 Kgs 6:15) to hide the brick work . . . ."[6]

Regardless of what method was employed in Solomon's temple, the latter method seems to have been employed in the second. The prophet Haggai ordered the people to go to the hills, to cut and bring in wood, and to use it to rebuild the temple (Hag 1:8). That text, moreover, knows nothing of the Persian king's supplying the funds for rebuilding the temple or of stones. It seems likely that the builders would have used the stones left from Solomon's temple, and needed only to secure satisfactory wood. One could argue then that Ezra 4:1-3, like Haggai 1:8, reflects the beginning of the process circa 538/7 and speaks of the role of Zerubbabel and Joshua, while Ezra 6:1-18 describes Darius's decree and the work's completion in 520–515. (See further in connection with vv. 16-18.)

In any case, Ezra 6:6-12 describes a beneficent King Darius, who commands that Tattenai and his associates (or investigators[7]) not hinder the work. Actually, it is not clear in Ezra 5 that they intended to do so, but they did think it prudent to check out the returnees' claim to have permission from the Persian king just in case. The chapter's plot also takes a bit of a twist with the command that the cost of rebuilding be paid from "royal revenue," i.e., tax money collected by Tattenai and his officials as tribute to Darius. That command is often cited as evidence of the generosity and leniency of the Persians, and that conclusion might well be correct. Still, the text might hint that the money would come from taxes Tattenai collected from locals on behalf of Persia, but it was used in carrying out his responsibilities. Since Ezra-Nehemiah seems to have been compiled throughout the fourth century and not actually finished until the mid-second century (see the Introduction to Ezra-Nehemiah, "D. Languages, Text, and Place in the Hebrew Bible Canon"), certainty about historical details is impossible.

Verse 9 depicts Darius as ordering that sacrificial animals be provided by Tattenai for offering at the temple. That order seems quite surprising since Zoroastrianism (the religion practiced by the Achaemenid dynasty in Persia) did not enjoin sacrificing animals. [What Was Zoroastrianism?] Still, it is possible that Darius made provisions for his subjects who did. According to v. 10, he also provided money for sacrifices to be made on his behalf, thereby asserting the Persians' dominion over local religions. The returnees should not only offer those sacrifices in compliance with the practices of their own religion but also pray for the life and well-being of Darius himself. Disinterested practices, i.e., practices followed for their own sake and not for personal benefit, are rare in any culture or any religious tradition. Darius himself is portrayed here as covering all possibilities, although the reader perhaps was expected to read v. 10 as Darius's own recognition of Yʜᴡʜ's power. Similarly, Isaiah 45:1-7 is a message from God telling Cyrus that it was Yʜᴡʜ (not Ahura Mazda, god in Zoroastrianism) who placed Cyrus on the throne of Persia and gave him victory over Babylon. Theologically, Ezra and Second Isaiah agree about God's sovereignty over and use of the other nations to accomplish divine purposes.

Next, Darius pronounced a twofold curse on anyone (presumably Tattenai, members of his retinue, and/or people in Judah and Jerusalem) who altered his command by not carrying it out properly. A supporting beam would be pulled out of such a traitor's house, allowing or causing the house to fall on the disobedient occupant and impaling him in the process. The use of passive verbs probably indicates that Darius was calling for divine punishment. Regardless, v. 12 then invokes Yʜᴡʜ ("the God who has established his name there"), not a Persian or some other god who would have no interest in protecting a temple to Yʜᴡʜ, to destroy

What Was Zoroastrianism?

Zoroastrianism is named for its founder Zarathustra or Zoroaster, who lived in India perhaps in the late second millennium, or else in the seventh century ʙᴄᴇ, and who wrote hymns to the deity Ahura Mazda. Zoroaster appears to have been a monotheist who thought that Ahura Mazda created the dualities of good and evil. The Achaemenids (rulers of Persia from 559 to 331 ʙᴄᴇ) acknowledged him as their chief deity, but they never mention the man Zoroaster. Zoroastrian priests were known as magi, and fire was the chief symbol of their religion. Their religious practices were consistent with teaching in the Avesta, the scriptures of Zoroastrianism. Approximately 18,000 Zoroastrians survive today in Iran, but most live in and around Bombay, India.

See briefly W. G. Oxtoby, "Zoroastrianism," *Abingdon Dictionary of Living Religions* (ed. Keith Crim; Nashville: Abingdon, 1981) 827–29, here 827; and Martin Schwartz, "Zoroastrianism," *Funk & Wagnalls New Encyclopedia* (ed. Norma H. Dickey, Ramsey, NJ: Funk & Wagnalls, 1986) 28.172–74.

any person (e.g., Tattenai) who altered the decree or anyone (e.g., the opponents of the returnees in Judah) who interfered with efforts to carry out the rebuilding project. That warning employed the Deuteronomic idea that God caused God's "name" to dwell in the temple. (The phrase meant that God was present uniquely in the temple.) That warning also recognized the tension in Jerusalem over who would rebuild the temple, and it sided with the returnees and claimed imperial Persian authority and protection for them. It also formed an inclusio with Ezra 1:1-3, in which the Persian king Cyrus also recognized YHWH. The author then repeated the point in Ezra 6:22 to close out Ezra 1–6.

Completion of Rebuilding, 6:13-15

Ezra 6:13-15 offers the only description in the Bible of the work done in rebuilding the temple. Verse 13 might seem redundant in light of vv. 1-12, but its rhetorical effect is powerful. It reports that Tattenai and his envoy, armed with instructions from King Darius, returned to Jerusalem and "with diligence" did just what the king had commanded. These verses also constitute the second time in six chapters that the author insisted Persia authorized the returnees and them alone to do the building. The letter, therefore, was crucial to the politico/religious agenda of Ezra 1–6, indeed the whole book of Ezra, concerning who was allowed to rebuild and use the temple.

Verse 14 specified that the "elders" of the Jews built the temple. There is no mention of Sheshbazzar, despite his prominence in Ezra 1 and his mention in Ezra 5:14, or of Zerubbabel, despite his prominence in the predictions of both Haggai 2:20-23 and Zechariah 4:6-10a, as well as his being mentioned elsewhere in Ezra. Nor does the text of Ezra mention Joshua, the high priest, despite his prominence in Zechariah 3:1-10 and 6:9-15. The omission of Zerubbabel here suggests that Ezra 6:13-15 was crafted with the intention of excluding him from the narrative. Scholars sometimes explain his omission with the suggestion that he had died, and that is possible, although he may have simply returned to Babylon. Regardless, he is not mentioned. More important, the verses also reflect the late sixth-century reality that community influence among the returnees lay with their family heads, their elders, not with appointees of the Persian government. Differently stated, the authority to direct many kinds of behavior among the returnees was family based, and certain kinds of behavior were limited to those who had been in exile and returned. The verses intended, moreover, that life in the new Jerusalem would reflect that reality.

Ezra 6:14 does contain one anachronism, however. In speaking of the dedication of the temple in the sixth year of King Darius, it also says the returnees "finished their building by the command of Cyrus, Darius, and Artaxerxes" (r. 465–424). The mention of the latter king was clearly an anachronism, since the temple was finished in 515, some fifty years before the beginning of his reign. The eleventh-century Jewish teacher Rashi got around that conclusion by understanding the name "Artaxerxes" as a dynastic title like "Pharaoh," but it is clearly the name of the Persian ruler mentioned in the next chapter.[8] Mentioning him, therefore, was apparently a touch of the redactor who inserted the narrative about rebuilding the wall (actually directed by Nehemiah after 445) into the narrative about the temple. (See the discussion of the Persian kings under "The Use of Two Languages" in the comments on Ezra 4.)

The role of Haggai and Zechariah in the rebuilding process was mentioned again in v. 14, thus rounding off the narrative that began in Ezra 5:1 with the mention of the action of the two men. Both verses content themselves with mentioning the two prophets, and neither quotes them nor ascribes to them any specific action other than "prophesying." Prophetic endorsement was important to the author of these chapters, but the agenda of the author was so focused on the rebuilding of the temple that there was no need to quote either man directly or to ascribe any particular role in the events to them. Indeed, the books that bear their names ascribe them no function other than prophesying.

The discussion of rebuilding the temple concludes with the statement that the temple was finished on the third day of the month of Adar in the sixth year of the reign of King Darius, often calculated as March 12, 515. The Deuterocanonical 1 Esdras 7:5 gives the date as the twenty-third day of the month of Adar. Either the word for twenty dropped out of the MT, or it was added to 1 Esdras. Either way, the date was five years later than the date the work stopped in Ezra 4:24, and the inquiry was directed to Darius. What actually happened during those five years was left untold, as was the time between 539 and 520.

Dedication of the Temple, 6:16-18

Those who dedicated the temple were listed as "The people of Israel, the priests and the Levites, and the rest of the returned exiles . . . ." At first glance, the sentence sounds all-inclusive, but that glance is illusive. Thus far in Ezra, the term "Israel" had been used several times in the phrase "the God of Israel," which is a traditional title for God; in Ezra 2:59, where it distinguished ethnic Israelites from others among people who had returned from the exile; in Ezra 3:10 in connection with David, king of Israel; and in Ezra 4:3, where it distinguished those who had returned from exile from other people living in Yehud. In view of the exclusionary bent of the narrative of the rebuilding of the temple, it seems likely that the phrase "the people of Israel" at the beginning of v. 16 referred only to the returnees. The phrase "the priests and the Levites, and the rest of the returned exiles" then constitutes an appositive, specifying who was meant by the phrase "people of Israel." Williamson points to its use in Ezra 1:5 to describe the exiles in Babylon.[9] If this understanding of the phrase is correct, this text perhaps casts light on and is illuminated by Haggai 1:1–2:9, which also reflects tension between the prophet and citizens of Jerusalem/Judah who had done little to nothing to rebuild the temple between 539 and 520. It would appear that the impetus for the rebuilding project still lay with the former exiles in 520. People in the land during the exile presumably sacrificed elsewhere, perhaps in a northern shrine like Bethel (see Zech 7:1-7; 8:18-23). Be that as it may, Isaiah 56:3-8 insists that God would welcome foreigners to the new temple in Jerusalem. The exclusivistic voice of Ezra was not the Hebrew Bible's only word on who was welcome at the temple.

The builders celebrated their achievement with joy and with abundant sacrifices: one hundred bulls, two hundred rams, and four hundred lambs, plus twelve male goats as a sin offering for "all Israel" (i.e., the returnees). The description of the celebration is modeled after the description of the dedication of Solomon's temple in 2 Chronicles 7:4-7, which, in turn, was modeled after 1 Kings 8:62-63, although both of those passages report vastly more animals sacrificed on that occasion. The comparatively moderate numbers in Ezra 6, therefore, speak for the accuracy of its report.

Verse 18 concludes the account of the dedication with the statement that the people "set the priests in their divisions and the Levites in their courses for the service of God at Jerusalem . . . ." The relationship between priests and Levites was long and bumpy, and it is difficult to sort out to say the least. [Priests and Levites] This verse, however, does little more than assert that the two groups were properly installed for their service at the temple. The verse does end with a note that has attracted scholarly discussion: "as it is written in the book of Moses." J. M. Myers thinks the allusion is to texts like Exodus 29 and Leviticus 8 (in connection with priests), Numbers 3:5-39 (in connection with priests and Levites), and Numbers 8:5-19 (in connection with Levites),[10] but those texts do not actually deal with what each group did. Other scholars point to 1 Chronicles 23–26 as the more pertinent source and assume the citation was erroneous.[11] The Chronicler devotes those chapters to David's census of the families of Levites and the divisions of the priests and their respective functions. In fact, 1 Chronicles 26 adds gatekeepers to the list of officials who received Davidic instructions. The immediate context for 1 Chronicles 23–26, however, is David's charge to Solomon that he observe "the statutes and the ordinances that the LORD commanded Moses for Israel." Even if the actual source the author of Ezra 6:18 had in mind was 1 Chronicles 23–26, that passage itself cites Moses, and the author of Ezra 6:18 appealed to him.

Ezra 6:18 concludes the Aramaic-language section that began in Ezra 4:8. (The book of Ezra-Nehemiah also employs another Aramaic document in Ezra 7:12-26.) The use of Aramaic in 4:8–6:18 was probably to lend a more authentic tone to the reports in which it appears. The verses that follow in Ezra 6:19-22, although in Hebrew, continue and conclude the discussion of sixth-century Jerusalem and its temple.

Priests and Levites

Levi was the third son of Jacob by his first wife Leah, according to Gen 29:34, and the Bible traces both Moses and Aaron back to him, though in some traditions Aaron is more a troubler than a priest and Exod 32 portrays him unorthodox. During the period in the wilderness, Levites are portrayed as acting as priests, though Moses' Midianite father-in-law Jethro did as well. Thus priesthood was not exclusive to Levites even in Israel. Priestly traditions in the Pentateuch, however, do portray the priesthood as Levitical and even Aaronic. That portrayal looks to be an after-the-fact revision of earlier traditions. In the Deuteronomistic books (Joshua through 2 Kings), the triumph of the Levites as the priestly clan comes through, and all Levites are deemed priests (Deut 18:1-8).

The reality before the time of Josiah (r. c. 640–609) may have been less strict. One of David's two priests, Zadok, simply appears on the scene, and he may have been a priest in Jerusalem before it became Israelite. In any case, the thrust of Josiah's reforms as spelled out in Deuteronomic 2 Kings 22:3–23:25 was to (re)install Levitical priests in full control of the temple in Jerusalem. Moreover, there were Levitical groups in northern Israel as well as in Judah, but they seem to have been out of luck. The latest development temporally seems to be the ascendance of Aaronites only as priests, with other Levites relegated to lesser roles than offering the sacrifices. The exilic prophet Ezekiel divides them into two groups, one (the sons of Zadok) in charge of sacrifices and the other in charge of caring for the temple itself. In post-exilic 1 and 2 Chronicles, Levites are composed of three different groups, each with particular duties.

For more, see Merlin D. Rehm, "Levites and Priests," *ABD* 4.297–310.

As just mentioned, v. 19 switches from Aramaic back to Hebrew without acknowledgment, unlike the switch from Hebrew to Aramaic, which was acknowledged in Ezra 4:7. The explanation for that switch might be that Aramaic was used simply to establish the legitimacy of rebuilding the temple as an act ordered by Persia, while the observance of Passover was a purely Yehudite matter.

Keeping the Feast of Passover, 6:19-22

That festival was observed on the fourteenth day of the first month (Nisan) of the new year (515). It is interesting to note in passing that the Aramaic passage dated events in terms of the Babylonian calendar, but the Hebrew passage beginning in v. 19 gives the number of the month, the most common dating system in the Hebrew Bible. This difference is further evidence that the book of Ezra was cobbled together from different sources, and that no unified dating or other system was superimposed on the whole of Ezra, let alone of Ezra-Nehemiah.

Ezra 6:19-22 relates the first Passover in the rebuilt temple. According to Exodus 12:1-10, Passover was instituted as a home observance, but according to Deuteronomy 16:5-6 (perhaps dated to the time of Josiah [r. 640–609]), it was to be observed in Jerusalem. The issue became moot when the temple was destroyed, but it came alive again when the temple was rebuilt. Verse 20 says that the priests and Levites purified themselves and killed the Passover lambs for the returned exiles, their fellow priests, and themselves. Verse 21 specifically includes both returnees and "all who had joined them and separated themselves from the pollutions of the nations of the land to worship the LORD, the God of Israel." That description recognizes the participation of at least some of those who had remained behind. Ezra 9–10 will reduce this larger group of celebrants exclusively to returnees again, however, suggesting that v. 21 rests on old traditions. The concluding verse, Ezra 6:22, says that the people celebrated the feast of unleavened bread (which was observed the first seven days after Passover) with great joy.

That verse also adds a strange note: YHWH "had turned the heart of the king of *Assyria* to them, so that he aided them in the work on the house of God, the God of Israel." It was—according to the narrative just completed—Darius, the king of Persia, who had helped them. Why, then, speak of him as the king of Assyria? Technically he was Assyria's king, of course, since Persia captured Assyria as part of its empire. Still, Assyria was a small part. J. G. McConville argues that this unexpected reference to Assyria marks Darius as "the true descendant of [the Assyrian kings] Sennacherib and Shalmaneser," enemies who had attacked Judah 9 (2 Kings 18-19; 2 Chronicles 31)," and that Nehemiah 9:32 shows a similar perspective.[12] That may be too strong a statement, although modern readers should not overestimate the generosity and open-mindedness of the Persians. Williamson is probably more correct when he suggests that Assyria was thought of sometimes as the stereotypical foreign kingdom and that the Persians thought of themselves as the successors of Assyria/Babylon.[13] Perhaps the thinking was this: if the Persians were the successor of Assyria/Babylon, it was appropriate for them to pay for the restitution of the temple destroyed by Babylon. Moreover, Joseph Fleishman maintains that these verses "conclude the history of the celebration of the festival as well as the period of the destruction of Israel since the Assyrian invasion. These verses contain elements by means of which the author wished to give the reader a feeling of hope which permeated the people who returned."[14]

The first part of the tripartite plan for Ezra-Nehemiah comes to a close with Ezra 6:19-22. Ezra-Nehemiah is composed in three parts, each with its own purpose. The narrative designed to legitimate the returnees as the proper religious and local political leaders of Yehud was complete. They had come back under the commission and with the assistance of the Persian emperor Cyrus. As far as the *redactor of Ezra-Nehemiah* was concerned, the temple was for their exclusive use. Ezra 7–10 will skip ahead a couple of generations, but it too was written to defend the prerogatives of the returnees over against any claims that the people who had remained behind in Yehud might claim or desire for themselves. Ezra returned with another small group of returnees to assure the ethical purity of worshipers there, a purity guaranteed by descent from the original returnees. That claim had political ramifications, which is why Ezra 1–6, 7–10 and the narrative of Nehemiah place so much emphasis on their appointment by the Persians and their careful compliance with the Persians. Finally, the book of Nehemiah will defend the ongoing rights and privileges of the returnees over against those of the Samaritans and those in Yehud who cooperated or at least sympathized with the Samaritans. It will describe the rebuilding of the walls of Jerusalem by the descendants of returnees only, making the city a holy zone/area around the temple, thus protecting it from ritual and ethical contamination. Overall as well perhaps, Ezra-Nehemiah was written to legitimate the claims of the returnees in the eyes of the *captives still in Babylon* and gain their agreement with and approval of the actions the returnees had taken.

CONNECTIONS

1. The returnees' exclusion of persons desiring to participate in the construction of the temple and participation in worship there was

wrong, just as exclusionary practices are wrong for Christians today. I am old enough to remember when deacons in a local church in my hometown threatened personally to block any African Americans who attempted to enter for Sunday morning worship. Such an affront to Southern segregation would have to be stopped. This threat was made despite the fact that the janitor of that church was a black man who had on at least one occasion to my knowledge brought a significant number of people from his church to that white church to hear a well-known evangelist. That night the pastor at the time had recognized him and his friends and welcomed them. I am sure that well-meaning adults thought their janitor would have been sincere and that his presence and that of his friends was appropriate. They also seem to have thought that anyone who came on Sunday in the heat of civil rights conflicts would have come "just to cause trouble."

I am not naïve. I know perfectly well that behind Jim Crow laws and behind segregated facilities, churches, lunch counters, and restrooms, and behind various laws and other practices lay the fear of losing one's job to someone who would work for less money, seeing the value of one's house plunge if the neighborhood desegregated, and a genuine but prejudiced fear that one's child might want to marry one of "them."

If the truth be known, my most recent trips back to my hometown have revealed mixed marriages, or at least mixed couples with children. The "worst fears" of segregationists came true, perhaps in their own families. Still, I have to ask whether the important issue is the color of a person's skin. Is it not, rather, the quality of a person's character? It has not escaped my attention that during my adult life, the entertainment and the sports worlds have accepted black performers and athletes on a broad scale, while 11:00 on Sunday morning remains what has been termed "the most segregated hour of the week in America." I salute denominations that have elected or appointed black or other minority pastors as presidents or bishops. I do not, however, see many thoroughly integrated churches.

A black friend of mine observed at a Martin Luther King Jr. Day celebration a few years ago that he thought the real barriers to integrating churches now are more cultural than racial. I do not know if he is correct. I do know that I love the music played and sung in my church, and it resembles the kind of music I buy or listen to in the media (especially public radio and television). I am not sure what to do about that situation. Do I go to a church, white or black, for the purpose of "integrating" it? As far as I know, I would

Segregation in the South

Jack Delano, photographer. At the bus station in Durham, North Carolina. May 1940. (Credit: Library of Congress, Prints and Photographs Division, Washington, DC)

be welcome in any church in my town, and anyone would be welcome in my church. Still, my presence would make some people uncomfortable. I am a retired college professor of religion. I love a sermon that stimulates me to think, and I relish and teach a Sunday school class that thrives on open discussion. I know, however, that my church does not appeal to a large percent of people in our community, even if they give us credit for our ministries to people in need. I am not the victim of deliberate exclusion, and I pray that our church does not deliberately exclude people.

2. It is worth noting that Persia is said to have paid for the reconstruction of the temple, and it is clear from the book of Ezra and other post-exilic texts that Persia controlled much that went on there. The returnees ran it, and the investigation by Tattenai shows that Persians controlled everything public in the province, including the temple. We might find such control objectionable because our sympathies lie with Judah, and maybe just the returnees only. That is clearly true for the sympathies of the author(s) of Ezra 1–6. We might remind ourselves, however, that what government pays for, government will (and perhaps even must) control.

3. The Persian kings were Zoroastrians who did not offer animal sacrifices, although Ezra 6 shows them not just permitting the people of Israel to do so but also paying for rebuilding the altar and the initial sacrifices. Worship in the Hebrew Bible, however, centered on sacrifice, although prayer, singing, dancing, and other actions were also included. The New Testament depicts Jesus going to the temple, although not having sacrifices offered on his behalf. Mark 12:33 quotes Jesus as saying that loving God and other people was superior to offering sacrifices. The New Testament also portrays Jesus as sinless and not needing some type of sacrifice, and the Synoptics portray his final meal as the feast of Passover. The Gospel of John, by contrast, times his death to coincide with the slaying of the Paschal lamb, thereby depicting Jesus as the perfect sacrifice (cf. 1 Cor 5:7). Thus, the New Testament seems not to condemn the practice of offering sacrifice, but it does say that Jesus's death was the great sacrifice, offered once for all (Heb 10:1-18). For early Christians, it eliminated any need for sacrifices.

Jews also abandoned the offering of sacrifices after the Romans destroyed the temple and prohibited Jews from using it. The Rabbis then taught that contemplating the sacrificial texts was what was really required. How could they make such a change? For one thing, they had no choice, since no altar except the ruined one at the temple would be legitimate. For another thing, though, they came to see that repentance was what really counted. Without repentance, a sacrifice was of no avail. It was a logical step after the destruction of the temple in 70 CE simply to repent and to meditate on sacrifice.

NOTES

1. *Matthew Henry Commentary on the Whole Bible*, http://www.biblestudytools .com/commentaries/matthew-henry-complete/ezra/6.html, on Ezra 6:3-5 (accessed 6 January 2014).

2. Ralph W. Klein, "The Books of Ezra and Nehemiah," *New Interpreter's Bible* (ed. Leander E. Keck; Nashville: Abingdon, 1999) 3.708.

3. One might note also that Ezekiel's vision of the new temple (Ezek 40:48–42:20) had different measurements than Solomon's as well, although those dimensions also are cumbersome and describe a future temple.

4. Bede, *Homilies on the Gospels* 2.1, in Marco Conti, ed., *Ancient Christian Commentary on Scripture: Old Testament. V. 1-2 Kings 1-2 Chronicles, Ezra, Nehemiah, Esther* (Downers Grove IL: Intervarsity, 2008) 317.

5. See the footnote on Ezra 6:4 in *Biblia Hebraica Stuttgartensia*, p. 1420. Phillip A. Noss and Kenneth J. Thomas (*A Handbook on Ezra and Nehemiah* [USB Handbook Series; New York: United Bible Societies, 2005] 132) recommend that Bible Society translators adopt that reading.

6. Roland de Vaux, *Ancient Israel: Its Life and Institutions* (trans. John McHugh; New York, Toronto, London: McGraw-Hill, 1961) 316. Emmett Willard Hamrick ("Ezra," *The Broadman Bible Commentary* [ed. J. Clifton Allen; Nashville: Broadman, 1970] 452) suggests that the wood was used to reinforce the walls against earthquakes.

7. Frithiof Rundgren, "Über einen juristischen Terminus bei Esra 6 6," *ZAW* 70 (1958): 209–15, here 214.

8. See Judah J. Slotki, *Daniel • Ezra • Nehemiah* (Soncino Books of the Bible; London, New York: Soncino Press, 1985) 146. Diane Edelman (*The Origins of the "Second" Temple: Persian Imperial Policy and the Rebuilding of Jerusalem* [Bible World; London: Equinox, 2005]) proposed a drastic reinterpretation of post-exilic chronology, situating this dedication at a time early in the reign of Artaxerxes I (465–425 BCE), an attempt rejected by Ralph W. Klein ("Were Joshua, Zerubbabel, and Nehemiah Contemporaries? A Response to Diane Edelman's Proposed Late Date for the Second Temple," *JBL* 127 [2008] 697–701) on the grounds that her dates conflict with Haggai, Zechariah 1–8, and the basic flow of Ezra 1–6.

9. H. G. M. Williamson, *Ezra, Nehemiah* (WBC; Nashville: Thomas Nelson, 1985) 84.

10. Jacob M. Myers, *Ezra-Nehemiah* (AB 14; Garden City: Doubleday, 1965) 53.

11. See, for example, D. J. A. Clines, *Ezra, Nehemiah, Esther* (NCB; Grand Rapids MI: Eerdmans and London: Marshall, Morgan & Scott, 1984) 96.

12. J. G. McConville, "Ezra-Nehemiah and the Fulfillment of Prophecy," *VT* 36/2 (1986): 205–24; here 208, 223–24.

13. Williamson, *Ezra, Nehemiah*, 85–86.

14. Joseph Fleishman, "An Echo of Optimism in Ezra 6:19-22," *HUCA* 69 (1998): 15.

PART TWO: REBUILDING THE TEMPLE COMMUNITY, EZRA 7:1–10:44

PREPARATION IN BABYLON FOR A RETURN WITH EZRA

Ezra 7

COMMENTARY

[Outline of Ezra 7:1–10:44] Ezra 7–10 constitutes the second major section of Ezra-Nehemiah. If Ezra 1–6 was designed to legitimate the returnees as the proper religious and local political leaders of Yehud, Ezra 7–10 skips ahead a couple of generations to defend the prerogatives of the returnees over against any claims that the people who had remained behind in defeated Judah might claim or desire for themselves. Ezra returned with another small group of returnees and decided to assure the ethical purity of worshipers there, a purity guaranteed by descent from the original returnees. That claim had political ramifications, which is why Ezra 1–6, 7–10 and the book of Nehemiah place so much emphasis on their appointment by the Persians and their careful compliance with the Persians. As will be seen in connection with the book of Nehemiah, Ezra-Nehemiah was written to defend the ongoing rights and perks of the returnees over against those of those in Yehud who had not been in Babylon.

> **Outline of Ezra 7:1–10:44**
>
> Preparations in Babylon, 7:1-28
>   Narrator's Introduction of Ezra and his Task, 7:1-10
>   Letter of Artaxerxes to Ezra in Aramaic, 7:11-26
>   Ezra's Praise of God in Response, 7:27-28
> Initial Implementation of the Task, 8:1-36
>   List of Returnees by Fathers' Houses, 8:1-14
>   Assembly and Recruitment of Levites, 8:15-20
>   Further Preparations: Sanctification, 8:21-30
>   Journey and Arrival, 8:31-34
>   Offerings for the Temple, 8:35
>   Support for Temple and People, 8:36
> Conflict Concerning the Purity of the Community, 9:1-15
>   Report about Mixed Marriages, 9:1-2
>   Ezra's Reaction: Mourning and Prayer, 9:3-15
> Resolution: Separation from Foreign Wives, 10:1-17
>   Ezra's Action and Communal Reaction, 10:1-6
>   Communal Assembly to Bring about Separation, 10:7-17
> Conclusion: the Separated Community, 10:18-44
>   List of People Involved, 10:18-43
>   Concluding Summary, 10:44

A preview of Ezra 7–10 is in order. Some exiles had returned home, the altar and temple had been rebuilt, but still not all was well. In Ezra 7 a complication carries over from Ezra 1–6, namely the presence within Yehud of people or children of people who had not been in Babylon. In chapter 7, readers begin the second major section of Ezra-Nehemiah, which focuses on rebuilding the Yehudite (Returnee) community by restoring the Law to its preeminent position in the community. Readers also finally meet the book's namesake. He was a priest who descended from a long line of priests said to reach back to Aaron (Ezra 7:1-6). (See the discussion of Ezra in the Introduction to Ezra.) He was born in Babylon, but he chose to journey to Jerusalem in the seventh year of King Artaxerxes. His work was to study and enforce the Law of Moses in Jerusalem. P. R. Davies cautions, however, that modern readers need to realize that despite the impression possibly given that the laws of the Pentateuch had been "inherited" exclusively from the past, much of that material was produced during the Persian Period.[1] In other words, the exact contents of the "law" read by Ezra (in Neh 8:3-8) are not clear. In fact, where Ezra seems to quote Torah (Ezra 9:11-12), what one reads appears to be allusions to Leviticus 18:15; Deuteronomy 1:38-39; 6:11; 7:1, 3; 11:8; 18:9; 23:6; *and* 2 Kings 21:16.[2] It is not, therefore, an allusion exclusively to Torah in the canonical sense,[3] but it comes close. Readers also ought to remember that the book of Ezra-Nehemiah itself arose sometime after the career of Nehemiah, in its final form centuries after that time.

In recounting that return, Ezra 7 repeats the exodus theme from Ezra 2. Ezra 7:1-10 reports that Ezra and others from Babylon gathered to return to Jerusalem. Ezra 7:11–8:36 then relates the events of their journey. Within those verses, Ezra 7:11-24 reports the contents of a letter from Artaxerxes commanding Ezra to convey silver and gold from Artaxerxes to Yehud to underwrite the expenses of the temple and commanding heads of provinces through which they passed to aid when necessary. Next, according to Ezra 7:25-26, Artaxerxes commissioned Ezra to teach the law of Ezra's God and of the Persian Empire. (Like Ezra 4:8–6:18, this letter was written in Aramaic.) Ezra 7 closes with an exclamation (Ezra 7:27-28) in which the narrative abruptly switches from Aramaic to Hebrew and from the third person limited to the first person singular point of view, a perspective that extends through the end of the book.

Those two verses also provide a transition to Ezra 8:1-14, which lists the names of leading families and the numbers of families who returned with Ezra. The families themselves had already been mentioned briefly in Ezra 7:7, but not discussed. According to chapter 8, they numbered 1,378, with 135 more families coming "later." Assuming at least four persons per family on average, that group of returnees would have totaled ± 6,000. (Though smaller than the nearly 50,000 said to have returned in 539 [Ezra 2:1-65 // Neh 7:5-73a], thousands of additional newcomers would have constituted a large group of new returnees to be assimilated.) They gathered at "the river that runs to Ahava" (v. 15), where Ezra discovered he had no Levites in his company. He sent eleven men back to a place named Casiphia to find Levites willing to go to Yehud. Eighteen Levites answered the call, plus 220 descendants of temple servants. [Ahava and Casiphia] Both groups presumably brought their families, adding a total of 1,000 or more to Ezra's company. After fasting, praying, and making preparations (Ezra 8:18-30), the group traveled to Jerusalem (Ezra 8:31-39).

Ezra 9:1-4 reports the intermarriage of "the people of Israel" with people from surrounding areas. Their behavior constitutes the last major complication in the plot of the book of Ezra. Its namesake offered a prayer of confession for the offending returnees, which he ended by confessing that God was angry over such transgression (Ezra 9:5-15). Who were these people that had behaved so poorly? The answer is that the offending people were returnees from 539 who had married local people. Those locals were the people who had remained behind in Judah after the exile and then joined the returnees as mentioned in Ezra 6:21. Ezra became adamant that the returnees divorce those wives, i.e., send them away along with their children. Many of the accused returnees responded by confessing their sins (Ezra 10:1-5) and divorcing the "foreign" wives (Ezra 10:6-44). No matter how satisfied Ezra might have been at the outcome, the events discussed in Ezra 9–10 raise serious ethical questions about the treatment of these families. Even if the people sinned by marrying non-returnees (and it is not clear to me, nor had it been to them, perhaps, why such behavior was sinful), did their wives' status (as people of Yehud left behind after the fall of Jerusalem) warrant breaking up the families?

The Narrator's Introduction of Ezra and his Task, 7:1-10

[Outline of Ezra 7] With little notice (simply the words "After this"), the narrative of the book of Ezra jumps forward in time from 515 BCE (Ezra 6:15) to the reign of "Artaxerxes." The king in view apparently should be understood as Artaxerxes I

Ahava and Casiphia

Ezra 8:15 speaks of a river that runs to a place called Ahava, while vv. 21 and 31 speak of the river (or canal) Ahava. It appears that the author thought the river and canal had the same name. The locations of Ahava and Casiphia, however, are unknown, though they seem to have been located near Babylonia on a westward route, Casiphia east of (or closer to Babylon than) Ahava. Scholars sometimes point to Ophis, Awana, and Itus as possible sites for Ahava, and to Ctesiphon on the Tigris River for Casiphia.

Outline of Ezra 7

Narrator's Identification of Ezra and his Task, 7:1-10

Letter of Artaxerxes to Ezra (in Aramaic), 7:11-26

Ezra's Praise of God in Response, 7:27-28

(r. 465–424) not Artaxerxes II (r. 404–358), and it is possible that the author of Ezra-Nehemiah did not know there was more than one. (See [Artaxerxes I or II?].) In any case, he lists only Cyrus (r. 539–c. 531), Darius (r. c. 520–486), Ahasuerus or Xerxes (r. 486–465), and Artaxerxes, omitting Cambyses (r. 530–522) and mentioning none later. The activities narrated in Ezra 7–10 could have occurred during the reign of either Artaxerxes, and there is no *compelling* way to settle the debate. On the whole, however, Artaxerxes I may be more likely. If so, the date would be 458. If Artaxerxes II was in view, the date would be 398, and any actual overlap between the careers of Ezra and Nehemiah would have been practically impossible (assuming that Nehemiah himself flourished during the reign of Artaxerxes I), which few scholars contest.

Scholars have offered other dates for Ezra in view of the problems connected with corroborating Ezra's career with Nehemiah's. One suggestion is to date his activity shortly before 448 on the basis of comparisons with Persian texts or to take the reference to the "seventh year of King Artaxerxes" in Ezra 7:7 as designating a *sabbatical* year, in this case 444/443.[4] Variations such as these last two arise in connection with trying to ascertain more particularly the context for Ezra's return, and are important, but they derive from accepting the date in the career of Artaxerxes I as approximately correct. One last suggestion, advanced originally by A. van Hoonaker and defended by a host of other scholars including H. H. Rowley, is that Ezra flourished in 428, the thirty-seventh year of Artaxerxes, but that the Hebrew word for "thirty" fell out of the text. J. A. Emerton, however, carefully discussed the reasons adduced for that view, found them all unconvincing, and argued instead for 398, during the reign of Artaxerxes II.[5] O. Margalith, by contrast, suggested that a strong, pro-Persian government in Yehud would be beneficial to Persian interests along the Mediterranean coast, which led Artaxerxes I to send Ezra to Jerusalem.[6] Such enlightened self-interest appears to offer a possible explanation for a Persian ruler to allow Ezra's journey to Yehud. This commentary, then, will follow the traditional view that Artaxerxes I was in view. Otherwise, even the basic, chronological sequence of Ezra-Nehemiah must be taken as in error. In addition, the placing of the Ezra narrative in Nehemiah 7:73b–8:18 would have to be seen as completely anachronistic. Taking both dates as more or less correct makes Ezra and Nehemiah contemporaries, but men with different missions.

Readers of the book of Ezra-Nehemiah first encounter King Artaxerxes (i.e., Artaxerxes I, r. 465–424) in Ezra 4:7-23, an anticipatory narrative in which the king postponed the rebuilding of the city of Jerusalem, especially its wall, while he investigated the matter. Ezra 7:73b–8:18, dated in the seventh year of his reign (i.e., 458), shows no cognizance of that letter or the issue it raised. Nor need one expect it to do so, since the date of that letter would fall later during the time of Nehemiah's work in Jerusalem beginning thirteen years later in 445, the twentieth year of Artaxerxes' reign and about the beginning of the reign of Sanballat (r. c. 445–408).[7]

Ezra 7:1-5 traces Ezra's lineage back to Aaron, the brother of Moses. All the men named were pre-exilic priests; none was from the period of the exile or the time covered by Ezra 1–6. Given his illustrious lineage, the legitimacy of Ezra's priestly status was above reproach; he had roots not just back to the original temple but to the very first priest Aaron as well. Except for the last three (Phineas, Eleazar, and Aaron), the names in this list also appear in lists of priests in 1 Chronicles 6. [Ezra's Lineage according to Ezra 7:1-5]

Ezra's Lineage according to Ezra 7:1-5

Name	Information	Where Mentioned Elsewhere
Seraiah	Son Jehozadak taken into exile in 586	1 Chr 6:14
Azaria	Father of Seriah	1 Chr 6:14
Hilkiah	Father of Azariah	1 Chr 6:13
Shallum	Father of Hilkiah	1 Chr 6:13
Zadok	One of two concurrent high priests under David	1 Chr 6:53; 18:16
Ahitub	Son of Amariah; grandfather of Zadok	1 Chr 6:12; 6:52; 18:16
Amariah	Son of Azariah	1 Chr 6:10
Azariah	Son of Merioth	1 Chr 6:9; 6:52
Meraioth	Son of Zerathiah	1 Chr 6:5; 6:52
Zerahiah	Son of Uzzi	1 Chr 6:6; 6:51
Uzzi	Son of Bukki	1 Chr 6:5; 6:51
Bukki	Descendant of Aaron through Abishua	1 Chr 6:5; 6:51
Abishua	Son of Phineas	1 Chr 6:4-5; 6:50
Phineas	Son of Eleazar	1 Chr 6:4; 6:50
Eleazar	Third son of Aaron by Elisheba	1 Chr 6:3; 6:50
Aaron	Brother of Moses	1 Chr 6:3; 6:50

Many of the names are mentioned twice in 1 Chronicles 6, but vv. 50-53 list all but Azariah, who is picked up from the longer list in vv. 3-15.

What is a reader to make of this genealogy? First, there are no post-exilic priests in it. That omission is startling, since those names presumably would have been the easiest to come by, at least the name of Ezra's father. Second, no priest is mentioned that is not known from Chronicles, which the opening verses of Ezra quoted verbatim. The entire genealogy, therefore, *could* have been drawn from 1 Chr 6. Third, in the ensuing narratives, Ezra undertakes no priestly duties. Finally, Ezra was explicitly called a scribe as well. These observations have led some scholars to conclude that Ezra was not really a priest and the genealogy was simply drawn from 1 Chr 6. That conclusion is too drastic, but readers should note that Ezra exercised no priestly duties, though his role in the issue of mixed marriages in chapters 9–10 might well have been of interest to the priests. At least this much seems clear: the author provided Ezra's priestly background to enhance Ezra's prestige and his right to say who could and who could not worship in the temple.

The priests named come from different periods. The first name, Seraiah, also appears in 1 Chronicles 6:14. The name Seraiah was quite common in the Hebrew Bible, which mentioned ten different men by that name. The one in view here was the father of Jehozadak, who was taken into exile in 586. Seraiah, therefore, was the last high priest before the exile to fulfill his whole term. The next name, Azariah, was common too, being held by perhaps twenty-five different men. The one in view here was the grandfather of Jehozadak. The third, Hilkiah, was the name of a number of different people too, including (here) the priest who discovered the law book in the temple in 622, during the reign of Josiah (640–609), and who was a leader in the ensuing reformation (2 Chr 34:9-28).

Then the genealogy jumps back from the late seventh to the tenth century. The first name from that period was Shallum, another common name, but the one in view here is the Shallum who was the son of the high priest Zadok (1 Chr 6:12-13), the man next mentioned. Zadok, of course, was the priest in Jerusalem named co-chief priest with Abiathar by David. Abiathar had been a companion of David during the time he was running from Saul. Zadok may have been a resident of Jerusalem when David captured it, since he simply appears in the narrative after that event.

Priests by the names Ahitub, Amariah, Azariah, and Meraioth (see Ezra 7:2-3) appear twice in 1 Chronicles: 6:7-12 and 6:50-53. They appear to have lived before the career of David, so they would not have served in Jerusalem. Both 1 Chronicles 6:5 and 6:50 call Abishua, the next priest (Ezra 7:5), the descendant of Phineas. He is the earliest person named in the material common to Chronicles and Ezra.

The last three names in the list, Phineas, Eleazar, and Aaron, are known from the Pentateuch. The first two were direct descendants of the third and earliest, Aaron. He was, of course, a Levite, the brother of Moses, and the patriarch of the Aaronic priests as far as Exodus through Numbers, Chronicles, and Ezra-Nehemiah are concerned. Numbers 3:9-10 makes absolutely clear that Aaron and his sons alone were the priests and that the Levites functioned merely as assistants. Joshua, Judges, and 1 Samuel, however, seem to recognize the legitimacy of other priestly groups and other sanctuaries. Archaeological data partly corroborate this latter view. Sacrifices were offered at a number of Israelite sanctuaries, some excavated by archaeologists: e.g., Hazor, Megiddo, Taanach, Dan, Lachish, Arad, and Beer-sheba.[8] Once the sanctuary in Jerusalem was built, however, 2 Samuel through 2 Kings insist (in accord with Deut 18:1-8) that only Levites could be priests and (in accordance with Deut 12:2-14) that only the one place where God would make God's name dwell, understood as the temple in Jerusalem, was a legitimate site for offering sacrifices to God.

That opinion clearly was not shared by people in northern Israel, who worshiped in their shrines (e.g., Dan, Bethel, and especially Samaria) throughout the Old Testament narratives. [Excavation of the Altar Site at Dan] In fact, exclusivity of worship was not always practiced even by all the people in pre-exilic Judah either. Micah 6:16, for example, blames the eighth-century people of Jerusalem for following the syncretistic practices of the ninth-century northern kings Omri and Ahab, and Jeremiah 8:1-2 condemns seventh/sixth-century Judeans for worshiping the host of heaven, i.e., astral deities. Between the time of the destruction of the temple by Babylon in 586 and its rebuilding in 515, the issue was mute. There is, however, no reason to suppose that those who remained in Judah (and Samaria) failed to offer sacrifices to God at other sites. Zechariah 7:3 mentions priests at Bethel, although not sacrifice. Still, what is the purpose of having priests except to offer

---

Excavation of the Altar Site at Dan

While no remains of the ancient temple and altar in Jerusalem have been found, archeologists have recently uncovered an altar at Dan, one of the sanctuaries of the northern kingdom of Israel. Such altars sat on a prepared area and might reach several feet in height. Typically, altars were constructed of unhewn stone, minimizing work by human hands.

One Israelite altar was at this site in the city of Dan, which lay near the southern foot of Mt. Hermon in northernmost Israel. It was founded (according to Josh 19:40-48; Jdg 18:1-31) by the tribe of Dan, but it was charged immediately with idolatry and was declared illegitimate in the tenth century after

A cult place behind the gate of the fortification of Tel Dan was probably built by King Jeroboam of Israel in the 10th BCE. Dan, Israel. (Credit: Erich Lessing/Art Resource, NY)

the construction of the temple in Jerusalem and the division of the Davidic/Solomonic kingdom. Jeroboam I made Dan and Bethel royal sanctuaries, and drew the wrath of the Deuteronomistic Historian, the redactional author of Joshua through Kings, for doing so (1 Kgs 12:25–13:13-34). That author read the Deuteronomistic claim for the Jerusalem temple as the exclusive place for the legitimate worship of God back into the early monarchy with his account of Jeroboam's setting up golden bulls at both sanctuaries. The Deuteronomistic author wanted his readers to see the bulls as deities or at least representatives of deities other than YHWH. It is quite likely, however, that the bulls were intended to represent animals the invisible deity rode. In Jerusalem, by contrast, the ark of the covenant with its cherubim on top served that same purpose. To be sure, the bulls at Dan and Bethel lent themselves to easy construal as objects of worship. Then their worship was ripe for condemnation as a violation of the Ten Commandments, which is precisely what the Old Testament did.

On the history of shrines in ancient Israel, see, briefly, William G. Deever, "Temples and Sanctuaries: Syria—Palestine," *ABD*, 6.376–80, esp. p. 380.

Elephantine in Egypt

Around or soon after the Babylonian attacks on Jerusalem in 598/7 and 587/6, perhaps during the reign of Pharaoh Hophres (r. 588–566), a Jewish military group settled on an island in the Nile River in southern or Upper Egypt (i.e., upstream from, but south of Lower Egypt where the Nile empties into the Mediterranean Sea), in the area of the modern-day Aswan Dam. Among their accomplishments was the building of a temple to God. They appear to have enjoyed Persian recognition, but they eventually raised the ire of Egyptians, perhaps for offering animal sacrifices, and an Egyptian named Vidaranag, at the instigation of Egyptian priests, destroyed the temple in 410. The transplanted Judeans were literate, leaving a variety of texts behind, discovered by archaeologists in 1893. A few records deal with their desire to rebuild their temple, and they sent letters to Bagoas, the Persian-appointed governor of Yehud, detailing the destruction of their temple and asking Bagoas to intercede with the Persians on their behalf to allow the temple's rebuilding. A memorandum from the group to Egyptian officials indicated that they had also contacted the governor in Samaria, and both men approved the plan to rebuild the temple in Egypt. These records are instructive because they perhaps show lay officials in Jerusalem and Samaria, who were prepared to function side by side in cooperation with each other as well as the Persians.

The letters referenced may be found in Pritchard, ed., *ANET* (2011), 450–51.

sacrifices? Worship at the temple in Elephantine in Egypt (built in the sixth century by Judeans who had fled Jerusalem and the Babylonians) included sacrifice, and worship at sites in Israel and even Judah *may* have done so as well. It is difficult to imagine no sacrifices being offered in either Israel or Judah for the entire exilic period, since offering sacrifices was the people's main form of worship. The rebuilding of the temple in Jerusalem in the late sixth century renewed the debate about legitimate worship with a twist: the returnees insisted that only they could worship (i.e., offer sacrifices) in the temple. [Elephantine in Egypt]

The post-exilic period also saw the limiting of the full priesthood to the descendants of Aaron, a change that was read back into the Mosaic period and spelled out in Leviticus and Numbers, which offer a variety of priestly additions to the law. If the authors/editors of Joshua through Kings based their perspective on the second giving of the law on the eastern bank of the Jordan (i.e., Deut 12–28), the compilers of the laws in Exodus through Numbers based theirs on what they saw as the first (i.e., the prior, definitive) giving of the law on Mount Sinai. Modern readers should not, however, try to hold ancient writers accountable to modern standards of consistency in this regard. Instead, they should read such laws as attempts to make clear to later generations what God speaking through Moses intended from the beginning. [The History of the Priesthood in Ancient Israel]

Ezra 7:6 introduces the protagonist Ezra as "a scribe," i.e., a literate man, one who could read and write and support himself thereby. It is very difficult to know the literacy rate in ancient Yehud. Even later in the Greco-Roman world, literacy among *free males* has been estimated only at 20–30 percent, with a lower rate for women, slaves, and lower classes who made up most of the population.[9] How low that leaves the rate of literacy in sixth/fifth BCE Yehud is unclear, but it was not likely to have extended far beyond scribes and some other specialists. It is not surprising, then, that Nehemiah 7:73b–8:12 describes the people as assembling to *hear* the reading of the law and its explication. They did not have their own copy and would not have been able to read it if they had. Ezra 7:11 elaborates, calling Ezra "the

The History of the Priesthood in Ancient Israel

Discerning the history of the priesthood is among the most difficult tasks in Old Testament research. It is complicated by modern readers' limited knowledge of the history of the rise of the Old Testament. It is difficult to know what laws about the priesthood actually existed in the Mosaic period, although it is clear that all laws came to be ascribed to Moses—regardless of when they were written. Starting, however, with the narratives in Joshua and Judges, readers encounter a situation in which various sorts of people presented themselves as priests, but Levites were preferred. In addition, sacrifices were offered at a number of Israelite sanctuaries, including some excavated by modern archaeologists: e.g., Hazor, Megiddo, Taanach, Dan, Lachish, Arad, and Beer-sheba. Solomon perhaps built the temple in Jerusalem as a royal chapel, but 2 Kgs 22:3–24:27 records the discovery of the Law (most likely Deut 12 28, based on Josiah's reaction) and prohibits sacrificing anywhere else in all Israel but the temple (see Deut 12:2-14), thereby limiting the observance even of Passover, a home rite, to Jerusalem. In particular, Solomon ordered destroyed the ancient worship center at Bethel, where Jeroboam had erected a golden bull. These behaviors so closely follow the ideas in Deuteronomy that the identification of the law code with at least Deuteronomy 12–26 is widely made among scholars.

The post-exilic period saw the limiting of the full priesthood to the descendants of Aaron, a change that was pushed back to the Mosaic period and spelled out in Leviticus and Numbers, which offer a variety of priestly additions to the narrative of the giving of the law. If the authors/editors of the Former Prophets based their perspective (i.e., Deut 12–28) on the second giving of the law on the eastern bank of the Jordan, the compilers of the laws in Exodus through Numbers based theirs on the first (i.e., prior, definitive) giving of the law on Sinai.

priest . . . , the scribe, a scholar of the text of the commandments of the LORD and his statutes for Israel." In a context where legitimacy was going to be an issue, the narrator makes it clear that Ezra was God's priest for Jerusalem as well as King Artaxerxes' representative.

Ezra 7:7-10 takes the first step in the narrative by means of a broad statement that "some of the people of Israel, and some of the priests and Levites, and the temple singers and gatekeepers, and the temple servants also went up to Jerusalem." This grouping anticipates the list in Ezra 8:1-20 and the narrative in Ezra 8:21-36. Ezra 9–10 will develop a new theme.

The year of Ezra's journey was the seventh year of Artaxerxes (I), i.e., 458.[10] It began the first day of the first month (March/April), and it ended the first day of the fifth month (July/August, both dates according to the post-exilic calendar). (See the discussion of calendars in the comments on Ezra 6.) This report ends with two comments. (1) God's gracious hand was on Ezra. That is, God had cared for him and the travelers on their possibly dangerous journey. (2) Ezra had a threefold purpose in going: to study Torah, to obey Torah, and to teach its "statutes" (*ḥōq*, a singular noun designating something prescribed) and "ordinances" (*mišpāṭ*, again a singular noun specifying a judgment or justice) within Israel. The singular was used perhaps to signify the unity of the law. To "study" the law was to study it industriously and gain the ability to expound and apply it to life.

The Letter of Artaxerxes to Ezra in Aramaic, 7:11-26

As was characteristic of Ezra 1–6, in Ezra 7 too written records and letters are important. In vv. 12-26 the author quotes a letter Artaxerxes gave to Ezra (according to v. 11). Its inclusion was intended to eliminate all doubts about the authority of Ezra to undertake the measures the remainder of the book would narrate. While the text does not say so, this letter too, like Ezra 4:8–6:18, was written in Aramaic. In v. 27 the narrative switches back to Hebrew and for the first time assumes the first person singular point of view. Ezra 10 reverts to the third person. In the book, only Ezra 7:27–9:15, fifty-three verses, were written in the first person, and Ezra 8:2-14 is a third person genealogy.

As was typical of ancient letters, this one opened with the name of the sender: Artaxerxes. He mentioned his retinue of seven advisors (v. 14, see also Esth 1:14), and he called himself "king of kings." That was a self-appellation not noteworthy for its modesty. Moreover, it would have fit better Darius I, who succeeded in conquering territory all the way to Greece, only to be stopped at the battle of Marathon. Artaxerxes I was one of the lesser important (i.e., less powerful!) kings. Regardless, he is portrayed in Ezra 7 as having been as powerful and as congenial to exiles as Cyrus had been in Ezra 1. (It never hurts to praise the people who aid you.) Overall, Artaxerxes extends to Ezra a greeting of peace, honors the God of Israel, and reproaches Yehudites who do not honor YHWH and himself. He tells Ezra to make inquiries about Yehud and Jerusalem with respect to "the law of your God" and to "convey the silver and gold that the king and his counselors have freely offered to the God of Israel" together with "all the silver and gold that you shall find in the whole province of Babylon" to Jerusalem for the house of God there (Ezra 7:14-16). It is not clear whether that silver and gold would be collected from exiles (some of whom might have amassed some wealth during their families' sojourn in Babylon) or the population more generally (as commanded by Cyrus in Ezra 1:4). The parallels between Ezra 1 and 7 suggest the latter, but nothing as explicit as Ezra 1:4 appears in Ezra 7.

Moreover, like Cyrus, Artaxerxes decreed that any of the people, priests, and Levites still in Babylon were free to accompany Ezra, although his proclamation clearly implies that they should not be coerced. One might have assumed Persian permission from Ezra 1, but Ezra 7 repeats it, emphasizing the explicit permission of Artaxerxes to go. Any offering they gave was to be of their free will, not coerced (v. 16). The tripartite division of this group of travelers follows the pattern of laity and two groups of religious officials seen also in Ezra 2:70 and 6:16. It is a way of including all people allowed and expected to participate. It directs that those returning with Ezra would have the same rights of access to the temple as those who had rebuilt it in 520–515. This point was crucial for the Ezra narrative. Still, it enfranchised people who had been gone from Jerusalem over a century, and—along with the rest of the book of Ezra—the letter disenfranchised people who had remained in Jerusalem or Judah during the whole period.

Artaxerxes gave directions about how the money was to be spent (Ezra 7:17-20). The first priority was to pay for animal, grain, and drink offerings at the new temple. The people were to buy bulls, rams, lambs, grain, and drink (i.e., wine, see the directions in Num 15:5) to sacrifice. (See also Ezra 6:17, where the returnees sacrificed a dozen goats, one for each tribe of Israel.) Thus, in the book of Ezra two pagan emperors paid for sacrifices, but foreign wives and children of returnees living in Yehud would eventually be excluded from worshiping there by Ezra (Ezra 10:6-16)! In any case, the offering was not to be skimpy; anything lacking, Ezra could pay for with funds from the royal treasury, i.e., probably the treasury of the satrapy.[11]

The author of Ezra 7 was not finished, however, with the instructions from Artaxerxes. He next reported a decree to "all the treasurers in the province Beyond the River" (v. 21), i.e., the large province of which tiny Yehud was a part. Those people would have been employees of the Persian king, whom Ezra and his entourage would encounter on their lengthy journey. Artaxerxes ordered that they too supply Ezra with provisions for the temple: silver, wheat, wine, oil, and unlimited salt. The first four are specified in hundred weights. Clines thinks that these levies were to be annual,[12] but the text does not say so. It seems more likely that the text envisions a one-time contribution to help the exiles as they journeyed to Jerusalem. The same holds true for v. 23. It would be unnecessary to prohibit those officials from exacting annual fees from persons who had passed through their areas but once. To be sure, v. 23 mentions "the house of the God of heaven," but Ezra's whole ministry was presented as a ministry to the temple. Verse 24, by contrast, appears to concern a separate issue. It prohibits those officials from taxing cultic officials in the future, lest they incur divine displeasure, a prohibition that Williamson argues was in line with Persian practice elsewhere.[13] In addition, the categories of official returnees are basically the same as in Ezra 2:36-57: priests (vv. 36-39), Levites (vv. 40-42), temple servants (vv. 43-54), and other servants (see "Solomon's" servants in vv. 55-57), although the number reported as returning under Ezra was a fraction of those said to return under Zerubbabel.

The value of 100 talents of silver would be significantly higher than the value of the other goods, even "limitless" salt. Clines notes that Herodotus (the great fifth century BCE Greek historian) reports that the annual income of the whole satrapy at that time was only 350 talents. A gift of 100 talents to the temple would be nearly one-third, a huge amount for even a one-time gift. Clines suggests that the word "talents" perhaps should read "minas," one sixtieth the weight, but even that would still be a sizeable amount, whether paid one time or annually.[14] His suggestion is without textual support, but it shows how overwhelming 100 talents would have been, whether paid once or annually. Modern readers can do little more than note that the reported amount probably was intended to be stunning.

The report of Artaxerxes' directives to Ezra ends in vv. 25-26 by granting Ezra the authority to judge and punish "all the people in the province of Beyond the River who know the laws of your God." Presumably this charge applied only to religious issues; Persians maintained final control in others. The identity of those laws is unclear, and scholars divide over whether it was the Torah, in toto or in part.[15] Moreover, the king gave Ezra explicit permission to punish offenders by death, banishment (NRSV) or beating, confiscation of goods, or imprisonment. This authority will become crucial in Ezra 9–10. Davies points out, however, that the text does *not* say that Ezra brought the law code with him. It had already been mentioned in Ezra 6 in connection with the ordering of the priests and Levites, "as written in the book of Moses."[16] What he did bring was the imperial authority to teach and enforce the code, apparently on his own best judgment, and to execute or banish people who did not obey him. That understanding of Ezra's authority was crucial to the book of Ezra, and according to the book the people accepted that authority. What this verse does for its later post-exilic author and reader, according to T. B. Dozeman, is to articulate "the environment (i.e., the nomos) for the transformation of Yahwism from a . . . religion centered in a monarchy to a religion of law, constituted in the Torah of Moses."[17]

Ezra's Praise of God in Response, 7:27-28

At this point, the narrative returns to the Hebrew language, and it takes up the first person singular point of view for the first time. [The First Person Singular as a Literary Point of View] Technically, the two verses do not identify the speaker as Ezra, but he had been the addressee of the letter given to Ezra. No other person seems to fit. The first person singular will continue through Ezra 9:15. Ezra 10:1 reverts to the third person singular.

The subject matter of vv. 27-28 is Ezra's expression of thanksgiving to God for putting such thinking as expressed in the letter into the head of the Persian king. No claim is made that the temple was singled out for special favor on that occasion. The author perhaps neither knew nor cared whether other priests at other sanctuaries had such authority. What was important for the agenda of the book of Ezra was that its namesake could claim such permission. Emboldened by God's commission, Ezra's first course of action was to gather leaders from among the exiles to make the trip with him.

The First Person Singular as a Literary Point of View

AΩ In everyday conversations, the use of the first person singular typically designates the speaker's own point of view. In addition, speakers often address others as "you," and speak of a person or persons in the third person: he, she, it, they or them. Generally speaking, literary authors observe those same conventions, but not always. Sometimes an author will write a short story or novel using the first person "point of view." In the case of a murder story written in the first person, no one would consider arresting the author for murder and looking for a corpse. Likewise, someone writing a personal account or even an autobiography could choose to write in the third person. One classic example of such writing is Julius Caesar's account of his actions in the Gallic wars, written in the last century before Jesus. Likewise, the use of the first person singular in Ezra 7:21 is not proof that Ezra wrote the book that bears his name. That is particularly so since Ezra 7:1, 6, 11 and 10:1-17 are written in the third person. It is possible, but not necessary, that the author had access to writings by Ezra which he used in Ezra 7:27–9:15. In any case, the basic narrative of Ezra 7–10 is the third person narrative, which is supplemented by first person materials.

Summary

Ezra 7 first introduces Ezra, the son of a line of priests reaching all the way back to Aaron (vv. 1-6), then reports that he led a large

The Relationship between the Decree of Artaxerxes in Ezra 7 and the Activities of Ezra throughout Ezra 7–10

Decree of Artaxerxes	Activities of Ezra
Ezra is a scribe of the law of the God of heaven (7:21)	Ezra reads the law and the people keep the Feast of Booths (*Neh* 7:79–8:18)
"People of Israel," priests and Levites, are allowed to go to Jerusalem (7:13)	Ezra assembles people, priests, and Levites to return to Jerusalem (7:1-28)
	Mixed marriages are dissolved because they were contrary to the law (9:1–10:44)
Gifts of silver, gold, vessels from the king, counselors, and people for the temple (7:15-19)	Much gold and silver plus vessels transported and delivered (8:24-34)
Other necessities to come from the state treasury (7:20-23) No tribute on temple or personnel (7:24)	Ezra thanks for God's putting it in the king's heart to beautify the temple (7:27)

Based on Lester L. Grabbe, "What Was Ezra's Mission?" *Second Temple Studies. 2. Temple Community in the Persian Period* (ed. T. C. Eskenazi, K. H. Richards; JSOT Sup 175; Sheffield; JSOT Press, 1991) 286–99, here 287.

group of exiles from Babylon to Jerusalem (vv. 7-10). Next, Ezra 7 and 8 describe the action of 7:7-10 in more detail. The narrative proper begins in 7:11 with Artaxerxes supplying Ezra with a letter announcing Artaxerxes' largess for the temple and Ezra's permission to appoint magistrates and judges for Persia in the entire region Beyond the River.[18] Ezra's response closes the chapter. Ezra 8 will detail the trip to Jerusalem and its temple, while Ezra 9–10 will discuss the painful issue of mixed marriages, and in Nehemiah 8 Ezra will read the law for the people of Yehud to keep. A chart will illustrate the relationship between Ezra 7 and the remaining Ezra narratives. [The Relationship between the Decree of Artaxerxes in Ezra 7 and the Activities of Ezra throughout Ezra 7–10]

CONNECTIONS

1. In his attempt to make this narrative relevant to his readers, Bede (the eighth-century British, Catholic monk) asserted that Ezra was a "type" of Christ:

> By his name too, which means "helper," Ezra openly stands for the Lord. For it is he by whom alone the people of the faithful are constantly liberated from tribulations and, as though from captivity in Babylon to freedom in Jerusalem, are brought from the "confusion" of the vices to the "peace" and serenity of the virtues as they advance by the steps of meritorious deeds.[19]

Bede's sentiment is noteworthy, but it conveniently ignores the text on which it is based. There was little serene about Ezra in his confrontations with people in Jerusalem.

2. Colonialism may be defined as "imposed foreign rule [in which] one people or government extends its sovereignty and imposes political control over an alien people or territory."[20] The ancient world saw the Egyptians, Babylonians, Persians, and Greeks operating as colonialists. What is pertinent in the book of Ezra is that Babylonian colonies simply passed into the possession of Persia. Colonies in the ancient world varied in the number of people who came from the colonizing area and in their severity, although they all treated the colonies as their possessions that could be used to increase the imperial coffers. From extant accounts, however, the Persians seem to have been more lenient than their predecessors in the Levant. What is remarkable about the accounts in Ezra is the leniency they ascribe to the Persian king in his treatment of exiles, in particular of Jewish exiles in Babylon: those wishing to return home were allowed to do so and were aided on their journey and in rebuilding their communal religious life.

In Ezra 7 readers encounter a Judean portrayal of the ideal foreign king with Judeans living among his colonies. He was respectful of his subjects and non-belligerent towards them. He respected their gods, including specifically the God of Judah. He sent money back to the needy province, and did not just take from it. Finally, he guaranteed the right of his displaced subjects to return to their homeland, and even assisted them.

Modern readers might well learn some things from this portrayal of the pagan king. Readers might learn to be respectful of foreigners among them, whether dislocated professionals fleeing Iraq or migrant Latino workers harvesting crops on American farms or roofing American houses. Modern readers might learn to respect houses of worship and centers of cultural exchange operated by Muslims, Hindus, Buddhists, Jains, or others instead of lashing out at those people in hate when a person or group harms Americans abroad. Modern readers might seek to aid families of workers who still live in the homeland and depend on money from their loved ones working in America. Modern readers might seek to aid workers here in their attempts to visit their families back home or to help them bring their families here. Modern readers might simply learn to act kindly and hence lovingly to foreign workers and other strangers living among us. They might discover that by doing so they had "entertained angels without knowing it" (Heb 13:2).

Islamic Center of America

The Islamic Center of America, the largest mosque in the United States, located in Dearborn, Michigan. (Credit: Dane Hillard, Wikimedia Commons, CC-by-2.0)

The United States rightly congratulates itself on religious tolerance. This beautiful mosque stands as a place of worship for Muslims in America, as they too express their freedom to worship how, where, and as they see fit. It and other such houses of worship deserve the same respect as churches and synagogues.

NOTES

1. Philip R. Davies, *On the Origins of Judaism* (London, Oakville: Equinox, 2011) 16.

2. D. J. A. Clines, notes on Ezra in *The HarperCollins Study Bible* (San Francisco: HarperCollins, 1993) 714. See also p. 660 in the revised edition of 2006.

3. Rolf Rendtorff, "Esra und das 'Gesetz,'" *ZAW* 96 (1984): 165–84, here 183–84.

4. Ulrich Kellermann, "Erwägungen zum Problem der Esradatierung," *ZAW* 80 (1968): 55–89; Aaron Demsky, "Who Came First, Ezra or Nehemiah: The Synchronic Approach," *HUCA* 65 (1994): 1–19, here 15; and Demsky, "Who Returned First, Ezra or Nehemiah?" *BRev* (1996): 28–33, 46.

5. J. A. Emerton, "Did Ezra Go to Jerusalem in 428 B.C.?" *JTS* n.s. 17/1 (1966): 1–19.

6. Othniel Margalith, "The Political Role of Ezra as a Persian Governor," *ZAW* 98 (1986): 110–12.

7. See "Sanballat," *NIDB*, 5.96. Interestingly, Bede ("On Ezra and Nehemiah," in *Ancient Christian Commentary* [ed. Marco Conti; Downers Grove IL: InterVarsity, 2008] V, 321) devotes three lengthy sentences to this historical issue, in which he cites

Josephus (*Ant*. 11.5.1), who attempted to settle the issue by saying Artaxerxes was actually Xerxes, who ruled 486–465

8. Beth Alpert Nakhai, "Altar," *Eerdmans Dictionary of the Bible* (ed. D. N. Freedman; Grand Rapids MI: Eerdmans, 2000) 45–48.

9. Ruben B. Dupertuis, "Literacy," *NIDB*, 3.672.

10. If the date Ezra departed for Jerusalem was the seventh year of the reign Artaxerxes II, it would have been 398 BCE.

11. Judah J. Slotki, *Daniel·* • *Ezra·* • *Nehemiah* (New York: Soncino Press, 1985) 151.

12. D. J. A. Clines, *Ezra, Nehemiah, Esther* (NCB; Grand Rapids MI: Eerdmans; London: Marshall, Morgan, & Scott, 1984) 104.

13. H. G. M. Williamson, "Exile and After: Historical Study," *The Face of Old Testament Studies: A Survey of Contemporary Approaches* (ed. David W. Baker and Bill T. Arnold; Grand Rapids MI: Baker, 1999) 236–65, here 251.

14. Clines, *Ezra, Nehemiah, Esther*, 104.

15. Conservative scholars tend to argue that the "law" was the Torah, more or less as it was canonized, while others are less certain. Edwin M. Yamauchi ("The Archaeological Background of Ezra," *BSac* 137 [1980]: 195–211, here 206) is cautious with his endorsement of the first option: "There is no reason to doubt that Ezra could have brought back with him the Torah, that is, the Pentateuch." Critical scholars might well respond that there is a great deal of doubt about Yamauchi's statement though, since as noted above what one finds in Ezra are allusions to Lev 18:15; Deut 1:38-39; 6:11; 7:1, 3; 11:8; 18:9; 23:6; and 2 Kgs 21:16, but not direct quotations.

16. Davies, *On the Origins of Judaism*, 65–66.

17. Thomas B. Dozeman, "Geography and History in Herodotus and in Ezra-Nehemiah," *JBL* 122 (2003): 449–66, here 459.

18. J. C. H. Lebram ("Die Traditionsgeschiche der Esragestalt und die Frage nach dem historicschen Esra," *Archaemenid History, I. Sources, Structures and Synthesis. Proceedings of the Gronigen 1983 Archaemenid History Workshop* [ed. Heleen Sancisi—Weerdenburg; Leiden: Nederlands Institut voor het Nabije Osten, 1987] 103–38, here 137) calls attention to Artaxerxes' generosity to a subject people and concludes that this motif is not historically accurate. Rather, he claims, it arose in the Hellenistic Period as an expression of Judean hate aimed at Greece, expressed by means of a false contrast between the current, hated Greeks and the earlier, allegedly beneficent Persians. If some scholars overemphasize the openness of the Persians, Lebram seems to be guilty of denying it. Both extremes are to be avoided.

19. Bede, "Ezra as a Type of Christ," *Ancient Christian Commentary on Scripture*, 321.

20. Michael Mastanduno, "Colonies and Colonialism," in *Funk & Wagnalls New Encyclopedia* (ed. Norma H. Dickey; vol. 6; United States: Funk & Wagnalls, 1986) 443.

RETURN OF EXILES
WITH EZRA

Ezra 8

COMMENTARY

[Outline of Ezra 8] Ezra 8 continues the first person narrative of Ezra's return from Babylon to Jerusalem begun in Ezra 7:27-28. It opens (vv. 1-14) with a list of the male heads of the families that returned to Yehud with Ezra and the number of males returning with each head.[1] In v.15 the first person singular narrative resumes from Ezra 7:26. Ezra assembled his group at "the river that runs to Ahava," where he took stock of his entourage, discovering that no Levites were returning with him (vv. 15-20). He sent for several Levites and their families. Then he proclaimed a fast to invoke God's protection, set aside twelve of the leading priests, entrusted them with gold and silver for the temple, presumably the gift of Artaxerxes mentioned in Ezra 7:16 (vv. 21-30), and departed for Jerusalem (vv. 31-32). On the fourth day after their arrival in Jerusalem, they delivered the ritual vessels they were carrying to the priests at the temple (vv. 33-34). Ezra 8:35-36, however, reverts to the third person. It reports that Ezra and his companions offered burnt offerings to God (v. 35), presumably in gratitude for their safe journey. Finally, the chapter says they delivered the king's orders to the satraps and governors to support the temple and the returnees (v. 36).

Outline of Ezra 8

Tally of Returnees by Fathers' Houses, 8:1-14
Assembly and Recruitment of Levites, 8:15-20
Further Preparations: Sanctification, 8:21-30
Journey to Jerusalem and Arrival, 8:31-32
Offerings for the Temple, 8:33-34
Worship at the Temple and the Delivery of Artaxerxes' Gifts, 8:35-36

Tally of Returnees by Fathers' Houses, 8:1-14

Ezra 8 opens with a list of the heads of the houses to which those returning to Jerusalem with Ezra belonged, i.e., the real Israel, since not all residents of Yehud did. (Ezra 2 served the same purpose in Ezra 1–6.) Not surprisingly, the list begins with priests, namely

The Heads of Families

Family	Head	Number of Returnees
Aaron	Phineas/Gershom, Ithamar/Daniel, David/Hattush Parosh	150 men
Pahath-Moab	Elihoenai	200 men
Zattu	Shecaniah	300 men
Adin	Ebed	50 men
Elam	Jeshaiah	70 men
Shephatiah	Zebediah	80 men
Joab	Obadiah	218 men
Bani	Shelomoth	160 men
Bebai	Zechariah	28 men
Azgad	Johanan	110 men
Adonikam	Eliphet, Jeiel, & Shemaiah	60 men
Bigvai	Uthai	70 men

Based on H. G. M. Williamson, *Ezra and Nehemiah* (WBC 16; Waco: Word, 1985) 107.

Phineas, a grandson of Aaron, to which line Ezra belonged (compare Ezra 7:1-5 and Exod 6:25). The remaining eleven families mentioned in vv. 2-14 were non-priestly. The lay families are listed according to a common pattern: the name of the extended family or father's house, the name of the current head of the family, and the number of people in the family.[2] Somewhat surprising is the note in vv. 13-14 that the descendants of two of the houses (Adonikam and Bigvai) "came later." The verse appears to mean that they were not part of Ezra's entourage, but followed at some unspecified time. Their inclusion raises the real possibility that the list was compiled later and by someone other than Ezra and that it was employed here for the sake of completeness by (1) Ezra's biographer, (2) the editor of Ezra 7–10, or (3) the editor of the book of Ezra-Nehemiah. The number of returnees totals about 1,500 males. The information in vv. 2-14 can be most clearly represented by a chart. [The Heads of Families] Nothing, however, was said about the women and whether they had a say in the matter of the move. [What about the Wives?] [Eliehoenai]

Assembly and Recruitment of Levites, 8:15-20

The first person narrative that had begun in Ezra 7:27-28 and had been interrupted by the list of returnees in Ezra 8:1-14 resumed in these verses. As mentioned, the name of the place where Ezra and his co-travelers met was "Ahava," which was mentioned in Ezra 8:15 as a town and in Ezra 8:21 and 31 as a river or canal. (The river/canal perhaps took its name from the town or vice versa.) Its site has not been identified. The same is true for the place named

Casiphia, which may have been a settlement of Judean exiles, to which Ezra sent messengers seeking Levites to return to Jerusalem.

Ezra says (in v. 16) that he sent for nine men who were leaders and two (Joiarib and Elnathan) who were "wise men." They were dispatched to Casiphia to recruit Levites for the trip to Jerusalem. They would be needed at the temple, presumably. The nine names of leaders at least look suspicious. Two were named Elnathan, the same as one of the "wise men," and another Nathan. Yet another of the nine was named Jarib, very similar to the wise man Joarib. It is at least possible, therefore, and maybe even probable, that there were only six priests in view (Eliezer, Ariel, Shemiah, Jarib, Zechariah, and Meshullum) and in addition two "wise men" (Joarib and Elnathan). One can easily imagine names being changed slightly and being dropped out of the list in one manuscript and being added back in a later one, the whole chain of events resulting in the longer list in the Hebrew Bible. In any case, Ezra's messengers traveled to Casiphia seeking Levites, who would be needed at the temple in Jerusalem to aid with the sacrifices.

What about the Wives?

Ezra 8, like much of the Bible in general, concerns itself with men, in particular with priests and Levites. Clearly the chapter and, indeed, the whole book of Ezra-Nehemiah, is concerned with the actions of leading men. The rationale for such limitations probably would have been that "that was simply the way things were!" Why, however, should things have been that way? Or, differently stated, what was the excuse for such views? The practice in the ancient Levant was much older than Israel and *perhaps* was rooted in biology. Women bore the babies and nursed them; mothers were restricted in their ability to move about as long as that was going on; and they might bear another child quite soon after weaning one. Since having numerous progeny was valued as the means to ensure that a family survived, pregnancy, motherhood, and restrictions on women's work and other behavior came to be seen in ancient Israel not just as physical or societal norms but as divine mandates. Let it be noted, however, that women (mothers or not) were expected to aid in agriculture, and so were the children as soon as they were able.

Why, though, would they also need to be banned from the priesthood or ritually cleansed from the "pollution" of menstruation or the issuance of blood in childbearing before they could even participate in religious ceremonies? The answer may lie partly in that blood was seen as the life force and had to be shed under particular circumstances and handled ceremonially in precise ways. Its use in sacrifices was conceived of as celebration before God or as a means to atone for particular kinds of sins, but using it did not contaminate priests. (They did, however, have to be ritually cleansed before offering sacrifices.) A woman's menstruation (and a man's seminal emissions too), however, was seen as a "pollutant." That is, menstruation was seen as rendering one unclean for contact with sacred areas, people, food, and other objects. That conclusion was neither necessary nor moral. One suspects that a hefty dose of male supremacy stood behind the view and its accompanying prohibitions and restrictions on women.

The recruiting trip was successful. Two Levites—Sherebiah, with eighteen sons and other relatives, and Merari, with his relatives and their twenty sons—answered Ezra's call to return to Jerusalem for service at the temple. In addition, 220 temple servants traveled with them. The word for servants, *nĕtînîm*, derives from a root meaning "give," and suggests that they had been "given" to the temple. Verse 20 attests that David had instigated this class of temple personnel. Regardless, they are referred to as temple servants and may have descended from temple slaves. Ezra had requested only Levites and got thirty-eight volunteers; perhaps they were not

Eliehoenai

AΩ The name Eliehoenai appears in Ezra 8:4. It means "my eyes are unto God." It affirms the dependence of its bearer on the law of God for guidance and the mercy of God in times of difficulty.

Judah J. Slotki, *Daniel • Ezra· • Nehemiah* (London, New York: Soncino Press, 1985) 156.

enough to manage a temple. In any case, F. C. Ensham suggests that the willingness of the *nĕtînîm* to return to Jerusalem may have been a factor in the Levites' willingness to return.[3]

These numbers call for further comment. Ezra 2:36-39 says 4,289 priests returned with Zerubbabel and company, and Ezra 2:40-42 numbers the Levites returning with him at seventy-four. Neither Ezra 7 nor Ezra 8, however, takes account of them. The comments on Ezra 2 questioned the high numbers of returnees and dated that list late. Here it is appropriate to note that the narrative in Ezra 7–8 shows no awareness of the return of a large community of priests and Levites, or indeed of *any* previous return of exiles, let alone a crowd of circa 50,000. Moreover, the Ezra narratives (Ezra 7–10 and Neh 7:73b–9:37) do not recognize the legitimacy of the worship that was taking place at the temple in Jerusalem when Ezra and company arrived. Modern readers of Ezra, therefore, should not expect a description of a welcome to Jerusalem/Yehud being extended to Ezra and his entourage by earlier returnees, and they do not find one.

Preparations for Departure, 8:21-30

The narrative mentions first a fast proclaimed by Ezra. [What Is a Fast?] It was prompted by his awareness of the danger of an overland journey, especially in view of the valuables described in Ezra 7 that he was carrying to Jerusalem. In particular, however, in v. 21 Ezra mentions his fear for the safety of the travelers. Interestingly, he does not explicitly mention the "silver and gold" given him by King Artaxerxes for the "house of God" in Jerusalem (see Ezra 7:15-16), though that should be part of the "possessions" in view. Another factor played a role as well: shame. Ezra says that he "was ashamed to ask for a band of soldiers and cavalry to protect [him and the other travelers] against the 'enemy' [probably highway bandits, but possibly other officials] along the way." He had said nothing to the king of Persia about needing soldiers to guard the king's gifts from robbers or other disloyal persons. If he had done so, he might have "lost face" before the king. Here, though, the narrative lets the reader know of such dangers by revealing Ezra's personal insecurities. Ezra then did

What Is a Fast?

Simply stated, a fast was a voluntary forgoing of food and perhaps even water associated with an act of mourning. A fast might also call for tearing one's clothing, wearing sackcloth, covering one's head with ashes, or other such acts of abasement. Though fasts often accompanied funeral rights, they sometimes accompanied prayer as a testament to its fervor and sincerity. That seems to be the nature of Ezra's fast.

David A. Lambert, "Fast, Fasting," *NIDB*, 1.431–34.

what any rational and cautious believer would do: he asked God for protection. At once Ezra confirmed what readers would expect: God did protect him, his entourage, and the treasures and belongings they took with them. There is no suspense in the telling of this trip, no narrow escapes from bandits, or even of hardships along the way.

Next, Ezra narrated the actions he took to protect the king's gold and other gifts bestowed on him and his traveling companions. He does imply thereby, of course, that the travelers were in danger of being attacked and at least robbed of their valuables if not killed by highwaymen. His trip without a royal guard stands in marked contrast with Artaxerxes' sending officers and cavalry, apparently on his own initiative, with Nehemiah on his return to Jerusalem (Neh 2:9). The absence of guards is all the more remarkable in light of the value of the gifts from the Persian king.

Then, according to many translations (e.g., the NRSV), Ezra selected twelve priests, i.e., Sherebiah, Hashabiah, and ten of their kinsmen (Ezra 8:24). That sentence is problematic, however, since vv. 18-19 list both men as Levites. It makes more sense to understand the text to mean that Ezra chose twelve priests, plus the Levites Sherbiah and Hashabiah, and ten more Levites as well. [An Issue of Translation and Punctuation] He weighed out to each of them a portion of the six hundred talents of silver and one hundred talents of gold plus a number of vessels (vv. 26-27). The weight of a talent fluctuated somewhat, but in Mesopotamia one weighed about seventy-five pounds.[4] Williamson estimates the weight of the silver at over 24.5 tons and of the gold at 3.75 tons.[5] Both in terms of the worth of the minerals and of their weight (how many camels would it take to carry that much weight for hundreds of miles?), one should perhaps conclude that the numbers were disturbed in transmission. An alternative understanding would be to suppose that the weights were exaggerated to praise the generosity of Artaxerxes and/or to glorify God and the temple.

Of the remaining gifts, the weight of the hundred silver vessels is missing, giving likely

An Issue of Translation and Punctuation

ΑΩ It appears in a number of English translations of Ezra 8:24 as if the priests Ezra selected to transport the gold given him by Artaxerxes numbered twelve, specifically Sherebiah, Hashibiah, and ten others (cf. NRSV, which renders the phrase in question as follows: "twelve of the leading priests: Sherebiah, Hashabiah, and ten of their kin with them"). The problem with that translation is that vv. 18 and 19 had specifically identified Sheribiah and Hashabiah as Levites, not as full priests as this translation clearly implies. Batten, basing his translation on 3 Esdras, argues that the text originally read, "and I set apart from the leaders of the people twelve, and from the priests of the temple Sherebiah and Hashabiah and with them ten of their brethren." That reading, however, still presumes that Sherebiah and Hashabiah were priests, indeed "leading priests." It would appear better, instead, to think of the group as consisting of twelve priests on the one hand and of Sherebiah, Hashabiah, plus ten more Levites on the other. One could translate then as the NIV does: "Then I set apart twelve of the leading priests, together with Sherebiah, Hashabiah, and ten of their brothers . . . ." Similarly, Slotki advises translating the Hebrew preposition *le* with the English words "besides."

L. W. Batten, *The Books of Ezra and Nehemiah* (ICC; Edinburgh: Clark, 1913) 322.

Judah J. Slotki, *Daniel• Ezra• Nehemiah* (Soncino Books of the Bible; London, New York: Soncino Press, 1985) 160.

evidence that the list suffered in the transmission of the text. The two "copper" vessels are modest. Williamson calculates their weight at less than twenty pounds. He also cites scholars who speculate that they were made of orichale, "an alloy of copper highly prized in the ancient Near East."[6]

This section of the narrative closes (vv. 28-30) with Ezra's charge to those transporting the gifts to Jerusalem. He proclaimed both the gifts and the gift-bearers "holy" to the Lord. That is, the bearers were dedicated to God for service at the temple, and the vessels would be used in the worship at the temple. Those bearing the gifts were supposed to guard/protect them (from both contamination and loss) on the trip and to deliver them to the temple in Jerusalem upon their arrival. The report of the preparations ends with the weighing of the gold and silver for distribution among those bearing it.

Journey to Jerusalem and Arrival, 8:31-32

Let it be noted first that this trip to Jerusalem is the second of five programmatic texts in Ezra-Nehemiah. Ezra 2:1-70a had described a huge party of returnees coming to reclaim their land and to rebuild the temple acting on the direct command of Cyrus. Ezra 7–8 now details the journey of a second group of returnees under the priest Ezra acting on the direct command of "Artaxerxes." Ezra 9–10 will show the necessity of purging members of the original company of returnees who had removed themselves from the "true" community by marrying local Judean women. The reuse of the list in Ezra 2:1-70a in Nehemiah 7:5-73a will show the continued viability of that community, guaranteed now by the reconstruction of the wall around the city, and Nehemiah 13:23-31 will describe one final purging of the community by Nehemiah.

According to Ezra 7:1-10, the journey from Ahava to Jerusalem took four months, beginning the first day of the first month (March/April) and ending the first day of the fifth month (July/August). The actual start of the journey was delayed until the twelfth day of the first month

Journey of Ezra

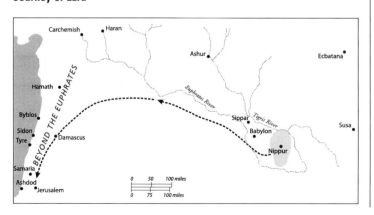

(Ezra 8:31), due to Ezra's desire to enlist Levites. Ezra 8:31-32 emphasized God's protection of the travelers during the journey. Readers may infer no loss of life, possessions, or offerings for God along the way. Nothing is said about their route, but readers may consult the opening remarks on Ezra 1:1 for some information about the geography of the trip.

Offerings for the Temple, 8:33-34

Ezra 8:33-34 records a strict accounting of the silver, gold, and vessels Ezra brought from Babylon to priests in Jerusalem, namely to Meremoth, the son of Uriah, and Eleazar, son of Phineas. Neither man was mentioned in the list of returnees in Ezra 2, but that list named travelers said to have returned in 539 BCE. (See the discussion of "The Date of the Return" in the comments on Ezra 2.) Those returnees could hardly be expected to be alive in 458, let alone 398 if Ezra traveled to Jerusalem then. Verse 33 lists independent witnesses of the accounting of Artaxerxes' gifts in Jerusalem, specifically by the Levites Jozabad ben Jeshua and Noadiah ben Binnui. Jeshua and Binnui were mentioned in Ezra 3:9 as two Levites who worked on the foundation of the temple. Appropriately, therefore, Ezra 8 names leaders in Jerusalem belonging to the generation *following* the return. Even then probably they would not have been young men.

Klaus Koch suspects more tension among the returnees than these verses disclose on the surface. He notes that none of these priests is designated the "high priest," even though Haggai and Zechariah use that term in the late sixth century. [7] (Readers of this commentary might profit from looking at the role of the high priest Joshua in Hag 1:1, 12, 14; 2:2, 4. In addition, Zechariah 3 details a vision of something like Joshua's institution as the high priest.) In Ezra 8, when Ezra first arrived, he acknowledged the status of Meremoth by delivering to him the wealth Ezra had brought from Persia, though interestingly the book does not call Meremoth high priest. A glance at Ezra 10:36, moreover, shows that he, like a number of other men, had married a local woman whom he sent away (divorced). Koch argues that his whole division of priests was removed from office, though later Jeshua again regained control of the temple and the priesthood. [8] Some of Koch's reconstruction is inferential, but in any case Ezra 10:36 mentions Meremoth as a priest who had to divorce his local wife, and one may note that Ezra himself took up residence in the temple (Ezra 10:6).

Worship at the Temple and the Delivery of Artaxerxes' Gifts, 8:35-36

Verses 35-36 revert to a third person narrative (cf. Ezra 7:1–8:15) and do not mention any names, though the obvious worshipers are Ezra and those who traveled to Jerusalem with him. They sacrificed burnt offerings consisting of twelve bulls, ninety-six rams, seventy-seven lambs, and a sin offering of twelve male goats for all Israel. In a burnt offering (sometimes called a "whole burnt offering" in English translations), the entire body of the sacrificial animal, and not just a part like the juicy tail, was burned. Such offerings were appropriate for dedicating altars or for other auspicious events.

They were meant basically to honor God and generally were portrayed as being costly.[9] A celebration involving the sacrifice of one hundred eighty-five animals would certainly be costly, and presumably would be appropriate for envoys of the Persian government. They also sacrificed twelve goats as a "sin offering": i.e., an offering for unintentional infringements of moral or ritual laws by the travelers.[10] [An Oddity in the Hebrew Text of Ezra 8:35]

Ezra 8 concludes with the notice that Ezra and the other travelers delivered King Artaxerxes' commissions to the local authorities, who in turn supported the people and the temple. While Ezra's trip was shown to be a complete success, the ensuing narrative in Ezra 9–10 about "mixed marriages" will reveal tensions in Jerusalem and Yehud.

An Oddity in the Hebrew Text of Ezra 8:35

AΩ Ezra 8:35 recounts the sacrifices offered by Ezra and his companions when they reached Jerusalem. It says clearly that they offered burnt offerings and sin offerings. Then the verse concludes with a phrase that may be translated "All of it was a burnt offering." That conclusion seems to dangle, so Norman Snaith suggests moving those words to a place earlier in the sentence before the reference to the sin offering. The text would then list the animals employed in the burnt offering and sum up its description" ". . . all these were (offered as) a whole-offering to the LORD" (p. 151). Regardless, all the animals mentioned in the verse would have been slaughtered and burned.

Norman Snaith, "A Note on Ezra viii. 35," *JTS* 22 (1971): 150–52.

CONNECTIONS

1. In the box titled "What about the Wives?" I raised the issue of male supremacy in Ezra-Nehemiah. It is not, however, an issue for the Old Testament and Old Testament times exclusively. In modern America, most women and children receive proper medical care, but not all. Of course, not all men do either. Still, it took an act of Congress to assure that things like childbirth and early childcare did not adversely affect the pay and promotions due women, and a "glass ceiling" is said to preclude women's advancement to top corporate or political positions.

I wish I could say that the church quickly saw not only how demeaning to women (and thus immoral, sinful) such restrictions are, but it did not and often still has not. In Acts 16:40, Paul and Silas went to the home of Lydia, apparently an economically independent woman who allowed a church to meet there. Early churches that met in homes presumably did so under the watchful eyes of the women of the household. First Timothy 3:11 admonishes "deaconesses" serving beside deacons to be serious, truthful, temperate, and faithful, and Romans 16:1 calls Phoebe a "deacon."[11] How widespread deaconesses may have been during the ministry of Paul is unclear, but soon enough the church embraced the *surrounding cultural prejudice* concerning roles women might play. First Timothy 2:12 speaks in the name of Paul, forbidding any woman to teach or have authority over a man. Thus, early on the church fell captive to the male supremacy of its environment. Those behaviors may have been adopted to make the church more attractive to its environment, but they relegate women to second-class status in the church. Likewise, some early Christians (e.g., Philemon) also owned slaves, but few would argue today that owning slaves is moral, let alone ordained by God.[12]

I spent my entire working career as a college (and occasionally, part-time seminary) professor, and this is what I have been seeing for decades. Fifty-five percent or more of college students are women. Up to two-thirds of academic and leadership awards go to women. In the corporate world, to be sure, there is still a glass ceiling keeping women out of many upper-level positions, but that ceiling is cracking. I have been saying to male students for years that the chances are very good and improving constantly that they

Georgetown College

Of the 1043 students who attend Georgetown College, where the author taught from 1986–2008, 54.2 percent are female, a statistic that mirrors the national trend.

View of Giddings Hall from Memorial Drive on the campus of Georgetown College in Georgetown, Kentucky. (Credit: Sydney Poore and Russell Poore, Wikimedia Commons, CC SA BY 3.0)

will one day work for a woman. It is time for men and women to readjust their thinking about women leading men. That statement is even truer for the church than for business and politics.

2. Ezra 8, like Ezra 1, is notable for its portrayal of the good ruler: he is one who is kind to his people and to sojourners, and one who is willing to give freedom and money to his foreign subjects. Warriors and conquerors though they were, there is little doubt that the Persians were kind to their subjects at least in comparison to the Assyrians and the Babylonians. Might American politicians, therefore, if they wish to be Christian, pay more attention to helping people and less to military power and big corporations?

3. Note should also be taken of Ezra's meticulousness in receiving, transporting, and delivering the king's money. Perhaps such care was merely a function of common sense; he was after all bearing the treasure of a powerful man. Perhaps, though, Ezra's care for those items offers readers an object lesson when caring for the goods of other people, whether powerful rulers, good friends, or total strangers. Ezra guarded the gifts as if they were his own and delivered them to the institution and persons for whom they were intended.

NOTES

1. J. P. Weinberg ("*Das bēit 'ābōt im* 6.-4.Jh.v.u.Z," *VT* 23 [1973]: 400–14, here 413–14) argues that the "father's house" of the Persian Period was a paternal association or bonding of the exiles and returnees that united a number of real or figurative families into functioning units. This type of association appears in Ezra 8:2, 5, 10 and Neh 1:1 and 3:4.

2. Ralph W. Klein, "The Books of Ezra and Nehemiah," *NIDB*, 3.725.

3. F. Charles Fensham, *The Books of Ezra and Nehemiah* (NICOT; Grand Rapids MI: Eerdmans, 1982) 115.

4. See H. G. M. Williamson, *Nehemiah* (WBC: Nashville: Thomas Nelson, 1985) 67. See more fully Raz Kletter, "Weights and Measures," *NIDB*, 5.834.

5. Williamson, *Ezra, Nehemiah*, 119.

6. Ibid. Bernhard Pelzl ("Philologisches zu Esra 8:27," *ZAW* [1975]: 221–24) offers the translation ". . . two vessels of wonderfully shinning copper, objects valuable as gold."

7. Klaus Koch, "Ezra and Meremoth: Remarks on the History of the High Priesthood," *Sha arei Talmon: Studies in the Bible, Qumran, and the Ancient Near East*

Presented to Shemaryahu Talmon (ed. Michael Fishbane, Emanuel Tov, and Weston W. Fields; Winona Lake IN: Eisenbrauns, 1992) 105–10.

8. Ibid., 110.

9. Philip J. Budd, *Leviticus* (NCB; London: HarperCollins; Grand Rapids MI: Eerdmans, 1996) 42–43.

10. Frank H. Gorman, "Sacrifices and Offerings," *NIDB*, 5.25-26. Lev 4:5-7, 16-18 gives the instructions for such sacrifices.

11. In 1 Tim 3:11 one finds the Greek word *diakonesantes*, female deacon, and Rom 16:1 calls Phoebe a *diakonos* (deacon).

12. The so-called "curse of Canaan" by Noah (in Gen 9:25) did not consign blacks to slavery, despite the claims of Americans in the nineteenth and twentieth centuries. The man Canaan was not African. Rather he was the progenitor of the Canaanites and the other olive-skinned people with whom Israel shared its homeland and whom it wanted to dominate. Besides, it was Ham, Canaan's father, who "saw [Noah's] nakedness." See Gen 10:15-19. Nor is it clear exactly what Ham did, though presumably it was worse than simply seeing his drunken father with no clothes on. See Stephen R. Haynes, *Noah's Curse: The Justification of American Slavery* (Oxford: Oxford University Press, 2002).

THE PROBLEM OF
MIXED MARRIAGES

Ezra 9–10

COMMENTARY

If Ezra's journey to Jerusalem turned out to be a success, the developments that ensued there were sometimes less than ideal, in one respect in particular as the author of Ezra saw it. Some returnees from 539, including priests and other temple officials, had not kept themselves separate from the "peoples of the lands" (i.e., people who had not been in exile) as required in Exodus 34:11-16 and Deuteronomy 7:1-6. [Parallel Laws in Exodus 34:11-16 and Deuteronomy 7:1-6] Specifically, Ezra 6:21-22 reported (without comment) that Judeans that had not been in exile joined the returnees in observing the Passover. What to do about those Judeans and other non-returnees constitutes the narrative climax of the book of Ezra in the last two chapters of that book. [The Nature of the Problem]

That action offers a specific example of a larger problem in the Bible identified by William P. Brown: divergent traditions and the issue of community.

Parallel Laws in Exodus 34:11-16 and Deuteronomy 7:1-6

The laws in Exod 34:11-16 and Deut 7:1-6 (or something much like them) stand behind the charges against intermarriage in Ezra 9–10.

Exodus 34:11-16	Deuteronomy 7:1-6
God will drive out of Canaan the Amorites, the Canaanites, the Hittites, the Perizzites, the Hivites, and the Jebusites [Girgashites not listed].	God will drive out of Canaan the Hittites, the Girgashites, the Amorites, the Canaanites, the Perizzites, the Hivites, and the Jebusites.
Make no covenants with them.	Make no covenants with them. Show them no mercy.
You will, but should not intermarry.	Do not intermarry with them.
Tear down their altars, etc.	Tear down their altars, etc.

For all the divergent traditions contained in the Hebrew Bible, for all its striking incongruities and tensions, it is the continuity of community that undergirded it. Through its tangled history, ancient Israel suffered schism, dissentions, exile, and fracture, and yet it remained, in its own eyes, a community. Amid the ever-changing course of history, Israel evolved as a community that productively borrowed from the cul-

The Nature of the Problem

The prohibition of marriage between Ezra's returning group and those left in Yehud during the exile is probably better called ethnic exclusivism than racial prejudice. Either attitude, however, demeans the persons rejected.

tures and religions of its neighbors as much as it polemically engaged the cultures and religions of its neighbors. The sheer variety of Scripture points back to the validity of the community behind it.[1]

It was indeed the constituency and the continuity of the community that were at stake in Ezra 9–10, but the "community" was defined quite narrowly, particularly, divergently, and incongruently to use Brown's terms. Brown's perspective is informed by a larger canon; the perspective of the author of Ezra-Nehemiah was informed by and articulated for a particular subset within the post-exilic community of Yehud: "The people of Israel," God's community, was understood by the redactor of Ezra 1–10 as the exiles who returned home to Jerusalem from Babylon. Their neighbors are not likely actually to have been Canaanites, Hittites, Perizzites, Jebusites, and others mentioned specifically in the text because those groups were ancient and had long since been absorbed into Israel—rather to the disgust of the redactors of Joshua–2 Kings. That means, of course, that the returnees themselves were as likely as anyone else in Judah/Yehud to have ancestors from those ethnic groups. Worshipers of YHWH who lived and worshiped elsewhere in Samaria and Yehud, however, were excluded from Ezra's particular community, even if they were ethnically as "pure" as anyone returning from Babylon.

For the redactor of Ezra-Nehemiah, the "real" Israel had been carried away into exile. Those who remained behind, no matter how many such persons there were and no matter where and how they might have worshiped YHWH during the exile, were considered unfit to worship in the rebuilt temple. Indeed, even early returnees who had married spouses from Yehud instead of from the returnees were deemed unfit to worship there until they divorced their "foreign" spouses and joined in with the returnees (Ezra 10:6-44). The author/editor of Ezra-Nehemiah defines all "uncontaminated" returnees as the new "in-group." It is by no means clear, however, that twenty-first-century readers of the Bible must agree. [An Alternative Biblical View of Who Belonged to Israel] In any case, the issue here is not simply whether to believe the Bible, but what to do about texts that flatly disagree with other texts. Isaiah 56:6-8 specifically says that in the new temple

foreigners who join themselves to the LORD, to minister to him,
to love the name of the LORD, and to be his servants,
all who keep the Sabbath, and do not profane it, and hold fast my
covenant—

these I will bring to my holy mountain [the temple in Jerusalem],
and make them joyful in my house of prayer;
their burnt offerings and their sacrifices will be accepted on my altar;
for my house shall be called a house of prayer for all peoples. (NRSV)

Readers of the Old Testament are caught between these two perspectives. In categories employed by scholars who study the history of religions, the difference is between ethnic religions (those into which one is born, adopted, or married) and universal religions (those that make membership or inclusion a matter of choice by individuals). Ezra was firmly entrenched in ethnic thinking, while Isaiah 56 draws deeply from inclusivity and individual choice. Paul and others led the early church into that second camp as well. (That issue lies at the heart of the book of Acts.) For Paul, all people are welcome before God, regardless of ethnicity, class, education, or any of the other particulars of human existence. There is an important lesson here for careful readers of the Bible, who try to keep the whole sweep of its contents in focus as they develop their own theology: just because religious folks, whether today or important people in the Bible, think and say they are doing the will of God is no guarantee that they are.

Ezra 9–10, then, constitutes the climax of the book of Ezra. If Ezra 1–6 reports a return of exiles from Babylon and their rebuilding the altar and temple in Jerusalem, Ezra 7–10 reports a return of still more exiles and the tension over who controlled and was fit to worship at that temple. (The fact, incidentally, that the book of Ezra recounts no other returns by exiles in Babylon to Jerusalem does not prove that there were none. The book of Ezra simply does not mention any others if there were any.) By connecting the Ezra narratives to the narrative of the return in 539, the redactor forged a link between those two groups of returnees, seeing them as the authentic part of old Judah/Israel, blaming any of them guilty of intermarrying, and by implication rejecting as non-Israelites *all* other residents of post-exilic Yehud who had not gone into exile including those who had joined themselves to the returnees as discussed in Ezra 6.

An Alternative Biblical View of Who Belonged to Israel

Despite the fact that the returnees' perspective dominates the Ezra narratives, one biblical text was far more inclusive: namely the book of Ruth, whose heroine was a Moabitess. According to Gen 19:30-38, Moabites were descendants of Abraham's son Lot. In pre-exilic times they seem not to have been hated, though they were not loved either. After the exile they were seen as impure. The book of Ruth, probably written in the post-exilic period, combats exclusivism by means of a brief postscript that identifies its Moabite heroine as an ancestress of David, the great king whose son Solomon built the temple. If, then, the Davidic line included a Moabitess, such people cannot all have defiled their partners and children. To be sure, the date of the book of Ruth is contested, but scholars who study the development of biblical Hebrew typically see the language of Ruth as fitting a transition period between the late pre-exilic and the early post-exilic periods. The acerbic tone of Ezra-Nehemiah is lacking in Ruth, and the short genealogy linking David and the royal line to a Moabitess has a "gotcha" effect to it.

In addition, moreover, J. L. Wright argues that Ezra 6 (written in the third person) and 9 (written in the first person) derived originally from different authors, that the first person account in Ezra 9 draws on distinctive features of Nehemiah 1:1-11 and 13:23-29, and that it therefore was composed secondarily as a new introduction to Nehemiah's account.[2] Regardless, the author of Ezra 9–10 thought that Ezra tried to build an exclusive community before the Yehudites rebuilt the wall of Jerusalem to keep out foreigners and their influence. Ezra 10, however, employs the third person limited point of view, so the oscillation observed in Ezra 7 and 8 between first person (Ezra 7:27-29; 8:1-34) and third person (Ezra 7:1-26; 8:35-36) continues in Ezra 9 (first person) and 10 (third person). That whole complex narrative (Ezra 7–10), nevertheless, defends the same ethno-biological view about who constituted the "real" Israel: the returnees.

By also adding the narrative of Nehemiah and interlocking that narrative with the work of Ezra by means of the narrative of Ezra's reading the law in Nehemiah 7:73b–8:18, the redactor of Ezra-Nehemiah did not tell three separate stories but one story covering three periods. Ezra 1–6 reported difficulties in rebuilding the temple, and restricted the workers to returnees (Ezra 6:16-18) who observed the Passover (Ezra 6:19-22). Likewise, Ezra 9–10 limits worship in the temple to returnees—even at the cost of divorce. [Outline of Ezra 9–10] The book of Nehemiah concludes the overall narrative by describing the rebuilding of the wall—an event anticipated already in Ezra 4:7-23. By adding the narrative of Nehemiah, which also condemns intermarrying with people not part of the exclusive sect of returnees, and by interlocking it with the Ezra narratives, the author/redactor claimed Nehemiah and his builders as part of the narrative of the "true Yehud."

Outline of Ezra 9–10

With regard to Ezra 9–10, then, the observation of Wolfgang Oswald is correct: "the balance of power in [Yehud] is at stake"[3] in these chapters.

Conflict Concerning the Purity of the Community, 9:1-15

As stated above, Ezra 9:1-15 places front and center the issue of intermarriage between returnees and non-returnees. The narrative seems to take at face value the report in 2 Chronicles 36:15-21 that Nebuchadnezzar had killed all the inhabitants of Jerusalem. (On the temporal priority of 1 and 2 Chronicles to Ezra-Nehemiah and the relationship between them, see the "Introduction to Ezra-Nehemiah" under the section titled "E. The Relationship of Ezra-Nehemiah to 1 and 2 Chronicles.") Clearly, Nebuchadnezzar destroyed the city and killed or exiled all inhabitants necessary to carry out its capture, but 2 Kings 25:11-12 also notes whom he killed/exiled and whom he spared. The latter were called "the poorest people of the land." (Cf. Jer 39:10, which also says Nebuchadnezzar spared "some of the poor people who owned nothing," and adds that he "gave them vineyards and fields.") Since virtually all persons who lived outside of cities would have constituted the "poor" in his view, they surely accounted for the overwhelming majority of the tiny population in 586. No doubt some of the poor, maybe even many, died in the fighting or starved as a consequence of the Babylonian siege, in which its soldiers ate or destroyed much of the farmers' crops. Still, the reality was that rural life continued. In addition, some inhabitants of Jerusalem may well have fled to the countryside in advance of the Babylonians' siege. Second Kings 25:22-26 narrates the activities of Gedaliah, the man the Babylonians put in charge of Judah after the destruction of the city. Clearly there were people for him to govern, and not all of them fled to Egypt with those who assassinated Gedaliah. Thus, the land was not bereft of Judeans or others.

Report about Mixed Marriages, 9:1-4
Such a disclaimer as the one in the previous paragraph probably would have been seen as nitpicking by the redactor of Ezra-Nehemiah. His sympathies and concern lay exclusively with the returnees (see Ezra 7:7, where they are distinguished from the other people of Israel, priests, and Levites in exile in Babylon), some of whom at least had married locals after they reached Yehud. ["The People of Israel"] H. Maccoby argues that the author of Ezra

> invented a new concept of the "holy seed" as equivalent in sanctity to the Temple and its appurtenances. . . . [He] extends Deuteronomy's prohibitions against intermarriage with Canaanites to "all exogamous marriages" [i.e., marriages with Judeans who had never been in exile]. Then he concludes from Deuteronomy that Israel is a "sanctum" and that the adulteration of the "holy seed" is a desecration of the *sancta*, for which, when inadvertent, the expiation is a [guilt offering].[4]

(The material within brackets was added to clarify Maccoby's meaning.)

"The People of Israel"

The book of Ezra uses the phrase "people of Israel" exclusively in connection with the returnees, as the following list will show.

• Ezra 1:3 uses the term "people" in connection with the exiles.

• Ezra 2:1 speaks of the exiles as the "people of the [Babylonian] province."

• Ezra 3:1 says that when the Israelites were settled in their towns, the people—led by Jeshua and Zerubbabel (conspicuous returnees mentioned in Ezra 2:2)—set up the altar in Jerusalem.

• Ezra 3:8 mentions Zerubbabel, Jeshua, their people, plus all the other priests, Levites, and people who had returned from exile, and credits them with making a beginning on the temple.

• Ezra 3:13 reports on other priests, Levites, and heads of families who had not been in exile and who cried in disappointment at the sight of the new (but shabby) temple, a note highly reminiscent of Hag 2:1-9.

• Ezra 6:21 discusses "the people of Israel who had returned from exile and all who had separated themselves from the pollutions of the nations of the land."

• Ezra 7:7 (speaking of those who traveled with Ezra) says that "some of the people of Israel, and some of the priests and Levites," etc., went up to Jerusalem.

• Ezra 7:13 has Artaxerxes grant permission for more of "the people of Israel or their priests or Levites" in his kingdom to relocate to Yehud if they so chose.

• Ezra 7:16 repeats that permission.

• Ezra 8:15-20 has Ezra review his volunteers, discover that there are no Levites among them, and send an envoy to Iddo and Casiphia to recruit some.

• Ezra 8:36 reports that Ezra's envoys supported the people and the house of God.

This list of texts shows that in the book of Ezra, the returnees were the ones designated the "people, priests, and Levites." The exception in Ezra 3:13 was based on Hag 2:1-9, which did not, however, speak of the returnees as the only people of the community. A mention of people, priests, and Levites appears again Neh 10:28, along with other cult officials. Also Neh 10:34 and 37 mention them in regulations about financing temple services and its officials, but that is a different issue.

Ezra, thus, perceived those returnees who married outside that group as traitors to their cause, which group/community should have been preserved by endogamy within the ranks of the earlier returnees. Everyone else was dismissed as foreign. As proof of God's demand for endogamy, v. 1 cites the injunctions against intermarrying with Canaanites, Hittites, Perizzites, Jebusites, Ammonites, Moabites, Egyptians, and Amorites as a precedent in v. 2 for forbidding intermarriage with anyone already in Yehud when the first returnees arrived (see Deut 7:1-4). As Bob Becking expresses the matter, "The idea of divine election is thus reformulated in biological categories."[5] [Parallels between the Peoples Listed in Exodus 34:11-16, Deuteronomy 7:1-6, and Ezra 9:1] Of course, the term "biological" must be used carefully here. This issue is not racial; all participants were Near Eastern residents of Yehud. It did not matter to the redactor that many or most of those involved were as "Israelite" as the returnees and, moreover, had been born and lived their entire lives there.

Returnees wanting and needing wives were in no position to be picky, however. They had to marry people available. Besides, a few people who had remained behind might have been or become as well as or better off financially than many returnees who had

---

Parallels between the Peoples Listed in Exodus 34:11-16, Deuteronomy 7:1-6, and Ezra 9:1

Exod 34:11-16	Deut 7:1-6	Ezra 9:1
Amorites	Hittites	Canaanites
Canaanites	Girgashites	Hittites
Hittites	Amorites	Perizzites
Perizzites	Canaanites	Jebusites
Hivites	Perizzites	Ammonites
Jebusites	Hivites	Moabites
	Jebusites	Egyptians
		Amorites

A comparison of the lists in Exod 34:11-16 and Deut 7:1-6 with Ezra 9:1 shows several differences. For one thing, the third list does not mention the Hivites, but they do not appear in post-exilic texts other than 1 and 2 Chronicles, where the Chronicler is following Samuel/Kings. Perhaps they were no longer of interest to the Jerusalemite community. Second, the order of the remaining peoples varies somewhat, but that was true even between Exodus and Deuteronomy. Of more interest, third, is the addition of the Ammonites, Moabites, and Egyptians. The Moabites and the Ammonites became bitter foes of Judah at the time of the destruction of Jerusalem (see Zeph 2:8-11), perhaps for not aiding refugees. The Egyptians constitute the most intriguing addition. Jews at the military colony of Elephantine built their own temple in the sixth century BCE, which the Persians destroyed a century or so later. Modern readers know of its existence from a papyrus from that colony written in 407 BCE to Bagoas, the governor of Yehud, asking for help in rebuilding their temple. It was perhaps worshipers at that temple that the author of Ezra 9:1 had in mind as specifically barred from the rebuilt temple in Jerusalem.

See "Petition for Authorization to Rebuild the Temple of Yaho," *ANET* (2011), 450–51.

---

brought back only what they could carry. Returnees might have seen people living on former land holdings of returnees, moreover, as "squatters," although such charges are not leveled in the text. Still, those who had remained in Yehud after the fall of Jerusalem would have been understandably unwilling to cede property in 458 that had been vacated (forcibly or not) more than a hundred years earlier in 586. Besides, they may well have considered the exiled Davidides, priests, and other upper-class persons guilty of inhospitality, usury, and similar offenses (the Old Testament prophets certainly did often), and they may have believed that the former leaders (i.e., the exiles) got exactly what they deserved. One need only read texts like Jeremiah 1:1-10; 13:15-27; 18:13-17; 21:11-14; and Zephaniah 1:2–2:3 to find just such sentiments among the biblical prophets.

Ezra 9:1-4 portrays "officials" (a conveniently nonspecific identification; see [Officials]) reporting to Ezra that "the people, the priests, and the Levites," all presumably from the returnees in 539, were guilty of committing abominations, namely of intermarrying with "the peoples from the lands." The charge seems reminiscent of the warning in Deuteronomy 12:30-31 against committing the abomination of the inhabitants of Canaan. The list of people with whom intermarriage was forbidden

Officials

AΩ The term for "officials" (*śārîm*) appears six times in Ezra 7-10. In Ezra 7:28 it designates officials of the Persian king; in Ezra 8:20 officials of David; in Ezra 8:24 and 29 leading priests; and in Ezra 10:8 people rendering judgments along with elders. Its use in Ezra 9:1 is singularly vague, perhaps intentionally so. Perhaps Ezra simply did not want to disclose the identity or office of his informants.

reads like those in Exodus 34:16, Deuteronomy 7:3, and Nehemiah 13:32. The reference to Israel as the "holy seed" appears elsewhere too: e.g., Exodus 19:26 and 22:31; Deuteronomy 7:6 and 14:2; and Malachi 2:15. T. C. Eskenazi and E. P. Judd suggest an identity for those people that is completely consonant with the view expressed above, namely that "the women of Ezra 9–10 could have been ethnic Judeans or Israelites who had not been in exile and who, in the eyes of the early returnees, were appropriate marriage partners."[6] Those women claimed legitimacy, a claim that had been accepted in Jerusalem prior to Ezra's arrival, and modern readers might well ask, "Why not?" [What Did the Law Say?] Ezra's response, though, was to mourn before God. He tore his clothes as a sign of grief, pulled some of his hair, and sat, appalled at such behavior. Likeminded persons, presumably the officials who reported the "misbehavior" to Ezra, joined his period of silence.

Ezra's Reaction: Mourning and Prayer, 9:5-15

At the time of the evening sacrifice [Evening Sacrifices], Ezra arose from his seat where he had been fasting (v. 4), fell on his knees (a posture of humility in prayer), and prayed to God. The contents of the prayer, at least in summary form, appear in vv. 6-15. It is a model for such prayers. Ezra approached God in shame and contrition over the (perceived) sins of the people. They had been unable to hide their sins from God. Indeed, those sins themselves had risen to heaven. Nor, Ezra confessed, was his generation the first to do so. He and all the readers of this book would know of the centuries of sins that had led to the destruction of Jerusalem and the exile. Still, God had not abandoned the city for the depravity of its inhabitants, but had shown divine favor or grace by remembering the exiles in Babylon and by giving the returnees a "stake" in God's "holy place," i.e., the temple. In v. 9, Ezra employs the image of a fence, a protective surrounding, as a metaphor for the temple. Their condition of ongoing servitude Ezra terms "slavery," a description that reveals how many/most of the people of Yehud conceived of their lives in the hands of the Persians. No matter how kind an occupying power may conceive of itself as being, locals paying taxes and obeisance to them are almost certain to perceive them differently. Ezra could understand their power over Jerusalem only as a function of what moderns sometimes call God's "permissive will." God would permit such things to happen in the first place if and only if God's people deserved it. God would continue to allow such domination to continue in the second place if and only if God's people deserved it. Such domination would continue

What Did the Law Say?

The issue of what kinds of marriages were or were not permissible in the Old Testament is a thorny one that Sara Japhet has discussed at some length. First, she reminds readers that there is no law in the Pentateuch forbidding intermarriage *in general* (italics Japhet's). Exod 34:11-16, however, warns against making covenants with the people of Canaan, and Deut 7:1-3 prohibits marriage with them. Finally, Deut 23:1-3 excludes from the "congregation of the Lord" (JPS Bible) those whose genitals are damaged, bastards, Ammonites and Moabites, and Edomites and Egyptians. All those laws seem to offer the basis for Ezra's pronouncement.

The issue for Ezra was this: how should people settle issues not directly covered by the Law? Japhet's answer is that Ezra's speech utilizes all these texts from Deuteronomy. The table below shows the overlap among them.

Ezra 9:1, Peoples with whom Israelites, priests, and Levites had intermarried	Deut 7:1, Peoples Israel was supposed to put to death	Deut 23:3, Peoples not to be admitted to the assembly of YHWH
Canaanites	Canaanites	
Hittites	Hittites	
Perizzites	Perizzites	
Jebusites	Jebusites	
Ammonites		Ammonites
Moabites		Moabites
Egyptians		
Amorites	Amorites	
	Girgashites	
	Hivites	
		Anyone with testicles crushed or penis cut off

It appears that the Girgashites and Hivites in Deut 7:1 simply were omitted from Ezra 9:1. The first four peoples in Ezra's list (Canaanites, Hittites, Perizzites, and Jebusites) plus the Amorites were listed in Deut 7:1, however. Of the remaining three (Ammonites, Moabites, and Egyptians), the Egyptians had been omitted from the list in Deut 7:1, possibly because some of them had aided Israel's escape. Ammonites and Moabites were not on the list in Deut 7:1, either. They were named in Deut 23:3, though, where they (along with any man whose testicles had been crushed or whose penis had been cut off) were to be *barred from the assembly of YHWH*.

Ezra 9:1, therefore, contains a list drawn from *two* Deuteronomic texts. Of its eight nations, the first four (the Canaanites, Hittites, Perizzites, and Jebusites) no longer existed in Ezra's time, and the seventh (the Egyptians) had been exempted from the list of the banished in Deut 23:7 because of kindness offered by some of them to Israelites. According to that verse, Egyptians could be admitted to full status in their third generation in Israel. Japhet argues, then, that the author(s) of Ezra 9 and 10 created a new list of people to which the law against intermarriage would now apply. It draws on Deut 7:1 and forbids intermarriage with people from five of the nations mentioned there, *as well as* from Egypt. It also draws on Deut 23:3, which bans Ammonites and Moabites from the assembly of YHWH and the others from the list of nations Israel was supposed to put to death according to Deut 7:1. These last three nations, Egypt, Ammon, and Moab, then, are the only three really in view.

Further on, Ezra 9:11-12 also brings in two more originally unconnected texts: Lev 18:27 and 20:24. The first speaks of earlier inhabitants defiling the land, and the second promises it to Israel. Ezra 9 puts the two passages together, arguing thereby that intermarriage was banned because of the uncleanness of the peoples. It was an easy step in Ezra 9:11-12, then, to ban marriages with such people, and another in Ezra 10:3 to have the scribe Ezra urge the people to send away the offending wives as a necessary step toward Israel's regaining the land. Why, though, send away the children? The answer may be that ethnic affiliation goes with the mother. Thus a foreign mother bears foreign children, so the Moabite and Ammonite mothers should take their children with them.

Sara Japhet, "Law and 'the Law' in Ezra-Nehemiah," *Proceedings of the Ninth World Congress of Jewish Studies* (Jerusalem: Magness, 1985) 99–115, esp. 106–11.

Evening Sacrifices

Evening sacrifices are mentioned occasionally in the Old Testament. The first occurrence appears in Lev 6:20, where God tells Moses that Aaron (and his successors) was to prepare a meal (flour) sacrifice on the day he was anointed as priest. He was to burn part in the morning and part in the evening. The evening offering is mentioned again in 2 Chr 2:4, which specifies that evening offerings be made daily. In 2 Kgs 16:10-15, King Ahaz ordered a new altar built in Jerusalem, dedicated it with offerings, and ordered that various offerings, including an evening grain offering, be made daily. 2 Chr 31:2 says that King Hezekiah ordered burnt offerings every morning and evening, and Ezra 3:3 says that Joshua and Zerubbabel set up the altar in Jerusalem again, and that "they" offered burnt (i.e., animal) offerings every morning and evening. The practice, obviously, was well known and needed no explanation in Ezra 9:4-5.

until God's people had paid the price of their sins. Only God's grace could change the situation.

In v. 10, the prayer makes a turn with Ezra's words, "And now . . . what?" Ezra had confessed to God the sins of the people, which explained the past and current condition of Yehud, so next Ezra would lay out what the people must do to improve their lot. If the problem was that they had forsaken the commandments of God (Ezra 9:10), the response of the people should be to confess their sins (Ezra 10:2) and to amend their ways (Ezra 10:19). First (Ezra 9:11-12), however, Ezra specified the nature of the sins of returnees. He imaginatively positioned the people around him outside Yehud, in the Sinai and east of the Jordan before Joshua led them into Cisjordan. He strung together a series of allusions to verses from Leviticus, Deuteronomy, and 2 Kings in this sequence: Deuteronomy 18:15; Leviticus 18:24-30; Deuteronomy 18:9; 2 Kings 21:16; Deuteronomy 7:3; 23:6; 11:8; 6:11; and 1:38-39. Then he fast-forwarded to his own time. He concluded that the exile and the current condition of Yehud and Jerusalem were *less* punishment than the people actually deserved. The hearers (or at least the readers) were left to suppose, perhaps, that Ezra thought God would have been justified in wiping out the whole countryside and leaving it empty.

In Ezra 9:15, Ezra asked God (and his readers rhetorically) if the "remnant" (the returnees) now would break faith with God by marrying those who had remained in Yehud. God had been just to punish old Judah and to send the exiles to Babylon. Ezra questioned how the returnees in his presence could stand before God if they incurred guilt by marrying the contaminated people who had remained behind in Judah.

Resolution of the Problem by Public Divorce, 10:1-17

Ezra 10 divides nicely into two parts. The first part, vv. 1-17, describes the positive result of Ezra's confession. The second part, vv. 18-44, lists the priests (vv. 18-22), the Levites (vv. 23-24), the singers and gatekeepers (v. 24), and the laypeople, the "people of

Israel" (vv. 25-43), eighty-four men altogether, who had divorced their wives. The chapter concludes with an enigmatic verse that reports the divorce. The comments on Ezra 10 will follow the divisions of that analysis, except that Ezra's actions and the community's reactions will be discussed under two headings.

The Community's Reaction, 10:1-5

The verbs in Ezra 10:1 change voice from the first person to the third person, suggesting a switch in sources, but the narrative of Ezra 10 nevertheless presupposes the action described in the "memoirs" in Ezra 9. The phrase "While Ezra prayed and made confession . . ." summarizes Ezra 9:5-15, and while the second half of the verse recalls the setting described in Ezra 9:1-4, Ezra 10:2-5 begins to narrate the people's response to Ezra's prayer. A Returnee named Shechaniah, son of Jehiel (who was an exile from the area of Elam in eastern Persia; see Ezra 2:7), spoke up to confess his own guilt and that of other returnees. They had indeed broken faith with God by marrying "foreign" women, "foreign" to the returnees, that is, but local inhabitants of Yehud/Jerusalem. He urged his co-returnees to join him in divorcing their local wives, since it was their duty to God. Ezra seized the moment and compelled all other guilty returnees (priests, Levites, and "all Israel") to promise to do so. Ezra 10 clearly presents that outcome as morally right and God ordained. (I, however, find his perspective to be theologically and ethically flawed, and I will reflect on this issue below in Connections 2.)

Ezra's Fast and the Community's Assembly to Bring about Separation, 10:6-15

These verses describe the banishment of the local wives of early returnees. Readers learn that Ezra mourned—over the "faithlessness" of early returnees, not over what was happening to those families. He went to the home of a priest named Jehohanan son of Eliashib [Jehohanon Son of Eliashib] and fasted all night as an act of mourning over their perceived disobedience. Next, the narrator says that "they" (no names cited) issued a proclamation throughout Judah and Benjamin (i.e., the parts of the old alignment of tribes that belonged to tiny Yehud) summoning all returned exiles (designated here as "the people of Judah and Benjamin") to an assembly in Jerusalem. The

Jehohanon Son of Eliashib

The identity of this priest is intriguing. Williamson devotes a lengthy discussion to it, listing five different solutions. He considers the list in Nehemiah defective, since it names only six high priests during the period of 539–322. In any case, this "son of Eliashib" is not named in the list of six high priests found in Neh 12:10: Jeshau, Joiakim, Eliashib, Joida, Jonathan, and Jadua. He notes, moreover, that the name "Eliashib" was fairly common, so the priest mentioned here was not necessarily the high priest.

H. G. M. Williamson, *Ezra and Nehemiah* (WBC; Nashville: Thomas Nelson, 1985) 152–53.

text does not say to how many people that summons applied, but the empty area that was old Jerusalem around the temple would have held that part of the population of Yehud. The assembly, held three days later on the twentieth day of the ninth month (Chislev, so the meeting was held in December), was for returnees only. It was a cold, rainy day, which made the people shiver—both because of the weather and because of the gravity of the matter according to v. 9. The people sat in an open place in front of the temple, awaiting Ezra's words and actions.

What followed was a nasty scene. Ezra demanded first that the accused returnees confess their sins to the Lord God of their Ancestors. That sin, of course, was their marriage to local women construed as "peoples (plural) of the land" and "foreigners," although they clearly hailed from Yehud. The guilt-stricken returnees, perhaps afraid of Ezra and clearly afraid of what God might do to them, agreed at once. They did, however, make one (humane) request: postpone the mass divorce (the expulsion of the affected women and children) for three days. One might suppose they would need that much time to gather belongings and to make arrangements for the wives and children to move somewhere. One can only hope that they did not simply kick the women and children out of house and home. They were to leave in an orderly manner on the third day (v. 14).

The decision was not, however, unanimous. Two priests and two Levites demurred. The author carefully records their names, presumably so that their apostasy would be remembered and their actions held against their descendants. One of the names, that of the Levite Meshullam, was the same as the name of one of Ezra's hand-picked Levites who aided him on his journey (Ezra 8:15). Perhaps his defiance of Ezra's decision was seen as especially blameworthy. In any case, the four men left. To carry out the action, Ezra personally selected heads of each family. They appear to have examined each case, beginning their investigation after ten days. The situation may have been more complex than the narrator made it seem because it took them two months to review all the cases and be sure all the directives had been carried out.

List of People Involved in Intermarriage, 10:18-43

Ezra chose heads of families among the returnees to investigate who had married non-returnees. The investigators did as they were told. The book of Ezra concludes (vv. 18-33) with a list of returnees who had married locally, but agreed to divorce (lit., "send away") the wives (and children). The first group of guilty men (vv. 18-21) consisted of priests from four families: Jeshua, Immer, Harim, and Pashhur. These four priestly families were also listed in Ezra 2:36-39. [Priestly Families Who Returned from Exile with Zerubbabel and the Number of Descendants Who Apostatized] The list continued, classification by classification: Levites, temple singers, gatekeepers, and families of laypeople. Among the families listed here, six were also listed among those returning with Zerubbabel: Parosh, Elam, Zattai, Bebai, Bani, and Hashum. The family of Bani is listed twice, permitting one perhaps to wonder if the second occurrence was originally Bezai, named third from last in Ezra 2. Regardless, these six names are enough to prove the narrator's point: returnees among the first group had intermarried with people who had not been in exile. Since many returnees were listed by town rather than by name in Ezra 2, the names Harim, Hashun, Binnui, and Nebo probably conveyed the same message as the names of the priests: all were men who returned from Babylon to Yehud earlier than did Ezra and had married local Judean women who had not been in Babylon.

Priestly Families Who Returned from Exile with Zerubbabel and the Number of Descendants Who Apostatized

Ezra 2:36-39	Ezra 10:18-22
From Jeshua: 973	From Jeshua: Maaseiah, Elizer, Jarib, and Gedaliah
From Immer: 152	From Immer: Hanani, Zebadiah
From Harim: 1017	From Harim: Maaseiah, Elijah, Shemaiah, Jehiel, and Uzziah
From Pashhur: 1247	From Pashhur: Elionai, Maaseiah, Ishmael, Nethanel, Jozabad, and Elasah

Concluding Summary, 10:44

Verse 44 is the conclusion of the book of Ezra, although it is strangely worded—perhaps in keeping with its strange sentiments, perhaps because it was damaged in transmission. It might be translated, "All of them had taken [as wives] foreign women, and some of them were wives that bore children." The second part of that verse is muddled, although its general sense is fairly clear. The offending males had married local Judean women, and some of those wives had borne children. Read that way, the verse wraps up the author's discussion of what he considered a wrong and deplorable situation, but it actually leaves the outcome open. (That issue will rear its head again in Neh 9:1-3.) The NRSV, however, follows the parallel passage in 1 Esdras 9:3b, and renders the verse, "And these had married foreign women, and they sent them away with their children." If 1 Esdras 9:3b has the correct ending, the solution (divorce with the children going with their mothers) compounded a perceived wrong with action that perpetuated the consequences of the "sin" to another generation. Commenting on this and other passages in Ezra-Nehemiah, Mark McEntire observes, "Human beings have become the initiators of covenant, and God's response is hoped for but not explicitly present."[7]

This discussion of Ezra and his reforms is not intended to make him out as a bad man but to show him—as the Bible typically does with its heroes—as a sinful man and also one flawed like all other human beings. God's justice and God's grace sometimes are channeled through human agents, even the best of whom sometimes err in judgment and conduct, even as they try to carry out God's will. God's manner of acting also stands as a warning to all of God's servants in positions of authority. They are to be careful how they exercise that authority. Just because people act for God does not guarantee that they will be God-like in their actions. (See further below in Connections 3.) R. W. Klein is kinder to Ezra and the returnees than I, condemning the action but suggesting that intermarriage with those who had remained might mitigate the rights of the returnees to the land in case their standing might be compromised in the future.[8] If so, would even that fear justify their actions? Klein and I are agreed on what happened but perhaps disagree on its defensibility.

As the book of Ezra stands in the MT, however, God's action in the restoration of Jerusalem and Yehud had only begun. It had not reached its full development. The book of Nehemiah would narrate the ensuing actions of God and God's people in Yehud. In the middle of that book, Ezra emerges again as a key actor. J. P. Lange wrote a paragraph from a thoroughly Christian perspective that, with a few modifications, might well serve as a postscript for the entire book of Ezra and a transition to the book of Nehemiah.

> It is true that [the returnees] still for a long time . . . could not entirely dispense with externalities. It was necessary that their God should ever have a temple, in which to dwell among His people, though apart from them. . . . [S]o Israel itself [deemed that they, the returnees,] still needed a city in which they might be near the temple, in which more than anywhere else they might live in a religious community, and they must still secure it with walls and gates. But in view of their higher and proper aim, they were no longer called to reconquer their political independence and re-establish a worldly kingdom.[9]

CONNECTIONS

1. If indeed the redactor/author of Ezra-Nehemiah thought that the true Israel consisted only of persons who had been exiled to Babylon and that they and their descendants alone were worthy of being considered children of Israel, he held a view quite at variance from the author of the book of Ruth. That post-exilic author told the story of the union of not just one but two men from old Judah with the same Moabitess wife: Ruth. The first husband, Chilion, died childless (Ruth 1:1-5), but the second, Boaz, was the progenitor of King David. (See the brief genealogy in Ruth 4:18-22.) The message of that book for its original audience and for its reader today was clear: all people matter to God.

Ruth and Boaz

In Ruth 2, the Moabitess Ruth finds work in the field of Naomi's kinsman, Boaz, and secures permission from him to glen in his field. This picture depicts that first meeting.

Rembrandt Harmensz van Rijn (1606–1669). *Meeting of Ruth and Boaz in the Fields*. c. 1640. Pen and bistre ink on paper. Louvre, Paris, France. (Credit: © RMN-Grand Palais/Art Resource, NY)

It is very difficult to get over prejudice of any sort, and doubly so when other people are perceived to threaten one's perks or financial status, let alone one's faith. Throughout American history the same difficulty is encountered in connection with perceived political "rights" based on gender, race, or ethnic background. Native Americans represent a repressed indigenous group disparaged by the people who conquered them. An old saying that epitomizes this feeling runs, "the only good Indian is a dead Indian." Our nation's experience, moreover, is that one group of immigrants discriminated against others, including Native Americans. Even many Europeans (especially eastern Europeans) entered the United States as refugees. All those persons became second-class persons, often designated by labels: e.g., wetbacks, niggers, Japs, coolies, and wops (people who entered "without passport"). Even now some people (immigrants or not) are often condemned as "freeloaders," "bums," or "shiftless," with little or no consideration given to their contributions to American society, let

Hardship and Suffering

Eldon Garnett and Francis LeBouthillier. *Memorial to Commemorate the Chinese Rail Workers in Canada.* 1989.

Located where the main rail line crosses Spadina Avenue, just north of the Rogers Centre stadium (formerly Skydome), this massive monument commemorates the thousands of workers brought from China to build the Canadian Pacific Railway in the late 19th century. (Credit: Shaun Merritt/Wikimedia Commons CC-by-2.0)

Immigrants just arrived from foreign countries—Immigrant Building, Ellis Island, New York Harbor. (Credit: Library of Congress, Prints and Photographs Division, Washington DC)

These three images capture the hardship and danger suffered by many groups in the United States, in particular European and Asian immigrants and Native Americans.

Navajo Men at Fort Sumner NM. Detail. c. 1866. (Credit: National Archives, 111-SC-87976)

alone their humanity. One cannot eat or wear respect, but a lack of respect and concern is deadly to human growth and relationships. The struggle not just for equality but also for respect wages on in our beloved country, even among Christians.

2. People trying to do the "right thing," i.e., to obey God in perplexing times, may well face ethical decisions like those of the returnees (the heroes of Ezra 2) in confronting such basic issues as whom to marry and (as in Old Testament laws) what to eat or drink. Indeed, a religion that does not deal with such issues is not very useful to everyday life. Readers of the Bible are apt to read these verses on the assumption that "if Ezra did it, it must have been correct." Bede, for example, argued that those who were innocent (i.e., who were married to other returnees) flocked to Ezra, while those who had married locals had thereby sinned.[10] It seems to me, however, that Ezra and his companions erred in the way they attempted to correct what they considered sins and moral failings on the part of the earlier returnees. Ezra and his people

demanded that the earlier returnees divorce their local wives and send them and their children away. Perhaps those women were able to return to their fathers' homes; perhaps they would have been able to remarry; perhaps not. If what those early returnees did was morally repugnant to God and deserving of censure, so be it— although I must confess I see no sin incurred by some in the first wave returnees marrying the women there, but I see great wrong, indeed sin, in banishing those women and their children. What would seem to me better for them to have done—*if anything*—was to request repentance for their marriages and then for the community to accept those women, children, and all other would-be worshipers of God at the temple. I am not alone in that sentiment about post-exilic Yehud. Isaiah 56:7 (probably from the early post-exilic period but traditionally understood to be from eighth-century Isaiah) articulates such an open perspective by quoting God as saying of the temple, "my house shall be a house of prayer for all peoples." Zechariah 14:16-21 likewise envisages a future temple/Jerusalem, where peoples from all over the world who chose to do so could come to observe the Feast of Tabernacles. According to both prophets, the people of God and their places of worship are to be open to all who come.

People are often guilty of condemning someone for actions the observers consider wrong, only to conclude later that they (the observers) were the ones in error. Sometimes observers act on the basis of incomplete information, but other times for selfish reasons. The perceived moral (or other) failures of others may actually rest on distortions of the truth—even the will of God—based on one's own self-interests.

3. These reflections raise a question about the nature of the Bible itself. Some people, of course, consider the Bible to be the actual w-o-r-d-s of God, *literally* true word for word. Even they, however, agree that the Bible contains poetry (though they might not agree that all poetry is symbolic and that it works on various levels besides the literally obvious) and would concede that the reference in Ecclesiastes 1:4 to the sun's rising, going down, and hastening to the place where it rises is not literally, scientifically accurate. The exegesis of Ezra 9–10 given above, however, involves making a distinction between what the Bible says in one place versus what it says in another and choosing between them. Such a choice is not usually an issue for Christians when the distinction is between what the Old Testament said and the New Testament makes of it, though often those differences are minimized (unconsciously or deliberately) by reading the New Testament back into the Old. For

example, people often insist that Isaiah the prophet was predicting Jesus in Isaiah 7:14 (based on Matt 2:22-23). Actually, the eighth-century BCE prophet clearly was speaking of a child who already had been born and was living in Jerusalem, who was to be understood by the king of Judah as a sign concerning the danger the kingdom was facing, and the impending end of that threat. The situation and all the persons mentioned belong to the reign of King Ahaz of Judah sometime between 735 and 732.

The issue in Ezra 9–10, then, is how to read Ezra's demands for divorce. One could simply say that divorce was the will of God, perhaps the "permissive" though not "real" will of God. Or one could appeal to the New Testament's teachings against divorce to settle the issue, and maybe that is what I have done. Such an appeal leaves open the issue of how to handle ethically or theologically challenging passages in the New Testament itself, however. It also leaves open challenging texts like Ezra 9–10 that are not addressed in the New Testament. Differently stated, is one permitted as a Bible-believing Christian to evaluate negatively the actions and sayings of people in the Bible that are uncontested by the Bible itself?

Once again, I think the answer is affirmative. Let me cite one experience from my classroom teaching. Several years ago, a student told me that she had just become a Christian and had decided to read the Bible through. She started with Genesis. When she reached chapter 19, which concludes with the sordid story of Lot's incest with his daughters that resulted in the births of Moab and Ammon, my student was appalled. She complained that the text did not even say their behavior was wrong. I asked her if it really needed to do so. She quickly replied, "No." Almost any reading of that text would result in the same answer.

In the case of the divorce of the women in Jerusalem by their husbands, returnees from 539, the text also makes no comment. Perhaps the author thought that the decision to divorce the women was morally defensible. Contemporary readers do not have to share that opinion, however, in order to read the Bible as God-inspired literature. Readers, therefore, do not have to approve the actions of Ezra and his supporters as dutiful adherence to God's will. In fact, readers might do the Bible as a whole more justice by criticizing that heartless solution. I belabor this issue because contemporary believers too might face situations for which biblical narratives or even outright instructions might seem to offer disturbing teachings, when the words of those verses might better be read as descriptive than as prescriptive.

NOTES

1. William P. Brown, "From Apology to Pedagogy: Interpreting the Bible Past and Present in the Seminary Classroom," *Int* 66 (2012): 371–82; here 377.

2. Jacob L. Wright, "Seeking and Writing in Ezra-Nehemiah," *Unity and Disunity in Ezra-Nehemiah; Redaction, Rhetoric, and Reader* (ed. Mark J. Boda and Paul L. Redditt; Hebrew Bible Monographs 17; Sheffield: Sheffield Phoenix Press, 2008) 277–304; here pp. 287–88. Most scholars, traditional or critical, take the term literally as descendants of those ancient neighbors. See the 1708 classic *Matthew Henry Commentary on the Whole Bible*, http://www.biblestudytools.com/commentaries/matthew-henry-complete/ezra/, on Ezra 9:2.

3. Wolfgang Oswald, "Foreign Marriages and Citizenship in Persian Period Judah," *Journal of Hebrew Scriptures* 12, article 6, 16.

4. Hyam Maccoby, "Holiness and Purity; The Holy People in Leviticus and Ezra-Nehemiah," *Reading Leviticus; A Conversation with Mary Douglas* (JSOTSup 227; ed. John F. A. Sawyer; Sheffield: Sheffield Academic Press, 1996) 153–69, here 167.

5. Bob Becking, "Continuity and Community: The Belief System of the Book of Ezra," *The Crisis of Israelite Religion: Transformation of Religious Tradition in Exilic and Post-exilic Times* (ed. Bob Becket and Marjo C. A. Korpel; Leiden, Boston, Cologne. Brill, 1999) 256–75, here 270.

6. Tamara C. Eskenazi and Eleanor P. Judd, "Marriage to a Stranger in Ezra 9–10," *Second Temple Studies 2: Community in the Persian Period* (ed. T. C. Eskenazi and H. K. Richards; Sheffield: Sheffield Academic Press, 1994) 266–85, here 285.

7. Mark McEntire, "Portraits of a Mature God: What Would a Theology of the Hebrew Scriptures Look Like if Ezra-Nehemiah Was at the Center of the Discussion?" *PRelSt* 39 (2012): 122. The word "covenant," in fact, is used only here in Ezra and in Nehemiah only in Neh 1:5 and 9:32 (where it quotes or paraphrases Deuteronomy), and in Neh 9:8 (which alludes to Gen 15).

8. Ralph W. Klein, "The Books of Ezra & Nehemiah," *The New Interpreter's Bible* (Nashville: Abingdon, 1999) 3:747.

9. John Peter Lange, *Commentary on the Holy Scriptures. Critical, Doctrinal and Homiletical. Ezra* (Grand Rapids MI: Zondervan, n.d.) 1.

10. Bede in Marco Conti, ed., *Ancient Christian Commentary on Scripture: Old Testament V. 1-2 Kings, 10-2 Chronicles, Ezra, Nehemiah, Esther* (Downers Grove IL: InterVarsity, 2008) 330.

INTRODUCTION TO NEHEMIAH

The book of Nehemiah continues the book of Ezra.[1] [Outline of the Book of Nehemiah] It depicts the last and longest part of a three-part story: an original return under Sheshbazzar (see Ezra 1 and its mention of Sheshbazzar in Ezra 5:13-17) and under Zerubbabel and Jeshua and others (Ezra 2:1–5:12 + 6:1-22); a second return under Ezra (Ezra 7–10); and a third return under Nehemiah, along with his efforts to strengthen the city and its defenses. Another part of the Ezra narrative, however, stands separate from the first part, namely in Nehemiah 7:73b–8:18, and Nehemiah 12:26 and 36 mention Ezra the scribe editorially. (Neh 9:5 in the LXX also mentions him editorially. The NRSV adopts that reading, though Ezra is not mentioned in the MT.) It appears, therefore, that the scribe(s) responsible for the canonical collection Ezra-Nehemiah linked Ezra 1–6 to Nehemiah by means of identical lists of returnees in Ezra 2 (which mentioned Nehemiah third, even though he played no role in the action in the book of Ezra) and in Nehemiah 7. This oddity in Ezra 2, combined with the large number (nearly 50,000) of reported returnees, has caused a number of modern scholars to surmise that the list itself originated *after* the return of Nehemiah, maybe even well after. (See further the discussion "H. The Date of Ezra-Nehemiah" in the "Introduction to Ezra-Nehemiah.") It is quite possible, however, and maybe even probable that Ezra's career did overlap Nehemiah's; the previous sentences simply describe the literary situation. Indeed, the position of this commentary is that both Ezra and Nehemiah flourished during the reign of Artaxerxes I.

Nehemiah's first trip to Yehud occurred in the twentieth year of Artaxerxes' reign (445; see Neh 2:1), and the text says he remained there until the thirty-second year (Neh 13:6), when he returned to Susa. Then, "after some time" (apparently brief), he sought and received permission to return to Jerusalem, where he discovered that non-returnees had gained a foothold in the temple and that the Levites had not been paid, forcing them to return to their farms to make their living (Neh 13:10-14). Nehemiah brought them back to Jerusalem to work. While the activities of Nehemiah himself are related largely in the first person singular, material from various other

Outline of the Book of Nehemiah

Nehemiah Learns of the Ruined State of Jerusalem, 1:1-11

The Transition from Ezra to Nehemiah, 1:1a

The Setting for Nehemiah, 1:1b-3

The Prayer of Nehemiah, 1:4-11a

The Status of Nehemiah, 1:11b

Nehemiah Goes to Jerusalem, Inspects Its Walls, and Decides to Repair Them, 2:1-20

The Confession of Israel's Rebellion against God's Commands, 9:16-31

Nehemiah Secures Permission from Artaxerxes to Repair Jerusalem, 2:1-8

Journey and Initial Meeting with Sanballat, 2:9-10

Nehemiah's First Three Days in Jerusalem, 2:11-16

The Decision to Repair Jerusalem, 2:17-20

Organization of the Work, 3:1-32

Opposition from Leaders of Samaria, 4:1-23

The Work on the Wall and the Opposition of Sanballat and Tobiah, 4:1-9

Nehemiah's Response, 4:10-15a

Work on the Wall Resumed, 4:15b-23

Financial Mistreatment and Generosity, 5:1-19

Complaints from Workers about Financial Mistreatment, 5:1-13

The Generosity of Nehemiah, 5:14-19

Opposition Overcome and the Wall Repaired, 6:1–7:73a

An Invitation to Meet with Sanballat, Tobiah, and Geshem, 6:1-9

An Invitation to Plot with Shemaiah in the Temple, 6:10-14

The Completion of the Wall, 6:15–7:4

The Census Taken by Nehemiah, 7:5-73a

Ezra Summons the Returnees to Obey the Law, 7:73b–8:18

The Setting of the Narrative, 7:73b

The People Gather and Direct Ezra to Read them the Law, 8:1-8

The People Return Home and Celebrate the Harvest, 8:9-12

The People Build Booths and Observe the Festival of Booths, 8:13-18

Confession Signed by the Returnees and Details of a New Covenant, 9:1–10:39

A Prayer of Confession, 9:1-38

The Setting for the Confession, 9:1-5

The Prayer of Confession, 9:6-37

Praise for Creation and the Promise to Abraham, 9:6-8

Praise for God's Victory at the Red Sea and for Leading Israel, 9:9-15

The Confession of Israel's Rebellion against God's Commands, 9:16-31

The Returnees as "Slaves" in Their Own Land, 9:32-37

The Result of the Confession: An Agreement in Writing, 9:38

Those Who Signed the Agreement, 10:1-27

Obligations under the Agreement, 10:28-39

Population of the City and Villages Increases; Dedication of the City Wall, 11:1–12:43

The Resettlement of Some Returnees, 11:1-2

The Names of the Returnee Families Living in Jerusalem, 11:3-24

The Returnees who Lived in Surrounding Villages, 11:25-36

Priests and Levites who Returned with Zerubbabel and Jeshua, 12:1-26

The Dedication of the City Wall, 12:27-43

The Reforms of Nehemiah, 12:44–13:31

The Assignment of Temple Responsibilities, 12:44-47

An Introduction to the Encounter between Nehemiah and Tobiah, 13:1-3

The Reforms of Nehemiah, 13:4-31

Everything Foreign Cleansed, 13:4-14

Sabbath Observance Reformed, 13:15-22

Mixed Marriages Condemned, 13:23-27

Priesthood and Temple Purified and Offerings Enabled, 13:28-31

Nehemiah. Illustration for *Old Testament Portraits* by Cunningham Geikie. Engraving. English School, 19th century. Portraits drawn by A. Rowan and engraved by G. Pearson. (Credit: Private Collection/© Look and Learn/Bridgeman Images)

sources also was used in the retelling, following the pattern in Ezra of enhancing an act or event by showing that the hero acted with the full knowledge and permission of the Persians, as well as on his own initiative in carrying out his commission from God.

Modern scholars have often compared the book of Nehemiah to extra-biblical literature. The ancient writer Josephus, for example, retold the narrative portions of Nehemiah in condensed form, giving more prominence to the priest Ezra. At the same time, he emphasized Nehemiah's service to King Artaxerxes and his respect for law, aspects of Judaism important to Josephus in his defense of his faith. He also made Nehemiah into another Joseph, effective in leadership and generous in using his own money to aid God's cause.[2] G. von Rad argues that the book shows affinity with inscriptions detailing the actions of Near Eastern and Egyptian officials in terms of phraseology and the descriptions of official tasks.[3]

A. The Role of Nehemiah in the Canonical Book that Bears His Name

Unlike Ezra, Nehemiah was not a priest. When the narrator needed to include instructions on how to worship, he used a narrative about Ezra the priest (Neh 7:73b–8:18). Nehemiah's primary role was to direct the repairing of the wall around Jerusalem. The political reason for the Persians to allow that project is never given, though scholars have speculated. (No surprise there!) Apparently that repairing activity marked a change in status of the still largely ruined and scarcely populated city. Resettlement of the city was confined to the central part of the old city. Estimates put its population at only 1,500 at most to as few as about 625 people in Nehemiah's time.[4] [Archaeologists' Estimates of Populations of Ancient Sites] Whatever purpose the Persians might have had in allowing the repairing of the wall of Jerusalem was irrelevant to the scribe(s) responsible for Ezra-Nehemiah. To him, the key mover was

Archaeologists' Estimates of Populations of Ancient Sites

Archaeologists estimate the size of the population of ancient sites by a number of means: old records, the size of a settlement, the number and size of buildings, the size of the walls if present, and the number of grave sites, to name but a few. Simply put, human occupation leaves remains. Moreover, and surprisingly, density varies little down to modern times. Archaeologists determine the type and size of an occupied site, and then they can make a fairly accurate estimate of the population of an area. What is at issue in post-exilic Jerusalem is how much of the older city was reused and when. By New Testament times, Jerusalem was far larger that in Old Testament times. Still, even if a considerably larger city was rebuilt than the returnees needed (since they were repairing older walls), Persian period settlers left precious few artifacts that have been discovered.

Will more be recovered? Quite possibly. Will the conclusions change? That would require major new discoveries in the area that appears to have been occupied. For the time being, it appears as if Nehemiah repaired the old city walls because that was easier than building new ones, although the population was sparse. Certainty is impossible, though, because archaeology in the old city is difficult both for political reasons and because modern Jerusalem was built right over it. For the time being, probably most respected archaeologists now hold to a figure from a 600+ to c. 1,500, however sad that figure might make some of them.

God, who worked through Nehemiah. The people of God had returned to the city of God and rebuilt its temple already. The next task was to repair its wall. Readers might suppose the purpose of the wall was security, and that may well have been part of the motivation. One may doubt, however, that a repaired wall around such a sparsely populated city would have fended off for long a siege by Persia. In repairing the wall, however, the returnees did prepare Jerusalem to be the city of God housing the temple of God for the people of God.[5] Unlike Ezra, then, Nehemiah was no priest; but like Ezra, his work was essential to Jerusalem's new role as the spiritual hub for the returnees.

B. The Structure of Nehemiah

The book of Nehemiah constitutes a threefold narrative, as analyzed by E. S. Gerstenberger.[6]

Nehemiah 1:1– 7:73a	**Nehemiah 7:73b– 10:39**	**Nehemiah 11–13**
Commission, 1:1– 2:10	Proclamation of Torah, 7:73b–8:18	Population Delineated, chapter 11
Repairing, 2:11– 6:10	Prayer of Petition, chapter 9	Priests, Levites, other Officials, 12:1-26
Lists, 7:1-73a	Covenant Commitment, chapter 10	Dedication of the Wall, 12:27-43
		Dedication of the Community, 12:44–13:31

Torah proclamation, prayer, and commitment to God and community stand in the center of the book and at the heart of their experience.

C. The Plot of the Book of Nehemiah

As has already been noted in comments on Ezra, the book of Ezra-Nehemiah offers a carefully redacted narrative of the return of the "true" Israel from Babylon to Jerusalem. Five passages anchor this case. (1) Ezra 2:1-70a shows a huge party of returnees coming to reclaim their land and to rebuild the temple acting on the direct command of Cyrus (Ezra 1:1–6:22). (2) Ezra 7–8 details the journey of a second group of returnees under the priest Ezra acting on the direct command of "Artaxerxes," and the list of returnees in

Ezra 8:1-14 ties Ezra 7–8 to the original group of returnees. (3) Ezra 9–10 shows the necessity of purging members of the original company of returnees who had removed themselves from the "true" community by marrying local Judean women. Ezra 10:18-44 anchors that narrative. (4) Nehemiah 7:5-73a employs (apart from transmission errors) the same list as Ezra 2:1-70a, and it shows the continued viability of that community, guaranteed now by the reconstruction of the wall around the city. Finally, Nehemiah 12:1-26 repeats a little of that list, describes one final purging of the community by Nehemiah, and assures the readers that their descendants, their "group," were the ones who repopulated Jerusalem.

An analysis of the narrative portion of Nehemiah reveals the following typical narrative structure: setting, complications, climax, and denouement. Viewed from that perspective, the book of Nehemiah opens with its hero safely and productively at work in Susa, one of the capitals of the Persian Empire. The time is the twentieth of the month of Chislev, i.e., the ninth month, or November/December in modern calendars. Verse 2 ties Nehemiah to the exiles in Babylon and identifies them as "those who escaped the captivity," i.e., those who had survived the demise of the city by being taken to Babylon. The fate of the city, long known to the exiles themselves, was described—for the benefit of the later reader. That "news" saddened Nehemiah, who prayed to God for the city and implored God's help/mercy.

The complications begin with Nehemiah 2. The sadness Nehemiah felt over the state of Jerusalem showed on his face and in his demeanor before King Artaxerxes. The king, therefore, granted Nehemiah's request to go to Jerusalem. After surveying the broken condition of the walls, Nehemiah planned a course of action, organized a workforce under priests, and rebuilt/repaired the walls. The chief impediment, or obstacle to be overcome, was the opposition leader of Samaria, a man named Sanballat. No reason is given for his actions; he is

Tomb of Artaxerxes

Prospective tomb of Artaxerxes I in Naqsh-e Rustam, Iran. (Credit: Anatoly Terentiev, Wikimedia Commons, CC-BY-SA-3.0)

The Tomb of Artaxerxes remains as a reminder of his power.

portrayed as fully vile, a portrayal he might have strongly denied. The repair work was finished speedily. The people met to confess their sins (Neh 9), the population of the city increased by casting lots to see who would move there (Neh 11), the wall was dedicated (Neh 12:27-43) and duties assigned. The climax had been reached and presented. Things had moved toward a satisfactory conclusion. When it seemed that all would end well, Nehemiah returned to Susa. Such a denouement was not to be the case, however. Those nearby residents of "foreign descent" (i.e., people who had remained behind in Jerusalem during the exile) wanted to worship in Jerusalem too, but they were banned (Neh 13:1-3). Rather than ending peacefully, the narrative reports a new crisis in the temple. Twelve years after his arrival in Jerusalem, Nehemiah returned to the presence of Artaxerxes, but then trouble arose in the temple in connection with Tobiah, a Yahwist whose name meant "Yahweh is good." That turmoil (or something else) brought Nehemiah back to Jerusalem (Neh 13:6-7). He banned Tobiah from the temple. Then he instituted Sabbath observance reforms and condemned "mixed marriages," thus ending the book of Nehemiah on the same exclusivist note that closed the book of Ezra.[7]

D. Memoirs of Nehemiah and Other Sources

As mentioned in the Introduction to Ezra-Nehemiah, "C. The Historical Reliability of Ezra-Nehemiah," scholars typically note that the book of Nehemiah contains an extensive amount of first person singular narrative material that plausibly can be attributed to Nehemiah himself: Nehemiah 1:1–2:20; 3:33 [Engl. 4:1]–7:3; 12:27-42; and 13:4-31. Nehemiah 3:1-32 is a list of work groups that by its nature is not first person singular. That it is authentic to its context is possible but not provable. In the following discussion, it will be treated in its context in the "Memoirs of Nehemiah." These texts offer a coherent portrayal of the activities (and thought) of Nehemiah.

First person plural verses appear in Nehemiah 9:38–10:39, which includes a list of people said to have signed a covenant to separate themselves from the "people of the land," the Judeans who had not been in exile in Babylon. It lists Nehemiah's name as a signee, and it is quite consistent with the overall thrust of Ezra-Nehemiah that the returnees made such an agreement to worship at the temple and underwrite its needs and supply its priests. That the non-priestly wall-builder Nehemiah had anything to do with that pledge is not said explicitly, though Nehemiah is clearly included among the signees.

The rest of the material in the book consists of the following: Nehemiah 7:5-73a//Ezra 2:1b-67 (the numbers of returnees),[8] Nehemiah 7:73b–8:18 (a third person narrative about Ezra), Nehemiah 9:1-37 (a prayer of penance, in which the MT does *not* mention Ezra), Nehemiah 10:1-37 (the signees of a covenant and its stipulations), Nehemiah 11:1-36 (another list of groups of inhabitants), and Nehemiah 12:1-25 (another list of returnees). The chapters do not mention Nehemiah, and they are written in the third person. They appear to be separate traditions picked up by the redactor of Ezra-Nehemiah and used in connection with his discussion of Nehemiah's career. Finally, the book of Nehemiah, like that of Ezra, draws in places on laws in the Pentateuch, although it is not always clear exactly what the text received by the redactor said. Likewise, he may well have modified his received texts to make them fit his context.[9]

E. The Message of the Book of Nehemiah

Despite the rancor and exclusivism that permeate Nehemiah, what is its abiding message? Is it not that God desires that God's people cooperate with each other and God to live the godly life in their rising up and in their sitting down, in their work and in their celebration and leisure, and even in their marrying? In Nehemiah, that life is marked by celebrating life with God and trying to obey God's commandments. The book of Nehemiah portrays that ideal in exclusivist terms, but the ideal itself should not be lost on modern readers. What might we do to reflect better the love of God for all people? On Sundays, let us worship with all of God's children who care to join us. At Thanksgiving, let us eat and celebrate in the name of God and in inclusive ways. Let us thank God for loving us, not just in spite of but maybe because of all our differences. At Christmas, let us honor our Jewish friends with a Hanukkah card. If we are ever near a mosque, let us pause for prayer ourselves at the call from the minaret. Yes, and we may share our faith and listen as they share theirs. We all might learn more about God, whether anyone converts or not.

Worship: Christian, Muslim, and Jewish

Carol A. Highsmith (1946–). A congregation sings God's praises at the Freewell Missonary Baptist Church in Montgomery, Alabama (Credit: Library of Congress, Prints and Photographs Division, Washington DC)

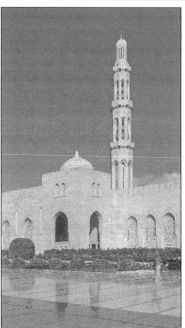

Main minaret of Sultan Qaboos Grand Mosque, Muscat, Sultanate of Oman. (Credit: Richard Bartz, Wikimedia Commons, CCA-SA 3.0)

President Obama hosts a traditional Passover Seder Dinner on Thursday night, 9 April 2009. Some friends and White House employees and their families joined the Obama family. (Credit: Pete Souza, White House photographer)

CONNECTIONS

1. What might a book about the repairing of the wall around Jerusalem and the handling of legalistic issues teach modern readers? One thing is that in biblical faith and worship, material things matter. Humans are ventilated bodies capable of a proper, worshipful relationship with God. Nowhere does the Bible, and particularly not the Hebrew Bible, describe them as eternal spirits encased or captured in unspiritual, mortal bodies. That Christian view arose after the time of the writing of the New Testament and was derived from the church's Greek culture after the completion of the writing of those books. Modern inheritors of that Greek anthropology read it back into the Bible. In biblical anthropology,

we are bodily beings before God, created to worship and to have communion with God. In the Old Testament, the book of Daniel in particular looked forward to the *resurrection* of martyrs and others. So too in the New Testament, believers are promised that they will be raised (as bodies, though perfected ones) to eternal life. The material world, moreover, is God's creation.

The construction of the wall around Jerusalem, insofar as its purpose was to "fence in" the holy God and protect the temple from the impurity of outsiders, misunderstood the inclusive nature of God. As we have seen in places in Ezra and will see again in Nehemiah, that exclusivism brought about extreme, unnecessary heartache for some of the people of God and set up roadblocks against others who wished to be part of that people. We must be careful to note the difference. In Nehemiah as in Ezra, the issue lay within people who considered themselves descendants of Abraham. The returnees saw themselves as the legitimate heirs of Jerusalem and the temple and of their benefits. They described those descended from Judeans and others who had remained in Judah as the "out group." In the new Persian-period Yehud, the returnees alone would hold both religious and political power.

Some time before the New Testament period, Pharisees and Sadducees divided over such basic questions as what books belonged in the Hebrew Bible and whether there would be a resurrection, questions no living human being could answer definitively. The Essenes (the sect most likely responsible for assembling the books that constitute the Dead Sea Scrolls) seem to have rejected both Pharisees and Sadducees. Even modern western Judaism is divided among Orthodox, Conservative, and Reform believers.

Nor has the church, ancient or modern, escaped such thinking. Its barriers are sometimes subtler, but historically they have far-reaching consequence. In Europe, not only did Roman Catholicism and Eastern Orthodoxy divide, but Eastern Orthodoxy developed its own various lingual and national divisions. Likewise, Protestants separated from Roman Catholics, and Protestantism itself was a splintered movement. Indeed, even Baptists in the United States exist in a bewildering array of sub-denominations. The divisions are sometimes quite acrimonious over differences some other Christians can hardly detect. The accompanying diagram, which lists only major divisions, will illustrate the splintering of the church. [The Three Basic Branches of Church Denominations]

The religion of ancient Israel was an ethnic religion, i.e., one into which people were born. In the Hebrew Bible, the act of circumci-

The Three Basic Branches of Church Denominations

Eastern Orthodox	Roman Catholic	Protestantism
Russian		Lutheran
Greek		Anglican
Slavonic		Presbyterian
Coptic		Baptist/Disciples
Ethiopian		Adventist
Syrian		Pentecostal

sion was the rite by which Hebrew males were initiated into the covenantal community. Non-Hebrew males living among Israelites also could gain permission to participate in the community's religious observances and rites by submitting to circumcision. Foreigners were not always welcome, nor did they necessarily always want to participate in Israelite rites, but Isaiah 56:6-8 anticipated the time when foreigners who joined themselves to God would serve and minister to God, offer acceptable sacrifices, and pray in the temple. The translators of the LXX, moreover, typically used different words to distinguish typical foreigners from converts.

How one reads texts, even Ezra-Nehemiah, can be important. If readers assume that whatever a biblical writer endorses is correct, such readers will buy themselves great difficulty. If Genesis 1–3 must trump evolution, must Ecclesiastes 1:5 trump the modern view of the solar system? ("The sun rises and the sun goes down, and hurries to the place where it rises.") Likewise, if Ezra and Nehemiah were correct that only returnees belonged to the true Israel, does that idea have any enduring relevance in a world where Herod's temple was destroyed by the Romans in 70 CE?

How, moreover, could the church possibly conceive of itself as the new Israel? Is it not clear that the New Testament itself reinvented the idea of Israel as a community for Jews *and* Gentiles (i.e., everybody) and replaced sacrifice at the temple with the understanding of the crucifixion as Jesus' offering of himself for the redemption of all people, Jews and Gentiles? Is it not just as clear that Jews did not accept that reinterpretation, though Judaism became quite open to converts? Ezra and Nehemiah ultimately did not win in Judaism.

Romans Destroying Jerusalem in 70 CE

Francesco Hayez (1791–1882). *The Destruction of the Temple in Jerusalem, 70 AD, by Roman Soldiers.* Galleria d'Arte Moderna Venice. (Credit: Alfredo Dagli Orti/The Art Archive at Art Resource, NY)

2. What is the basis for this shift between Ezra-Nehemiah and the New Testament, which saw the good news as applicable to all people? It appears to be the fundamental conclusion that God had deliberately included Gentiles by sending Jesus and founding the church. Indeed, the New Testament itself is clear that God had meant to include both Jews and Gentiles all along, and already in Genesis 12:3 God says to Abram that through him "all the families of the earth shall bless themselves." Before New Testament times, Judaism itself had come to accept proselytes, and the point of the discussion in Jerusalem in Acts 15 was that now God was admitting into fellowship all believers, Jews and Gentiles, on the basis of faith. [Proselytism] In short, from the perspective of the New Testament, exclusion was never part of God's plan, and the inclusion of Gentiles was. That shift represents a fundamental rethinking of the nature of who belonged to God's people that surfaced in Ezra-Nehemiah.

Proselytism

The act of proselytizing or making converts of adherents of one faith to another is a common theme in the New Testament, beginning as early as the narrative of the conversion of the Ethiopian eunuch in Acts 8:26-40. That man was a "God-fearer," one attracted to Judaism (for its monotheism or ethical standards), but unable or unwilling to convert fully. Neither his race, his nationality, nor his castration precluded his becoming a disciple of Jesus, however. Since Judaism, however, was an ethnic religion, the barrier was high but not absolute. He could have been circumcised as part of the ritual, presumably, so conversion would have been possible.

3. It is not difficult, however, to understand and appreciate why the authors of Ezra-Nehemiah took the stance they did. In the Old Testament, belief in Yahweh was conceived in ethnic terms: Yahweh was the God of the children of Abraham. Proselytism was acceptable, particularly in the case of spouses, slaves, and others who belonged to an Israelite household. Ezra-Nehemiah was something of an aberration, then. It made its case for the returning exiles on the grounds that they had lost their positions and perks due to their sinfulness, a point the prophets had thundered at them repeatedly. What was needed was for the returnees to get things right, to restore the temple, and thereby to ensure the future blessings of God upon the returning community. The problem with that perspective is simply that it was exclusivistic. God also loved the people who remained behind, people the returnees refused to see as part of the covenant. Are not our church splits and our denominational wars, however, due in part at least to the same kinds of disagreements? Even if we are no more successful than God's people in Yehud of getting along, can we not at least continue to try to love each other and to long for a time of peace—if only in heaven?

NOTES

1. For a more extensive introduction to the overall collection, see Introduction to Ezra-Nehemiah.

2. See Louis Finkelstein, "Josephus' Portrayal of Nehemiah," *JJS* 43 (1992): 187–202.

3. Gerhard von Rad, "Die Nehemiah-Denkschrift," *ZAW* 76 (1964): 176–87.

4. See the discussion in David Ussiskin, "On Nehemiah's City Wall and the Size of Jerusalem during the Persian Period: An Archaeologist's View," *New Perspectives on Ezra-Nehemiah* (ed. Isaac Kalimi; Winona Lake IN: Eisenbrauns, 2012) 101–30, here 116. The larger estimate of c. 1,500 has been offered by, among others, Oded Lipschits, "Archaemenid Imperial Policy and the Status of Jerusalem," *Judah and the Judeans in the Persian Period* (ed. Oded Lipschits and Manfred Oeming; Winona Lake IN: Eisenbrauns, 2006) 19–52, here 32.

5. See Manfred Oeming, "The Theological Ideas behind Nehemiah's Wall," *New Perspectives on Ezra-Nehemiah* (ed. Isaac Kalimi; Winona Lake IN: Eisenbrauns, 2012) 131–49, here 147.

6. E. S. Gerstenberger, *Israel in the Persian Period; The Fifth and Fourth Centuries B.C.E.* (Biblical Encyclopedia; trans. S. G. Schatzmann; Atlanta: Society of Biblical Literature, 2011) 14 (with modifications).

7. M. D. Goulder ("The Songs of Ascents and Nehemiah," *JSOT* 75 [1997]: 43–58) points out interestingly that Psalms 120–127 follow the first person singular narratives in Nehemiah 1:1–7:5a sequentially, and that Pss 133–134 follow the narration in Neh 13:4-31. What exactly those observations prove may be left open except to say that within later books of the Old Testament the Nehemiah narrative was known and his actions highlighted.

8. Neh 7:4-5 contextualizes for the book of Nehemiah the list that follows in Neh 7:6-73a.

9. See the discussion by Hannah K. Harrington, "The Use of Leviticus in Ezra-Nehemiah," *JHS* 13 (2013): 1–20. Harrington argues that at least some differences may be accounted for by text fragments found among the Dead Sea Scrolls. She may well be correct, but modern readers probably need to remember that Ezra-Nehemiah and the latter parts of the Pentateuch seem not to have been written until the post-exilic period. With the text in flux, post-exilic authors may have felt at liberty to make alterations when quoting it.

NEHEMIAH LEARNS OF THE RUINED STATE OF JERUSALEM

Nehemiah 1

COMMENTARY

[Overview of Ezra-Nehemiah] As mentioned in the Introduction to Nehemiah, the book constitutes the second part of a two-volume work describing the work and trials of the returnees, the descendants of the sixth-century exiles to Babylon who returned to Yehud under Sheshbazzar (Ezra 1:8-11 and 5:14) and Zerubbabel (Ezra 2:1–5:2; see also the book of Haggai and Zech 1–6). As discussed in the introduction to this entire volume, Ezra-Nehemiah itself was composed of three parts, each with its own purpose. Ezra 1–6 was designed to legitimate the returnees as the proper religious and local political leaders of Yehud. They came back under the commission and with the assistance of the Persian emperor Cyrus. As far as the redactor of Ezra-Nehemiah was concerned, the temple was for their exclusive use. Ezra 7–10 skips ahead a couple of generations, but it too was written to defend the prerogatives of the returnees over against any claims that the people who had remained behind in Yehud might assert or desire for themselves. Ezra returned with another small group of returnees to assure the ethical purity of worshipers there, a purity guaranteed by descent from the original returnees. That claim had political ramifications, which is one reason why Ezra 1–6, 7–10 and the narrative of Nehemiah place so much emphasis on their appointment by the Persians and their careful compliance with the Persians. Finally, the book of Nehemiah was written to defend the ongoing rights and perquisites of the returnees over against those of the Samaritans and those in Yehud who cooperated or at least sympathized with them. It described the rebuilding of the walls of Jerusalem by the descendants of returnees only, making the city a

Overview of Ezra-Nehemiah

Restoring the Yehudite community through rebuilding the temple, Ezra 1–6

Restoring the Yehudite community through reaffirming the Law, Ezra 7–10

Restoring the Yehudite community through rebuilding Jerusalem's wall, Nehemiah 1–13 holy zone/area around the temple, thus protecting it from ritual and ethical contamination. Overall as well perhaps, Ezra-Nehemiah was written to legitimate the claims of the returnees in the eyes of the captives still in Babylon and gain their agreement with and approval of the actions the returnees had taken.

Nehemiah 1 leaps ahead from the discussion of Ezra's career and the banishment of wives and children of returnees who married locals to the career of Nehemiah, set in the twentieth year of Artaxerxes (apparently in 445 BCE, but probably 446; see below in connection with Neh 1:1b-3), slightly more than a decade later than Ezra 7–10. Aside from Nehemiah 7:73b–8:18, the book of Nehemiah shows no awareness of Ezra. That silence does not prove that the two men did not know each other; it might simply reflect their different duties. Still, the population of Jerusalem was so small (estimated at 1,500 and possibly as low 625 as late as the time of Nehemiah) that they must have known each other if they lived there simultaneously. (See the discussion of the population of early post-exilic Jerusalem and [Archaeologists' Estimates of Populations of Ancient Sites] in the "Introduction to the Book of Nehemiah.") Regardless, the redactor or author of Ezra-Nehemiah makes it clear that their actions were part of one divine plan, although he does not have them interact.

Margaret Cohen distinguishes two types of narratives in Nehemiah: "Story-Telling Tales" and "Document Tales."[1] The former, of course, are narratives that emphasize the actions of their participants, especially their hero. Such narratives appear in Nehemiah 1:1b-11, 2:1-9, 2:10-20, 4:1-15/16, 5:1-13, 6:10-14, and 13:6-31, and they provide much of the plot of the book. The other narratives were built around documents that play a significant role. Those narratives include Nehemiah 3:1-28, 5:14-19, 6:1-9, 6:15-19, 7:1-72, 8:1-18, 9:1-37, 10:1-10, 11:1-36, 12:1-26, 12:27-43, 12:44-47, and 13:1-5. Since the English word "tale" often but not necessarily carries the connotation "untrue," "false," or even "lie," the more neutral term "narrative" will be used here. Narration is the act and art of telling events. (Again, however, readers are reminded that fiction can tell the truth about people and that biographers and autobiographers can lie or at least be mistaken.)

Readers will remember what has been argued before in connection with the book of Ezra, namely that the redactor of Ezra-Nehemiah presented the threefold return to Jerusalem (Ezra 1–2, Ezra 7–8, and Neh 1–2), the rebuilding of the temple (Ezra 3:1–4:5 + 5:1-22), the limiting of the "elect" community to returnees (Ezra 7–10), and now the rebuilding of the wall around Jerusalem (Neh 1–6) as parts of one piece of work by God. The redactor did so by interlocking the narratives. In the midst of the narrative about rebuilding the temple, Ezra 4 has the Persians grant returnees permission to rebuild the wall. That is a narrative one would expect and in fact gets in Nehemiah 2. In the midst of the narrative about Nehemiah, moreover, the redactor has Ezra read the Law (Neh 7:73b–8:18), thus completing his own mission by determining who was fit to worship at the temple in Jerusalem and who was not. Nehemiah 1 provides the transition from one hero to the other and introduces him. [Outline of Nehemiah 1]

> **Outline of Nehemiah 1**
> The Transition from Ezra to Nehemiah, 1:1a
> The Setting for Nehemiah, 1:1b-3
> The Prayer of Nehemiah, 1:4-11a
> The Status of Nehemiah, 1:11b

The Transition from Ezra to Nehemiah, 1:1a

The book of Ezra ended on the sad, even appalling note that earlier returnees who had married local wives were forced either to divorce (expel) them and their children or to leave the community of returnees with their families. Only four men refused to comply, and their names were duly noted as outcasts (Ezra 10:15). The book of Nehemiah begins with the phrase, "The words of Nehemiah, son of Hacaliah." That heading resembles the headings of the prophetic books Isaiah (see 1:1, 2:1, 13:1), Jeremiah (1:1), Hosea (1:1), Joel (1:1), Amos (1:1), Micah (1:1), and Zephaniah (1:1). It is not clear that that heading was intended to make Nehemiah into someone like a prophet, but he is portrayed as someone who spoke and acted for God as a genuine prophet would. As was true with Haggai (1:1; 2:1, 10, and 24) and Zechariah (1:1, 70), his work was dated during the reign of a Persian king.

As in the book of Ezra so also in the book of Nehemiah, one of the redactional motifs is the marking of time. Six date markers appear in Nehemiah, namely in Nehemiah 1:1, 2:1, 6:15, 7:73b, 9:1, and 13:6. (See also Ezra 7:1, but there the formula is not as clear, nor did it matter. Ezra's legitimacy derived from his priestly lineage, which was traced intermittently all the way back to Aaron.) The date formulae in Nehemiah sound like those in Haggai and Zechariah 1–8 in particular. The reader knows from the outset that this man Nehemiah, who turns out to be a wine steward in one of the Persian courts, will tell his own story in his own name, the story of a mission—as it turns out—that was carried out under the authority of the Persian king.

The Setting for the Narrative, 1:1b-3

With no further introduction to Nehemiah or his situation, v. 1b assumes the first person singular voice, dates what follows in "the month of Chislev" (i.e., November/December) and "the twentieth year," and locates him in Susa. (See [Months in the Hebrew Calendar] in the comments on Ezra 3.) Immediately readers want to know "twentieth year of what?" As it turns out, the answer seems to be the twentieth year of the reign of King Artaxerxes I, but the answer to the question of which Artaxerxes was in view is so debatable that scholars write articles and monographs about it. (That information may tell readers more about biblical scholars than readers want to know.) In the Introduction to Ezra-Nehemiah, the suggestion was made that Nehemiah may have served under, and the original narrator of his activities may have flourished during, the reign of Artaxerxes I (465–424). In that case, there would have been no question about his identity. It would only become an issue after the rise of Artaxerxes II (r. 404–358). Readers of the book of Nehemiah may have a question about which Artaxerxes was in question, but it is not necessary that even an editor from the fourth century, knowing Nehemiah not to be a contemporary, would have been uncertain as to which Artaxerxes was in view. Later still, the issue might emerge, but readers of the final version of the book in the Greek period might not have cared much which Persian king was in view.

The literary narrator also locates the hero Nehemiah in Susa, one of the several capitals of the Persian Empire. Situated near the southwestern border of modern Iran and Iraq, north of the western end of the Persian Gulf, it lay near the southern border of Persia. It had been the leading city of a culturally distinct group, the Elamites, who were assimilated into Persia under Cyrus. This background is intimated in Ezra 4:9, which mentions "the people of Susa, that is, the Elamites."

Another issue to resolve is the year of the action in Nehemiah 1. The problem is that the date of that action is given as the month of Chislev, in the twentieth year of Artaxerxes. (Chislev is the name of the *ninth* month of the year.) Nehemiah 2:1, however, is dated in the month of Nisan, the *first* month, of the same year. Taking the dates at face value, Nehemiah spoke to Artaxerxes about Jerusalem (in 2:1) eight months before he heard of its condition from his brother (in 1:1). Since that conclusion is patent nonsense and violates the sequence of the plot, there must be a problem with the date in Nehemiah 1 or 2. Since the dates in the rest of the book of Nehemiah seem consistent, and since Nehemiah 1 appears to be an introduction crafted to lay the groundwork for all that follows, many scholars simply assume that the date for Nehemiah 1 should have been given as the ninth month of the *nineteenth* year of Artaxerxes I. The rest of the dates then work fine. That solution will be adopted here and reflected in charts throughout this commentary. [Dates in the Book of Nehemiah] This dating scheme, moreover, helps to structure the plot of the book of Nehemiah, so it will be noted each additional place it appears: Nehemiah 2:1, 6:15, 7:73b, 9:1, and 13:6.

The action begins with the notice that one of Nehemiah's brothers, Hanani, who presumably had been born in exile as had Nehemiah and had moved to Jerusalem or Yehud, came back to Susa accompanied by others from there. Nehemiah asked him for a report about the condition of Jerusalem, and learned that it was still in shambles. D. J. A. Clines says that the description of the city "cannot refer to the destruction of the city in 587 BCE," and speculates that the destruction in view was a result of a subsequent defeat of the city, an allusion to which he thinks he finds in Ezra 4:23.[2] All that verse says, however, is that the Persian army forced the cessation of repairs to the (broken) city of Jerusalem until the permissibility of that work could be verified. It is quite clear from archaeological surveys, moreover, that post-exilic Jerusalem lay in shambles from its ruin at the hands of the Babylonians well into the Persian period if not the Greek, as was argued in the interpretation of Ezra 4. Thus, it appears as though Ezra 4:23 does indeed refer to the shambles left by the Babylonians in their destruction of Jerusalem.

Dates in the Book of Nehemiah

As in the book of Ezra so also in the book of Nehemiah, one of the redactional motifs is the marking of time. Six date markers appear in Nehemiah, namely in Nehemiah 1:1, 2:1, 6:15, 7:73b, 9:1, and 13:6.

Text	Date	Event
1:1	9th month (Chislev) of 19th year of Artaxerxes, 446(?)*	Hanani arrives in Susa
2:1	1st month (Nisan) of 20th year, 445	Nehemiah departs for Jerusalem
6:15	6th month (Elul) of 20th year, 445	Repairs on wall finished
7:73b	7th month (Tishri) of 20th year, 445	Reading of the Law in Jerusalem
9:1	7th month, (Tishri) of 20th year, 445 (implied)	Separation of "Israel" from others
13:6	Month omitted, 32nd year of Artaxerxes, 433	Nehemiah returned to Susa

* Neh 1:1 sets its action in twentieth year of Artaxerxes, i.e., 445. Neh 2:1 also sets its action in the twentieth year of Artaxerxes, but Nisan was the first month in the Babylonian year. D. J. A. Clines suggests plausibly a slight slip of the pen and dates Neh 1:1 four months earlier in year 446.

D. J. A. Clines, "An Introduction to and Notes on Nehemiah," in *HarperCollins Study Bible* (ed. Wayne A. Meeks; New York: HarperCollins, 1993) 717, n. on Neh 1:1.

The Prayer of Nehemiah, 1:4-11a

The reaction of Nehemiah to news of the condition of Jerusalem was to pray, an act he will repeat many times in the book.[3] The majority of the chapter reports the essence of that prayer. He sat to pray (see also Ps 137:1 and Job 2:13), a custom that has survived among Jews. Bereaved persons would sit on low stools to mourn during the time of mourning.[4] Nehemiah's prayer, appropriately, was preceded by a days-long season of mourning and fasting. Such mourning often took the form of accepting blame for one's sins or those of one's family, city, or nation. Fasting, or the voluntary limiting of food and perhaps even liquids, was a spiritual discipline designed to rid oneself of self-exaltation and self-satisfaction. Besides, a full stomach may lead to sleepiness instead of concentration on one's moral shortcomings. A moderate amount of food, water, and sleep may leave the worshiper alert and prepared to hear God and to take action.

Nehemiah prays not only on his own behalf but also that of his family. In this context, the "family" may well have included all the exiles in Babylon and its environs and perhaps even the returnees in Jerusalem. It would have been—perhaps—an even nobler prayer to include the well-being of his king and captors, but no such prayer is reported. Instead, Nehemiah's prayer reaches back to Moses and includes all Israelites between Moses and himself. The prayer is laced, moreover, with language and sentiments expressed in texts like Deuteronomy 7:7-9 and 30:1-5. His starting point was well taken. That last passage in particular works with a hypothesized or envisioned disobedient and exiled people scattered abroad that repents and that God brings back to the land of their forebears. Although the text does not say as much, Nehemiah appears to come to a decision to try to aid those returnees, for he invokes God's blessings on what he is about to do. In doing so, Nehemiah also prays to the "God of heaven." Of the five uses of that phrase in the Hebrew Bible, four occur in Nehemiah.[5] They are Nehemiah 1:4 and 5, 2:4, and 2:20. In Nehemiah 1:5-11 and 9:5-37 as well, God is portrayed as the Lord of history.

The Status/Position of Nehemiah, 1:11b

The chapter closes by having Nehemiah report his employment to the reader. All the reader knows up to this point is that Nehemiah lived in or at least was staying in Susa. He could have been any John Doe, like numerous other exiles simply living there, more or less assimilated into Elamite, now Persian, life. As it turns out, however, although the reader is expected to see God's providential hand at work here and not coincidence, Nehemiah was a "cup-bearer" to the king of Persia. His task was to keep wine cups filled at meals. He might not have been the only one, but as a cupbearer he had frequent, direct contact with the king. As one who kept the wine flowing, he may have been a servant the king enjoyed having around. In any case, Nehemiah was well known to the king. The beginning of Nehemiah 2 presupposes that connection, so the editor supplies it here.

CONNECTIONS

1. The situation in Nehemiah 1 involves displaced people trying to survive, even thrive, in a foreign land. Nehemiah was struggling in a foreign land, where his forebears had been dragged against their will. The status, indeed quandary, of displaced people is thus revealed. It was not the Persians' fault that Judeans in the Babylonian period had wound up in a foreign country. To their credit, they seemed willing enough for those displaced people to return home. Perhaps they hoped those people would be grateful. At some point, Nehemiah's brother seems to have availed himself of that opportunity. Although he was "home" in Yehud, the family was divided. He traveled to see his brother. One can at least surmise that it was the only time he expected to see Nehemiah. The text does not say whether Hanani wanted to stay in Elam, although that is unlikely. Nor does it say whether he hoped Nehemiah would return with him to Yehud. It remains aloof from such considerations. What it does focus on, however, is the longing for Nehemiah to see his homeland succeed. That success, in fact, became a goal, dare one even say an obsession.

Nehemiah may remind modern Americans of the numerous refugees or children of refugees now living in the United States. Some may have come here willingly; some may have been brought by their parents; some may have been brought in to work long hours in low-paying jobs or even to serve as prostitutes. They too perhaps long to see their homeland or at least see it and their families there succeed. They may want to send money there or relocate a relative to the United States. What they may encounter, however, is rejection or discrimination, especially if their English is accent-laden and hard to understand or if they do not speak English at all. They may be here through no fault of their own. They might even

Somali Refugee Children in St. Petersburg, Florida

To escape war, famine, and persecution during the Somali civil war, tens of thousands of Bantus fled to refugee camps. By 2007, more than 10,000 had been resettled to cities throughout the United States with the help of the United Nations High Commissioner for Refugees (UNHCR), the U.S. State Department, and refugee resettlement agencies across the country.

Bantu refugee children from refugee camps in Kenya in St. Petersburg, Florida; at a farewell party before being relocated to other places in the US. (Credit: Melvin "Buddy" Baker, Wikimedia Commons, CC-by-2.0)

have been born here—as Nehemiah had been born in Babylon. What they may well face is discrimination and hostility.

Many churches (and other groups) try to help such people. One possible result of a study of Nehemiah is the development of sympathy for such misplaced persons and their hopes for the homeland even if they prefer to remain here. What they may need is a helping hand from a church or church-sponsored organization to get food, shelter, jobs, hprayealth care, English lessons, and security for their old age. In those ways, they are just like most of the rest of the people in this their home away from home. They need help finding a place to live, new friends and neighbors, adjusting to a new language, perhaps adjusting to a new calendar, and certainly other new customs including diet. One thing readers of this commentary can do is to help support and even befriend such misplaced persons, some of whom at least may be prohibited by one thing or another from even practicing their trade or profession.

Habitat for Humanity at Fremont Fair, 2007

Habitat for Humanity is not actually a church-sponsored group, but many of its leaders and workers are Christians. Regardless, its work is an example of caring persons trying to help poor people with one of the basic necessities of life: livable housing.

Habitat For Humanity volunteers constructing a house during the 2007 Fremont Fair, Seattle, Washington. The house would later be moved to Snoqualmie Ridge in Seattle's eastern suburbs. (Credit: Joe Mabel, Wikimedia Commons, CCA-SA 3.0)

2. Nehemiah's immediate reaction upon hearing of the plight of his homeland was to offer an intercessory prayer on its behalf. A cynic might reply that talk, even prayer, is cheap. Such talk is not cheap, however. It involves persons in the concerns and woes of people other than them-

selves. It implores the mercy of God, who may well want to use the one praying in answering the prayer. It is a two-faced supplicant indeed, however, that asks God to act on behalf of someone but then declines to be part of meeting the needs of that person. Obviously no one can meet all the needs one sees, but individuals or groups can meet some of them. Examples of such aid include regular contributions to food pantries or banks, working with Habitat for Humanity builders, carrying immigrants (and others) for medical aid or assistance with government agencies, and even housing such persons for a while or adopting a homeless child overseas. In Nehemiah's case, it involved leaving his position at the king's palace to return to a "motherland" that he had never seen.

3. Readers might want to stretch themselves, however, and ask what happens when people pray and God does not answer? The old saying that "There are no atheists in foxholes" may not be completely true; some soldiers faced their deaths without recourse to faith. Even some Christians in foxholes, however, die horrible deaths. Praying to God for help offers no guarantee of a positive response. Such prayers do reveal a deeply felt sense that human suffering is not God's ultimate plan for God's children.

NOTES

1. Margaret Cohen, "Leave Nehemiah Alone: Nehemiah's 'Tales' and Fifth-Century Historiography," in Mark J. Boda and Paul L. Redditt, eds., *Unity and Disunity in Ezra-Nehemiah* (Hebrew Bible Monographs 17; Sheffield: Sheffield Phoenix Press, 2006) 55–74.

2. D. J. A. Clines, "An Introduction to and Notes on Nehemiah," in *HarperCollins Study Bible* (ed. Wayne A. Meeks; New York: HarperCollins, 1993) 717.

3. Mark J. Boda ("Prayer as Rhetoric in the Book of Nehemiah," *New Perspectives on Ezra-Nehemiah* [ed. Isaac Kalimi; Winona Lake IN: Eisenbrauns, 2012] 267–84) notes the ubiquity of prayer in the book of Nehemiah and argues that "prayer is utilized to accomplish many of the purposes often associated with direct discourse in ancient literature: internal characterization, dramatic effect, rhetorical structure, plot advancement, and ideological interpretation."

4. Judah J. Slotki, *Daniel • Ezra • Nehemiah* (Soncino Books of the Bible; London, New York: Soncino, 1951) 183.

5. F. C. Fensham, "Some Theological and religious Aspects in Ezra and Nehemiah," *JNSS* 11 (1983): 59–68, here 60.

NEHEMIAH DECIDES TO REPAIR THE WALLS

Nehemiah 2–3

COMMENTARY

While Nehemiah 1 introduces the book's narrator/hero, situating him in Susa (which lay in eastern Persia due north of the western end of the Persian Gulf), Nehemiah 2–3 describes his journey to Jerusalem, his inspection of the broken wall, and his decision to repair it, and it offers a report of who was to build the gates and set up the doors. [Outline of Nehemiah 2–3] Nehemiah 4 will describe problems encountered in repairing the walls themselves, although even it does not say the wall was finished. Rather, Nehemiah 5:1–6:14 describes internal struggles among the returnees, and Nehemiah 6:15 finally says that the repairing of the wall was completed. Last, Nehemiah 7:1-3 mentions the installation of the doors/gates of the city and the appointment of guards for those gates, and Nehemiah 7:4-73a repeats the list of names given in Ezra 2. This whole complex of narratives and documents, moreover, was anticipated in Ezra 4:7-23, which registered opposition to repairing the wall of Jerusalem in a context that otherwise described the repairing of the altar and temple in Jerusalem. Those verses served as a redactional anchor in the first part of Ezra-Nehemiah for Nehemiah's work, described in the third part of the overall literary product. Readers of Ezra-Nehemiah at this point will be expected to know about that tension long before they arrive at Nehemiah 2. These comments will focus on the action in that chapter and the next only.

Outline of Nehemiah 2–3

Nehemiah Secures Permission from Artaxerxes to Repair Jerusalem, 2:1-8
Journey and Initial Meeting with Sanballat, 2:9-10
Nehemiah's First Three Days in Jerusalem, 2:11-16
The Decision to Repair Jerusalem, 2:17-20
Organization of the Work, 3:1-32

Nehemiah Secures Permission from Artaxerxes to Repair Jerusalem, 2:1-8

Aware now (following the visit of Hanani and others from Judah) of the continuing sad condition of Jerusalem, Nehemiah determined to go to there to see to its restoration in the twentieth year of Artaxerxes. Here again, as in Nehemiah 1:1, the author uses a date as a structuring device to move the plot of his work forward. [Dates in the Book of Nehemiah] As a Returnee, Nehemiah might be assumed to have a voice in Jerusalem, but as a non-Levite he would not necessarily have the final say among the theocratic, priestly group in charge in Jerusalem and Yehud. Consequently, he sought his authority from the Persian king Artaxerxes. With Persian backing, he would be able to improve matters as he saw fit. The narrator describes the scene where Artaxerxes grants Nehemiah that authority.

In his role as wine steward, Nehemiah perhaps typically presented himself as a joy-filled servant who brought cheer to the king in the form of wine and perhaps even humor. The narrator, in fact, informs the reader that Nehemiah had never before been sad in the king's presence. (Was his disposition that sunny, or did he deserve an Oscar for playing his court role superbly?) Sensing his servant's unhappiness, the king inquired about its cause. Nehemiah's reaction was to become afraid. Therein readers get a glimpse into such one-sided relationships. It was the wine-bearer's task to select and pour joy-bringing wine. Had he displeased his master? Would his obvious sadness cause discomfort to the king? Would he be punished?

Dates in the Book of Nehemiah

As in the book of Ezra so also in the book of Nehemiah, one of the redactional motifs is the marking of time. Six date markers appear in Nehemiah, namely in Nehemiah 1:1, 2:1, 6:15, 7:73b, 9:1, and 13:6.

Text	Date	Event
1:1	9th month (Chislev) of 19th year of Artaxerxes, 446(?)*	Hanani arrives in Susa
2:1	1st month (Nisan) of 20th year, 445	Nehemiah departs for Jerusalem
6:15	6th month (Elul) of 20th year, 445	Repairs on wall finished
7:73b	7th month (Tishri) of 20th year, 445	Reading of the Law in Jerusalem
9:1	7th month, (Tishri) of 20th year, 445 (implied)	Separation of "Israel" from others
13:6	Month omitted, 32nd year of Artaxerxes, 433	Nehemiah returned to Susa

* Neh 1:1 sets its action in twentieth year of Artaxerxes, i.e., 445. Neh 2:1 also sets its action in the twentieth year of Artaxerxes, but Nisan was the first month in the Babylonian year. D. J. A. Clines suggests plausibly a slight slip of the pen and dates Neh 1:1 four months earlier in year 446.

D. J. A. Clines, "An Introduction to and Notes on Nehemiah," in *HarperCollins Study Bible* (ed. Wayne A. Meeks; New York: HarperCollins, 1993) 717, n. on Neh 1:1.

Joseph Fleischman recognizes a deeper dimension to this interchange. Fleishman notes that Artaxerxes would have been a Zoroastrian. One of the characteristics attributed to the God of that religion, Ahura Mazda, was positive thinking and good spirits. Thus, Fleischman suggests, Artaxerxes might have seen Nehemiah's bad mood "not as a transient condition, but as a source of evil, and therefore Nehemiah took a great risk when he compelled the king to address him."[1]

Nehemiah's answer (2:3-8a) was as measured as it was obsequious. He began with a typical salutation to a king: "May the king live on and on." [The Translation "on and on," not "forever"] Most translations, including the NRSV, render the Hebrew word used here "perpetually" as "forever," but "forever"—as Hebrew scholars routinely note—is too Greek a concept for the Old Testament. The Hebrew word is better rendered "perpetually" or "on and on." (See also the discussion of Ezra 3:11 in this commentary.) In this narrative at least, the king did not react with offense, but with concern for his servant. The passage gives at least two clues to this concern. First, the king assumes that something is amiss with Nehemiah,

---

The Translation "on and on," not "forever"

AΩ The translation "forever," although typical in English versions of the Old Testament, introduces an idea unknown to it. It is a truism for moderns that "Forever is a long, long time," but we typically mean that whatever is "forever" is eternal and will stretch beyond life or else that those who have died will be resurrected in a new world or even heaven. The Hebrew language and Bible had no such concept of "forever." The Hebrew word typically translated "forever" actually meant something like the modern idea of "open-ended" or "as far as the eye can see." It could run in either direction, past or future. It almost surely did not imply eternal life on earth, let alone in heaven with God. The burden of proof is on anyone to find that idea in the Old Testament as opposed to reading it into the text.

Several key texts on the subject warrant a brief glance. Isa 25:8 speaks of God's "swallowing up" death perpetually. There, however, "death" is a symbol for the tragedy of oppression and exile that had fallen (or would fall) upon the people of Judah. The prediction is that such a "death" would end and that God would protect Jerusalem and the people perpetually. Ezekiel's vision of the valley of dry bones (Ezek 37:1-10, 11-14) makes a similar point. Verses 1-10 predict (or, after the fact, look back on) the destruction of Judah, and vv. 11-15 predict the end of the exile and a return of the exiles to Judah. Likewise, the book of Daniel anticipated both the fall of the Greek Empire and its king Antiochus

Epiphanes IV, who had destroyed the temple and (apparently) defiled its altar, and also the resurgence of Judah. Martyrs would be restored to life on earth to enjoy the lengthy life they deserved, and Daniel would be included too (Dan 12:13).

On the interpretation of the texts mentioned above, readers might consult the following commentaries.

In the Smyth & Helwys Commentary Series:
Patricia K. Tull, *Isaiah 1–39* (Macon GA: Smyth & Helwys, 2010) 394–98.
Margaret S. Odell, *Ezekiel* (Macon GA: Smyth & Helwys, 2005) 449–53.
Sharon Pace, *Daniel* (Macon GA: Smyth & Helwys, 2008) 326–43.

In other series:
Joseph Blenkinsopp, *Isaiah 1–39* (AB 19; New York, London, Toronto, Sydney, Auckland: Doubleday, 2000) 368–73.
Walther Zimmerli, *Ezekiel II* (Hermeneia; Philadelphia, Fortress, 1983) 259–63.
Paul L. Redditt, *Daniel* (NCB; Sheffield: Sheffield Academic Press, 1999) 180–93.

In other sources:
Paul L. Redditt, Expository Article, Isaiah 26, *RevExp* 88 (1991): 195–99.

and second he cares enough to inquire what was wrong, inviting a request from Nehemiah.

Nehemiah's answer surely follows the protocol for addressing the king. Politely, he turned the king's question back on him rhetorically: "Why shouldn't I be sad?" Then he answered the king's question. He told Artaxerxes that he had just learned that "the city, the place of my ancestors' graves, lies waste." Its gates had been destroyed by fire, so whatever remained of the city wall was useless defensively. (See 2 Chr 36:19.) The king, like Nehemiah in the first chapter, is portrayed as not knowing of that state of affairs, and Nehemiah did not name the city. Ezra 4:12 and 15 report, however, that Rehum (a royal deputy) via Shimshai (his scribe) informed King Artaxerxes that Jerusalem was a "rebellious and wicked" city whose inhabitants were repairing the city. The time frame for that letter is impossible to assess. If it concerned the work of Nehemiah, Artaxerxes was the one who had authorized the work, however unwittingly. If it dated earlier in the reign of Artaxerxes and he had banned the work, Nehemiah was discrete in not naming the city and the author was coy in hiding that refusal. Since Ezra 4 does not relate the outcome of the audience of Rehum and Shimshai before Artaxerxes, readers are left in a quandary. What all this may represent, however, is simply a loose thread in the narrative. In Nehemiah 2:8, the king granted Nehemiah's request for wood to use in repairing the "gates of the temple fortress" (see below), the wall of the city, and for the house that Nehemiah would occupy. What the narrator wants to emphasize all the way through is that the returnees were led by God and that the Persians fully endorsed and underwrote what they did.

At any rate, Artaxerxes recognized the direction the conversation was taking and asked what he could do. Since such concern for the distant background of a servant would be unusual, the reader is (or should be) caught off guard. Nehemiah is portrayed as properly pious and dependent on God in that he prayed (quickly and silently, presumably) before answering. He then asked to return to the city of his ancestors' graves in order to repair it.

The king, in turn, was pleased to grant the request, but the text does not say why. Is the reader supposed to infer that the king was so kindly disposed toward his servant that he would immediately grant permission for an open-ended sojourn in an unknown city to repair it? Perhaps so. At a deeper level, however, the author probably wants the reader to see that the hand of YHWH the God of Israel was at work behind the scenes by means of the king of Persia, who thought—mistakenly—that he was in charge of matters in Jerusalem. (See the overall conclusion in Neh 2:8b.) The king's answer was so self-evidently positive that it is not even recorded. He and Nehemiah negotiated the length of Nehemiah's absence (twelve years according to Neh 5:14 and Neh 13:6), and the queen acted as the witness to the verbal agreement. Who on earth could challenge Nehemiah's authority?

Next, Nehemiah asked for letters to the appointed rulers of the Persian province named Beyond the River, i.e., the Euphrates. (Please see [The Extent of the Persian Empire].) The king directed them to allow Nehemiah to pass through en route to Jerusalem. Such a notice perhaps would also imply that they were to assist Nehemiah as he needed with wood and other materials. (See comments on v. 10 below.) That permission would also put the two local opponents of Nehemiah, the villains of the account, on notice that Nehemiah was traveling and working with Persian backing. Nehemiah had requested and received the promise of timber for the gates of a "temple fortress" (the Tower of Hananel mentioned in Neh 3:2?), the wall (as supports?), and the house Nehemiah would occupy (v. 7). The king granted the request because—as Nehemiah reports in v. 8—the hand of God was on him to direct and empower him. Those materials were to be delivered by "the keeper of the king's fortress," so someone in the king's employ had to know the name of the city.

Nehemiah Pleading to Repair Wall
Nehemiah pleads with King Artaxerxes for permission to go to Jerusalem and rebuild its wall.

Friedrich Peypus (1485–1534) printer. "Nehemiah's Request." From *The Bible of Both Testaments*. (Credit: Pitts Theological Library)

Journey to Jerusalem and Initial Meeting with Sanballat, 2:9-10

The setting changes in 2:9-10. Nehemiah seems to have traveled to Jerusalem alone or with his brother; he mentions no companions. En route he presented the letters from Artaxerxes to the Persian-appointed governors of the larger area: Sanballat, a Horonite official [Beth-Horan/Horonite], and Tobiah, called the Ammonite [Ammon/Ammonite]. That description is often taken at face value, and scholars often assume he descended from the Ammonites and lived

Journey of Nehemiah

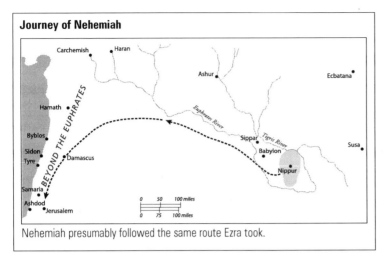

Nehemiah presumably followed the same route Ezra took.

Beth-Horan/Horonite

AΩ The term "Horonite" quite possibly denotes that he was a resident of Beth-Horon (which meant "place of the hollow"), the name of two towns northeast of Jerusalem expanded and fortified by Solomon. The two towns belonged to the tribe of Ephraim and lay on the border with Benjamin. They appear here to be part of post-exilic Yehud near the area of Samaria.

E. W. G. Masterman and J. F. Prewitt, "Beth-Horon," *ISBE*, 1.469.

Ammon/Ammonite

In the Old Testament, Ammonites were descendants of Ammon, one of the two sons of Lot conceived during a drunken, incestuous act of intercourse after the destruction of Sodom and Gomorrah. See Genesis 19:30-38.

in Yehud. The name "Ammonite" probably was used as a slur, however, reminding readers of the baseness of the Ammonites depicted unforgettably in the narrative of the conception of Ammon and of his brother Moab in the wake of two consecutive nights of drunken incest between Lot and his two daughters (Gen 19:30-38). B. Mazar, however, thinks Tobiah was "a Jew (not half-Ammonite and half Jew, or even pure Ammonite, . . .) but one of the heads of the Jews and a relative of the high priest. . . . What is meant [by the term the 'Ammonite servant' in Neh ii, 10 19] is the *servant of the king . . .* of Persia in residence at Ammon, [perhaps even] the governor of Ammon."[2] Apparently, then, the author of this narrative was indicting the two men as base and worthless, not welcome even to set foot in Jerusalem! This instance will not be the last time readers encounter these men in the book of Nehemiah, and the relationship will be contentious and contemptuous. Sanballat will be mentioned nine more times in the book and Tobiah thirteen. Readers might need to remember, however, that the name Tobiah actually means "Yah (a shortened form of the divine name YHWH/Yahweh) is good." His parents, therefore, acted like devout Yahwists, and he may well have conceived of himself that way too.

Nehemiah's First Three Days in Jerusalem, 2:11-16

The first thing to notice in this account of Nehemiah's activities is that he did not just rush right into his repairing project. Instead, he took three days to rest from his trip. Then, he and "a few good men" of his choosing arose during the night. He made an inspection of the city then, when, presumably, he would be unseen and unaccompanied by people already in Yehud who had their own agenda. Although other people arose with him (to help him prepare for the inspection?), he does not say they went along. His words can be translated, "and there was no other beast [of burden] with me, only the beast that I was riding." If attendants accompanied him, they walked, and he does not mention them. Still, why mention them at all if they did not go?

The comment, moreover, that he "inspected the walls of Jerusalem that had been broken down and its [wooden] gates had been destroyed by fire" has inspired a wide-ranging debate among scholars: What wall? Where did it run? Archaeologists have not been able to resolve that issue. Traditionally, authors of biblical studies have assumed a fairly large city, but more recently some have suggested a much smaller one.[3] The issue impinges heavily on the proper understanding of the historical background of Nehemiah, but caution in the exegesis of the text will allay the awkwardness in not knowing the size of the city or the extent of its early resettlement—except to say that it must have been sparse.

Differently stated, thus far archaeologists have been unable to discover any wall that can be assigned comfortably to Nehemiah's time. That means that modern readers cannot know its exact dimensions. Was it the old wall from 586 or something smaller? That gap in knowledge does not prove, of course, that no such wall was built, though some modern archaeologists are of that opinion. It does suggest, however, that readers pay close attention to what the text actually says. It does not say he built a new wall; it says he repaired an old wall. It does not say to what height he repaired it, let alone that it was repaired to the same height all around. Artists' renditions of a massive, new stone wall are without attestation archaeologically and arise from the artists' imagination. The reality was likely something more mundane: the repair of broken walls up to whatever height was practical. *The important thing to the returnees building it was that it demarcated the holy space of the temple.*

Nehemiah Surveying the Wall

Gustave Doré (1832–1883). "Nehemiah's Survey of Jerusalem's Ruined Walls." Illustration from *The Holy Bible containing the Old and New Testaments, according to the authorised version.* (Credit: Creationism.org)

This painting captures the broken condition of part of Jerusalem's wall as described in Neh 2:11-16 and 4:1-20.

The author knew, of course, as does the reader, that already the temple area had been refurbished and the temple rebuilt. These verses relate what could be seen when Nehemiah visited the ruins of the wall. The narrative of the tour began and ended at the Valley Gate, which was on the southwestern edge of the pre-exilic city, the end away from Babylon. It seems probable today that that area suffered less damage than the northern side in the destruction of the city in 586. (Besides, Nehemiah presumably had already seen that part of the city upon his arrival from Babylon.) He then traveled basically eastward to the Dung Gate, on the south end of the oldest part of the city. There the wall had been damaged and the gate destroyed. Next he proceeded to the Fountain (or Water) Gate at the southern edge of David's city and to a pool there called the King's Pool. Then he turned to inspect the east wall of the city, traveling as far as he could. Blocked from further inspection, he turned back and reentered the city through the Valley Gate. It is not clear, then, how much of the wall he actually examined, but it was enough for him to know that the damage to the old city itself was extensive. He closed his description of his nighttime inspection with the observation that the "officials" of the city did not know where he had gone or what he was doing. (A reader might assume that they thought he was asleep.) He defines those officials in the last half of v. 16 as "the Jews, the priests, the nobles [i.e., the "rank"], and the people [i.e., the "file," the other people in the community]."

The Decision to Repair Jerusalem, 2:17-20

Armed with firsthand information of the dire circumstances of Jerusalem, and although the text only implies that he summoned the rank and file, Nehemiah spoke to them. He acknowledged what they already knew: the city wall lay in ruins, and he told them that God had sent him to restore it. Presumably they would reuse what they could and repair what they had to. The "people" were thrilled at the prospect. Those in view presumably included the returnees with Ezra (thirteen years earlier according to the dating scheme of Ezra-Nehemiah) and descendants of returnees in 539/520.

The petty bickering between returnees and those who had remained behind began at once. Sanballat and his partner Tobiah are named again as ringleaders in the opposition, but a third name is added: Geshem the Arab.[4] He will appear again in Nehemiah 6. Actually, his mention here serves mainly to foreshadow his mention in that chapter, and neither chapter says he does anything independently from Sanballat. In both places, then, basically he indicates the existence of other surrounding groups that opposed Nehemiah. Any concession Nehemiah won from Persia for Yehud and Jerusalem would probably come at the expense of the surrounding local groups, none of whom—presumably—would want to lose power or revenues to new leadership in Jerusalem.

Their first tactic was to mock and ridicule the idea. They appear to have assumed that Nehemiah had no Persian authorization for the work, an assumption the reader knows is fallacious. Interestingly, however, in v. 20 Nehemiah appealed to God as his authority and the one who promised success. Then Nehemiah announced his intention to begin repairing the wall right away, and declared that the three men and their supporters would have no part in the process.

That tension between Nehemiah 1 and 2 might be taken as an indication that Nehemiah 1 was added later. Still, Nehemiah 1 was written in the first person singular and in any case introduces the hero, Nehemiah. Something had to precede Nehemiah 2. Perhaps then readers might give the redactor of Ezra-Nehemiah credit for building into his carefully fashioned narrative a sly critique of the three antagonists: Nehemiah was in league with God, while the other three were in the dark. In any case, in the book of Ezra-Nehemiah YHWH was the one really in charge in Jerusalem and the one whose permission and commission to build the temple really mattered.

People Who Rebuilt the Gates, 3:1-32

[The Typological Interpretation of Artaxerxes, Sanballat, Tobiah, Nehemiah, and the Places and Names Mentioned in Zechariah 3] Perhaps the place to begin the discussion of Nehemiah 3 is that archaeologists today cannot point to any section of any recovered wall and say with confidence, "This is the wall that Nehemiah repaired." If he had repaired no wall, however, it is hard to see why anyone would have believed and treasured a work claiming he did, at least until after the time of the Maccabees when the wall again was refurbished and enlarged. While it is not impossible that Ezra-Nehemiah arose en toto that late, that explanation is not the most convincing. (See the discussion "The Number of Returnees" in the Introduction to Ezra-Nehemiah.) Still, the list in Nehemiah 3:1-32 makes no mention of Nehemiah and uses no first person verbs. It appears, actually, to be a list added to his Memoirs. (See comments in the

The Typological Interpretation of Artaxerxes, Sanballat, Tobiah, Nehemiah, and the Places and Names Mentioned in Zechariah 3

The Venerable Bede saw the pagan king Artaxerxes "as a type of the Lord, who builds a city for himself from living stones." Sanballat and Tobiah were figures of heretics and enemies of the church, and Nehemiah was a model teacher. Bede also treated the meanings of the gates, three in particular, and the pool of Shelah. The fish of the Fish Gate stood for those faithful to God. The Dung Gate represented those ordained people through whom the filth of vices was removed. The pool (correctly equated with the pool of Siloam in the New Testament) "stands for the Lord Savior who was sent by God the Father for our illumination." The Horse Gate anticipated the entrance of Gentiles (Horses!) into the church. Bede gets an A for imagination and an F for attention to the text of Nehemiah.

See the *Ancient Christian Commentary on Scripture: Old Testament V; 1-2 Kings, 1-2 Chronicles, Ezra, Nehemiah, Esther* (Downers Grove IL: Intervarsity, 2008) 336–41.

Introduction to Ezra-Nehemiah and on Ezra 2, 7, and 12 about the age of these the lists.) The list does not appear to be all of one piece, moreover, and its purpose was to honor all the people named. Taking the list at face value, O. Lipschits argues that the twofold list "comprises both those who organized and financed the construction of the various sections of the wall and those who organized and financed the building of the six gates."[5] The editor's aim was to emphasize the role and importance of Nehemiah as the one who instigated the project and saw it through to a successful conclusion.[6] D. J. A. Clines offers the plausible suggestion that the people named in Nehemiah 3 may well have been those who financed the work rather than those who actually did the building.[7] One of those persons was named Meremoth son of Uriah son of Hakkok. N. Avigad notes that the Hakkok family is known to have been one of the important families serving in Solomon's temple.[8]

It is also worth noting that v. 8 actually says "they restored Jerusalem as far as the Broad Wall." The word translated "restored" often means "forsake" or "leave," but Jewish commentators sometimes have explained that the word suggests that the builders filled in something with dirt. Modern commentators sometimes emend the text to read a word meaning "strengthened," but J. J. Slotki (following others) plausibly suggests that the circumference of the old city was larger than they needed, so at that point they abandoned the old outer wall and "left" the inhabited part outside of Jerusalem.[9] D. Ussishkin differs slightly, arguing that Nehemiah restored the whole wall, but that most of the city remained unoccupied, just as Nehemiah 7:4 reports.[10] There is but the one reference to the "Broad Wall" in v. 8. R. Grafman argues that it had run from a point just south of the Siloam Pool in an irregular semicircle on the western side of the temple mount, but he also points out that there is no mention that it was actually rebuilt.[11] C. G. Tuland draws the conclusion that its omission "was part of Nehemiah's premeditated plan to limit the area of Jerusalem to the needs of a greatly reduced population."[12] Modern readers, obviously, are left somewhat in the dark.

Regardless, Nehemiah 3:1-32 mentions two towers (the Tower of the Hundred, the Tower of Hananel, both in v. 1) and ten different gates: Sheep (vv. 1, 22), Fish (v. 3), Old (v. 6), Valley (v. 13), Dung (v. 13), Fountain (v. 15), Water (v. 26), Horse (v. 28), East (v. 29), and Muster (v. 32). As mentioned in the Introduction to Ezra-Nehemiah, however, this description presupposes a city similar in size to Jerusalem in the seventh century or the second. (See [Map of Jerusalem in the Time of David and Solomon] in the Introduction to Ezra-Nehemiah) I am unable to resolve this issue further, but it is possible to discern differences in the book of Nehemiah in how Jerusalem as "conceived" differs from how Jerusalem is "perceived" and from how Jerusalem would have been experienced as "lived space" in the fifth century BCE. Each perspective will be discussed in turn.[13]

In terms of how Jerusalem was *conceived*, it is useful to distinguish Persian from Yehudian views. Persian permission to repair Jerusalem's wall, according to K. G. Hoglund, would have come as a means to enhance Persian interests in Jerusalem and Yehud. Hoglund notes that since Persians rarely allowed the construction of such walls, the repairing project "points to a new status for Jerusalem within the imperial system, a change also indicated by the establishment of the imperial garrison to the north of the city."[14] In other words, at Nehemiah's time, not earlier, Jerusalem replaced Mizpah (cf. 2 Kgs 25:23; Jer 40:7-12), which lay a few miles NNW of Jerusalem as the "capital" of Yehud.[15] Jerusalem's new status was conceived by Persia as part of its attempt to integrate large portions of the Levant into the imperial system, whatever that might have entailed for Jerusalem and Yehud.[16]

The book of Nehemiah, by contrast, conceived the repairing as the divinely sanctioned plan to restore Yehudite control of its own local affairs alongside the ambitions of rival Samaria, whose own mid-fifth-century temple and standing eighth-century wall[17] point to its importance in the area in the early Persian period. Incidentally, the returnees' desires for self-direction under Persian hegemony might have disturbed or even encouraged the Judean expatriates still in Babylonia, who had once ruled the area and perhaps wished to exercise influence themselves over the returnees in Judah.

Limited archaeological investigations of Jerusalem reveal the physical (or *perceived*) space behind these narratives. Had a photographer snapped pictures and a cartographer mapped the city, it would have looked plain and small during the Persian Period. It included the old city of David and at least part of the temple mount. Oded Lipschits estimates its population in the mid-fifth century at about 1,500 persons, probably composed of the Judean elite,[18] and some estimates put it much smaller.

That scholarly estimate has been falling for years in light of such archaeological investigation as is possible in the midst of the sprawling modern city and the presence today of the third holiest site in Islam. In 1992, Philip J. King still estimated the population at 4,500 in Nehemiah's time and acknowledged that some estimates ran twice that high.[19] The estimates used in this commentary are the latest known to this author. In addition, Judean territory would have extended no more than about twenty miles in any direction from the city itself.[20] One peculiar Hebrew word that appears in vv. 9, 12, 14, and 18 is often taken to refer to "districts" in the city, which might imply a more developed city than the one imagined here. M. Weinfeld, however, challenges that translation and thinks the word actually has to do with money or taxes.[21] In other words, the two men designated by the term might have been the two tax collectors for the small city. If so, they would have needed other means of income as well.

Descriptions of the returnees in Ezra-Nehemiah included some sectarian concerns, in particular the separation of true people of God from "foreign" wives (Ezra 9:1–10:44) and from important local figures who had never been in exile. One can understand the concern of the members of the Diaspora who returned to guarantee for themselves a preferred status. That their attempts were not entirely successful is shown by the final narrative in Nehemiah (13:4-29), which rails against the actions of the priest Eliashib. He had granted special privileges to his relative Tobiah, who had opposed Nehemiah earlier (Neh 2:10; 6:14, 17-19), who is mentioned by name thirteen times in chapters 2, 4, 6, and 13, and who, thus, was no minor character in post-exilic Yehud or the book of Nehemiah. In Ezra-Nehemiah, the issue was simple: who—i.e., what families—belonged to Israel[22] and deserved to lead the city in its new role within the Persian Empire? The answer for the author was equally simple: the returnees.

CONNECTIONS

1. Nehemiah 2:2 portrays the pagan king Artaxerxes as caring enough about his servant to inquire about the cause of Nehemiah's sadness and then caring enough for him to take action. Simply to

ask and to do nothing would signify curiosity but not necessarily empathy and compassion. To assume he knew what was wrong might well signify a kind of arrogance about always knowing. At least such actions based on assumptions on *our* part may misfire. We might notice that someone is despondent, but fear our being asked to do something to remedy matters, and never show any interest in a friend's change of demeanor and/or personality. Or we might ask and then be unwilling to act to alleviate the problem. Let readers recognize at least a modicum of concern on the part of Artaxerxes for his servant and a willingness to help. Can modern believers be justified in doing less than that ancient Zoroastrian king did? Could we be willing not simply to pray for the hungry but also to contribute monthly to a local food bank? Could we slip cash into an envelope and get it to a person we know is in need? Might we take an interest in political campaigns where aid for the poor is an issue and advocate for them?

"Votes for Women"

Suffragists Rose Sanderman (holding horn) and Elizabeth Freeman (right). c. 1913. (Credit: Library of Congress, Prints and Photographs Division, Washington, DC)

Attention by Christians and others in the early twentieth century led to women gaining the right to vote. Christians can also aid the poor in their struggle for better living conditions.

2. One question implied above was whether Nehemiah was justified in supporting the claims and aspirations of the returnees against those of people in Yehud and Samaria. The answer seems self-evident to readers who see only his side of the issue and accept his view as God's view to boot. One wonders, though, whether God was as opposed to worship outside of Jerusalem as were people who ran the temple. One finds that same view in Deuteronomy, only there the Canaanites were in control of the entire territory. One wonders as well whether God loved only the children of Abraham. Worship, privileges, wealth, and group membership have had and still have a way of coloring worshipers' perspectives about what God wants and whom God loves. In any case, Matthew 28:19-20 makes it perfectly clear that Jesus' followers are to begin where they are and reach out to all people, evangelizing them, baptizing them, and incorporating them into the family of

God. Jews and Gentiles, men and women, young and old, rich and poor, indeed "Red, brown, yellow, black, and white, [all] are precious in [God's and Jesus'] sight." It is not necessary, however, to denigrate the ethnic religion of ancient Judah in order to embrace the wider perspective of a world religion. It is necessary, though, to move beyond seeing God as the God of only some people.

3. Gordon F. Davies reflects on the significance of this decision to repair the walls of Jerusalem.

As much as the stone walls, what [will be] thrown around Jerusalem is living tradition, a rampart from which to survey the past and the future. The temple is already rebuilt because the community cannot change without liturgy, the link to the past that keeps memory—and tradition—alive. That tradition, out of which Ezra and Nehemiah speak, is now reinforced as the compass of the people's identity, but in ways whose circumstances are different again. If tradition is to be a source for reform new generations must always be at home in it, as Ezra and Nehemiah are in the language of Moses and Solomon. For two such different characters to speak through tradition in the modes of both ethos and pathos shows adaptability of interpreted tradition as a hermeneutic of changing realities.[23]

NOTES

1. Joseph Fleischman, "Nehemiah's Request on Behalf of Jerusalem," *New Perspectives on Ezra-Nehemiah* (ed. Isaac Kalimi; Winona Lake IN: Eisenbrauns, 2012) 241–66, here 250–51.

2. B. Mazar, "The Tobiads," *IEJ* 7/2 (1957): 137–45, here 144. The article continues in *IEJ* 7/3 (1957): 229–38.

3. See, for example, M. Avi-Yonah, "The Walls of Nehemiah—A Minimalist View," *IEJ* 4 (1954): 239–48.

4. J. J. Reeve ("Geshem" *ISBE*, 2.449) suggests that Geshem (which meant something like "rain storm") was probably chief of an Arabian tribe that settled in southern Yehud during the exile or that had been settled in or near Samaria by Sargon II in the late eighth century.

5. Oded Lipschits, "Nehemiah 3: Sources, Composition, and Purposes," *New Perspectives on Ezra-Nehemiah* (ed. Isaac Kalimi; Eisenbrauns: Winona Lake, 2012) 73–100, here 97.

6. Ibid., 98.

7. D. J. A. Clines, notes on Nehemiah 3:1-32 in *The Oxford Annotated Study Bible* (Oxford: Oxford University Press, 1989) 719.

8. N. Avigad, "A New Class of Yehud Stamps," *IEJ* 7 (1957): 146–53, here 149.

9. Judah J. Slotki, *Daniel • Ezra • Nehemiah* (Soncino Books of the Bible; London, New York: Soncino Press, 1951) 196.

10. The name "Israel" is used thirty-nine times in Ezra and twenty-two in Nehemiah, as opposed to fifteen times in Ezra and twenty-eight times in Nehemiah where the name "Judah" is used. Not surprisingly, a number of the usages of "Judah" appear in contexts where opposition between Samaria and Jerusalem is discussed. See David Ussishkin, "Nehemiah's City Wall and the Size of Jerusalem," *New Perspectives on Ezra—Nehemiah; History and Historiography, Text, Literature, and Interpretation* (ed. Isaac Kalimi; Winona Lake IN: Eisenbrauns, 2012) 101–30, conclusion on p.125.

11. R. Grafman, "Nehemiah's 'Broad Wall," *IEJ* 24 (1974): 50–51.

12. C. G. Tuland, "*ZB* in Nehemiah 3:8; A Reconsideration of Maximalist and Minimalist Views," *AUSS* 5 (1967): 158–80, here 177. See further, Nicholas Andrew Bailey, "Nehemiah 3:1-32: An Intersection of the Text and the Topography," *PEQ* 122 (1990): 34–40.

13. This description of the city first appeared in a slightly different form in Paul L. Redditt, "Depictions of Exilic and Post-exilic Jerusalem in the Hebrew Bible, especially Haggai, Zechariah, and Malachi," *Die Stadt im Zwolfprophetenbuch* (ed. Aaron Schart and Jutta Krispenz; Beihefte zur Zeitschrift für die Alttestatamentliche Wissenschaft, 428; Berlin, Boston: Walter de Gruyter, 2012) 359–83, here 365–68.

14. Kenneth G. Hoglund, *Achaemenid Imperial Administration in Syria-Palestine and the Missions of Ezra and Nehemiah* (SBLDS 125; Atlanta: Scholars Press, 1992) 224.

15. Oded Lipschits, "Achaemenid Imperial Policy and the Status of Jerusalem," *Judah and the Judeans in the Persian Period* (ed. Oded Lipschits, Manfred Oeming; Winona Lake IN: Eisenbrauns, 2006) 34.

16. Ibid., 37.

17. Ibid., 31.

18. Ibid., 32, and Oded Lipschits, "Persian Period Finds from Jerusalem: Facts and Interpretations," *JHS* 9, article 20, p. 21, http://www.jhsonline.org.

19. Philip J. King, "Jerusalem," *ABD*, 3.747–66, here 753.

20. See the map labeled "Achoris and Evagoras" in A. F. Rainey and R. S. Notley, *Carta's New Century Handbook and Atlas of the Bible* (Jerusalem: Carta, 2007) 170.

21. Moshe Weinfeld, "PELEKH in Nehemiah 3," *Studies in Historical Geography and Biblical Historiography Presented to Zecharia Kellai* (ed. Gershom Galil and Moshe Weinfeld; VTSup 81; Leiden, Boston, Cologne: Brill, 2000) 249–50.

22. Avigad, "A New Class of Yehud Stamps," 146–53.

23. Gordon F. Davies, *Ezra & Nehemiah* (Berit Olam; Collegeville MN: Liturgical Press, 1999) 94.

OPPOSITION, EARLY WORK, AND COMPLAINTS BY WORKERS

Nehemiah 4–5

COMMENTARY

The work of repairing the walls had begun, but the displeasure of Sanballat the Horonite and Tobiah "the Ammonite" flared. Calling Tobiah an "Ammonite" was a slur in view of the appalling circumstances of Ammon's and Moab's births (Gen 19:30-37). Tobiah was mentioned in Nehemiah 2:10, but he took action to oppose the returnees first in Nehemiah 4. John M. Halligan says that these two men and Geshem (Neh 5) perceived a healthy (and walled) Jerusalem as constituting Yehud's "protection against their encroachment on the district."[1] Clearly Halligan has sided with Nehemiah, the narrator. Those three men, however, might well have rebutted that they were protecting their own proper interests in Yehud. Regardless, the returnees continued their rebuilding efforts, the description of which runs through Nehemiah 6. Contention between the returnees and their neighbors continued, moreover, even during Nehemiah's second stay in Jerusalem in connection with the high priest Eliashib, Sanballat's son-in-law, specifically over the special accommodations Eliashib provided for Tobiah (Neh 13:4-9). In other words, Nehemiah succeeded in rebuilding the wall, but not in ridding himself and Jerusalem of what he perceived and portrayed as the meddling of those two antagonists.

Before investigating Nehemiah 4 and 5, however, a glance back at Ezra 4:8-23 is in order. According to O. Lipschits, those verses reflect an attempt to build fortifications around Jerusalem sometime earlier in the reign of Artaxerxes I (465–424 BCE) than the arrival of Nehemiah.[2] (Readers may recall that this commentary dubbed those verses in Ezra "proleptic.") In favor of Lipschits's suggestion is the observation that the verses are clearly out of place chronologically in Ezra 4. There, they function as a redactional anticipation of and linking device to the career and the book of Nehemiah. The renewed efforts at rebuilding under Nehemiah, discussed as a new beginning, caused outrage on the part of Sanballat, the local puppet ruler of Samaria, and of his ally in Judah, Tobiah "the Ammonite." (See the discussion in connection with Neh 2:10).

Recently, moreover, A. Faust has discussed the issue of egalitarianism in the history of Israelite life. He argues that early Israel (down to the mid-eighth century) was characterized by an "egalitarian sentiment" that resisted ostentatious display in the form of elaborate burial places even for kings.[3] He may be correct; no such places have been discovered, although who knows what lies below the streets of the old part of modern-day Jerusalem? Such a sentiment clearly lay behind some of the critiques of Jerusalem and Samaria in the "Writing Prophets," beginning in the mid-eighth century BCE. Ezra-Nehemiah, however, may be accused of limiting that "egalitarianism" (if that term is even appropriate for the fifth century BCE) to the returnees. As Ezra-Nehemiah portrays the matter, only the returnees belonged to Israel. They and only they, therefore, should control Jerusalem and its temple. It follows further that they and they only should also control and direct the rebuilding of the wall around Jerusalem, which would define the larger holy space around the temple.

The Work on the Wall and the Opposition of Sanballat and Tobiah, 4:1-9

[Outline of Nehemiah 4–5] [Verse Numbers in Nehemiah 4 in the Hebrew Bible and in English Translations] Sanballat, governor of neighboring (and rival) Samaria to the north, along with Tobiah (see comments on Neh 2:10 and [Ammon/Ammonite]) and apparently an assistant of Sanballat of some sort, heard of Nehemiah's plan and opposed it in anger. The questions on the lips of Sanballat might also (better?) fit 520–515 BCE, when the returnees rebuilt the temple: "What are these feeble Jews doing? Will they restore things? Will they *sacrifice*? Will they finish it in a day?" (NRSV) The Hebrew is terse, so the REB translates these questions a little more fully as follows. "What do these feeble Jews think they are doing? Do they mean to reconstruct the place? Do they hope to offer sacrifices and finish the work in a day?" As questions directed against

Outline of Nehemiah 4–5

The Work on the Wall and the Opposition of Sanballat and Tobiah, 4:1-9
Nehemiah's Response, 4:10-15a
Work on the Wall Resumed, 4:15b-23
Complaints about Usury, 5:1-13
The Generosity of Nehemiah, 5:14-19

Verse Numbers in Nehemiah 4 in the Hebrew Bible and in English Translations

Verse numbers in Neh 4 differ between the Hebrew Bible and English translations. In the Hebrew Bible, Neh 3 continues through Neh 4:6 of modern English Bibles. Thus, Neh 4:7-23 in English translations constitutes Neh 4:1-17 in the Hebrew Bible.

the rebuilding of the altar and temple, they would make much sense. As questions *redirected* against the repair of the broken and decayed wall, they highlight the immensity and spoof the duration that the time-consuming task would require to do fully. Not to be outdone by Sanballat, Tobiah added his own comment of derision: "That stone wall they are building—any fox going upon it would break it down" (v. 3). The sarcasm is clear. If one little fox climbing on the wall or racing along its top would break it down, it would serve no useful purpose as part of the defense of the city. The image is also satirical, demonstrating the inadequacy of the wall. [What Is Satire?] The truth of the matter is, however—as already pointed out in this commentary (see the Introduction to Ezra-Nehemiah, "C. The Historical Reliability of Ezra-Nehemiah")—that the wall was not intended to keep out invaders, especially not the Persians. It was built, actually, with Persian permission, at least according to the book of Nehemiah. The reason Persia had for allowing its reconstruction most likely was to set up Jerusalem as some kind of *administrative* center for Yehud. Jealousy and/or a desire to maintain their own status and role(s) perhaps motivated Sanballat and Tobiah to oppose its new status.

> **What Is Satire?**
>
> Terry R. Clark defines satire as primarily "an act of inquiry or exploration into the truth, falsity, or reasonableness of a particular idea or practice." Tobiah used this satirical quip to belittle the returnees' efforts to repair the broken sections of the wall. His point was that the repaired wall would be ineffectual, because even the slightest disturbance, e.g., a fox scurrying along its top, would cause it to collapse again. Thus Tobiah ridiculed the whole venture of attempting to restore the wall as ill conceived and inadequately carried out.
>
> Terry Ray Clark, "Saved by Satire," *Understanding Religion and Popular Culture* (ed. Terry Ray Clark and Dan W. Clanton, Jr.; New York, Routledge, 2012) 13–27, here 16.

Those two men are not depicted as resisting Persia directly, but they would do anything they could to thwart the efforts of the returnees in order to ingratiate themselves to the Persians and gain control of local affairs. The weaker Jerusalem and Yehud remained, the happier those two men would be. The brief glimpse in Nehemiah 13 of Nehemiah's second trip to Jerusalem confirms that understanding of the situation. In Nehemiah's absence, the (high) *priest* Eliashib made available a large place on temple property ("in the courts of the house of God," v. 7) for Tobiah to stay when he visited the city. In fury the *non-priest* Nehemiah, upon his return to Jerusalem, evicted his old nemesis (Neh 13:8-9).

The returnees' response to the jeers of Sanballat and Tobiah was to commence work. When they had rebuilt the gaps in the wall to half its height (the text gives no indication of how long that work took or how high the walls reached, although the whole project was finished in fifty-two days according to Neh 6:15), armed forces under Sanballat, Tobiah, and the Ashdodites (people living in the old Philistine territory on the west side of Judah) plotted to disrupt the work. [Who Were the Philistines?] Their action forced Nehemiah to

Who Were the Philistines?

The Philistines were a group of people in the East Mediterranean who settled the coastal plain of Palestine, basically from Joppa to Gaza. They built five city states: Ashdod, Ashkelon, and Gaza along or near the Mediterranean coast, and Ekron and Gath somewhat inland. They are known from Egyptian records from about the late thirteenth century on, i.e., about the same time Israel is first mentioned by name in the Merneptah Stele. (The Merneptah Stela was a thirteenth-century monument erected by Pharaoh Merneptah of Egypt, recounting his battles in Palestine. See Pritchard, *ANET* [2011] 328–29.) In the Bible, that is roughly the age of Joshua and the Judges. The Philistines are men-tioned eight times in Genesis and twice in Exodus, all in connection with a place name or the name of a king. They appear numerous times in Judges 3, 10, 13, 14, 15, and 16, and frequently in 1 Samuel as well. They appear to have been defeated, subdued, or at least repelled during the early years of the Davidic monarchy, and they appear subsequently in both the Hebrew Bible and the Assyrian and Babylonian Chronicles, i.e., down to 586 BCE. In the book of Nehemiah, they reappear as allies of Sanballat and Tobiah, but they appear nowhere in the post-exilic period literature as a dis-tinct people. Part of their legacy, however, is the area name Palestine.

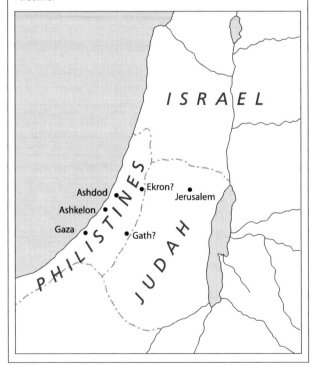

use some of his people as guards against possible attack by them. He also prayed to God for help, and well he might!

Nehemiah's Response, Nehemiah 4:10-15a

Not surprisingly, the returnees (called "Yehud" here) reported that their strength was failing from the double duty of watching and working. Their enemies (i.e., Sanballat, Tobiah, Geshem, their subjects—see Neh 2:19—and, pre-sumably, the unmentioned Judeans who had not been in exile and did not belong to the "real" Judah in the book of Ezra) plotted against them to attack them unawares while they were working. The "Jews" in v. 12 were the same people called Judah (Yehud) in v. 10. They had lived in exile or else they descended from those who had. They complained to Nehemiah ten times (!): "From all the places where they [the oppo-nents] live, [i.e., all over Yehud, Samaria, Ammon, the Philistine coast, and perhaps other sur-rounding areas] they will come up against us." In other words, the returnees in Yehud feared an attack by their hostile neighbors not only from within Yehud but also from their nearby neighbors.

Verse 13 reads strangely. The NRSV translates it as follows: "So in the lowest parts of the space behind the walls, I stationed people according to their fami-lies . . . ." The problem centers on one word in the Hebrew text: *mittaḥtîyôt*, translated "the lowest parts" in the NRSV and "lowest levels" in the REV. There is, though, no noun corresponding to the word "parts." The Hebrew word in question is a masculine plural form of the adjective *taḥat*, i.e., "those." It also might be understood to mean "those persons" instead of "those parts." One may also read the first letter "mem" partitively, i.e., with the meaning "some of." Then the text could be translated, "So *some of* the lowest (ones) I stationed behind the wall according to their families . . . ." That understanding will be adopted here. In that case, Nehemiah seems to have meant that he stationed some of the lowest-ranking returnees behind the wall to be the first line of defense in the event of a military breakthrough by the enemies. He armed them, moreover, with swords, spears, and bows. In other words, all fighters received weapons with which to fight, regardless of whether they already owned and kept them in a collective place or simply received them compliments of Nehemiah. All defenders, not just the wealthier ones, would have the means to defend the city. The further phrase "according to their families" probably means they were grouped by family rather than by some other arrangement. Fighting side by side with their family members, they might have fought harder than if they were standing next to someone with whom they had no family connection.

His fighters assembled, armed, and assigned to stations, Nehemiah gave them a pep talk epitomized in v. 15a: "Fear not! YHWH, who is great and awesome, will be on your side when you fight for your cause." That speech employs phrases that belong to "holy war" theology. [What Was Holy War, and How Holy Was It?] That theology is laid out in Deuteronomy 20:1-18. There Moses instructed the invading Israelites to fight to the death in Canaan, to take no prisoners, and to trust in God to fight for them. Nothing, though, is said in Nehemiah 4 about launching an attack. Most persons perhaps would say that, ethically speaking, Nehemiah was on firm ground in telling people they could defend themselves against attack, even if the language used here echoed more combative and less morally defensible language in Deuteronomy. Of course, pacifists might well say that the more moral course of action would have been for Nehemiah and the returnees to Yehud to pursue their objectives peacefully. Regardless, v. 15a then reports that the "enemies" learned that Nehemiah and his cohorts had found out about the intention to attack and armed themselves.

What Was Holy War, and How Holy Was It?

"Rules" or laws for conducting warfare were placed upon the lips of God as part of a speech to Moses in Deut 20:10-20. In that chapter as in the rest of Deuteronomy, the author states that the laws are designed for a time when the Israelites were living in their own land. The instructions for fighting fall into three basic parts. Part 1 (vv. 10-15) discusses how to treat enemies outside of Israel. When the Israelite soldiers approached a city, they were to offer it terms of peace: their lives in exchange for submission. If the city refused, a siege should follow. When the city was forced to surrender, all the men should be killed, but the women and children could be taken as booty.

Part 2 (vv. 16-18), however, says that the inhabitants of Canaan itself should simply be killed: men, women, and children. The stated rationale for this barbarism was fear that the people of Israel would succumb to the temptation to worship the gods of the Canaanites. The books of Joshua through 2 Kings and 1 and 2 Chronicles as well show how pertinent that warning was. Still, is fear that captors might convert to the religion of their captives justification for the cold-blooded murder of anyone, let alone the extermination an entire population? Ethically speaking, holocaust is indefensible regardless of the religious fear, motivation, or even perceived divine command behind it. Or

so it seems to me now; so it has seemed to me since I was about ten years of age; and so it seems to the representatives of the nations who have framed and at least claim to adhere to the Geneva Accords. In the midst of war, soldiers typically are not concerned about the rights of their enemies, even if their enemies are no longer in a position to harm them. That is the brutal reality of war, but it does not make such actions morally right.

Part 3 (vv. 19-20) urges a kind of restraint totally lacking in part 2. The invading Israelites were to spare the fruit trees! It would take years after the battle ended for new trees to bear fruit again. This decreed restraint is justified as being in the invaders' long-term interest, so it amounts to this: in achieving the short-term goal of starving or otherwise killing the inhabitants of a city, do nothing that would damage you in the long term. It is a rationally defensible command; trees outside a besieged city could benefit no inhabitants. It stands in contrast, however, with the bloodthirsty behavior demanded with respect to the Canaanites themselves in vv. 16-18. So vv. 15-20 command sparing fruit tree because they will be of use to the Israelites when they win, but the verses demand slaughtering all local inhabitants when Israel wins because those people might corrupt the religion of the conquerors.

Work on the Wall Resumed, 4:15b-23

Prepared to work or fight as necessary, the returnees resumed work on the wall of Jerusalem. Danger lurked from imminent attack. The workers, moreover, were spread out all along the wall, presumably inspecting everything and working on places that needed to be rebuilt or reinforced. Nehemiah, therefore, chose to use a trumpet or *shophar* (ram's horn) to call workers to assemble and mobilize for war. [Trumpet (Shophar)] Prudence suggested dividing the work force, moreover, so that only half worked at a time, while the other half stood watch, prepared for battle.

Nehemiah 4:16 describes their weaponry: spears, shields, bows, and body armor. The shields quite possibly were wickerwork, using willow branches or leather stretched over a wooden frame. The term translated "body armor" may

Trumpet (*Shophar*)

The word for "trumpet" was "*shophar*." Typically made from the horn of a ram or a wild goat (although the word could be used of a metal instrument), a *shophar* could be engraved, softened and reshaped, and even provided with a mouthpiece. It could sound only a few notes, but it could be loud and threatening. It was used often, therefore, as a warning instrument or—as here—to call people to assemble.

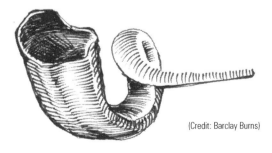

(Credit: Barclay Burns)

well designate protection covering the breast or torso, made of bronze. (Compare the description of Goliath's "coat of mail" in 1 Sam 17:5.[4] One may wonder, though, how many of the soldiers actually had such armor.) Staying armed slowed down their work on the wall and made it more burdensome. Half of the men worked, while half stood ready for battle. If someone spotted the enemy approaching, he was to sound the alarm and the warriors were to assemble before Nehemiah.

Interestingly, Nehemiah registers no recognition of the wear and tear such working hours and conditions took on the workers. Working double shifts, however, (i.e., "from the break of dawn until the stars came out," v. 21) left them no time for tending to their own farming and other necessary tasks, causing problems that raised their heads in Nehemiah 5. Nehemiah himself asserted that neither he nor his "brothers" (i.e., his kinsmen or relatives) nor the men of his guard ever took off their clothes. (Perhaps he meant they did not disrobe for sleep. One could hope, however, they changed clothes and washed occasionally!) The workers were armed for battle, and Nehemiah stood ready to direct the forces. Indeed, Nehemiah ordered the workers to spend the nights inside the broken walls (v. 22), not in their homes, ready to defend their work against nighttime vandals. That command might not mean the families were left at risk, however, if the target of any feared attack would be the wall itself and work thereon.

The chapter ends with an enigmatic phrase literally translated "each of his weapons the waters." The phrase is routinely emended, and the NRSV reads "each kept his weapon in his right hand." Other translations render the phrase similarly: REB, "each one kept his right hand on his spear"; NAB, "everyone kept his weapon at his right hand"; NJB, "each one kept his spear in this right hand." The ASV, however, renders the words thus: "everyone *went with* his weapon *to* the water." Some such understanding of the text may stand behind three other modern translations. The NIV renders the Hebrew construction in question, "I stationed some of the people behind the lowest points of the wall," while the NIB reads, "men took up position . . ." and the CEV simplifies the whole construction to read "so I set men . . . ."

H. J. Warner suggests an accidental copyist's inversion of the two words, and thinks the original reading was a phrase meaning "the Shiloah of the waters," i.e., the Siloam spring. As he understands the two-word phrase, it means the workers could not take off their clothes to wash them at the spring Shiloah.[5] Regardless, the overall point of the verse is clear: Nehemiah, his brothers, and their servants were on call from dawn to dusk, and they spent their nights inside the wall.

In conclusion, A. H. J. Gunneweg summarizes the thrust of Nehemiah 4 as follows: it depicts Nehemiah with the full support of the returnees, who with circumspection and complete legitimacy organized and dedicated themselves to the rebuilding of the wall.[6] The preparedness of the workers would be challenged soon, a challenge narrated beginning with the very first verse of the next chapter.

Complaints about Usury, 5:1-13

The heavy time constraints caused by building and guarding the wall around Jerusalem had the practical and predictable additional result that the workers had no time to tend to their own crops and their financial affairs. Those who had sown the grain had no time to reap it, so some even had to borrow against the value of their property in order to buy food. Verse 3 mentions a famine, so their diverted attention may have been compounded by a lack of the rain needed for a good yield (which, presumably, the women could have harvested). Of course, the famine might have been caused by sheer inattention due to working on the wall. Either way, the farmers among the returnees were suffering while moneylenders among them were compounding problems by foreclosing on their property. Complicating their poverty was the severity of the Persian king's taxes, specifically mentioned in Nehemiah 5:4.[7]

The complaint of the poor was not based on an appeal for a handout or even for fair business practices, but on belonging to a shared humanity and community. "Our flesh is the same as that of our kindred," and "our children are the same [i.e., just as important] as their children" (v. 5). Family counts; community counts. As John Donne observed, "no man is an island, entire of itself." It is easy to claim that one is a self-made person, although no one is. Some people do, however, refuse to recognize their interdependence with other people. In this case, some returnees seem to have wanted to foreclose on the property of other returnees.

Thus, the moneylenders stood to benefit one way or the other from the unpaid work of the builders. Since, moreover, those lenders lived or conducted business in Jerusalem itself and/or in other ways benefited from the rebuilding of the wall, their demands for timely payment during that crisis were at best two-faced. Regardless, their actions offer a study of finance, interest, ethics, and the overall best interests of Jerusalemite/Yehudian society as a whole and a perspective on the abuse of power against some of God's people in their society. If the charging of interest itself is necessary for the *business* of loaning money, concern for others, a sense of fairness, and at times even good business practices might limit the rate of interest charged. In that or any society, family members, friends, and persons wishing to help others might loan money at no interest. Here, however, the practice of the lenders amounted to charging interest on persons taking on debt to benefit themselves and the moneylenders as well. [Interest and Usury in the Old Testament]

Upon hearing of the moneylenders' confiscation of the property of other returnees, Nehemiah was indignant. Operating under the authority of the Persian government, albeit in the best interests of the returnees as a whole, Nehemiah chastised the moneylenders. It was bad enough for the poor workers/fighters possibly to have to face Sanballat, Tobiah, and their allies in hand-to-hand combat; it complicated their situation to be put in jeopardy of losing their very lands and homes in the countryside to other Yehudites benefitting from their work. Moreover, the city of Jerusalem itself, although *not* the land of Judah, was virtually unoccupied during the exile. Sacrificing to rebuild it would not enhance the financial well-being of many of the returnees, at least in the short term. Its rebuilding was a collective effort for the collective good. The returnees perhaps also knew that the city would be strengthened as the religious center of Yehud and its political center as well.

Nehemiah took public action against the moneylenders, here called "nobles and officials." He charged them with usury and put them on trial. The author places the following sentence in his mouth: "As far as we were able, we have brought back our Jewish kindred who had been sold to other nations [i.e., taken into captivity]." The "we" in this sentence (v. 8) *seems* to refer Nehemiah himself, since his account of his journey in Nehemiah 2:9-10 seems to speak in the first person of his coming alone. Even if he brought a small retinue, however, the "we" really in focus in Nehemiah 5:8 is the group that will be mentioned in Nehemiah 7:7-72 and that was mentioned in Ezra 2:2b-67: the returnees as a whole. Those "Jewish" brothers (or "Yehudim"), the very people working to rebuild the city wall, were being sold like chattel for the repayment of debts.

Interest and Usury in the Old Testament

Exorbitant interest (and what might be exorbitant could vary from individual to individual, society to society, time to time, and proposed use to proposed use) or usury appears as an issue in various places in the Old Testament. Mark Biddle reviews the issue. The three major legal codes of the Pentateuch (the Covenant Code in Exod 22:25, the Priestly Code in Lev 25:35-37, and the Deuteronomic Code in Deut 15:6-10; 28:12, 44) as well as Ezekiel (18:8, 13, 18) prohibit the charging of interest by one Israelite from another. Loans could be backed by collateral, however (Ps 109:11), which a lender could seize in cases of default, as Nehemiah 5 shows, or the debtors themselves could serve as human collateral in the form of indentured servanthood.

Mark E. Biddle, "The Biblical Prohibition against Usury," *Int* 65 (2011): 115–27, here 123.

Confronted by Nehemiah with their own greed, the officials were silent. Those who had been yelling for justice in the form of monetary repayment for seeds and other agricultural necessities from the very workers/soldiers they depended on for safety now deemed silence the wiser course of action. Nehemiah spoke for those workers/soldiers. He said that the moneylenders had enslaved the former exiles, and he ordered the lenders to stop taking interest. It is not clear how much interest (on seed, payable in kind) they were charging, but it presumably would preclude keeping enough seed to plant the next year.

Nehemiah shamed the moneylenders as well (vv. 10-11). In ancient societies, losing face was a serious issue. The pride that would come from being well-dressed, well-fed, and independent, i.e., a worthy member of society, could be overwhelmed by shame if one were found to be duplicitous and unworthy. The ultimate threat in the Old Testament, though, was the divine threat against those who harmed the poor. God might well take action against such people for not respecting the God to whom the poor prayed. Nehemiah demanded that the moneylenders return the fields, vineyards, olive orchards, and houses given as security for loans and taken by the moneylenders, and that they return the interest they had charged as well.[8]

The verbally chastised lenders promised both to restore the confiscated property and the interest charged on the loans and to refrain from charging it in the future. As N. P. Lemche notes, however, this action should be viewed as a "once-only measure," not as a binding law prohibiting forever the charging and collecting of interest.[9] Then Nehemiah engaged in what elsewhere might be called a "prophetic action" when he shook out the fold of his garment and uttered this oath/prayer: "So may God shake out everyone from [his] house and [his] property who does not [keep] this promise. Thus may they be shaken out and emptied" (Neh 5:13, taken with modifications from the NRSV). The people voiced their assent with an oral "Amen," and they praised God. Moreover, they kept their promise, and the crisis was eased.

The Generosity of Nehemiah, 5:14-19

While Nehemiah might not be a role model in all things, he turns out to be a paragon of sharing riches or at least of not getting wealthy at the public's expense. He notes that from the time he was appointed governor (in the twentieth year of King Artaxerxes), neither he nor his brothers (who already lived in Yehud—see

Neh 1:1) ate the food allowance of the local governor. This verse balances the claim in Nehemiah 4:23 that they, like their guards, never took off their clothes, but stayed ready to fight against Sanballat and company twenty-four hours a day, every day. Nehemiah 5:15 lists the demands of previous governors as "heavy burdens" on locals, specifically including food, wine, and forty shekels of silver (about one pound's worth). [Weighing Silver and Minting Coins] In other words, Persian appointees had been living off of the people they governed. In and of itself, that arrangement was as things should have been. It was (and still is), however, all too easy for people in power to control taxation, fees, and other costs and bene-fits to improve themselves and their friends financially.

The information that Nehemiah held the position of governor fits his actions, although it exceeds what a reader might have inferred from the narrative of the Persian king's permission for him to return to rebuild the wall (Neh 2:8), and that status had been stated explicitly nowhere earlier. Should readers assume that his brothers provided his and their needs? Had his family carried wealth into exile and managed it well? Or should readers assume that his status as wine taster at the court paid handsomely, or that he had come into money some other way in Susa? No answer is given as to the source of Nehemiah's and his brothers' material well-being. Perhaps the compiler of Ezra-Nehemiah did not know, and/or did not care, and/or did not wish to say.

Weighing Silver and Minting Coins

The phrase "forty shekels of silver" probably refers to an amount of silver poured onto scales and weighed, as opposed to forty silver coins worth one shekel each. In biblical lands, coinage began, among the Greeks especially, in the sixth and fifth centuries BCE. Its value was obvious. More or less standard coins, especially any minted by governments, facilitated trade and eliminated disputes about scales. Phoenician cities followed suit in the mid-fifth century, and from about 410 BCE coins circulated throughout the eastern Mediterranean. Tiny Yehud and ruined Jerusalem would have been in no condition to mint coins in the mid-fifth century. How early some coins might have circulated there is difficult to judge.

See Gerald M. Bilkes. "Money, Coins," *NIDB*, 4.130–37 (here pp. 134–35).

Two dish scale (libra). Bronze. Ancient Roman. Museo Archeologico Nazionale, Naples, Italy. (Credit: © Vanni Archive/ Art Resource, NY)

Regardless, v. 17 has Nehemiah portray himself as the model aris-tocrat and ruler. His servants worked on the wall instead of attending to him all the time. He fed his entire retinue. One hundred and fifty people, counting both Jews and various officials, ate at his table, in addition to state visitors. The meals included three kinds of meat (oxen, sheep, and fowls), not just the grains, fruits, vegetables, and drink that would be the ordinary daily fare.

What is more, Nehemiah bore the entire cost for this hospitality, and he prayed for God to bless his generosity.

By way of summary, one may note that Nehemiah 5 operates at three different levels at least. (1) As the private musings of Nehemiah himself, the chapter appears to offer his own assessment of his role in the rebuilding of the wall and its contribution to the rebuilding of Yehud. (It might not be the most modest self-assessment one will ever read, but it offers an insider's view of a crucial period in Yehudite history from someone crucial to those events.) (2) As a document in someone else's later retelling of the crucial years 539–432, it reflects another author's assessment and endorsement of Nehemiah's crucial role in a relatively unknown part of the history of post-exilic Yehud. It moves the plot of Nehemiah toward the showdown with Sanballat and Geshem and the completion of the wall (Neh 6:1–7:4). (3) As the word of God, it reminds readers of the necessity of being faithful to God's leading.

CONNECTIONS

1. The first and most obvious connection between Nehemiah 4 and 5 and today is their lesson on how to face adversity. Tiny Yehud had been ruined by Babylon, and its neighbors saw advantages in its poverty. Yehud posed no political threat to anyone; it could do little or nothing to harm them. For that matter, none of those other petty kingdoms could inflict much harm on one another either, but their petty jealousies kept them wary of each other. That was a behavior that played into the hands of the Persians.

Nehemiah devised a plan to improve the lot of Yehud. Working within the Persian sphere of influence, he tried to restore the city of Jerusalem, certainly as its political and religious center and probably as a business center too. The city and its surrounding territory had maintained a love/hate relationship since the days David captured Jerusalem and Solomon expanded and enriched it. Still, a centralized government, mutually beneficial building projects and trade, mutual defense against surrounding enemies, and a developing economy were benefits of the monarchy. After the destruction of Jerusalem, the state of Judah, and the monarchy by the Babylonians, Yehud and the rest of the area had to start over. The Persians adopted the policy of allowing exiled people to go home, in exchange, presumably, for unswerving loyalty to Persia. Nehemiah's plan can be seen as an effort to reestablish tiny Yehud as a local government loyal to Persia and serving Persia's needs with its center in its old capital, but as one sensitive to the needs of its own populace. Nehemiah could use his position to unify the population of returnees around the worship of YHWH in their rebuilt and refortified old capital without allowing the wealthy to take advantage of the laborers. In his actions, therefore, he also stands as a model of service by the more fortunate on behalf of the less fortunate. He used his position and fortune to help other people.

2. The conflicts between Yehud and its tiny neighbors show that international affairs may wax or wane for personal as well as political reasons. Judah, Samaria, and other remnants of former little kingdoms could have benefitted from mutual cooperation, but they languished instead in local disputes and both personal and political jealousies. Even today, deliberative bodies from city councils to state capitals to the American congress and the United Nations still stall over what can be either raw ambition or entrenched privilege.

United Nations Building in New York

1 United Nations Plaza, also known as DC-1 and DC-2. 2010. (Credit: Gryffindor, Wikimedia Commons, CC0 1.0)

3. Nehemiah's insistence on the restitution of seized property makes of him a role model for the distribution and redistribution of wealth for the upkeep of a society. Everyone who is expected to work and participate has a right to expect a living wage and a becoming existence. Ours is a society that will deliberately hire Latin Americans to do the farming and other hot, difficult work that most of us do not want to do. They follow in a long line of such workers: African slaves, European immigrants, and Oriental laborers derisively called "coolies."

We follow other, similar practices. We tax income, but not the wealth people keep or the rise in value of one's dwelling until one sells it. The wealthy do pay property taxes, but the poor pay the taxes on rental property through their rent. We grant income tax credit for those who pay interest on mortgages, while the poor pay tax on the money they earn to pay for rent. We allow those who can afford health insurance to avoid income tax on that income. To be sure, the lowest-paid workers

Heathrow Airport

London Heathrow, Terminal 5, London, England. (Credit: Warren Rohner, Wikimedia Commons, CC SA 2.0)

London's Heathrow Airport connects Great Britain to the rest of the world. Basically, it serves the needs of Britain's and the world's business people. As with the United Nation Building in New York City, many of those who use Heathrow are among (or otherwise benefit from) some of the wealthiest and most powerful people in the world.

and some retirees may fall below the taxable income floor and now may have access to subsidized health care. By no means, however, do all the needy have access to such care. I am thinking here of people who live in remote or impoverished areas, drifters, illiterates, and some elderly. In addition, the poor might not drive on interstate highways, and certainly do not fly out of government-built airports.

The truth is that many of our tax laws were carefully constructed to benefit particular constituencies and not others. Some of the poorest Americans benefit if and only if a particular government expenditure benefits the whole economy. Finally, I confess that the very fact that I could write this paragraph shows that I know how to benefit from some of those laws or at least that I employ a knowledgeable tax accountant to figure my federal and state income taxes. (My city and country income taxes, by the way, are calculated on a flat rate right off the top. That is, I pay the exact same rate as the lowest-paid, part-time, hourly worker in the city of Georgetown.)

NOTES

1. John M. Halligan, "Nehemiah 5: By Way of Response to Hoglund and Smith," *Second Temple Studies 1. Persian Period* (ed. P. R. Davies; JSOT Sup 117; Sheffield: Sheffield Academic Press, 1991) 150–55, here 155.

2. Oded Lipschits, "Achaemenid Imperial Policy and the Status of Jerusalem," *Judah and the Judeans in the Persian Period (Judah and the Judeans in the Persian Period* (ed. Oded Lipschits and Manfred Oeming; Winona Lake IN: Eisenbrauns, 2006) 19–52, here 33.

3. See, conveniently, Avraham Faust, "Early Israel: An Egalitarian Society," *BARev* 39/4 (2013): 45–49 + 62–63.

4. See the discussions of both "shield" and "body armor" in Philip A. Noss and Kenneth J. Thomas, *A Handbook on Ezra and Nehemiah* (UBS Handbook Series; New York: United Bible Societies, 2005) 336.

5. H. J. Warner, "A Simple Solution of Nehemiah iv. 23 (Heb. verse 17)," *ExpTim* 63 (1952): 322.

6. Antonius H. J. Gunneweg, *Nehemiah* (KAT XIX 2; Gütersloh: Gerd Mohn, 1987) 83.

7. Judah J. Slotki, *Daniel • Ezra • Nehemiah* (Soncino Books of the Bible; London, New York: Soncino Press 1951) 209.

8. See E. Neufeld, "The Rate of Interest and the Text of Nehemiah 6.11," *JQR* 44 (1954): 194–204, here pp. 200–201.

9. N. P. Lemche, "The Manumission of Slaves—the Fallow Year—the Sabbatical Year—the Jobel Year," *VT* 26 (1976): 38–59; here 54.

THE WALL COMPLETED

Nehemiah 6:1–7:73a

COMMENTARY

Nehemiah 6 and 7 complete the narrative of the rebuilding of the wall of Jerusalem under Nehemiah. All that was left from the work described in Nehemiah 3–5 was to install the gates (Neh 6:1, 15), an event whose retelling is almost lost in Nehemiah 6 as it stands. Nehemiah 7:1-4, moreover, is clearly the culmination of the narrative in Nehemiah 6, and Nehemiah 7:5-6 editorially connects vv. 1-4 to vv. 7-73a. Nehemiah 7:7-73a adds little by way of narrative, repeating almost verbatim as it does the list of returnees from Ezra 2. (There is no need to repeat here the information given in the comments on those verses. Readers should consult that discussion if they need to do so.) An outline of the two chapters will demonstrate their structure. [Outline of Nehemiah 6:1–7:73a] The discussion of the list in Ezra 2 showed that the numbers it uses presuppose a body of

> **Outline of Nehemiah 6:1–7:73a**
>
> An Invitation to Meet with Sanballat, Tobiah, and Geshem, 6:1-9
> An Invitation to Hide with Shemaiah in the Temple, 6:10-14
> The Completion of the Wall, 6:15–7:4
> The Census Taken by Nehemiah, 7:5-73a

people larger than the likely total population of Yehud before the end of the Persian period or even the mid-second century. (See the discussion of the date of Ezra-Nehemiah in the Introduction to Ezra-Nehemiah.) It was, perhaps, the latest material added. [Written Resources and Biblical Revelation] The list, moreover, closes the first section of the book of Nehemiah. In anticipation of it, Nehemiah 6:1–7:3 describes the rebuilding of the wall and the installation of the gates. After a two-verse transition, Nehemiah 7:6-73a closes the first section, repeating Ezra 2:2-72, thereby stipulating who belonged to the people of God and who did not.

Nehemiah 7:73b–8:18 will open the second part of Nehemiah (7:73b–10:39), and it will depict Ezra summoning the returnees to obey the law. Nehemiah 9:1-37 will show them repenting of the "sin" of intermarriage with people who had not been in exile. Nehemiah 9:38–10:27 will list the signees of the covenant who agree not to intermarry, and Nehemiah 10:28-39 will depict them accepting its

Written Resources and Biblical Revelation

While 2 Tim 3:16 says that "All scripture is inspired by God and is useful for teaching, for reproof, for correction, and for training in righteousness," it neither explains what constitutes inspiration nor states what writings it has in view. It would seem to include the Old Testament, although even that statement is anachronistic since Jews did not specify exactly what books belonged to the canon until the end of the first century of the Common Era. Theories of inspiration abound, of course, and some Christians insist that the Bible must be treated as errorless in every way. That is a remarkable claim since Genesis 1 describes the creation of light as the first creative act of God, the establishment of night and day thus ending day one, but then the creation of the stars, the sun, and the moon on day three. Likewise, Eccl 1:5 says that "The sun rises and the sun goes down, and it hurries to the place where it rises." I was taught in school, however, that the earth is part of the solar system and that it revolves around the sun. Were my teachers anti-Christian, anti-Bible, and wrong? Perhaps scientists do not know what they are talking about, and they would certainly admit that they do not know everything, but it seems imprudent, indeed impossible, to have to dismiss them in order to believe the Bible.

A careful reading of the Bible sometimes is troubling because it reveals that the Bible does not always agree in details. A return to Genesis 1, for example, shows days one through six as days of creation, culminating in the creation of human beings. God then creates the Sabbath, the day of rest, thereby building regular periods of rest into the divinely ordained tempo of life. (In Exod 20:8-11 God commanded Israel to observe Sabbath as a day of rest.) Gen 2:4b-25, however, paints a completely different picture of creation. That text begins, "In (or on) the day that the Lord made the earth and the heavens . . . ." In that narrative, God began with extant dusty earth, created a man, planted a garden, ordered the man to till it, and then put the man to sleep and removed a rib from which God made a "helper" for the man, one of flesh and bone just like the man. There is no mention of day-by-day action. None. Rather, the two passages are both creation accounts, and the two depictions are so different that a reader either recognizes the use of two different creation narratives or else distorts one or both to force them to agree.

It would seem more reverent to let the biblical authors say what they have to say and to do one's best to understand them and apply them to human life before God. If there are texts that do not agree in details, one might recognize that sometimes matters are so complex that "a single-minded consistency is the hobgoblin of small minds." In the case of the Genesis accounts of creation, no one before the modern era would have understood a creation account that talked in terms of a round earth, a solar system, and nebulae of stars. The job of Bible-believing Christians is to do their best to understand the texts in their context and to try to apply their spiritual insights, commands, and promises to the readers' spiritual lives. Modern readers cannot really retreat to an earlier worldview even if they wish, and it is not reverent to force the biblical authors to agree with each other if they do not. Their views can (and apparently must) be read in tension and measured by reason and by the teachings of Jesus insofar as the Bible records them. Sometimes the most readers can hope for is to apply biblical teachings and narratives to the best of their ability.

---

conditions. The entire second section of Nehemiah was carefully constructed to say exactly who was walled in and out of Jerusalem, so far as the redactor of Ezra-Nehemiah was concerned. The faithful among the returnees were in; the rest of the returnees and everyone who had not been in exile were out.

An Invitation to Meet with Sanballat, Tobiah, and Geshem, 6:1-9

Nehemiah 6 opens by mentioning Nehemiah's old nemesis Sanballat, plus Tobiah (called the Ammonite, probably a derisive sneer[1]), and Geshem,[2] an Arab mentioned earlier in Nehemiah 2:19 in passing. These three men form a triumvirate of antagonists in the account of Nehemiah. It is doubtful that they perceived their actions in the same light that the book of Nehemiah portrays them. Perhaps all is fair in love, war, and religious disputes. The following

phrase "the rest of our enemies" allows the possibility that other local representatives of the Persians were involved as well, although the book names no others and the author of the book of Nehemiah may have known no other names. These three men invited (summoned?) Nehemiah to a meeting in "one of the villages in the plain of Ono," a twofold phrase perhaps to be translated instead "with the lions (or princes) in the plain of Ono." [In the Villages/With the Princes: Ono]

Nehemiah recognized (or at least suspected) their intentions to harm him, and declined on the best of grounds: "Thanks, but I am too busy to come to a meeting; I have more important business to conduct." (How many modern Americans would love to decline some invitations with a similar response?) That the invitation was not simply social, but a political demand to meet is proven by the fact that it was repeated three times. Nehemiah, however, declined every time. Finally, Sanballat issued a written summons hand delivered by his personal courier or intermediary (the equivalent of a summons to appear in court delivered by a sheriff) to Nehemiah to appear before him. [Intermediary] The summons took the form of an open letter, i.e., one made public.

The letter (vv. 6-7) contained several charges. First, it charged Nehemiah with planning to rebel against Sanballat and (indirectly) against King Artaxerxes, i.e., with sedition. The evidence for that charge was that he was repairing the walls of the old royal city. The reader, of course, has Nehemiah's word that he had traveled to Jerusalem with the permission of Artaxerxes to rebuild the walls of the temple fortress/wall of the city (see Neh 2:8), but Sanballat shows (or at least admits to) no awareness of that permit. An impartial reader might concede Sanballat's point. Jerusalem was no longer the political center of Yehud. That center would have been wherever Persia said it was. There was, therefore, no obvious reason to rebuild the wall. (Readers of this commentary will recall that the purpose for

In the Villages/With the Princes: Ono

AΩ The plain of Ono was located about twenty miles north and slightly west of Jerusalem, i.e., in post-exilic Samaria, just east of Joppa. Neh 6:1-2 records an invitation (or summons) from Sanballat and Tobiah for Nehemiah to meet with them there. In that invitation, one Hebrew noun used with a prefixed preposition is problematic. Translators typically interpret it to mean *"in one of* the villages in the plain." Richard Schiemann, however, notes that the MT literally reads "with the lions" and not "in the villages." He suggests that the Hebrew word for "lions" was sometimes used figuratively to mean "princes," so that Sanballat and Tobiah actually were inviting Nehemiah to meet with the local rulers or "princes." In that case, since the proposed meeting was to take place outside Yehud and might not have been pleasant or safe, Nehemiah may have been wise to decline the invitation.

Richard Schiemann, "Covenanting with the Princes: Neh VI 2," *VT* 17 (1967): 367–69.

Intermediary

AΩ The Hebrew word rendered "servant" in the NRSV means "boy, lad, youth" or "servant, retainer" (BDB, 655). Williamson, however, argues that in Neh 4:16 (MT 4:10) it carries official overtones. The same seems to be the case here, hence the choice of the term "intermediary" to describe his status.

H. G. M. Williamson, *Ezra and Nehemiah* (WBC 16; Nashville: Nelson, 1985) 255.

the wall may well have been to set apart the city around the temple as holy space, not to make it a defensive center. Similarly, Zechariah 9:8, probably from circa 500 BCE, envisioned the new temple as a bastion guarded by God that no conqueror would ever again capture.)[3]

Second, in v. 7 Sanballat perhaps insinuates that Nehemiah wished to install himself as king. If Sanballat knew of them, he could have pointed to prophetic predictions that there would be a king in Judah to buttress his summons. In 520 Haggai 2:23 had proclaimed God's intentions to make Zerubbabel "like a signet ring," i.e., the ring used by a king to sign his name, a message repeated in Zechariah 4:14, which announced the presence of two anointed ones in Jerusalem: namely, the king and the high priest. Also, Zechariah 9:9-10 proclaimed the coming of a king, albeit a peaceful one. God would do the fighting! Such "king talk" died out in the prophetic corpus and elsewhere in the Old Testament afterward, but it resurfaced here as a political theme—regardless of whether Sanballat knew those texts or other such hopes. He may simply have been reacting to Nehemiah's "take charge" attitude or threatening to charge him with sedition.

That accusation was cleverly designed and ambitiously motivated. If Sanballat successfully insinuated to Artaxerxes that Nehemiah held such ambitions, the rebuilding project would come to an end and Nehemiah would be recalled if not executed. This chess match between the two men, therefore, was potentially a deadly game. It also reveals Sanballat's likely ambition: to retain or else to secure control over Yehud himself. It is difficult to tell how much control, if any, he might have exercised over Yehud before Nehemiah came and thus what he stood to lose by Nehemiah's actions. In any case, he may have wanted such control or at least he might have feared what trouble Nehemiah might have been able to cause him.

Nehemiah denied the charge vehemently (v. 8), as indeed he had to do. In fact, he accused Sanballat of inventing it himself. The reader, of course, is in a position that Sanballat was not: the reader knows that Nehemiah had acted with the expressed approval of the king and on the king's behalf. Besides, readers already are in full sympathy with Nehemiah. It appears as if, however, from the urgency of Nehemiah's retort, that he realized that his goals (ambitions!) had been and could be again misconstrued in political infighting. Indeed, readers should remind themselves that Ezra-Nehemiah was not created (over whatever amount of time that took) simply for the sake of potential posterity but as a polemical document defending the perquisites of the returnees in Jerusalem and the temple *during and after* Nehemiah's time. In any case, v. 9 constitutes an aside, attributing selfish motives to Sanballat, Tobiah, and Geshem, and imploring God to act on Nehemiah's behalf. It comes across as the prayer of a man fearful of failing in his God-given mission through the actions of those he considered nefarious opponents. Regardless, the proposed meeting does not seem to have taken place.

An Invitation to Hide with Shemaiah in the Temple, 6:10-14

An indeterminate amount of time passed until "one day" Nehemiah visited Shemaiah ben Deliah ben Mehetabel, who was under house arrest. Shemaiah posed as a diviner who had uncovered a plot against Nehemiah's life that very night and proposed that Nehemiah conduct him to the temple, where the two would remain. Nehemiah at first seems to have taken his request at face value, but to have denied the request on two grounds. (1) Leaders should not hide in fear, and (2) he had no right to enter the temple (since he was not a priest). Further reflection apparently caused him to see in the invitation a plot hatched by Tobiah and Sanballat to shame him for assuming the priestly right to enter the temple. It was an act also that, if performed, would have had profound implications. A. L. Ivry writes, "his very presence in the temple compound with his soldiers and followers such as Shemaiah would have been deemed an act of intimidation and offense."[4] The vignette concludes with a prayer to God to remember (i.e., not just to recall later but to punish) the two adversaries for their cunning attempts to deceive and to bring down Nehemiah, aided by the prophetess Noadiah and the prophets who attempted to scare him, presumably by predicting the failure of his work. [Prophetesses] Apparently much or all of the temple bureaucracy was aligned with Sanballat and opposed to Nehemiah. It is worth asking what the priests and others feared to lose at his hands, but the question cannot be answered. R. P. Carroll, however, points to the dilemma that Nehemiah (and the people) had to face: Yehud would either have its own indigenous ruler or the king of Persia.[5] Nehemiah opted for loyalty to the Persian king, whose power he knew firsthand and at whose beck and call he served. In doing so he acted wisely.

Prophetesses

ΑΩ Typically in the Bible the spokespersons for God are designated a "prophet" or simply a "man of God." A few prophetesses, however, are mentioned as well: Deborah (Jdg 4:4), Huldah (2 Kgs 22:14), and the wife (?) of Isaiah (Isa 8:3), all positively. Also Miriam, the sister of Moses, is called a "prophet" (Exod 7:15). Noadiah the prophetess (Neh 6:14), however, is mentioned negatively. Given the other texts cited here, it would be incorrect to say that women never served God as prophetesses. It might also be incorrect to cite their relative infrequency as proof that God only rarely or never calls women. It might, instead, be correct to speculate that few women could hear such a call given the male-centered cultures of the Bible, and of those who did, few could bring themselves to follow such a call, and fewer still would be recognized as legitimate prophets.

The Completion of the Wall, 6:15–7:4

The refurbishing of the wall took a total of fifty-two days, and was completed on the twenty-fifth day of Ellul (the sixth month or October). Clines dates it precisely on October 2, 445 BCE.[6] [Dates in the Book of Nehemiah] The number fifty-two reveals more than might meet the eye. Building a city wall was no small task, requiring as it would extensive site preparation, the quarrying and moving of stone, cutting and moving or importing timber, and careful planning, measuring, and construction. All it took, moreover, to render a wall useless was to create one or more gaps in it and/or break down its necessary opening(s), the city gate(s), by destroying it (them). Both had befallen Jerusalem at the hands of the Babylonians. The city served in Nehemiah's day as the site of the temple and perhaps some other public buildings, but few if any other houses, none new. (See Neh 7:4.) What Nehemiah describes, therefore, probably is not the rebuilding of an entire wall but a series of repairs made on an older, existing wall. If the wall was not to serve as a military defense, it did not have to be very high, although workers might well have rebuilt it as high as practical. As time passed, the city's inhabitants could add other walls or could strengthen further the one they had. Readers, therefore, should envision Nehemiah's directing the easiest, most practical repairs that would result in an enclosure for the temple. The city, readers should conclude, was repopulated slowly (contra the insistence of some modern scholars to the contrary).[7]

A flurry of correspondence ensued between Tobiah, the "nobles" of Yehud and Nehemiah himself. Nehemiah 6:16-19 constitutes a sampling of that correspondence and other actions presented by the

---

Dates in the Book of Nehemiah

As in the book of Ezra so also in the book of Nehemiah, one of the redactional motifs is the marking of time. Six date markers appear in Nehemiah, namely in Nehemiah 1:1, 2:1, 6:15, 7:73b, 9:1, and 13:6.

Text	Date	Event
1:1	9th month (Chislev) of 19th year of Artaxerxes, 446(?)*	Hanani arrives in Susa
2:1	1st month (Nisan) of 20th year, 445	Nehemiah departs for Jerusalem
6:15	6th month (Elul) of 20th year, 445	Repairs on wall finished
7:73b	7th month (Tishri) of 20th year, 445	Reading of the Law in Jerusalem
9:1	7th month, (Tishri) of 20th year, 445 (implied)	Separation of "Israel" from others
13:6	Month omitted, 32nd year of Artaxerxes, 433	Nehemiah returned to Susa

* Neh 1:1 sets its action in twentieth year of Artaxerxes, i.e., 445. Neh 2:1 also sets its action in the twentieth year of Artaxerxes, but Nisan was the first month in the Babylonian year. D. J. A. Clines suggests plausibly a slight slip of the pen and dates Neh 1:1 four months earlier in year 446.

D. J. A. Clines, "An Introduction to and Notes on Nehemiah," in *HarperCollins Study Bible* (ed. Wayne A. Meeks; New York: HarperCollins, 1993) 717, n. on Neh 1:1.

author as representative of the reaction to Nehemiah's work. (1) The fear of God fell on the surrounding people, for they perceived God's hand at work in the repairing of the wall. (2) The nobles of Yehud corresponded by letter with Tobiah, presumably about Nehemiah, the work on the wall around Jerusalem, and the implications of its repair for them. (3) Those nobles tried to repair the breach between the two men by praising each to the other. (4) In response, Tobiah sent Nehemiah letters in an attempt to intimidate him.

Nehemiah 7:1 mentions in passing that when the wall had been completed, Nehemiah had the gates set in place. The equation of the city with the temple area continues in that verse when Nehemiah notes that gatekeepers, singers, and Levites had been appointed, unless, as Clines suggests, the phrase was a scribal gloss.[8] As it stands, however, the verse implies, though it does not actually state, that Nehemiah appointed them. J. J. Slotki notes that gatekeepers normally were entrusted with guarding the temple only, although here they are to guard the whole city.[9] In any case, the author-redactor of Ezra-Nehemiah insists that Nehemiah, not the priests, was in charge of the city, the administration of which he delegated to his brother "Hanani." The text also says that he made "Hananiah" the commander of the citadel. The two names perhaps refer to the same man. As a walled city/temple, Jerusalem was more or less safe as long as the gates were shut and barred. Ingress and egress were to be controlled by Nehemiah's people, in particular his brother.

Archaeologist David Ussishkin (who thinks that Nehemiah restored old, large walls) argues, however, that readers ought to read the account of the rebuilding of the wall in light of the recovered archaeological data from the site. That data suggests—as does this reading—that the rebuilding project had been largely political or symbolic, not a military act. Archaeologists, moreover, have as yet discovered no discernible trace of that wall. Most of the city remained uninhabited, while its few inhabitants were concentrated around the central part of the city, i.e., the city of David and the area of the temple mount. What is more, it seems to have remained very small until the second century BCE.[10] In other words, archaeology does not reveal a city different from the one that this proposed reading of the text does. The large numbers of returnees in Ezra-Nehemiah, however, are implausible for such an early time, but that discrepancy might simply suggest that the numbers were added much later in light of the city's population in the second century.

There is still another, minor point of interpretation concerning the instructions about when the gates of the city were to be opened. Verse 3 is sometimes translated to the effect "Let not the gates of Jerusalem be opened *until* the sun be hot; and, while they stand on guard, let them shut the doors and bar them." G. R. Driver observes that that translation is sheer nonsense; no one would keep the gates barred until the heat of the day and then open them when people might be napping. He recommends reading the Hebrew preposition used there as meaning "while" or "at the time of."[11] The sense then would be that the people should close the gates at naptime. The NRSV follows the typical reading, and the sentence may mean simply that the gates were to be open from morning until late afternoon, but be closed before the guards went off duty for the night.

Finally, the aforementioned v. 4 is a redactional ending, not simply to Nehemiah 7:1-3 or even Nehemiah 6:1–7:3, but to the whole of Nehemiah 1:1–7:3. It is followed by the same list of returnees as in Ezra 2. The broken state of the wall was first reported to Nehemiah by his brothers in Nehemiah 1:3, and the completion of its restitution is reported in Nehemiah 7:4. The first major task of Nehemiah was complete, but his narrative was not at its end. The second section of Nehemiah, namely chapters 8–10, will move on to additional issues.

The Census Taken by Nehemiah, 7:5-73a

The first-person narrative has Nehemiah say (v. 5a) that God had placed it in his mind to take a census of the population. The list of returnees that appears in Nehemiah 7:6-73a, however, is almost identical to the list in Ezra 2:1-70. [Parallels between Nehemiah 7:6-73a and Ezra 2:1-70] (See the discussion of the lists in the Introduction to Ezra-Nehemiah, "C. The Historical Reliability of Ezra-Nehemiah," "1. The Number of returnees and the Import of that List for the Date of the Completion of Ezra-Nehemiah," and the discussion of the census lists in connection with the comments on Ezra 2:1-70.) The reuse of that list here in Nehemiah 7 creates an inclusio around everything in between Ezra 2:1 and Nehemiah 7:73a. Its purpose is to delineate the returnees and only the returnees as persons who might be considered the "true" Israel and guaranteed their right to worship in the temple. Ezra 2:1-70 showed a huge party of

Parallels between Nehemiah 7:6-73a and Ezra 2:1-70

People Who Led the Returns, Nehemiah 7:7 // Ezra 2:1-2a
A Tally by Fathers' Houses, Nehemiah 7:8-60 // Ezra 2:2b-58
People Who Could Not Prove Their Ancestry, Nehemiah 7:61-65 // Ezra 2:59-63
Totals for the Entire Assembly, Nehemiah 7:66-69 // Ezra 2:64-67
Totals of Gifts by the Heads of Some Families, Nehemiah 7:70-72 // Ezra 2:68-69
Concluding Statement about Where People Settled, Nehemiah 7:73a // Ezra 2:70

returnees coming to reclaim their land and to rebuild the temple acting on the direct command of Cyrus. Ezra 7–8 detailed the journey of a second group of returnees under the priest Ezra acting on the direct command of "Artaxerxes." Ezra 9–10 showed the necessity of purging members of the original company of returnees who had removed themselves from the "true" community by marrying local Judean women. Nehemiah 7:5-73a promised the continued viability of that community, guaranteed now by the reconstruction of the wall around the city. The reuse of the list is facilitated by the fact that the lists report only numbers and families, not the individual names of the returnees themselves. (See the discussion "J. The Purposes of Ezra-Nehemiah" in the Introduction to Ezra-Nehemiah.) Nehemiah 12:1-26 also will reuse a few names from that list, and Nehemiah 13:23-31 will describe one final purging of the community by Nehemiah.

Nehemiah 7:5 is a first-person singular statement that God inspired Nehemiah to assemble the people and to enroll them by genealogy. Instead of reporting such an action, however, the verse continues by reporting that Nehemiah found a list of the original returnees, the ones who returned to Yehud with Zerubbabel and company (Neh 7:6-73a), i.e., the same census list as the one reported in Ezra 2. Despite the fact that the totals reported in Ezra 2:64 and Nehemiah 7:62 (42,360 in Ezra) plus 7,337 slaves and 245 singers (200 in Ezra) are nearly identical, those within the list said to have returned from the exile actually add up to only 31,099 in Nehemiah and 29,818 in Ezra. Of them, 642 according to Nehemiah 7:62 (652 people according to Ezra 2:60) could not prove they descended from Judeans. Wherever the lists came from, only 29,260 (Ezra) or 30,455 (Nehemiah), i.e., about 60 percent of the total numbers, constituted what the redactor of Ezra-Nehemiah held to be true Israelites, including the priesthood. The remaining 40 percent or so of the returnees apparently did not pass his test. As in Ezra 2 so here also, not even all the returnees belonged to the real Israel. This list, thus, seems to have served the redactor's purpose of arguing that *even from the beginning of the return* not everyone in Yehud and not even everyone among the returnees qualified as members of the people of Yehud/people of God. As argued in the Introduction to Ezra-Nehemiah, Ezra 2 listed the leading families in Jerusalem, beginning with priests and Levites, from a time perhaps as late as the second century BCE, and it sought to defend their claim to legitimate leadership. Its repetition in Nehemiah 7 reasserted that claim.

The last clause, "and all Israel settled in their towns" (Neh 7:73a), is but the first half of the sentence that constitutes Ezra 2:70. The last half-verse (Neh 7:73b) is used redactionally to introduce the narrative that follows in Nehemiah 8, which begins the second main section of the book (Neh 7:73b–10:39). That variation is not evidence, however, as is sometimes argued, that the list itself constituted a census list from *Nehemiah's* time. In the first place, the numbers supplied do not add up to the totals given in either Ezra 2 or Nehemiah 7. In the second place, judged by the best estimates archaeologists can make, the population of Yehud was not so large until the Maccabean period. It appears, therefore, that here and in Ezra 2 a later list of unknown origin was pressed into service as a census count, this time dated to 445 instead of 539 as in Ezra 2. It also brings the first part of the book of Nehemiah to a close, in the process legitimating its hero—a non-Levite—and his role as an agent of the Persians in rebuilding the wall to enclose the whole city and stake its claim as holy ground at the center of the holy people. The repetition in Nehemiah 7 of the list from Ezra 2 also signals that the work begun when returnees moved from Babylon to Jerusalem to rebuild the temple was now complete. Rebuilding the wall of Jerusalem had been the final part of that project. Thus, the first section of the book of Nehemiah ends with 7:73a; the second section (Neh 7:73b–10:39) will focus on worship, confession, covenant, and the *limited* repopulation of the city itself.

CONNECTIONS

1. Nehemiah was concerned with erecting a wall around God's "house," i.e., with setting it apart from the mundane to protect it from ritual contamination. In one sense, that was the correct thing to do. That which is sacred should, perhaps even must, be delineated from that which is mundane. Sacred things belong to God and should be recognized as God's, whether those things are days (Sabbath, Sunday), people (rabbis, priests, ministers, imams, nuns, and the like), objects (the Bible, crosses, meeting houses, or temples), songs, speech acts (prayers, sermons), or something else. Erecting "walls" around such things is necessary to mark them as special. Erecting a building or other space to use as God's house, a place to worship God, and then fighting over access to it is, however, counterproductive.

The whole point of recognizing and utilizing the sacred is to claim and modify the profane, thereby reclaiming God's entire world and all of God's people in one whole creation. In Christian Bibles, Genesis 1 and 2 describe that holy state, Genesis 3 and virtually the rest of the Bible describe its corruption and God's desire and efforts to redeem it, and Revelation 21 and 22 promise its ultimate renewal. Occasionally, the beatific vision breaks through elsewhere (e.g., Isa 56:1-8 and 65:17-23), although more typically in the Old Testament such restoration is limited to Israel. The Gospel of John announces the motivation and breadth of God's salvific work: God so loved the world that God gave God's only begotten son so that whoever believes in God will not perish but have everlasting life (3:16). It is in that overall context that Christian readers should both critique and apply Ezra-Nehemiah. In his confrontation with Sanballat, Tobiah, Geshem, and others, Nehemiah was right to insist that God was in the process of redeeming the returnees. In his insistence that God and his temple were limited only to returnees (or Yehudians or the descendants of Abraham), Nehemiah's vision fell short of the view of Jesus that God loves the whole created order and every person in it. Indeed, it also fell short of the hopes of Third Isaiah.

Nehemiah cannot be blamed, humanly speaking, for not wanting to include his enemies. Neither can moderns. Nehemiah should not, however, be assumed to be completely correct in everything he said or did because he was a hero for God. God's heroes had (and have) a way of getting in the way of God's desire and efforts for the redemption of humanity and of God's world. The Bible is rife with examples, most notably in the Old Testament view that in taking the holy land Israel's holy war should be total. No prisoners should be taken; no animals should be spared; and no annual crops should be spared either, although fruit trees should be (Deut 20:16-20). Human history too is rife with war, typically justified as "restitution" or "preservation," often with little regard to the devastation it causes. These are extreme examples to be sure, but they are based on the same sense of exclusive entitlement (as opposed to sharing) that possessed Nehemiah. Let the reader not misunderstand. This comment does not equate the actions of Nehemiah with those of heinous criminals, but this reading does not accept

The Reception of the Righteous into Heaven

Hans Memling (c. 1433–1494). "The Last Judgment." c. 1467–1471. Oil on panel. National Museum, Gdańsk. (Credit: Wikimedia Commons, US-PD)

that Nehemiah's actions carry out the full intention of God with regard to Nehemiah's neighbors either.

2. Closely related to the first point is a second: there is an implicit danger in trying to limit or delimit God to temple, church, or a people. In such thinking, God too easily becomes "ours": our God, our Protector, and our Benefactor. If we are God's people, and God is our God, then those who oppose us or do not like us are not just our enemies; they are God's enemies. When we conclude that they are God's enemies, we dehumanize them and prepare ourselves to mistreat them and maybe even exterminate them. It was Christian Germany that executed millions of Jews and Christian America that dropped the only two atomic bombs dropped in human warfare—yet. Exacerbating this problem is the ease with which wars (or other conduct) that are in our best interests can be rationalized as being in God's best interests. [Buchenwald Slave Laborers' Liberation]

Buchenwald Slave Laborers' Liberation

At the end of World War II, allied forces liberated slave laborers from the infamous camp at Buchenwald, Germany. In such camps, an estimated 6,000,000 Jews were tortured and killed in the attempt to "cleanse" Hitler's Germany of Jews.

Former prisoners of the "little camp" in Buchenwald stare out from the wooden bunks in which they slept three to a "bed." Buchenwald, Germany, April 16, 1945. (Credit: National Archives and Records Administration)

3. The second point leads to a third about using God or God's supposed will for one's own personal or political gains. Such (ab)use of theist faith is not new, but it seems that much in public discourse in America today is less about what God wants and more about what people want. In my younger days, laws were used to deny rights both to people of color and to Native Americans. More recently, Latinos and Latinas are used to do some of the most difficult, dangerous, or odious work in American society. One reads and hears people complaining about the United States government exceeding its constitutional powers by feeding the poor, healing the sick, comforting the afflicted, releasing the captives, and seeing to it that even the poorest people have access to "life, liberty, and pursuit of liberty" or at least food stamps. Some people seem to be more interested in preserving their positions, advantages, and tax breaks than in meeting the needs of others of God's children. Perhaps

federal programs are not the best solution, but the voluntary feeding of the hungry, housing the homeless, and clothing the naked has simply run up against human greed and is not sufficient.

4. Finally, the sorry spectacle of the governor of Samaria and of Tobiah trying to trick Nehemiah by lying and threats possibly strikes us as not surprising. We live in an age when truth (verbal or otherwise) in public discourse is often unwelcome and can be drowned out. An annual event in Kentucky is a picnic at a place in the western part of the state. It is held as a fundraiser for a charity, and for many years it has kicked off the political season for the ensuing year's elections! Politicians attend to speak, swear, defame their opponents, and otherwise engage in free political discourse. Sometimes that discourse becomes so vulgar or defamatory that the group that stages the event has to caution speakers and threaten to shut off their microphones. Nationally, moreover, political speeches and campaign ads display a mastery of the art of twisting even moral pronouncements into instruments of division and advantage. One can make the case that many Americans, including some professing, Bible-believing Christians, accept such actions as "just politics" and not an indictment against our moral indifference.

On a more personal note, some years ago I attended a conference for religious writers. The conference ended around 11:00 A.M., and my flight was not until mid-afternoon. I accepted a kind invitation from several of the other attendees (all pastors of Baptist churches) to join them for lunch before heading to the airport. The talk at the table, however, was how to use the political process and the pastors' connections with politicians to make sure that their favored candidates were elected to office and their views defended. To be sure, they had every legal right to hold that conversation and to discuss such actions. They had every right, even the moral obligation, to speak to their congregations about moral issues in this country. They did not, and still do not, however, have the legal right to use their pulpits and their churches for political advantage without surrendering their churches' tax-exempt status. Perhaps they walked the fine line that divided partisan from religious, but their sympathies seemed to me more partisan than Christian, and the actions they discussed did not even seem ethical. Perhaps we have all learned well and use effectively the tactics of Sanballat, Tobiah, and Geshem.

NOTES

1. D. J. A. Clines, "Introduction and Notes on Nehemiah," in *The HarperCollins Study Bible* (New York: HarperCollins, 1993) 718. Calling a man named after Yahweh an "Ammonite" probably was intended as an insult. The gross narrative about Ammon's conception and that of his half-brother Moab (Gen 19:30-38) was intended to stigmatize both them and their descendants as worthless half-breeds.

2. Frank Moore Cross, Jr. ("Geshem the Arabian, Enemy of Nehemiah," *BA* 18 [1955]: 2:46–47) notes that the name "Geshem, king of Qedar" appears in a fifth century BCE inscription, providing extra-biblical evidence of his name and status.

3. See Paul L. Redditt, *Zechariah 9–14* (IECOT; Stuttgart: Kohlhammer, 2012) 33, 42–42, 53.

4. Alfred L. Ivry, "Nehemiah 6, 10: Politics and the Temple," *JSJ* 3 (1972): 35–45, here 43.

5. Robert P. Carroll, "Coopting the Prophets: Nehemiah and Noadiah," *Priests, Prophets and Scribes. Essays on the Formation and Heritage of Second Temple Judaism in Honour of Joseph Blenkinsopp* (ed. Eugene Ulrich, John W. Wright, Robert P. Carroll, and Philip R. Davies; JSOTSup 149; Sheffield: Sheffield Academic Press, 1992) 87–99, here pp. 98–99.

6. Clines, "Nehemiah," 721.

7. See, for example, the defense of a larger population by W. S. LaSor, "Jerusalem," *ISBE*, 2.998–1032, here 1020. He lists these three "facts" (his choice of words) as conclusive proof of the city's population. (1) Nehemiah describes the city as an eyewitness; (2) he uses names and locations used in the pre-exilic period; and (3) the walls are similar to those described by Josephus at the end of the first century of the Common Era. Some scholars find that last observation so compelling, however, that they date Nehemiah as a finished product to the second century when the city did reach such dimensions.

8. Clines, "Nehemiah," 724.

9. Judah J. Slotki, *Daniel • Ezra • Nehemiah* (Soncino Books of the Bible; London, New York: Soncino, 1951) 220.

10. David Ussishkin, "On Nehemiah's City Wall and the Size of Jerusalem," *New Perspectives on Ezra-Nehemiah* (ed. Isaac Kalimi; Winona Lake IN: Eisenbrauns, 2013) 101–30, here 125.

11. G. R. Driver, "Forgotten Hebrew Idioms," *ZAW* 76 (1966): 1–7, here pp. 4–6.

EZRA SUMMONS THE RETURNEES TO OBEY THE LAW

Nehemiah 7:73b–8:18

COMMENTARY

Nehemiah 7:73b–8:18 begins the second major section of the book of Nehemiah (7:73–10:39), a section situating Torah proclamation, prayer, and commitment to God and community at the heart of the book and at the center of community life. (See the discussion "B. The Structure of the Book of Nehemiah" in the Introduction to Nehemiah.) Following the repetition in Nehemiah 7:5-73a of the list of returnees given first in Ezra 2:2-7 and the report that they had settled in their towns, Nehemiah 7:73b–8:18 turns to another narrative of Ezra, thus redactionally connecting the careers and books of Ezra and Nehemiah and presenting the two men as contemporaries. (See the discussion of this issue in the Introduction to Ezra-Nehemiah, "G. The Authorship and Unity of Ezra-Nehemiah.") It functions to show that the returnees living around Jerusalem were the ones who could not only rightly come to the city but who also rightly observed the festival. Nehemiah 7:73b–8:1a, moreover, utilizes Ezra 3:1, the opening verse of the narrative describing the rebuilding of the altar in Jerusalem, to introduce a new narrative separated from that return in 539 by nearly a century. Differently stated, Nehemiah 8 as it stands presupposes Ezra 2 (which the book of Nehemiah repeats in Neh 7:7-73a) and Ezra 3–6, as well as Ezra's journey to Jerusalem and his taking his place of authority there (Ezra 7–10). As stated in connection with the comments on Nehemiah 6:1–7:73a, the entire second section of Nehemiah (i.e., Neh 6:1–8:18) was carefully constructed to say exactly who was walled in and out of Jerusalem, so far as the redactor of Ezra-Nehemiah was concerned. The faithful among the returnees were in; the rest of the returnees and everyone who had not been in exile were out.

Despite the intervening chapters about Nehemiah and the repairing of the wall of Jerusalem (Neh 1:1–7:77), in Nehemiah 7:73b–8:18, surprisingly, Ezra is the hero, and Nehemiah is mentioned only once (Neh 8:9) in what is probably a redactional addition.[1] The plot of Nehemiah 7:73b–8:18 is straightforward. On the first day of the seventh month (year not stated, allowing the author to situate the narrative where he wanted it), the people gathered and directed Ezra to read the law to them, which he did (Neh 7:73b–8:8). Then they were told to celebrate that reading with a meal (Neh 8:9-12). The next day they discerned from the Law of Moses that the impending Feast of Tabernacles/Booths should be observed by dwelling in booths (Neh 8:13-18), which they attempted to carry out. The following comments will follow that analysis of the chapter. [Outline of Nehemiah 7:73b–8:18]

One obvious preliminary question, however, is why this narrative about Ezra has been separated from the others. One answer already supplied in this commentary is that the redactor did so in order to present the careers of the two leaders as one seamless whole in the restitution of the community of God in Jerusalem and Yehud. A second answer is that Nehemiah 7:73b–8:18 is used to portray the building of the wall theologically. In the absence of an earthly king, the city was to be the seat of God, the heavenly king. Politics and religion did not simply mix; they were two aspects of one thing. The returnees were the people of God, and they were to worship God at the temple in God's holy city. Don Polaski offers a third reason. By having the Law read at this point in his narrative, the redactor of Ezra-Nehemiah makes Nehemiah himself subject to the law.[2] He could not act in his own interests or in those of the Persian king exclusively.

Outline of Nehemiah 7:73b–8:18

The Setting of the Narrative, 7:73b
The People Gather and Direct Ezra to Read them the Law, 8:1-8
The People Return Home and Celebrate the Harvest, 8:9-12
The People Build Booths and Observe the Festival of Booths, 8:13-18

Chapter and Verse Numbers

Readers of the Bible sometimes discover places where modern translations make content breaks that are inconsistent with verse or even chapter breaks. Why is that so? The division of the Bible into chapters and verses is not original in the texts. Various markings indicating divisions in content do appear in the Hebrew Old Testament, having been added to those books by later Jewish scholars called Masoretes, but the earliest, best-known division of the whole Bible into chapters was the work of Stephen Langdon, the Archbishop of Canterbury from 1207–1228. That work proved helpful for readers, so over the next several centuries other people divided the chapters into verses. There is, however, still some slight variation among the various numbering systems, and occasional idiosyncrasies such as the verse division between Neh 7:73a and 73b still exist.

The Setting of the Narrative, 7:73b–8:1a

[Chapter and Verse Numbers] Nehemiah 7:73b actually begins the introduction to the narrative told in Nehemiah 8; the chapter division divides the action from its temporal setting, which supplies its date. [Dates in the Book of Nehemiah] In its original context (i.e., Ezra 2:20), the clause rounded off the narrative concerning the return of 49,000+ exiles from Babylon to Jerusalem; in Nehemiah 7:73b, it provides a segue from a comment about where the people lived (Neh 7:4) to a meeting of

---

Dates in the Book of Nehemiah

As in the book of Ezra so also in the book of Nehemiah, one of the redactional motifs is the marking of time. Six date markers appear in Nehemiah, namely in Nehemiah 1:1, 2:1, 6:15, 7:73b, 9:1, and 13:6.

Text	Date	Event
1:1	9th month (Chislev) of 19th year of Artaxerxes, 446(?)*	Hanani arrives in Susa
2:1	1st month (Nisan) of 20th year, 445	Nehemiah departs for Jerusalem
6:15	6th month (Elul) of 20th year, 445	Repairs on wall finished
7:73b	7th month (Tishri) of 20th year, 445	Reading of the Law in Jerusalem
9:1	7th month, (Tishri) of 20th year, 445 (implied)	Separation of "Israel" from others
13:6	Month omitted, 32nd year of Artaxerxes, 433	Nehemiah returned to Susa

* Neh 1:1 sets its action in twentieth year of Artaxerxes, i.e., 445. Neh 2:1 also sets its action in the twentieth year of Artaxerxes, but Nisan was the first month in the Babylonian year. D. J. A. Clines suggests plausibly a slight slip of the pen and dates Neh 1:1 four months earlier in year 446.

D. J. A. Clines, "An Introduction to and Notes on Nehemiah," in *HarperCollins Study Bible* (ed. Wayne A. Meeks; New York: HarperCollins, 1993) 717, n. on Neh 1:1.

---

the people of Jerusalem at one of the newly repaired gates, the Water Gate (see Neh 8:1a), whose repair during the time of Nehemiah was reported in Nehemiah 3:26. J. M. Myers says that the Water Gate stood either at the northeastern corner of the city of David or further north (i.e., closer to the temple) toward the Ophel, the northern part of the ridge east of the city of David.[3] Joseph Blenkinsopp observes that the Water Gate was presumably an entrance/exit point in the old city wall down the ravine that led to the Gihon Spring.[4] In any case, it stood reasonably near the temple, where the people gathered.

The People Direct Ezra to Read them the Law, Nehemiah 8:1b-8

Writing about vv. 1b-3, T. Reinmuth says, "These first three verses represent the author's narrative technique of providing a proleptic summary before the more elaborate and detailed account in vv. 4-8."[5] They are not, therefore, an insertion as is sometimes argued. Still, this "prolepsis" runs as long as or longer than the following account, except that the second account also contains two lists of seven names. Continuing, Reinmuth thinks the audience mentioned in v. 1 is the whole population of Yehud, and explains away the description of the assembly in v. 17 ("those who had returned from captivity") as an addition.[6] Whether that phrase is secondary may be left open (although his assertion seems dubious), but the phrase the "people of Israel" in Ezra-Nehemiah typically refers to the returnees only. Their legitimacy *vis-à-vis* all those who had remained behind or moved in after the destruction of Jerusalem was one of the main points of Ezra-Nehemiah, as morally deplorable as such pettiness of spirit and exclusivity to being the sole children of God may be.

These comments require further elaboration about the whole of Nehemiah 7:73b–8:18. Reinmuth may be correct that it was not a part of an original "Ezra Memoir" but was the creation of the redactor of Ezra-Nehemiah. It "shows a much broader relationship to the Torah than does Ezra 7–10."[7] The specific issues with which Ezra was concerned do not appear here. The passage does show, however, what Reinmuth calls "remarkable parallels" with other texts in the Hebrew Bible (Deut 31:9-13; Josh 8:30-35, and 2 Kgs 22-23). Nehemiah 8:13-18, by contrast, parallels Leviticus 23 and Deuteronomy 31:9-13 content wise.[8]

The event occurred the first day of the seventh month, the time of the fall festival, the climactic festival in the agricultural year. "This day (Tishri 1) later became New Year's day (Rosh Hashanah)."[9] The people directed Ezra to bring with him "the book of the Law of Moses, which the LORD had given to Moses." That phrase perhaps designated the Pentateuch as a whole,[10] and readers should perhaps presuppose that the "book" was kept in the temple.[11] The initial readers are presumed to understand which "book" was intended, although its identity is not clear to today's readers. It is sometimes said to be the whole Pentateuch, but it would have taken more than one morning (v. 3) to read the whole Torah and make its meaning intelligible through explanation.

Regardless, Ezra brought the book to the Water Gate (see above), which seems to have led into a large open area inside the wall, an area that could be used for public assemblies in peacetime as well perhaps as a place to muster soldiers to defend that gate of the city. [The Necessity of Meeting Places]

Moreover, Ezra read to all who were old enough to be attentive and to understand. Reinmuth comments, ". . . in Nehemiah 8 the presence of God is believed to be due to the communication of the Torah." He adds that what was happening was that the Sinai covenant was recalled (see Exod 24:7), so Ezra was presented as the new Moses. Ezra read all morning, pausing to allow his assistants time to explain what he had read to the returnees (see v. 8). Under those conditions,

The Necessity of Meeting Places

Meeting places for large groups are almost always necessary in a society for conducting business, making community decisions, and building community. Traditionally in American culture those places have included vacant lots, parks with band shells, parade grounds, and town squares. (I can recall hearing presidential candidate Dwight D. Eisenhower speak at a bandstand in a public park in Little Rock, Arkansas, in the fall of 1952, but then I watched his inauguration in Washington, DC, on television in January, 1953, from a friend's house located only a few hundred yards from where I heard him speak.) Town squares in front of courthouses were and still are used as open-market places and spaces for public gatherings, music events, and political speeches. Recent American (especially urban) culture has often replaced them with stadia, indoor arenas, and convention centers (even complexes, as anyone who has been to McCormick Place in Chicago, for example, knows). The public's business requires public places.

it is difficult to see him reading the Pentateuch in its entirety. The end of chapter (v. 18), however, reveals that Ezra read from the law daily during the days of the Feast of Tabernacles that soon followed. Clearly, he could have read much more of the law during the entire week.

What appears to be a second, parallel account of the same event comes next in vv. 4-8. Ezra stood on a platform specially built for the occasion. It was large enough to accommodate fourteen men, Ezra and thirteen others who are named in v. 4. Ezra stood in the middle with six to his right and seven to his left. Apparently, these men were laymen.

Ezra Reads the Book of the Law

David Martin (1639-1721). "Ezra Reads the Book of the Law" *Historie des Ouden en Nieuwen Testaments: verrykt met meer dan vierhonderd printverbeeldingen in koper gesneeden.* (Credit: Pitts Theological Library)

They helped in some way with the reading of the text: "they gave the sense of the text." Did they read some of the verses, or did Ezra read them all? Did they hold the scroll for him as he read, those on one side rolling it out for him and those on the other rolling it up again? Verse 7, moreover, names thirteen Levites who stood in the crowd and are said (v. 8) to have interpreted (paraphrased or explained) the book for the other returnees, who remained in their places. It was important all the people assembled hear and understand the law. The explanations perhaps included both paraphrasing and further explanations, and they may well have taken longer than the readings themselves.

The People Return Home and Celebrate the Harvest, Nehemiah 8:9-12

The next section of the chapter hones in on the significance of the time of the meeting. It was a day holy to God, a day to hear God's word read aloud. Modern readers should remember that the overwhelming majority of the people in ancient Israel were illiterate and that copies of books were quite rare. Verse 9, however, is problematic grammatically. Literally following the Hebrew word order, it can be translated,

> Then said [a third person singular verb] Nehemiah, he was the governor, *and* Ezra the priest, the scribe, *and* the Levities, the ones instructing the people, to all the people: "This day is sacred to the LORD, your God; you [plural] shall not mourn, nor shall you weep, for all the people were weeping."

The mention of Nehemiah here is the sole place in the entire chapter that he is mentioned, so scholars often (and probably correctly) say that his name was added as part of the process of including this narrative about Ezra in the narrative of/about Nehemiah, thereby tying together the activities of the two men. The text says that the Levites "helped the people to understand the law" (v. 7). Ezra and his assistants read, and the Levites helped them understand.

In v. 9, Ezra commanded the people to return to their homes and enjoy a feast before God. It was a holiday in the true sense of the word, a holy day. On that holy day, they were to share their bounty with those who had nothing to eat. (What is Thanksgiving if one has nothing for dinner?) They were not to bemoan their sins or berate themselves. The people obeyed. It is a comment on our culture when we equate having fun with misbehaving and assume that our faith is and must always be solemn. In the Old Testament, there were periods of fasting and repenting, but, before God, harvest time was not one of them. In this chapter's context in the book of Nehemiah, moreover, the activity last narrated had been the completion of the repairing of the wall (Neh 6:15–7:3) and the settling of the people "in their towns," i.e., outside Jerusalem (Neh 7:73a). In the seventh month, the harvest gathered, they assembled to hear the law book read, and then, according to the scribe Ezra in Nehemiah 8:10, it was time to go home and celebrate the harvest with a party! [The Agricultural Year]

The People Build Booths and Observe the Festival of Booths, Nehemiah 8:13-18

The day after the harvest feast the people, the priests, and the Levites returned to the temple to study the law. They discovered therein that they should observe the impending Festival of Booths (or Tabernacles) by living in booths. (Readers may wish to review the discussion of the Jewish calendar in the comments on Ezra 3.) The crops harvested would have included grapes and olives. Since

The Agricultural Year

Preparations for the agricultural year may be said to have begun in the fall. Grain was planted soon after the olive trees and vines bore their fruit. Seed was scattered over the growing area and plowed in to keep it away from birds. It would grow during the winter growing season and be harvested in the spring. Barley matured first in April, then wheat up to six weeks later, depending on the weather. Reaping was done by hand, usually by the whole family. In that process the stalks were cut off several inches above the ground, leaving stubble. Threshing was done at threshing floors, which were well-prepared and well-ventilated areas. It was done by the feet of oxen or donkeys or by a drag with studs on the bottom. The grain and chaff were then tossed into the air. The heavier grain would fall to the ground, and the wind would blow the chaff away. Isaiah 5:1-6 describes the harvesting of grapes in the late summer and the making of wine. (The process of pasteurizing grape juice so that it would not ferment is a late, Western development.) Olive trees had to be pruned, but they did well in the climate of Palestine. Some olives were kept for eating, and others used for oil to use with greens in eating.

The oldest known calendar in Palestine, the so-called "Gezer Calendar" from the tenth century BCE, actually laid out this whole pattern. It began in the fall with two months of ingathering, and then moved through the year.

> His two months are (olive) harvest,
> His two months are planting (grain),
> His two months are late planting;
> His month is hoeing up of flax,
> His month is harvest of barley,
> His month is harvest and *feasting*;
> His two months are vine-tending,
> His month is summer fruit.

W. F. Albright, trans., "The Gezer Calendar," ed. James B. Pritchard, *The Ancient Near East* (Princeton and Oxford: Princeton University Press, 2011) 287.

The ancient agricultural calendar that was found in Tel Gezer. The tablet discovered here is one of the oldest surviving Hebrew texts, written in the 'paleo-Hebrew' letters that were the norm in Judah before the Babylonian exile in the 6th century BCE. This text also provides key information about the agricultural cycle in ancient Israel. (Credit: http://www.inature.info; Yuval Mendelson via the PikiWiki, Israel free image collection project, CCA 2.5)

Rainfall in Israel

Ancient Israel experienced two seasons, the rainy season and the dry season. The Bible speaks of the "former" or "early" rains and the "latter" rains, i.e., those at the beginning and end of the cool/wet season. Average annual rainfall in ancient Israel varied from about forty inches on the Mediterranean coast near Sidon, to thirty-two inches near Mount Carmel, to twenty inches in the middle, to as little as four in the driest areas in the south, and to two around the Dead Sea. Even the rainy season was and is unpredictable. The first showers, the early rains, need to come, and rain needs to continue throughout the season. December may bring a little snow and usher in the coldest weather. Rainfall rises and then diminishes during the winter season, perhaps reaching its peak in the middle. The lengthy duration of the rains (i.e., the Latter Rains) is very important for a bountiful grain harvest.

J. A. Patch and C. E. Armending, "Agriculture," *The International Standard Bible Encyclopedia* (Geoffrey W. Bromiley; Grand Rapids MI: Eerdmans, 1979) 1.72–75.

James C. Vanderkam, "Calendar," *The New Interpreter's Dictionary of the Bible* (ed. Katherine Doob Sakenfeld; Nashville: Abingdon, 2006) 1.521–27, here 522.

they required special care, ancients often spent the nights in flimsy huts nearby to protect them. Rain would not be an issue. [Rainfall in Israel]

The basic laws for this festival may be found in Leviticus 23:33-43. Those verses, however, should be divided. Verses 33-38 give the basic laws, and vv. 39-43 go further, explaining what to do and adding that future people should live in tents as had the people in the time of Moses. In those verses, Moses instructed the people to observe the Feast of Booths or Tabernacles for seven days, beginning of the fifteenth day of the seventh month.[12] On the first day of the festival, they were to hold a holy convocation and not work. Beginning that day, they were to celebrate by offering sacrifices and by rejoicing before the Lord. Farmers who had experienced the heat of the summer and had reaped their harvest could perhaps be counted on to follow those instructions— especially in a good year. They were to present offerings to God the next six days as well, but presumably they could work, play, and conduct their normal chores. The last day of the festival, they were to observe convocation and not work that day either. Rather, they culminated the festival on a solemn note with an assembly. One act was to present animal, grain, and liquid offerings to God, and another was to pray for the expected rains that would pave the way to planting the next year's crops. Verses 39-43 offer further instructions and are often taken to reflect later reflection. Original or not, those verses serve to tie the directions for observing the festival to Moses himself.

Nehemiah 8:13-18 mentions the preparations for and the observance of the Feast of Tabernacles and shows the returnees following the directions of Moses. On the second day of the month, they gathered to hear Ezra read the law and to learn therefrom. In doing so, though Ezra did not bring the Torah back to Yehud with him (as is sometimes claimed), he did bring it back into the consciousness of his people.[13] Learning that they should dwell in tents or booths for the week (see Lev 23:34 and Num 19:12[14]), they quickly cut branches from olive, myrtle, palm, and other leafy trees and constructed booths for themselves on top of their (flat-roofed) houses to sleep in. The narrator disparagingly notes (v. 17) that the people had not done so since Joshua led them into Canaan, i.e., not even during the days of the first temple. Readers might note, moreover, that Nehemiah 8:18 describes Ezra's reading of the Torah in a way reminiscent of Deuteronomy 31:9-13, not of Leviticus 23:33-43.

Finally, and somewhat technically, scholars sometimes suggest that this narrative ties the reform of Ezra to the establishment of the Torah as "canon," i.e., an official standard by which to measure belief and/or conduct. Helge Stadelmann notes that that conclusion was invented by Pentateuchal scholars after the rise of the so-called "Four Source Hypothesis" concerning the Pentateuch. (That hypothesis arose in the late eighteenth and early nineteenth centuries, and it distinguished four basic underlying sources. While the hypothesis has undergone considerable refinement, it remains one way of understanding the rise of those books. Further discussion of it will lead readers too far from Ezra-Nehemiah, however.) The question Stadelmann asks is if the Pentateuch as it exists today, which arose over time culminating in the post-exilic period, was the law that Nehemiah read? Her answer is that the question is an invention of modern scholarship![15] These comments on Nehemiah 7:73b–8:18 have shown simply that this narrative presupposes acquaintance with some, even many, laws found in the Pentateuch, but it does not establish a date before which the Pentateuch must have reached its final form.

CONNECTIONS

1. The most obvious connection between Nehemiah 7:73b–8:18 and modern readers is the need to recognize that humans are not self-sufficient, that they depend on God for the very means of their existence—food, water, and shelter; that they belong to a community that can and will love, nourish, and sustain them; and that they have obligations to God and that community as an ongoing entity. John Donne described that horizontal dimension unforgettably.

> No man is an island entire of itself; every man
> is a piece of the continent, a part of the main;
> if a clod be washed away by the sea, Europe
> is the less, as well as if a promontory were, as

well as any manner of thy friends or of thine
own were; any man's death diminishes me,
because I am involved in mankind.

Ezra 9–10 described in vivid detail a community that, in an
effort to follow God strictly, demanded that men among early
returnees turn their backs on their own wives taken from non-
returnees and their own children. Sometimes the worship of God
may be costly in ways far beyond mere money. Believers need to be
on guard, however, lest in empha- sizing the vertical dimension of
their being they destroy its hori- zontal dimension. This chapter,
Nehemiah 7:73b–8:18, recognizes and depicts the wholeness, the
oneness of life before God in human community.

"No Man Is an Island"

Island of Lower Saranac Lake, Adirondack Mountains, New York, USA (Credit: Mwanner,
Wikimedia Commons, CC-SA 3.0)

2. The people who met were illiterate, but ready to hear the
word of God and to put it into action in their own lives. To be
sure, having a feast before God is
not a burdensome task, but it is the task of people who remember
even in good days that they are not self-sufficient; that God
enabled the success of their efforts by means of earth, rain, and sun;
and that it is good, even necessary, for humans to recognize their
abject dependence on God and each other. In our own culture,
those responsible for this volume and its readers as well have much
to be grateful for. All of us need to create and utilize collective as
well as individual opportunities and rituals to celebrate our collective dependence on God and to thank God for divine love.

3. The American holiday of Thanksgiving is—or at least originally was—a celebration like the one described in Nehemiah
8:8-18. It is rooted in a narrative about the first Thanksgiving
observed by the Pilgrims after their arrival in the United States. In
that narrative, local Indians joined them to celebrate the year, and
they remembered their successful journey to *New* England. It was a
time to celebrate life, community, the goodness of God, and the
bounty of the earth. To an extent, it remains so today. Families
gather; some people even travel considerable distances to "go

The First Thanksgiving at Plymouth

Jennie A. Brownscombe (1850–1936). *The First Thanksgiving at Plymouth.* 1914. (Credit: Wikimedia Commons, CC-PD-Mark)

home." In the early years of our marriage, i.e., seminary and graduate school years, my wife and I alternated families to visit. When I took my first teaching position in Ohio, a weekend trip for Thanksgiving became more problematic, and after the birth of our first child, Pam, too difficult to continue. Our church in Columbus at that time was composed largely of people from elsewhere, many from the South. We were immediately included in the family celebrations of other church members also too far away to go back home. Those Thanksgivings of turkey, televised football games, and Christian fellowship still stand out in our minds as special, even sacred. As the years passed, we also became involved in sharing the rest of the weekend with international students, who often had nowhere to go over a short break. We typically had Middle Easterners or Africans as our guests. Such celebrations, focused on God, family, food, and good times, still nourish our whole being in our maturity.

Writing about eating and food, T. W. Mann observes more broadly,

> As a material expression of God's grace, *all* food assumes a sacramental dimension. We are used to thinking of ritual meals as sacramental—Passover, the Lord's Supper. But every meal is a blessing, pointing to "the sacramentality of all of all daily eating and drinking." All food participates in "holiness," which is why eating requires sacerdotal regulations.[16]

Still, the special meals, the meals of ritual, call the partakers to take cognizance of their Maker who provides for them and should call the partakers to share with people who do not have enough to eat.

NOTES

1. Readers of this volume should remember that this comment, like other similar comments in this volume, describe literary, not historical aspects of the text.

2. Don Polaski, "Nehemiah: Subject of the Empire, Subject of Writing," *New Perspectives on Ezra-Nehemiah* (ed. Isaac Kalimi; Winona Lake IN: Eisenbrauns, 2012) 37–59, here 51.

3. Jacob M. Myers, *Ezra-Nehemiah* (AB14; Garden City NY: Doubleday, 1965) 115.

4. Joseph Blenkinsopp, *Ezra-Nehemiah* (OTL; Philadelphia: Westminster, 1988) 238.

5. Timothy Reinmuth, "Nehemiah 8 and the Authority of Torah," *Unity and Disunity in Ezra-Nehemiah: Redaction, Rhetoric, and Reader* (ed. Mark J. Boda and Paul L. Redditt; Hebrew Bible Monographs 17; Sheffield: Sheffield Phoenix Press, 2008) 241–62, here 246.

6. Ibid., 246, n. 12.

7. Ibid., 252–53.

8. Ibid., 257.

9. D. J. A. Clines, a note on Neh 8:1 in *The HarperCollins Study Bible* (New York: HarperCollins, 1993) 726.

10. It is clear, however, that the editing and copying of those books resulted in additions, omissions, and clerical errors. Extant copies of Old Testament books show some variations, although Jewish scribes standardized the texts after the destruction of Jerusalem by the Romans. For a discussion of the manuscript evidence, readers could consult S. K. Soderlund, "Text and MSS of the OT," *ISBE*, 4:798–814.

11. Reinmuth, "Nehemiah 8," 230.

12. Let the reader note that Moses would not have had to instruct Israelites wandering through the desert to live in tents. This instruction, therefore, provides some evidence that the laws in Deuteronomy arose over time but were ascribed to Moses as their fountainhead, and that their promulgation was read back to his period.

13. So Rolf Rendtorff, "Noch Einmal: Esra und das 'Gesetz,'" *ZAW* 111 (1999): 89–91.

14. C. Houtman ("Ezra and the Law," *Remembering All the Way* [Oudtestmentische Studien 21; Leiden: Brill, 1981] 91–155, here 104–105) notes that some of the details in this narrative do not jibe with Lev 23:36, 39 and Num 19:35. He suggests that the variations point to other versions of those laws elsewhere than in the Pentateuch. That is possible, but no such texts are known today. It is quite possible, instead, that they simply reflect a less-than-literalist relationship to the Pentateuch. James W. Watts ("Ritual Legitimacy and Scriptural Authority," *JBL* 124 [2005]: 401–17, here 406) notes that Ezra 3:4 says the returnees celebrated the Feast, suggesting an intertextual critique of the manner of that celebration.

15. Helge Stadelmann, "Die Reform Esras und der Kanon," *Der Kanon der Bibel* (ed. Gerhard Maier; Basel: Brunnen; and Wuppertal: Brockhaus, 1990) 65.

16. Thomas W. Mann, "Not by Word Alone: Food in the Hebrew Bible," *Interpretation* 67 (2013): 351–62, here 352–53. See also the superb collection of essays edited by Duke Divinity School professor Norman Wirzba, *The Essential Agrarian Reader* (Washington, DC: Shoemaker & Hoard, 2003).

CONFESSION SIGNED BY THE RETURNEES AND DETAILS OF A NEW COVENANT

Nehemiah 9–10

COMMENTARY

A brief review of the redactor's cues to reading Ezra-Nehemiah thus far will be helpful at the outset of the discussion of Nehemiah 9 and 10, which close the second major section of Nehemiah (Neh 7:73b–10:39). The redactor had concluded the account of the building of the temple with the words, "they built [the temple] and finished by command of the God of Israel and by the decree of Cyrus and Darius and Artaxerxes" (Ezra 6:14, author's translation). The narrative continued with the observance of the Feast of Unleavened Bread, "for YHWH had made them joyful and turned the heart of the king of Assyria [Persia[1]] toward them to strengthen their hands in the work on the house of God, the God of Israel" (Ezra 6:22). The theme of Persian permission for the returnees to journey to Jerusalem to build was repeated essentially toward the end of the book (in Ezra 9:9).

The redactor also presented Ezra's mission as the direct consequence of a letter of Artaxerxes in Aramaic (Ezra 7:11-24) with orders to execute or banish and also to confiscate the goods of anyone who disobeyed Ezra or the law, an order followed unflinchingly in Ezra 9–10. The text also mentions the kindness of Artaxerxes to Ezra and has Ezra bless God for putting into the heart of that Persian king the idea of beautifying the temple (Ezra 7:27-28). Nehemiah likewise gained permission from the Persian king to travel to Jerusalem, but to repair the walls of city around the temple (Neh 1–7). The second section of Nehemiah consists of 7:73b–10:39 and the third of 11:1–13:31. Within the second section, Nehemiah 7:73b–8:18 focuses on the reading of the law by Ezra to instruct people how to obey the law and how to worship God. It studiously avoids mentioning the Persians, even though it mentions the pharaoh of Egypt and the kings of

Assyria and bemoans the returnees' plight within the Persian Empire. Nehemiah 9–10 closes that section by having the people confess their sins and sign a covenant "to adhere to the law of God." [Outline of Nehemiah 9–10] Short though this section may be (only three chapters), it is the center of the book of Nehemiah, both in terms of location and in terms of theology.

A Prayer of Confession, 9:1-37

Nehemiah 7:73b–8:18 had related the events of the celebration of the autumnal Feast of Booths. Now Nehemiah 9:1-37 reports a time of separation from foreigners and confession of sin. (Compare Ezra 9–10.) If intermingling with locals is a recurring theme in Ezra-Nehemiah, that is so because intermingling was an ongoing phenomenon, one seen as troubling to the returnees with whom Nehemiah sided, but apparently regarded as a matter of course and not a moral issue by people who had not been in exile and even some who had. (See Ezra 9–10.) The prayer of confession in Nehemiah 9:1-37 is complex, so it will be divided into three basic components: vv. 1-5[2] constitute the setting and the rest of the chapter reports the prayer itself, with vv. 6-31 reciting God's past great actions and Israel's sinfulness, and vv. 32-37 lamenting that the people of God were slaves in their own land. In the discussion of vv. 6-31 that follows, the recitation of God's past great actions will be subdivided into three parts: praise for God's act of creation and God's promise to Abraham (vv. 6-8), praise for God's victory during the exodus and for leading Israel into Canaan (vv. 9-15), and confession for Israel/Judah's rebellion against God's commands justifying God's punishment of them (vv. 16-31).

The Setting for the Confession, 9:1-5
Nehemiah 9:1-5 carries over the place of action—Jerusalem—from Nehemiah 8, and it supplies the date of the action that Nehemiah 9:1–10:39 will relate: namely, the twenty-fourth day of "this month." The antecedent for the word "this" appears to be the seventh month mentioned in Nehemiah 7:73b. Both notices (7:73b and 9:1) are redactional, moving the action forward

Dates in the Book of Nehemiah

As in the book of Ezra so also in the book of Nehemiah, one of the redactional motifs is the marking of time. Six date markers appear in Nehemiah, namely in Nehemiah 1:1, 2:1, 6:15, 7:73b, 9:1, and 13:6.

Text	Date	Event
1:1	9th month (Chislev) of 19th year of Artaxerxes, 446(?)*	Hanani arrives in Susa
2:1	1st month (Nisan) of 20th year, 445	Nehemiah departs for Jerusalem
6:15	6th month (Elul) of 20th year, 445	Repairs on wall finished
7:73b	7th month (Tishri) of 20th year, 445	Reading of the Law in Jerusalem
9:1	7th month, (Tishri) of 20th year, 445 (implied)	Separation of "Israel" from others
13:6	Month omitted, 32nd year of Artaxerxes, 433	Nehemiah returned to Susa

* Neh 1:1 sets its action in twentieth year of Artaxerxes, i.e., 445. Neh 2:1 also sets its action in the twentieth year of Artaxerxes, but Nisan was the first month in the Babylonian year. D. J. A. Clines suggests plausibly a slight slip of the pen and dates Neh 1:1 four months earlier in year 446.

D. J. A. Clines, "An Introduction to and Notes on Nehemiah," in *HarperCollins Study Bible* (ed. Wayne A. Meeks; New York: HarperCollins, 1993) 717, n. on Neh 1:1.

---

through time. [Dates in the Book of Nehemiah] D. J. A. Clines notes that rituals of mourning were often used to express penance. Like mourners, penitents wanted to depict themselves as resembling the dead; hence they might fast, wear sackcloth, and put dirt on their heads as if they had been buried.[3]

The keynote of Ezra-Nehemiah was struck in v. 2: "Then those of Israelite descent [i.e., the returnees] separated themselves from all foreigners and stood and confessed their sins and the iniquities of their ancestors." More than ritual separation stands behinds this verse, however, and that is the issue of separating the returnees from their neighbors in Yehud. If that separation simply meant that the returnees had nothing to do with people from—say—Egypt, Greece, Arabia, or the like, it would still be exclusionist, elitist, prejudicial, and contrary to the call of Abraham that through his descendants "all the families of the earth will be blessed" (Gen 12:30). That verse called Abraham and his descendants to a lifestyle and an ethic that were open and inviting to all other people, i.e., all Gentiles. To be sure, few Gentiles then chose and only a minority today of the

Mourners' Attire, Medieval Style

This 15th-C. depiction of mourning suggests that mourning and penance have been linked through the centuries.

Tomb of Philippe Pot, Grand Senechal of Burgundy. Detail of mourner with coat of arms. French, 1477–1483. Polychrome stone sculpture group. From the St. John the Baptist Chapel at the Abbey church of Citeaux, Burgundy. Musée du Louvre, Paris, France. (Credit: © Musée du Louvre, Dist. RMN-Grand Palais/Art Resource, NY)

world's population chooses to enter that proffered covenant with God, but that should be up to them. Their freedom of choice—like Abraham's (and like ours)—obliged (and obliges) God's people to be open and receptive to others of God's children.

The returnees (as portrayed in Ezra-Nehemiah) can be forgiven if they believed that the Gentile world hated them and their God, and readers can perhaps even be sympathetic to them because to a considerable extent, faith in the God of Abraham came down through the returnees. Still, the evidence from the book of Ezra-Nehemiah itself is pretty clear that others in Yehud at least claimed to worship God, and the existence of temples to God in Egypt and Samaria give tangible proof that that was so. Moreover, the thinking in Isaiah 56:1-8 and 66:18-24 stands as testimony within the Bible itself that the thinking of the redactor of Ezra-Nehemiah on the subject of who belonged to the real people of God was not the Bible's only perspective.[4] [All God's People]

All God's People

Nehemiah rejected mixing with different people lest he and his followers somehow be ritually contaminated. Still, God does not judge people by the color of their skin or their place of origin, but by their love of and fidelity to God and to God's other children.

Staff of President Clinton's One America Initiative, the Initiative on Race. 1998. (Credit: White House, PD)

Isaiah 56:3-4, 7 specifically includes foreigners and eunuchs, indeed "all peoples." If it seems strange to modern readers that foreigners and even Jewish eunuchs would be disqualified from entering the temple for some thing or things over which they might have had no control, those readers will understand the force of Isaiah 56. If, as modern scholars often think, Isaiah 56–66 arose in the early post-exilic period, those chapters stand as an early post-exilic voice opposing the kind of exclusivism that surfaced in Nehemiah and apparently earlier among the returnees or others. If, however, those chapters arose from Isaiah himself, they stand as an eighth-century prophetic voice against the exclusivism advocated and established by Nehemiah among the returnees.

In any case, certain returnees—Jeshua, Bani, Kadmiel, Shebaniah, Bunni, Sherebiah, Bani, and Chenani—cried aloud to God, and were answered antiphonally by the Levites Jeshua, Kadmiel, Bani, Hashabneiah, Sherebiah, Hodiah, Shebaniah and Pethahiah. The Levites then called the people to pray to God, and they began the prayer with the line, "Blessed be your holy name, which is exalted above all blessing and praise." To bless the "name" of God was to bless God, the One whom the name represented.

Modern readers should not overlook the devotion of the people to God portrayed in the description of their worship of God. It describes a commitment to prayer at which the Christian Father Origen marveled in admiration.

> [W]ho would not be amazed that such a great people had such an extraordinary concern for devotion that four times a day—that is at the first hour of the morning, the third, the sixth, and the ninth, when time was to be made for prayer and psalmody—they gave themselves over to listening to the divine law in order to renew their mind in God and come back purer and more devout for imploring his mercy; but also four times a night they would shake off their sleepiness and get up in order to confess their sins and beg pardon.[5]

The Prayer of Confession, 9:6-37

The people offered a prayer of confession. In v. 6 the NRSV prefixes the words "And Ezra said," based on the LXX, but they are lacking in the MT, which is very likely original. The LXX translators seem to have added the words from the chapter's context in Nehemiah 8, thus tying the two chapters closer together by making the prayer Ezra's. The chapter itself, however, found its place as part of the overall intention to unite into one coherent narrative tradition about early returnees under Sheshbazzar and/or Zerubbabel, returnees under Ezra, and the work of Nehemiah. The prayer proper is composed of four parts: vv. 6-8 (which praise God for creating the world and for God's promise to Abraham); vv. 9-15 (which praise God for delivering Israel, understood, obviously, as the people marching with Moses at the Red Sea); vv. 16-31 (which confess the sinfulness of God's people); and vv. 32-37 (which complain or mourn that they, the returnees, are little more than "slaves" in their own land).

Analyzing that prayer, R. J. Bautch observes that vv. 6-31 constitute a recital of God's dealings with Israel, while vv. 32-37 constitute the complaint proper.[6] More fully stated, the recital in vv. 6-31 begins by retracing the election of Abraham, the exodus, the giving of the Law on Sinai and of manna and quail in the wilderness, the giving of water from the rock to Moses and the people of Israel, the defeat of Kings Sihon and Og, and the subjugation of the land of Canaan (vv. 16-25). Next, the prayer alludes to the period of the Judges and mentions the prophets of Israel (vv. 26-31), although not any by name and not necessarily those in the Major and Minor Prophets since none is cited, and also not the kings. Those kings were presumably of no concern to a people under the authority of the king of Persia. Then, vv. 32-37 complain that the returnees were "slaves in the land that [God] gave to their ancestors" and bewail the returnees' predicament under Persian power without mentioning Persia by name. Each part of the prayer will be analyzed in turn.

Abraham and Abram

The use of the name Abram in Neh 9:7 is significant. The name for the father of Israel is given as Abram fifty-seven times between Gen 11:26 and 17:5. Then in Gen 17:5 God renames him: "No longer shall your name be Abram [i.e., exalted father/ancestor], but your name shall be Abraham [i.e., multitudinous father]; for I have made you ancestor of a multitude of nations." The name Abram appears only twice more. The first is 1 Chr 1:27, which brought the ancestry of Shem down to Abram and then added: "that is Abraham." The second is Neh 9:7. The name Abraham appears, however, c. 180 times between Gen 17:5 and the end of the Hebrew Bible. Apparently, therefore, both Neh 9:7 and 1 Chr 1:27 were aware of the narrative of the changing of the name of Abram to Abraham in Gen 17:5 and must be dated later. A relative chronology, however, is not an absolute chronology, so the verse gives no absolute date later than which Neh 9:7 must have been written.

The Location of Ur

Ur lay southwest of or down the Euphrates River from Babylon (in modern Iraq), not far from where it joins with the Tigris before continuing on to the Persian Gulf. It measured about 1000 by 800 yards, and at two different times it was the major city in its environment.

W. S. LaSor, "Ur," *ISBE*, 4.950–55.

Praise for Creation and the Promise to Abraham, 9:6-8. Nehemiah 9:6-8 opens with a confession of God's mighty works: God and God alone created the sun, moon, and stars, i.e., the universe. God also made everything on the surface of the earth, including the seas. One hears overtones of Psalm 24:1: "The earth is the LORD's and the fullness thereof," and also of the creation story in Genesis 1:1–2:4a. That similarity does not prove that the verses in Nehemiah were written later than the other two or depended on them, although such dependence is quite possible. The similarity does show, however, that the author of Nehemiah 9:6 at least was familiar with thinking like that in those verses.[7] Verse 7 turns its attention to Abraham, called Abram [Abraham and Abram] and said to have come from Ur of the Chaldeans. (See Gen 11:31–12:3.) [The Location of Ur] Interpreters often read v. 7 to mean that God reacted to the previous actions of Abram. In other words, they argue that in vv. 6-9 God operated on a principle of justice: since Abram had proven himself faithful before God, God made a covenant with him. The statement, thus, is not an articulation of pure grace; instead it "works with a bilateral understanding of covenant."[8] Both sides have obligations to keep. M. J. Boda also comments that this prayer, like those in Ezra 9, Psalm 106, and Daniel 9, exhibits strong links with the laments of the Psalter, but the divergences from laments were too great to categorize those four songs simply as laments. In all four, complaint against God was muted, and the emphasis shifted to admitting the guilt of the supplicants and justifying Yahweh's actions of judgment.[9] In other words and importantly, the basis for the implored intervention of God was not the innocence of the returnees but the nature of God.

Because of Abraham's faithfulness (see also Heb 11:8-12), God promised to give to him and to his descendants the land of the Canaanites. The verse also lists the other traditional inhabitants of Canaan: Hittites, Amorites, Perizzites, Jebusites (pre-Davidic inhabitants of Jerusalem), and Girgashites. Those were the groups that God promised to defeat (see Gen 15:1-21, especially vv. 19-21). That task eventually fell to Joshua, who did not drive them all out, to the chagrin of the author of the book by his name.

Praise for God's Victory at the Red Sea and for Leading Israel, 9:9-15. Nehemiah 9:9-15 celebrates God's deliverance from Egypt at the Red Sea and God's leadership of the people of Israel in the wilderness. It opens by mentioning the "distress" or enslavement of the people of Israel in Egypt, a distress graphically portrayed in Exodus 1, 2, and 5. The "signs and wonders" (v. 10) God performed against Pharaoh were the so-called "plagues," enumerated as ten in Exodus 7:14–12:32. (See, however, Pss 78:44-51 and 105:28-36, which list only seven and eight, respectively.[10]) Those plagues, as described in Exodus, consisted of the turning the water of the Nile and its tributary streams into blood, frogs, gnats, flies, disease on livestock, boils on humans and animals, thunder and hail, locusts, darkness that could be felt (sometimes understood as a blinding sandstorm), and the death of the firstborn sons of the Egyptians. Only the first (unless only the color of the water is the issue) and the last were what moderns speak of as "supernatural." All ten, nevertheless, pointed to the activity of God to those who had the eyes to see, and none pointed to divine activity for the Egyptians who typically worshiped numerous gods but not the real God.

Other great deeds of God are listed next. The first was God's rescue of the people fleeing from Pharaoh at the "Sea of Reeds." [The Sea of Reeds] It was necessitated by the cruelty of the Egyptians toward the enslaved Hebrews. God led them by a pillar of cloud by day and a pillar of fire by night (Exod 13:17-22). On Mount Sinai, God gave them the Law, i.e., instructions on how to live before God and humans alike (Exod 20:1–Lev 27:34), and in the process God gave them Sabbath as a day of rest (Exod 20:8-11). When they hungered, God blessed them with manna (Exod 16:16-35), and when they thirsted God brought forth water from a rock (Exod 17:1-6; but see also the account in Num 20:1-13). Finally, God had promised to give them a land, beginning with Abraham (first in Gen 12:1-10 and then in Gen 15:1-21, where the list of nations to be displaced is first given), the land the redactor was claiming for the returnees at least in part.

The Sea of Reeds

The people of Israel came to a body of water called the "Red" Sea in English translations of Exod 15:4, but the word actually refers typically to "reeds" or even "weeds." See Jonah 2:5: "weeds were wrapped around my head at the roots of the [underwater] mountain." This sea is referred to about two dozen times in the Hebrew Bible, but its location is difficult to determine. J. Philip Hyatt examines this issue, noting that in places it could refer to either the Gulf of Aqaba (see 1 Kgs 9:26) or the Gulf of Suez (see Num 33:10); and that an old Egyptian text equated it with a "lake of reeds" near Raamses-Tanis in the Nile Delta near the Mediterranean Sea (see Exod 1:11). He cited other scholarly suggestions for the proposed trek: across the southern tip of the Sinai Peninsula; in the vicinity of Lake Timsah; across the northern end of the peninsula near Lake Menzaleh, where a marshy area is located (Hyatt's choice); and across a narrow strip of land on the very coast of the Mediterranean Sea.

Only one of these suggested sites lies anywhere near the actual Red Sea: the one across the southern tip of the Sinai Peninsula. Readers accustomed to maps in their Bibles may be familiar with maps purporting to trace Moses's stops, which are fairly evenly spaced down the west side of the peninsula and back up the east side. Many mapmakers will concede that none of those is known. In other words, what readers of the Bible actually know is (1) the escaping Hebrews left from northern Egypt, (2) did not follow the main highway to Palestine and beyond, and (3) wound up near Kadesh Barnea in the northern Sinai Peninsula. The "Sea of Reeds" was not the "Red Sea," and it perhaps was in a low area between Egypt and the Sinai Peninsula somewhere along what is now the Suez Canal.

J. Philip Hyatt, *Exodus* (New Century Bible; Grand Rapids MI: Eerdmans; London: Marshall, Morgan and Scott, 1971) 156–61, esp. 158–60.

The Confession of Israel/Judah's Rebellion against God's Commands, 9:16-31. After God had been so gracious, what had gone wrong? Why had God's people divided into two small kingdoms, and why had those kingdoms fallen into the hands of the foreign powers Assyria (who captured and annexed the kingdom of Israel) and Babylon (who defeated Judah and destroyed Jerusalem and the temple in the process)? The answer according to Nehemiah 9:16-31 was simple: they had acted presumptuously and "stiffened their necks" or rebelled instead of obeying God humbly. The rebellion was made all the more inexcusable by God's direct gift of God's commandments—in plain Hebrew, so to speak! Indeed, even while they were yet in the wilderness they had longed to return to the relative security of slavery in Egypt. (Living by faith can be a dangerous-appearing adventure.)

Verse 17b quotes a confession of faith familiar to readers of the Bible from Exodus 16:2-3 and Numbers 14:11-12: "You are a merciful God ready to forgive, gracious and merciful, slow to anger and abounding in steadfast love" (NRSV). Verse 17b adds that God did not forsake them.[11] J. H. Newman subjects this citation to scrutiny and argues as follows. The rhetorical effect of historical retrospects, this one in particular, was to show "how God had acted in the past as well as by divine promises made in the past. In the post-exilic period, the record of those acts and promises lay in texts and so the remembrance of history was shaped by the words in those texts. . . . Exodus 34:6-7 . . . came to be used as a focus and refrain . . . [in Neh 9:17] as a true representation of God's gracious and compassionate character."[12]

Verse 18 alludes to the narrative of Israel's worship of the golden calf (Exod 32:1-35), v. 19 again to God's leadership of the people by the pillar of cloud/fire that led them by day and night, and v. 20 to the gift of manna to feed them (see Num 11:4-9). God sustained them forty years in the wilderness (v. 21), during which time neither their clothes nor their sandals wore out (see Deut 8:4)! God gave them kingdoms and peoples as subjects (v. 22), specifically King Sihon of Hesbon (Num 21:21-31) and King Og of Bashan (Num 21:33-35). God multiplied their numbers "like the stars of the heavens" (v. 23, see God's promise to Abraham in Gen 22:17) and brought them into the land God had promised the patriarchs. They defeated the Canaanites and possessed their land (detailed in the book of Joshua[13]), including fortified cities, houses, vineyards, orchards, olive trees, and fruit trees. Nevertheless, they disobeyed God and rebelled (v. 26), so God sent conquerors (v. 27). After they repented, God sent saviors (the Judges) to deliver them. But they repeated their mistakes over and over (vv. 28-30; see Judg 2:16-23).[14] Still, the ever-faithful God did not abandon them, but warned them through the prophets (e.g., Nathan, Elijah, Elisha, Micaiah ben Imlah). Then God handed them over to the "people of the lands," here, apparently, a term for the Babylonians, Assyrians, and Persians.

Let readers note that Nehemiah 9:6-30 sketches the narrative of the Pentateuch starting with Genesis 12 as well as the Former Prophets, including an allusion to the judges as a time of backsliding and consequent tyranny. The review, however, shows remarkably little interest in the monarchy. Why so? Why would the review ignore Israel's kings? Perhaps it did so because the authors of Ezra-Nehemiah, written in the time of the Persian Empire and by people accountable to the Persians, did not want to offend and rile their overlords. The less said about indigenous former kings, good or bad, the better off they might have been perceived themselves. This recital also does not mention the great Major and Minor Prophets of Bible. Of course, Ezra 5:1-2 and 6:14 do mention Haggai and Zechariah of the temple. Why did Nehemiah 9:6-30 not mention any others? Perhaps their words were not known, but if they were, perhaps their denunciations of kings domestic and foreign and of the temple were blunt enough to ensure their omission from emperor-sensitive and temple-affirming Ezra-Nehemiah.

The Returnees as "Slaves" in their own Land, 9:32-37. Nehemiah 9:32-37 makes a definitive turn in Nehemiah's prayer from confession of sins to complaint proper. It also marks a turn in the use of the term "Israel." No longer does it refer to the generation of Moses and the pre-exilic people to whom God gave the land. In vv. 32-37, "Israel" in the post-exilic period was the returnees, to the authors of Ezra-Nehemiah the legitimate descendants of Moses and the pre-exilic traditions and thus the true heirs of God's promise.[15] "Whereas in Nehemiah 9:7-8 God is called righteous in light of Abram's faithfulness, in Nehemiah 9:33 the people's wickedness is used as the foil to God's righteousness. In the latter verse, the faithfulness once attributed to Abram has slipped from the human realm and now refers exclusively to God."[16] The irony, indeed the tragedy, for them was that they were "slaves" in their own land. Indeed, the people complained (Neh 9:36-37; NRSV):

Gleaners in the Field

Jean Francois Millet (1814–1875). *The Gleaners.* Musee d'Orsay, Paris, France. (Credit: Scala/Art Resource, NY)

Behold! We are today servants in the land which you gave to our fathers to eat its fruit and its goodness. Behold! We are servants upon it. Its rich yield goes to the kings whom you set over us on account of our sins; for they rule over our bodies and our animals at their pleasure, and we are in great distress.[17]

What, then, might a reader make of Nehemiah 9:6-37 overall? Two apparently opposing scholarly views will be mentioned. D. L. Smith-Christopher argues that this complaint (and other similar passages) articulated the resentment of these people *against* Persian domination. The returnees were reduced to being Judeans living as servants in Judah, the land God had given their ancestors. A portion of their hard-earned produce went as taxes to foreign rulers, who controlled them, their work, and even their animals. Although they confessed that they deserved such punishment by God, it was still punishment at the hands of foreigners, and they felt distress.[18] In connection with Ezra 1:1, Cyrus's proclamation authorized the building of something (the temple) they should have needed no foreign permission to build, and it determined who was permitted to participate in that building process. By contrast, M. Oeming situates Nehemiah 9 in the context of a series of international struggles against Persia by a group of Egyptians attempting to wrest Egypt from Persian control. He argues that the chapter was designed to portray Nehemiah and his work (indeed the whole mission of Ezra and Nehemiah) as part of a pro-Persian piece of writing. Indeed, Oeming calls it "propaganda."[19] Still, the verses contain ambiguity so that they can *also* be read negatively in an anti-Persian manner. Such vacillation on the part of subject peoples would be understandable, perhaps even inevitable, so modern readers should not press too hard to choose which understanding to adopt.

The Result of the Confession: An Agreement in Writing, 9:38

Nehemiah 9:38 is actually a transitional verse. Its first half concludes the narrative of Nehemiah 9:1-37, and its second half looks ahead to the list of names that constitutes Nehemiah 10:1-27. Such transitional phrases avoid the choppiness that might otherwise appear when previously existing, written texts are simply juxtaposed. This transition continues the first person plural from verses vv. 32-37, and it anticipates the resumption of first person plural verbs in 10:32-39. Its subject matter is simple: because of God's fidelity to Israel from Abraham to the time of Nehemiah, the people would remake their covenant with God and sign it.

Those Who Signed the Covenant, 10:1-27

R. J. Bautch says that Nehemiah 10 as a whole describes a covenant as an "agreement that a single community swears to uphold. The community's members are united as kin, with the more prominent persons mentioned by name. Moreover, their agreement mandates the performance of certain *mitzvot* [obligations] (10:30, 33), most of which pertain to the Sabbath."[20] What appears first in 10:1-27 is a list of names of the officials, Levites, and priests who signed the covenant, followed by a list of stipulations agreed to by the signatories and others.[21] The leaders may well have been the only returnees in Yehud capable of signing their names. Full literacy was limited, although the ability to sign documents was perhaps more widespread. At any rate, the verse as written presupposes their literacy as well as their legal right to sign a document for the returnees as a whole. In that sense, the document was presented as having legal force. Williamson hypothesizes that those entries were from individuals who signed using family names on behalf of their whole families.[22] The list of lay leaders (vv. 14-27) corresponds largely to names that appear in Ezra 2 and Nehemiah 7 as early returnees.

Obligations under the Covenant, 10:28-39

The point of the (very short) list of other signers in v. 28 was to show that not only the "rank" but also the "file" (the rest of people) agreed to the terms of the contract. These people included (rural) priests, Levites, lesser temple officials and servants, and all the returnees (those who "separated themselves from the peoples of the lands," an allusion to Ezra 9 and 10), not just the ranking citizens mentioned in vv. 1-27. Their agreement also bound their wives, children, and all responsible persons to the covenant. The curse they invoked ("may God condemn us") was a curse on all who broke the law. The terms used ("commandments" and "ordinances") are reminiscent of Deuteronomy but seem to include all laws, i.e., the Pentateuch or whatever parts of it were available to Nehemiah and his people. (See the discussion of the phrase "the Book of the Law of Moses" in connection with Nehemiah 8:1b-8. It is difficult to imagine that a different law book is intended here, and this verse emphasizes the divine origin of the Mosaic Law.) If any returnees failed to observe the law, i.e., to live and worship by it, family members should join the nobles and disinherit them.

Verse 30 had lifestyle issues in view, namely marrying outside the community of returnees, worshiping other gods, and siding with Sanballat and company, but not individual transgressions against God or one's associates. Religion is intimately intertwined with the whole of life, in this case marriage in particular. The people promise first not to arrange marriages for their children with the sons and daughters of non-returnees. In ancient Israel, young people did not date around and choose their own mates. Instead, parents arranged marriages for them. (The narrative of the marriage of Samson [Judg 14:1-4] shows that even ancient Israelites might have to deal with headstrong children who might want to marry someone from the outside, but the narrative of the choice of a wife for Isaac and his subsequent marriage to Rebecca [Gen 24:1-67] shows the system working as it was designed. Abraham even sent back to Mesopotamia to find Isaac a suitable wife.) [Arranged Marriages] In any case, in biblical times it was the fathers' responsibility to arrange marriages with suitable partners, and the children's responsibility to marry those partners. Here responsibility clearly involved living among the returnees and participating in the worship of YHWH with their families. The "curse" alluded to in Nehemiah 10:29 is either curses pronounced in the Law or self-curses made by individuals before God concerning the possibility that they sinned by worshiping improperly or by worshiping other gods. It was balanced by an oath swearing to keep God's law.

Verse 31 contains two vows to abstain from specific behaviors. The first was a vow not to buy grain from non-returnees on the Sabbath. Apparently there were no "blue laws" prohibiting such sales, but the returnees promised not to buy on the Sabbath or any

Arranged Marriages

In cultures such as ancient Israel, marriages were arranged between the families of the groom and bride, and monetary considerations might be part of the arrangement. Goods of one sort or another, what some people call a "bride price," might go from the groom's family to the bride's to recompense them for the loss of a daughter. A dowry might go with the bride into the marriage. That dowry would have belonged to her, although if it took the form of land, for example, her husband might "manage" it for her. Jewelry would have been hers to keep, wear, and pass down to her daughters. If moderns object that marriage is basically a matter of love between two people, they may find out that even a modern marriage has an economic side if it ends in divorce and there are children to provide for and/or property to divide.

José Pina (1830–1909). *Samson and Delilah*. 1851. National Museum of Art, Mexico. (Credit: Gianni Dagli Orti/The Art Archive at Art Resource, NY)

Simeon Solomon (1840–1905). *Isaac and Rebecca*. 1863. Watercolor. (Victoria and Albert Museum, London, Great Britain. (Credit: V&A Images, London/Art Resource, NY)

The Bible offers two well-known narratives about arranged marriages, those of Isaac and Samson. The contrast between the two only-sons could not be starker. Isaac accepted and loved the woman his father's servant brought back from Mesopotamia. Their story is one of an arranged marriage that turned out well, although their sons were less than ideal brothers. Samson, however, demanded that his parents secure a particular Philistine woman for him, and the ensuing marriage was a disaster. Undaunted, he pursued other women, at last losing his liberty and his life with the "wrong" woman, Delilah.

other holy day when all should be observing time off. The second was a promise to observe Sabbath years, when no crops were to be planted in a field. (See Exod 23:10-11, where the poor are allowed to glean the "volunteer crops" that came up in those fields.) These promises amount to increases in abstention. As Clines points out, no previous law had forbidden selling grain on the Sabbath. Besides, the promises reflect limits that worked to the disadvantage of different groups.[23] Foregoing the planting of crops in the seventh year would work to the disadvantage of farmers, although the land itself might well benefit. (That requirement appeared already in Exod 23:10-11, part of the so-called "Covenant Code," typically understood by scholars to be an early law code included in the Pentateuch.) Not selling on Sabbath would be a disadvantage to merchants. Since they are described as non-returnees, perhaps no one cared.

Continuing, Nehemiah 10:32-39 contains laws for the support of the temple. Any insistence that only returnees be allowed to worship there would limit the group who might provide that support. The text delineates the promised support first as an annual fee of one-third of a shekel. (How burdensome that tax would be is difficult to determine.) That tax was unusual, although not without precedent. Second Kings 12:4-15 relates the episode of a voluntary tax for the repair of the temple. Nehemiah 10:32 perhaps reflected the difference that a lack of royal support for the business of the temple would make as well as the aforementioned preferred limitation on which people were to be allowed to worship there and thus pay for the temple's upkeep. This money went for regular temple expenditures, including bread (to be kept at the temple), grain (for offerings) and animal burnt offerings (daily, sabbaths, new moons, and festivals, expenses to be met by donations), and sin offerings. These items are mentioned elsewhere in the Hebrew Bible but are drawn together in one list here. In addition to the third of a shekel per family per year, the temple received additional funding. Other kinds of revenue included first fruits (probably the best) of crops, firstborn baby animals, dough, first fruits from the trees, wine, and oil. The Levites would collect these offerings for their own upkeep and bring a tithe or tenth of them to the temple for its needs in worship and those who lived and worked there. The people concluded their prayer with the promise not to forget (neglect) the temple (v. 39).

Overall, then, Nehemiah 10:28-39 offers insight into the nitty-gritty business of running the temple. That institution required support from every family in order to carry out its God-given function. Malachi 3:8-10 envisioned a similar, although community-wide support for the temple, based, however, on the tithe, i.e., more or less according to one's ability to pay. (Obviously wealthy people could more easily afford to give a tithe than poorer ones, who needed all the grain they raised to keep themselves alive. From those able to give more, their gifts would be gladly received.) The same thought underlay the two different passages: all who used the temple and/or benefitted from its services should help pay for the temple's upkeep and its ministries.

With this analysis of Nehemiah 10:28-39 complete, it is now possible to investigate its nature. Clines calls it "a set of *halakot* (a Hebrew word literally meaning 'ways,' i.e. ways to go; in other words instructions on how to behave) probably devised by priestly or Levitical lawyers and thereafter assented to by the populace," and each *halakah* (the singular form of *halakot*) has something "novel" about it, but each also "represents the result of exegetical work upon previously existing laws."[24]

Clines distinguishes five different types of development in these verses. (1) Verse 35 constitutes a facilitating law, which establishes the machinery for carrying out a prescription. The petitioners pledge to bring the first fruits of plants and trees to feed the priests. (2) Verse 39 revises a facilitating law by stipulating that the Levites will collect the tithe for use by themselves, priests, gatekeepers, and singers. (3) Verse 33 creates a new prescription from a precedent in Pentateuchal law; what had been occasional levy for the sanctuary in Exodus 30:11-16 (a half shekel per person, regardless of one's personal wealth) here becomes an annual tax. (4) Several verses redefine categories. Verse 31 for the first time prohibits marriage with foreigners; v. 32 prohibits buying on the Sabbath; and v. 36 includes the fruit of trees among the first fruits to be tithes. (5) While one might argue that the laws in the Pentateuch constituted alternative methods of raising revenues, vv. 36-40 make them all simultaneously binding.[25]

Clines also deduces a set of principles lying behind these *halakot*. (1) Every one of them has some connection with a Pentateuchal prescription; none is simply invented on the spot. (2) Extension or reapplication is possible, even to the extent of bypassing the letter of the law for the sake of its spirit. (3) Pentateuchal law requires ancillary law in order to be effectual. (4) Pentateuchal law, nevertheless, is regarded as essentially harmonious; tensions are resolved by addition rather than by mediation or compromise. Clines, in short, finds the *halakot* to be *ad hoc* responses to problems encountered by Nehemiah.[26]

CONNECTIONS

1. Recognition of the kind of infighting within the post-exilic Yahwistic community that Neh 9:2 reports and *extols* reminds us even today that exclusivism within the community of God is not a good or healthy thing. It may well grow out of a commendable desire to preserve the faith in all its purity. The truth is, though, that biblical faith was flawed ethically, from Adam and Eve and from Abraham who expelled Hagar and Ishmael to the pious, religious priests and others who turned Jesus over to the Romans, and to those early Christians causing problems in the churches of Paul. God's work of redeeming the world is made no easier by God's children who see themselves as special. God's people are sinners like everyone else. The mere fact that God led later Jews to see God

Two Hymns

Nehemiah 9:5 says that the Levites Jeshua, Kadmiel, Bani, Hashabneiah, Sherebiah, Hodiah, Shebaniah, and Pethahiah called on worshipers to "Stand up and bless the LORD your God from everlasting to everlasting." The 18th/19th-century songwriter James Montgomery used the gist of that verse in his song of praise, "Stand Up and Bless the Lord."

From Stanza 1
Stand up and bless the Lord, All peoples of His choice;
Stand up and bless the Lord your God, With heart and soul and voice.

From Stanza 4
Stand up and bless the Lord, The Lord your God adore;
Stand up and bless His glorious name, Henceforth for evermore.

Another appropriate hymn for ancient Yehud and for modern God-lovers to sing, at least according to Isa 56:6-11, would be the first verse of "O God of Every Nation."

O God of every nation, of every race and land,
Redeem the whole creation with your almighty hand.
Where hate and fear divide us and bitter threats are hurled,
In love and mercy guide us, and heal our strife-torn world.

revealed in Ezra-Nehemiah and canonize that book does not prove that the actions of Ezra and Nehemiah were necessarily carried out as God intended. If a reader of these words objects that the Bible does not say Ezra and Nehemiah were wrong in their exclusivism, the point here is that it certainly does say so in passages like Isaiah 56:3-4, 7. God was (and is), however, not forestalled from acting until God's people learn to discern and follow perfectly the full word of God. Thank God! [Two Hymns]

2. Nehemiah 9:14 is the first place in Ezra-Nehemiah to use the word "sabbath." It appears eleven more times between Nehemiah 10:31 and 13:22, and the word "sabbaths" appears in Nehemiah 10:33. All those texts have in view practices associated with observing the Sabbath properly. Exodus 20:8-11 describes the Sabbath as a day to do no labor personally and to require no labor of one's children, servants/slaves, livestock, and resident aliens living in one's country. Despite the obvious pecking order lined out in those verses (putting resident aliens below not only one's family but also one's animals), the text makes clear that the Sabbath was a day for rest, for reflection on God's goodness, and for the general renewing of oneself. Sabbath, in other words, does not, or at least should not, consist of doing the chores one did not get around to during the week. For working adults, our Sundays (not the seventh day or Sabbath, of course, but the day the early church chose to observe in honor of the Resurrection of Jesus) may become the day for catching up on unfinished tasks from the previous week or (in the case of people like schoolteachers and college professors!) for grading papers and preparing for classes the next week.

Norman Wirzba offers a vibrant rationale for Sabbath observance.

Sabbath [observance] fosters in us an appreciation for creation as God sees it. We cannot acquire this divine point of view on our own. We need our [rest] to be properly inspired and formed, and for this formation we need to depend on God. The Hebrews learned this dependence in a humbling journey: forty years in the wilderness relying on God for direction and for the satisfaction of their every need.[27]

The point of the Sabbath is not to be busy, even at worshiping God, but to rest, to attune oneself to God, to share time with one's family, and—yes—even to sit down together for a good meal and a long talk. Of course, as the concept of Sabbath developed among Jews, the food for that day was to be prepared on the sixth day. (That tradition rested on the commandment to do no labor on the seventh day in given Exod 20:8 and elaborated in vv. 9-11.) A day of rest perhaps might include a walk, but the Rabbis realized that a walk late on the Sabbath to one's worksite or place of business might simply be a way to fudge on the end of Sabbath and get a jump on the workweek. Thus they limited how far and for what causes one might walk. Besides, most people in that culture probably got in all the walking they needed. Modern Americans, by contrast, often get so little exercise that biblical writers might admonish them now to walk to church together—both ways—as some Jews do to Synagogue services. I confess that when I teach Monday classes (yes, although retired I still sometimes teach a course or two in a given semester), Sunday evening may be dedicated to last-minute preparations that I could and should have completed Saturday or earlier. I also confess as well that I sometimes write on Sundays.

3. The custom of arranged marriages did not die out in some parts of Europe until the twentieth century, and young men in the United States sometimes (often?) still ask permission to propose to a couple's daughter. The delightful musical *Fiddler on the Roof* gently spoofs the entire system of arranged marriage beginning with the singing of "Matchmaker, Matchmaker" by the daughters of Tevye and Golde, continuing to the arrangement of the marriage of their oldest daughter to a butcher, followed by her refusal to comply and her insistence on marrying the tailor (whom she loved) instead. After the

Israel Gathering Manna/Quail

Master of the Manna (2nd half 15th C.) *The Gathering of Manna*. Wood. Musee de la Chartreuse, Douai, France. (Credit: Erich Lessing/Art Resource, NY)

hullabaloo surrounding that refusal subsides, Tevye and Golde sing an endearing duet.

Tevye sings to her: "Do you love me?"

Golde replies in a screech: "Do I what?"

"Do you love me?" he repeats.

"Do I love you?" asks Golde, and launches into a long list of things she has done for him their whole marriage long: cooked his food, washed his clothes, kept his house, and bore his children. Still he persists; he wants to know if she loves him. She answers that if all those years of living with him and doing for him do not constitute love, she does not know what love is. Pressed further, Golde finally says that she guesses she does love Tevye, and he confesses that he guesses that he loves her too. They conclude that after all those years of marriage, knowing that they love each other does not change a thing, but it is nice to know.

Times change, and so do marriage customs and expectations about marriage. Moderns marry for love. Still, marriage is about more than love or sex and excitement. It has to do with suffering with and caring for one another, working together, bearing children (where possible), supporting one another, and forgiving one another. Ideally, a marriage ends only when one partner dies, although now as in the past not all marriages work out. Some end in divorce, some for more solid reasons than the ones forced by leaders of the returnees—or so I think. Marriage is always partly about who we are and who we are becoming. Our faith can be part of the success of marriage. It need not be part of the problem, even if married partners do not share the same faith.

4. Modern readers need to recall that there were no weekly "temple" services to attend in Ezra's and Nehemiah's time, nor were there any "blue laws" prohibiting selling things on the Sabbath. Likewise in modern America, farmers may want to remind city dwellers that they have animals to feed and possibly cattle to milk daily, and harvest season allows no days off except when it rains. Sunday morning worship, especially among Protestants, seems to have been set as late as it was to allow time for milking and other such chores before farmers attended church. Modern stores, factories, and service businesses that run twenty-four hours a day, seven days a week, present contemporary challenges to taking Sunday off. What will be churches' and Christians' reaction to those challenges? Many churches already hold Saturday evening services in addition to those on Sunday morning and/or evening. Roman Catholic churches, which often serve urban congregations, have long held

Mass on Saturday evening or early Sunday morning. Will churches need to be even more creative and flexible? If so, what will be the cost in loss of community within churches? In any case, Christians might want to remember that God is God of all seven days, and that worship on any day is as appropriate as worship on Sunday morning and Sunday evening.

NOTES

1. The Persian king was intended, but he was called the king of Assyria here. Technically, of course, the Persian king was the king of Assyria, but of much more as well, more even than the old Assyrian Empire. See the discussion under comments on Ezra 6:22, where he also was called the king of Assyria.

2. H. G. M. Williamson ("Structure and Historiography in Nehemiah 9," *Proceedings of the Ninth World Congress of Jewish Studies* [Jerusalem: Magness, 1985] 117–31, here 117–18) thinks vv. 1-5a are based on an Ezra source and may have originally stood between Ezra 10:15 and 16. As the text stands now, however, the verses do not mention Ezra, nor did Neh 9:6 in the MT, and Neh 10 names Nehemiah, not Ezra. The issue in this commentary, in any case, is how the passage functions and what it means in its current context. Also, M. J. Boda ("Chiasmus in Ubiquity in Nehemiah 9," *JSOT* 7 [1996]: 55–70) takes exception to scholars who find a chiasmus in Neh 9. The comments on this chapter will heed Boda's warning.

3. D. J. A. Clines, "Notes on Nehemiah" in *The HarperCollins Study Bible* (ed. Wayne A. Meeks; New York: HarperCollins, 1993) 727.

4. See H. G. M. Williamson, "The Concept of Israel in Transition," *The World of Ancient Israel* (ed. R. E. Clements; Cambridge, New York, Port Chester, Melbourne, Sydney: Cambridge University Press, 1989) 141–61, here 150–51.

5. Origin, from "On Ezra and Nehemiah 3:.28," in Marco Conti, ed., *Ancient Christian Commentary on Scripture. Old Testament V* (Downers Grove IL: InterVarsity Press, 2008) 359.

6. Richard J. Bautch, "An Appraisal of Abraham's Role in Post-exilic Covenants," *CBQ* 71 (2009): 42–63, here 53.

7. Actual dependence might seem self-evident to readers of this commentary, but biblical scholars sometimes date the latest hypothesized Pentateuchal source "P" (or Priestly Source) as late as or later than Nehemiah. Volker Pröbstl (*Nehmia 9, Psalm 106 und Psalm 136 und die Rezeption des Pentatuechs* [Göttingen: Cuvillier, 1997] 60–62), however, takes this passage in Nehemiah as proof that the Pentateuch had reached its canonical form by the time Neh 9 was written. Still, readers are reminded that that date was later than the life of Nehemiah, probably in the fourth century or so. See the discussion in the Introduction to Ezra-Nehemiah.

8. See Bautch, "Abraham's Role," 54. See also Mark J. Boda, *Praying the Tradition: The Origin and Use of Tradition in Nehemiah 9* (BZAW 277; Berlin/New York: de Gruyter, 1999) 105; and H. G. M. Williamson, *Ezra-Nehemiah* (WBC; Nashville: Nelson, 1985) 304 n. 8a.

9. Boda, *Praying the Tradition*, 41.

10. The two psalms were songs containing allusions to the events, while Exod 7:14–12:32 was a carefully constructed narrative designed to single out exactly ten such wonders. Differences in the order prove nothing about the possibility of the events. Indeed, some of the wonders were natural occurrences, the timing of which was what was revelatory.

11. Volker Pröbstl (*Nehemia 9, Psalm 106 und Psalm 136 und die Rezeption des Pentateuchs* [Gottingen: Cuvillier, 1996] 68–69) finds this use from the two passages (from Exodus and Numbers) to be one piece of evidence that the redactor of Ezra-Nehemiah had the entire Pentateuch in hand when he wrote.

12. Judith H. Newman, *Praying by the Book; The Scripturalization of Prayer in Second Temple Judaism* (SBLEJL 14; Atlanta: Scholars Press, 1999) 114–15.

13. Pröbstl, *Nehemia 9, Psalm 106 und Psalm 136*, 68–69.

14. Ibid., 77

15. Readers may follow this use of the term in the comments on Ezra 1 (in v. 5 they are the exiles in Babylon); 2:59; 3:1; 4: 3, 16; 7:7-9; 9:1-4 (indeed the whole of Ezra 9–10); Neh 2–3; 7; and in Neh 9, particularly in vv. 1-2 and 32-37.

16. Bautch, "Abraham's Role," 56.

17. Sarah Japhet, "Sheshbazzar and Zerubbabel," *ZAW* 94 (1982): 73–75.

18. Daniel L. Smith-Christopher, *A Biblical Theology of Exile* (OBT; Minneapolis: Fortress, 2002) 44.

19. Manfred Oeming, *Judah and the Judeans in the Persian Period* (ed. Oded Lipschits and Manfred Oeming; Winona Lake IN: Eisenbrauns. 2006) 571–88, here 584.

20. Richard J. Bautch, "The Function of Covenant across Ezra-Nehemiah," *Unity and Disunity in Ezra-Nehemiah* (ed. M. J. Boda and Paul L. Redditt; Hebrew Bible Monographs 17; Sheffield: Sheffield Phoenix Press, 2008) 8–24; here 21.

21. Alfred Jepsen ("Nehemiah 10," *ZAW* 66 [1954]: 87–106) studied this chapter, noting that it contains both a three-part list of names and a document. He sets aside the issue of whether they belonged together originally and concludes that the list itself belonged to the time of Nehemiah and not later.

22. In a pair of footnotes in *The HarperCollins Study Bible* (p. 729), Clines also says that the list derived from Nehemiah's time but constitutes a roster of names as opposed to the names of people who actually signed the document.

23. Ibid, note on 10:30.

24. D. J. A. Clines, "Nehemiah 10 as an Example of Early Jewish Biblical Exegesis," *JSOT* 21 (1981): 111–17, here 111.

25. Ibid., 112–13.

26. Ibid., 114.

27. Norman Wirzba, *Living the Sabbath* (Grand Rapids MI: Brazos, 2006) 80.

DEDICATION OF THE WALL AND TEMPLE RESPONSIBILITIES

Nehemiah 11:1–12:43

COMMENTARY

Nehemiah 11–13 constitutes the third and final section of the book of Nehemiah. (See the discussion "B. The Structure of the Book of Nehemiah" in the Introduction to Nehemiah.) Following as it does the discussion of the repair of the wall of Jerusalem and a confession of sin, the section reports that one-tenth of the people moved to Jerusalem (11:1-2), names the Returnee families living there (11:3-24) and lists the surrounding villages where returnees lived (11:25-36). Nehemiah 12:1-26 repeats the names of people who returned with Zerubbabel and Jeshua. Since this is the third time the redactor has employed such a list, its significance for him cannot be overstressed. This list also explores a new subject, however, since—after the first few names in v. 1—it lists priests and Levites down to the beginning of the Greek period in vv. 2-26. (Thus the date for the *completion* of Ezra-Nehemiah cannot predate the end of the Persian or beginning of the Greek period, and its completion probably occurred even later, given the size of the numbers reported for the return in 539. (See the discussion in the Introduction to Ezra-Nehemiah.) Such lists and narratives constitute the basis for the final author's understanding of who belonged to the real Israel. As argued several times already in this volume, and first in the Introduction to Ezra-Nehemiah ("C. The Historical Reliability of Ezra-Nehemiah, 1. The Number of Returnees and the Import of that List for the Date of the Compilation of Ezra-Nehemiah"), the lists date from the final stage of the book in the first forty years of the second century BCE and help to defend the authority of the leaders in Jerusalem in that period.

The next narrative, Nehemiah 12:27-43, describes the dedication of the repaired wall, and from v. 31 on is the only part of Nehemiah 11–12 written in the first person singular and thus the only part that should be assigned to "Nehemiah's Memoirs." Readers often *assume* that Nehemiah was the author of the whole book, based on Nehemiah 1:1a, and the heading does state that the following material constitutes "the words of Nehemiah son of Hacaliah." Much of the book does relate his story in the first person singular. It is also clear to readers of this commentary, however, that various, previously existing lists were employed, and Nehemiah 7:73b–8:18 narrates an episode from the life of Ezra. Nehemiah 11:1–12:26, moreover, constitutes a collection of diverse materials used to contextualize the first-person narrative in Nehemiah 12:31-43. None of those verses carries a date.

Nehemiah 12:44-47 reverts to the third person, revealing itself as not part of the first person account it follows. It *appears* to conclude the discussion of Nehemiah's first sojourn to Jerusalem, reaching back to Zerubbabel (who first appeared in Ezra 2:2) to close the account of the rebuilding of Jerusalem. It, along with Nehemiah 13:1-3, describes the tension within the community that forced Nehemiah to return there, and Nehemiah 13:6-31 relates (again in the first person) the actions Nehemiah took to rectify matters. In between, Nehemiah 13:4-5 clearly introduces vv. 6-31, and something like it may have belonged to Nehemiah's "Memoirs." Thus Nehemiah 12:44–13:3 is transitional, filling in a little information about Jerusalem, ostensibly during Nehemiah's first term, but perhaps not. If these verses are read as belonging to Nehemiah's second term (discussed in Neh 13:4-31), the entirety of Nehemiah 11–13 can be understood as a discussion of it.[1] Either way, these comments will address only Nehemiah 11:1–12:43, which contains an inordinate number of names of people and places. [Outline of Nehemiah 11:1–12:43] Nehemiah 12:44–13:31 will be treated separately.

The Resettlement of Some Returnees, 11:1-2

The impression given thus far in Nehemiah that the city of Jerusalem was uninhabited (or nearly so anyway) before the wall was repaired is now made explicit. With the wall complete, the returnees cast lots to choose one out of ten of the returnees to resettle in Jerusalem. [Casting Lots] The assumption was that God guided the casting of the lots, and v. 2 says that the selected families willingly moved to Jerusalem and that the other returnees blessed them. (Another way to read the verse, however, is that some of the people simply volunteered to move to Jerusalem, which was in terrible condition, and the people blessed those among them who did not wait to be drafted, but volunteered.) It is anyone's guess how many of those new settlers might have been able to earn their living within the city. Some, possibly, would have had to travel to their farms to work their land and reap their harvest. Indeed, throughout Yehud all farmers would have had to travel at least a short distance to work; they lived in villages, towns, or cities, not on farms, and they walked or rode to their lands to farm them. Cities, however, also were the special locale of rulers, priests, merchants, and moneyed people who did not farm.

It is worth noting that Jerusalem is called "the holy city" in vv. 1 and 18. What made a place "holy" was that it was set aside for service to God. The old Jerusalem had been the locus of government, business, and diplomacy. It also housed the principal shrine to God, Solomon's temple, and after the time of Josiah its leaders claimed its royal temple as the sole legitimate place of worship in Judah. (Readers might note, however, that the eighth-century prophets Amos and Hosea condemned rulers and citizens of northern Israel and the nature of worship at shrines to God there, but did not condemn worship outside Jerusalem per se.) Ezekiel remarkably termed Jerusalem itself a whore (Ezek 16:15-22), although he said the same thing about the house of Israel as a whole and promised the cleansing of both (Ezek 43:/). Perhaps the new Jerusalem of Nehemiah's time had taken on or would take on some of the functions of government, indeed all eventually, but v. 1 emphasizes that it was the citadel of the temple. Its wall demarcated the sacred space, which was no longer just the area around the temple but the whole enclosed area, i.e., the whole "holy" city.

Casting Lots

Casting lots consisted of placing small objects of clay, wood, or other material into a container and shaking it until one was thrown out. The process was used to narrow a field of candidates for some particular action or even to determine guilt. 1 Sam 10:20-24 narrates the selection of Saul as king via casting lots. First the tribe of Benjamin was selected from the represented tribes, then the Matrite family, then Saul from the men of that family. Casting lots was used to determine the will of God, who was assumed to control the process.

D. E. Aune, "Lots," *The International Standard Bible Encyclopedia* (ed. Geoffrey W. Bromiley; Grand Rapids: Eerdmans, 1986) 3.172–73.

William Blake (1757–1827). *The Soldiers Casting Lots for Christ's Garments.* Pen, Indian ink, grey wash and watercolour on paper. 1800. Fitzwilliam Museum, Cambridge, Great Britain. (Credit: © Fitzwilliam Museum, Cambridge/Art Resource, NY)

The Names of the Returnee Families Living in Jerusalem, 11:3-24

Nehemiah 11:3-24 lists some of the new inhabitants, by ancestral names or by their personal names. Athaiah (v. 4), Maaseiah (v. 5), Sallu (v. 7), Gabbai and Sallai (v. 8), Joel and Judah (v. 9) are called "leaders." It gives the number of descendants of the sons of Perez alone as 468. (Perez, readers will recall, was a son of the patriarch Judah, born to him in a shameful encounter with his daughter-in-law [Gen 38:12-30]). Verse 9 mentions 928 more. No other numbers are given, but the verses certainly imply a much larger total figure. Verses 10 and 11 then list two priests, Jedaiah and Seraiah, and says they had associates. The number of associates, however, is staggering: 822 to take care of the temple, 242 more associates, and 128 said to have been valiant warriors (guards). In addition, v. 18 says there were 284 Levites, and v. 19 numbers the gatekeepers of the city at 172. All together the numbers given total 3,044 people said to have inhabited the city, and the passage may imply more. The numbers supplied clearly presuppose a large, functioning temple and thus derive from a later period, not from the time Nehemiah first resettled the ruined city. Such a large temple staff even a couple of generations later would seem burdensome for Yehud. In addition, the head of the Levites was a man named Uzzi, who was the overseer of the various types of work that went on in the temple. "Ophel," mentioned in v. 21, was the area between the old city of David and the temple hill and running east.

In any case, readers may wonder if the author actually meant to say that so many people lived in Jerusalem itself during Nehemiah's time and, if he did, whether he was correct. (See the Introduction to Ezra-Nehemiah, "C. The Historical Reliability of Ezra-Nehemiah, 1. The Number of the Returnees and the Import of that List for the Date of the Completion of Ezra-Nehemiah.") A population of even 3,044 would have constituted a high percentage of the estimated population of Yehud in Nehemiah's time: 13,350 in the early Persian period and only 20,650 in its second half (from the time of Nehemiah to the end of the Persian period in 323).[2] Modern estimates of the city's entire population run no more than 1,500 in the late fifth century,[3] or even as few as about 625.[4] Other biblical texts offer no help here. The book of Zechariah, for example, discusses the future of Jerusalem in four different chapters but gives no data about the size of its population. [Descriptions of the Future Jerusalem in the Book of Zechariah] The city's population perhaps did not reach the size implied in Nehemiah 11 until the Maccabean period. Thus, one may wonder whether the numbers were added to the narrative that late.

H. G. M. Williamson says, however, that the list of groups in vv. 4b-20 is more or less a list of those who lived in Jerusalem "after the city's population had been supplemented."[5] He dates the first stage or edition of Ezra-Nehemiah circa 400 BCE and a second (which includes Neh 12:1-20) circa 300 BCE. He does not supply numbers for the size of Jerusalem's population, and archaeologists' estimates of that size have steadily shrunk from the time of Williamson's commentary to the numbers just mentioned. Thus, if the numbers are to be retained, one needs to say that they were added (or modified) later, perhaps during the Maccabean period by which time the population of Jerusalem had grown to such a size.

Verse 24, moreover, is remarkable in one more respect. It says that Pethiah "was at the king's hand in all matters concerning the people." A man by the name of Pethiah was governor two generations after Nehemiah. *If* the phrase points to that man, it suggests strongly that the list in Nehemiah 11:3-23 derived from his time or later and was used here because it was the most relevant information about the care and status of the temple the later redactor of Ezra-Nehemiah had at his disposal. In any case, there was no Judean king in Jerusalem in the post-exilic period. The only king of Jerusalem was the king of Persia. His "presence" loomed over the city, which housed no local king of its own, Davidic or otherwise.

> **Descriptions of the Future Jerusalem in the Book of Zechariah**
>
> The post-exilic book of Zechariah also depicts the future city of Jerusalem in four places. (1) Zech 2:4 (c. late 520) predicts a future teeming population in contrast with the ruined city of 520. (2) Zech 9:8, traditionally dated 520 and often dated much later, but perhaps an early addition to Zechariah from c. 500, predicts that God will defend the temple, making it a garrison or bastion against attack. (3) Zech 12:1-9, which anticipates a siege of a rebuilt Jerusalem, dates later, i.e., after the reconstruction of the wall around the city under Nehemiah. Verse 2 depicts the city as being under a future siege. Verse 7 predicts victory for the city but portrays it as humbled by God. (4) Zech 14:2 anticipates a similar, future siege, while Zech 14:10 predicts the safety of the future city as guaranteed by God, and seems to presuppose standing walls and gates that will remain secure against any future threat.

The Returnees who Lived in Surrounding Villages, 11:25-36

By no means, moreover, did all the returnees live in Jerusalem, as Nehemiah 11:1-2 clearly says; 90 percent lived in seventeen villages around Jerusalem in Judah and in fifteen villages in what had been biblical Benjamin. Nehemiah 11:25-36 adds information about where some of them lived. Towns where they settled in *old* Judah are listed in vv. 25-30. Oded Lipschits attributes this list to the author/editor of the chapter itself. In other words, he sees it as an *ad hoc* creation.[5] The names include Beersheba and Ziklag, places well away from the action in Jerusalem. The list, then, appears to show where returnees settled, not necessarily where political lines might have been drawn. (Of course, Persia might not have drawn them very carefully, and residents might have disagreed.) Verses 31-35 number those residing in neighboring Benjamin separately. Jerusalem itself was located right on the border between old Benjamin and Judah, but near the middle of the post-exilic Persian province Yehud. The city had been a Hittite fortress belonging to no Israelites before David captured it and made it his city and the capital of his united kingdom. It became the sole place of worship in Judah later, during the reign of Josiah (2 Kgs 22:1–23:27). In the thinking of Nehemiah or at least that of the editor of Ezra-Nehemiah, however, the city itself would serve as the worship center of the returnees only. Perhaps inevitably, it would also become the political center of Yehud as well. Its importance to the returned exiles who gained and held power in Yehud would lead to that result.

List of Priests and Levites who Returned with Zerubbabel and Jeshua, 12:1-26

This commentary has devoted special attention to the overall narrative of the return of the "true Israel" from Babylon to Jerusalem connecting Ezra-Nehemiah. Five lists anchor this narrative, and the first four have already been discussed. (1) Ezra 2:1-70a describes a huge party of returnees coming to reclaim their land and to rebuild the temple acting on the direct command of Cyrus (Ezra 1:1–6:22). (2) Ezra 7–8 details the journey of a second group of returnees under the priest Ezra acting on the direct command of "Artaxerxes," and the list of returnees in Ezra 8:1-14 ties Ezra 7–8 to the original group of returnees. (3) Ezra 9–10 shows the necessity of purging members of the original company of returnees who had removed themselves from the "true" community by marrying local Judean women. Ezra 10:18-44 anchors that narrative. (4) Nehemiah 7:5-73 employs (apart from transmission errors) the same list as Ezra 2:1-70a and shows the continued viability of that community, guaranteed now by the reconstruction of the wall around the city. (5) The last list appears here in Nehemiah 12:1-26. It repeats a few names from Nehemiah 7:5-73a and reports which groups were assigned to perform what duties. Verses 1-9 provide a partial list of high priests down to Jaddua, who became high priest during the reign of Darius III Codomannus (r. 336–332) and served until 323.[6] Thus, these verses provide additional internal evidence that the book of Nehemiah was not complete before the early years of the Greek Empire, i.e., Williamson's circa 300 BCE, and it appears not to have been completed until later still.

The list of "priests and Levites who came up with Zerubbabel" in vv. 1-11 begins with a few names known from Ezra 2 and Nehemiah 7. [Leaders of Returnees in Ezra 2:2, Nehemiah 7:7, and Nehemiah 12:1-2] The names in v. 1 appear at the heads of those other two lists, but beginning with v. 2 the names listed as priests are almost all new to Ezra-Nehemiah. The Levites here are said only to be in charge of the songs of thanksgiving and to have formed an antiphonal choir.[7] (Are readers to assume that the author thought singing was their only function?) Finally, the list ends in v. 11 with the name Jaddua, the aforementioned high priest in 323.

Continuing, the name Jeshua in v. 11 is the same name as in v. 1, so vv. 10-11 list six high priests who flourished from 539 to 323: Jeshua, Joiakim, Eliashib, Joida, Jonathan, and Jaddua. If the list is complete (and it may be, although some scholars suspect it has holes), one or more high priests experienced a lengthy tenure. In both Ezra 2:2 and Nehemiah 7:7 the name Nehemiah appears, but it is replaced in Nehemiah 12:1 with that of Ezra, perhaps because Nehemiah was not a priest while Ezra was. Of course, neither was Zerubbabel; he was the Davidide who led the return and not included among the priests and Levites. Verse 8 turns from listing priests to listing Levites, but Jeshua (the first name in the list) was listed as a priest in Nehemiah 7:39. Perhaps two different men by the name Jeshua were intended.

If v. 10 mentioned the second high priest Joiakim (circa turn of the sixth to fifth centuries?), vv. 12-21 moved on to heads of priestly houses during his lifetime. Then vv. 22-25 list Levites who lived during the period of the last four high priests. This record is spotty indeed, and the names of the six priests include priests as late as the fourth century and despite the claim in v. 26 that these people belonged to the time of Jeshua, Ezra, and Nehemiah (i.e., 539–c. 432; see Neh 13:6). At any rate, Nehemiah 12:1-25 names some of the key figures who flourished between 539 and 323, not simply during the time of Nehemiah.

Leaders of Returnees in Ezra 2:2, Nehemiah 7:7, and Nehemiah 12:1-2

Ezra 2:2	Nehemiah 7:7	Nehemiah 12:1-2
Zerubbabel	Zerubbabel	Zerubbabel
Jeshua	Jeshua	Jeremiah
Nehemiah	Nehemiah	Ezra
Seriah	Azariah	Amariah, v. 2
Reeliah	Raamiah	
	Nahamiah	
Mordecai	Mordecai	
Bilshan	Bilshan	
Bigvai	Bigvai	
Rehum	Nehum	Rehum (v. 2)
Baaniah	Baanah	

Lyre

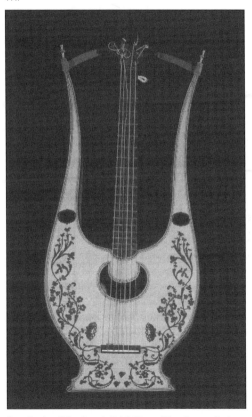

The lyre was one of three prominent stringed instruments, along with harps and lutes. The lyre consisted of a sound box and two uprights, not necessarily of equal length, topped by a bridge. The strings were attached to the sound box and the bridge. The accompanying photo is an ornate, 18th-century lyre, more elaborate than many. The harp, on the other hand, had strings of unequal length due to the curvature of the instrument. The third instruments mentioned here were not lutes but cymbals, flat percussion instruments that could be struck together, as today.

D. A. Foxvog and A. D. Kilmer, "Music," *ISBE*, 3.436–49, here 440 and 444.

Neapolitan lyre. Painted wood. 18th C. Museo di Capodimonte, Naples, Italy. (Credit: Gianni Dagli Orti/The Art Archive at Art Resource, NY)

The Dedication of the City Wall, 12:27-43

The dedication of the wall of Jerusalem, an event narrated in Nehemiah 12:27-43, set apart Jerusalem as the "holy city" (see Neh 11:1, 18 for that designation), so its walls and gates were purified just as the returnees themselves were (Neh 12:30).[8] The celebrants sang songs of thanksgiving, accompanied by cymbals, harps, and lyres (stringed, harp-like instruments). [Lyre] Such songs abound in the Psalter: e.g., Psalm 124 (perhaps the only pure example of a communal song of thanksgiving) and Psalm 30 (an individual song of thanksgiving), and a number of such songs combined with other genres.[9] Nehemiah 12:27 does not include any of the words of the songs, its author perhaps assuming that readers would be familiar with them or at least the tone and nature of the songs. The temple singers are said to have been gathered not only from the area around Jerusalem but also from other areas. One place was Beth-gilgal, which is not attested elsewhere in the Hebrew Bible. The word "gilgal" designates a circle of stones, so the place name would mean "house of a circle of stones." The name "Gilgal" is used in reference to three or more towns in the Hebrew Bible. Still, the reference in v. 27 might not have designated a town, but a house (beth) with a circle in front of, near, or around it. A second place, Geba, probably lay about nine kilometers (or about five miles) northeast of Jerusalem, and a third, Azmaveth, in the hills north of Jerusalem. Other singers lived similarly nearby in villages or clusters of houses. The redactor supplies a closing summary: the priests and Levites purified themselves, the people, and the gates and the wall of the city.

The first person account resumes in v. 31. Nehemiah says that he brought the leaders of Yehud (i.e., of the returnees) up onto the walls and divided the crowd below into two companies to give thanks and to process in opposite directions around the newly rebuilt wall, until they met at the temple. Nehemiah followed one of the groups of priests. When the two groups rejoined, they celebrated with offerings to God and with thanksgiving—the whole assembly, not just the men. Verses 41-43 round off and conclude the narrative. They do not employ first person verbs, but they do report that fifteen priests attended the event, seven of whom blew trumpets. A choir sang under the leadership of someone named Jezrahiah. The text explicitly says that women and children joined in too (v. 43). This verse is perhaps reminiscent of Ezra 3:15, which states that the people rejoiced when the foundation of the temple was laid, and the two verses would form an inclusio around the work in the city. That is, the restoration of the holy city began with the rebuilding of the foundation of the temple (Ezra 3:15) and was completed with the dedication of the wall around the temple/city (Neh 12:43).

The Pulpit Commentary treats this passage with the period of Nehemiah's second term (see Neh 13:4-31), and that understanding is defensible (as noted above), although not necessary.

> There was one day in the latter part in [Nehemiah's] administration which must have been to him a day of exquisite pleasure, and have almost repaid him for all the anguish that he had endured from the perversity of the people and the opposition of the nobles. After holding office for twelve years, he had occasion to visit the [Persian] court, either to make some special report, or because "his leave of absence had expired." While there, he had perhaps obtained permission to conduct a ceremony which he must have long had in his mind, but which he may have been afraid to venture on without the king's express sanction. That ceremony was the dedication of the wall. On returning to Jerusalem, in Artaxerxes' thirty-third year, BCE 431, he felt that the time had come to inaugurate his great work with appropriate pomp and circumstance.[10]

CONNECTIONS

1. Note was taken above that Nehemiah 11:1 called Jerusalem the "holy city" and that what makes any place "holy" is the presence of God. Today moderns travel to the "holy land" and visit Jerusalem and other sites. Christians visit the birthplace of Jesus in Bethlehem, the Jordan River where he was baptized, the city of Nazareth where he grew up and from which he launched his ministry, various sites where he preached or performed miracles, Calvary, and the tomb. What makes those sites sacred—for

Prayer at the Wailing Wall

American Colony (Jerusalem) Photo Department. Devout Jewish Women at the Wailing Wall. c. 1900–1920. (Credit: Library of Congress, Prints and Photographs Division, Washington, DC)

Christians—is their role or significance for the faith of the pilgrims. Contemporary Jews visit the Wailing Wall (part of the wall enclosing the grounds of Herod's temple that is still standing), and Muslims visit the Dome of the Rock, Islam's third holiest site built more or less on the location of the temple. To nonbelievers those places might—or might not—be places of interest for historical or other reasons, but they would not be sacred, i.e., places to meet and worship God. Holding something sacred, in other words, is an act of faith and will.

In the Bible and in the three religions mentioned in the previous paragraph people may participate in that kind of sacredness too by faith and obedience. "Holy" people also appear in other religions like Hinduism and Buddhism. They are treated with great respect and offered food, clothing, and other necessities by adherents to their faith or simply by well-intentioned admirers. The sacred completes (and even redeems) the mundane. ["Worthy of Worship"]

2. If worship at the temple under Nehemiah was marred (from some perspectives anyway) by its exclusivity, what about that of modern Christians? Christians are divided by denominations, socioeconomic status, race, cultural tastes, language, and a host of other important and not-so-important issues. I like classical music, but seldom country or modern rock. Church music seems best to me when accompanied by a piano, organ, or both, not guitars wired to a sound system. I like intellectually stimulating sermons, preferably under half an hour. I like to listen in quiet contemplation, not amid a chorus of "Amens" and shouting. All that is cultural, however, and a good meeting in an African-American church leaves me happy and singing, despite the length of the sermon. The delight on the faces of black friends and strangers alike because I am with them carries me for days. It is to be

hoped the days are long past when white men would block the door of their churches to keep "them" out. Hopefully, we can get over this sense of owning God's houses and God's being to say—based on prejudice, pride, or perceived financial worth—that some people are welcome, but others are not.

The Dome of the Rock

The Dome of The Rock Mosque, in the temple mount. (Credit: David Baum, Wikimedia Commons, CC by SA 3.0)

3. Cities thrive on the contributions both of people who live in them and people who do not. Each group needs the other. Our society, however, is wracked by suburban sprawl, inner urban decay, and much rural (as well as urban) poverty. We appear to be a nation of people striving to gain at the expense of each other. How are we any different from tiny post-exilic Yehud, where groups used religion to divide the community and where groups were determined to best one another?

"Worthy of Worship"

The motif of the worship of God finds expression in the modern song of praise and admiration, "Worthy of Worship," words by Terry W. York.

Worthy of worship, worthy of praise, worthy of honor and glory,
Worthy of all the glad songs we can sing, worthy of all of the offerings we bring.

Worthy of reverence, worthy of fear, worthy of love and devotion,
Worthy of bowing and bending of knee, worthy of this and added to these, . . .

You are worthy, our Creator, You are worthy, Creator, Sustainer,
You are worthy, worthy and wonderful, worthy of worship and praise.

Such praise is worship of the purest sort; it values God for God's sake, not for what God might do for the worshiper.

Words and music © 1988 by Van Ness Press, Inc./McKinney Music, Inc.

NOTES

1. See, for example, Joseph S. Excell, S. Spence Jones, Henry Donald Maurice et al., eds., *The Pulpit Commentary* (New York, Toronto: Funk and Wagnals, 1890) p. 9 of comments on Nehemiah.

2. Charles E. Carter, *The Emergence of Yehud in the Persian Period; A Social and Demographic Study* (JSOTSup 294; Sheffield: Sheffield Academic Press, 1999) 201.

3. Oded Lipschits, "Achaemenid Imperial Policy, Settlement Processes in Palestine, and the Status of Jerusalem in the Middle of the Fifth Century B.C.E.," *Judah and the*

Judeans in the Persian Period 9, ed. Oded Lipschits and Manfred Oeming; Winona Lake IN: Eisenbrauns, 2006) 19–52, here 32. He continues on p. 33: "I find it difficult to accept the idea that this [i.e., the list of returnees in Ezra 2, Nehemiah 7 and its shortened version in Nehemiah 12] was the list of those who actually returned from Babylon, whether at once or in several waves of immigration." Lipschits may, of course, be mistaken, but this much is clear: archaeological data do not support a mass return, regardless of what some archaeologists and/or some Bible scholars want to maintain.

4. I. Finkelstein, "Jerusalem in the Persian (and Early Hellenistic) Period and the Wall of Nehemiah," *JSOT* 32 (2008): 506–507. Of course, archaeological estimates are only estimates, but people do not inhabit a place and leave no trace.

5. H. G. M. Williamson, *Ezra and Nehemiah* (WBC 16: Nashville: Thomas Nelson, 1985) 346.

5. Oded Lipschits, "Literary and Ideological Aspects of Nehemiah 11," *JBL* 121 (2002): 423–40, here pp. 435–39.

6. See J. Crichton, "Jaddua," *ISBE*, 2.956.

7. Judah J. Slotki, *Daniel • Ezra • Nehemiah* (Soncino Books of the Book; London, New York: Soncino Press, 1951) 255.

8. David Janzen, "The Crisis of Jerusalem: Ethnic, Cultic, Legal, and Geographic Boundaries in Ezra-Nehemiah," *Unity and Disunity in Ezra-Nehemiah* (Hebrew Bible Monographs 17; ed. Mark J. Boda and Paul L. Redditt; Sheffield: Sheffield Phoenix Press, 2008) 117–35, here 133–34.

9. See Artur Weiser, *The Psalms: A Commentary* (Old Testament Library; Philadelphia: Westminster, 1962) 83–86.

10. Excell, Spence, and Maurice, *Pulpit Commentary*, p. 9 of comments on Nehemiah.

THE REFORMS OF NEHEMIAH

Nehemiah 12:44–13:31

COMMENTARY

How does Nehemiah 12:44-47 relate to Nehemiah 13:1-31? In answering that question, the place to begin is with Nehemiah 13:4-14, which renews the first person narrative found in much of the book of Nehemiah. (Actually, the first use of a first person verb is in v. 6, but vv. 4-5 introduce it.) Verses 4-14, however, follow information about actions taken in Jerusalem but not attributed to Nehemiah or his leadership. Nehemiah 12:44-47 is introduced with a very general connecting phrase "on that day" (NRSV) or "at that time" (NIV), but the phrase apparently does *not* designate the day of the dedication of the wall of Jerusalem (discussed in Neh 12:27-43) as the time frame for vv. 44-47. Nor do the verses directly attribute any action to Nehemiah. Instead they report (in v. 44) that unnamed "men were appointed over the chambers for the stores . . . ." Who appointed them is not said. There is actually no reason to suppose that Nehemiah did, since the text does not say so and the appointments would seem to have pertained to the temple only. Use of the passive voice, moreover, hides (intentionally or not) the identity of the appointer, although one might suppose that the high priest was the one who appointed temple functionaries. Finally, v. 47 speaks both of "the days of Zerubbabel" (i.e., 539/520) and of the "days of Nehemiah," so a redactor was clearly at work, reaching back over the whole narrative from Ezra 1 through Nehemiah 12.

The second passage is Nehemiah 13:1-3, which attaches directly to 12:44-47 with the phrase "on that day." The most obvious antecedent for the phrase is Nehemiah 12:47, which had just spoken of the *days* of Zerubbabel and the *days* of Nehemiah. The previous possible antecedent is Nehemiah 12:44-46, which discussed actions of persons other than Nehemiah appointed over the chambers for storage. The phrase "on that day" in Nehemiah 13:1, therefore, has no clear antecedent. Thus, it only loosely joins Nehemiah 13:1-3 to Nehemiah 12; it is actually a literary/redactional phrase that supplies a needed transition from 12:44-47 to what follows.

Nehemiah's old enemy Tobiah had been identified as an Ammonite the first time he was mentioned (see Neh 2:10). Whether he actually was of Ammonite descent or the term was simply a slur may be left open, but the book of Nehemiah called him one, and in so doing declared him unfit to be in the temple. (See Deut 23:3, which bars Ammonites and Moabites from the covenant community because they hired Balaam to curse them when the Israelites attempted to pass through their country en route to Egypt [Num 22:1–23:25]). Even Nehemiah 12:44-46 hangs in the air temporally, however. It describes the appointing of men over the storage chambers, whose usefulness in turn depended on the discussion of the sacrifices in Nehemiah 12:43.

Thus, Nehemiah 12:44-47 and Nehemiah 13:1-3 are both redactional pieces[1] that tie together Nehemiah's first mission (discussed in Neh 2:1–12:43 or just Neh 2:1–11:36) and his second mission (discussed in Neh 13:4-31 or the whole of Neh 11–13).[2] D. J. A. Clines thinks the seven verses paint an *idealized* picture of the postexilic community anyway.[3] Everything was running smoothly in contrast with the series of difficulties with which Nehemiah had to deal. Nehemiah 13:4, moreover, begins with a temporal phrase "before this." Before "this" what, however? Before "they" (unspecified people) read from the book of Moses (in Neh 13:1-3). In v. 4 itself, the high priest Eliashib (see Neh 3:1), whom Clines dubbed the "temple dean," prepared a place for the "Ammonite" Tobiah to stay in the temple. Finally, v. 6 discloses that Nehemiah was not in Jerusalem when all those events took place. Clearly vv. 4-6 have in view vv. 1-3, but vv. 1-3 are tied redactionally although not temporally to 12:44-47. It appears to be the case, therefore, that Nehemiah 12:44-47 and 13:1-3 together provide necessary background information for what follows in Nehemiah 13:4-14. These comments, therefore, will cover the whole last part of the book of Nehemiah. [Outline of Nehemiah 12:44–13:31]

The Assignment of Temple Responsibilities, 12:44-47

Nehemiah 12:44 appears to say that temple responsibilities were assigned (by someone not named, but presumably the high priest) on the same day that the wall around Jerusalem was dedicated.

Overall, however, vv. 44-47 form the first part of a two-part segue from the dedication of the city wall to the reforms of Nehemiah, and the verses idealize the community. Actually, vv. 44-47 contain two shorter reports, namely vv. 44-46 and v. 47. One might wonder if such business matters were the result of decisions and appointments over an undisclosed period. Each will be discussed in turn.

Verses 44-46 focus on the appointment of supervisors over storage chambers for all sorts of contributions: first fruits (part of the early produce) and tithes (one-tenth of the grain harvest). Verse 44 appeals to laws that required those offerings. (See, for example, Exod 23:16, 19; Exod 34:22, 26; Lev 2:12-14; Lev 23:10, 17, and 20.) Verse 45 says that someone also appointed singers "according to the command of David and Solomon." (That phrase might have in view instructions to musicians at the heads of some of the psalms, although only Psalm 72 mentions Solomon, and Ps 72:20 reads, "The prayers of David son of Jesse are ended.") Verse 46 mentions Asaph, a name that appears in the title of twelve psalms: namely, Psalms 50 and 73–83. [A Stage in the Rise of the Old Testament/Hebrew Bible]

A Stage in the Rise of the Old Testament/Hebrew Bible

Readers will note that this verse presupposes familiarity with much of the Pentateuch and the book of Psalms and recall that Neh 9:9-31 knows about the Law and the Former Prophets, Joshua through 2 Kings. Ezra 5:1-2, 3:2, and 6:14 also know of Haggai and Zechariah, although not necessarily the other Major and Minor Prophets. It is clear that many of the books that eventually formed the Hebrew Bible/Old Testament were treated as authoritative in some sense in Ezra-Nehemiah, although it would be anachronistic to call them "canonical" at that point. That designation per se did not come until the end of the first century CE. Ezra-Nehemiah gives readers a peek into the process along the way.

Verse 47, however, has the prophets Haggai and Zechariah in view, but it attributes to them a concern for the priests and attention to Levites totally missing in both prophetic books. The verse says that the people "gave the daily portions for the singers and the gatekeepers." (Haggai and Zechariah, however, make no such requirement, although both urge the rebuilding of the temple. Mal 3:10, however, does demand that people bring the full tithe [and offerings] to the storehouse of the temple. It sounds more like Neh 12:47 than do Haggai and Zechariah.) Of those offerings, the Levites kept their share (one might even say "took their cut") and passed on the priests' share to them. This verse depicts briefly, in other words, how the redactor/author of Ezra-Nehemiah thought the distribution of offerings should and did work.

An Introduction to the Encounter between Nehemiah and Tobiah, 13:1-3

Like Nehemiah 12:44-47, Nehemiah 13:1-3 connects the verses that follow (4-14) to the narrative about the repairing of the wall

(Neh 1:1–12:43). It opens with the typical redactional phrase "on that day," but the day in question cannot be the day the wall was dedicated because Nehemiah 13:6-7a makes it clear that "before this," Nehemiah had journeyed to Babylon and, "after some time" (two conveniently imprecise temporal indications), returned to Jerusalem, where what follows in 13:7-31 took place. The villain in vv. 4-9, moreover, is not the former main foe Sanballat, but Tobiah "the Ammonite," aided and abetted by the high priest Eliashib.

The narrative function of vv. 1-3 was to articulate the idea of the author that the temple was reserved for the use of returnees only. Tobiah clearly failed on that score; he had not been an exile, nor had he descended from one. In making that point, the three verses continued and made specific to the temple that same motif announced and argued in Nehemiah 9:1–12:47: the temple, like the walled city of Jerusalem itself, was for the returnees only. It was the holy (dedicated) city for the holy (consecrated) people who had returned from Babylon and kept themselves separate from the "local yocals" or non-returnees. The text appeals to the tradition about Balaam, found in Numbers 22–24 and mentioned in Deuteronomy 23:4-5, Joshua 13:22, Joshua 24:9-10, and Micah 6:5. Clearly a well-known tradition, it concerns a seer/prophet who was so clueless about what God wanted him to see (and thus say) that even his donkey could see danger that he, a famous seer, could not.

The particular issue in those traditions with which Nehemiah 13:1-3 dealt, however, was a small part of the content of God's messages the truth-blind seer/prophet could not see. Numbers 21:24 announced a woe upon the Ammonites, and Numbers 21:19 pronounced one against Moab. Appropriating those woes from their ancient context, Nehemiah 13:1-3 applies them to fifth-century Jerusalem, establishing the illegitimacy of any role in Jerusalem for Tobiah the Ammonite. How dare such a disqualified man be allocated space for lodging in God's temple by the high priest Eliashib himself! (We might wonder in response what sort of man dredges up seven-centuries-old issues to justify permanent, ongoing exclusion from God and community. More important, we might ask whether God is really a God who punishes children for the sins of their forebears from seven centuries earlier and not just take Ezra's and Nehemiah's word for it.)

The Reforms of Nehemiah

Example 1—Everything Foreign Cleansed, 13:4-14

The author of Ezra-Nehemiah was now ready to discuss Nehemiah's second mission in Yehud. In the thirty-second year of the reign of Artaxerxes (433), he had returned to Persia for a short but unspecified amount of time. A reader might have expected that return sooner based on Nehemiah's request for permission to travel to Yehud to repair the wall as reported in Nehemiah 2:1-8, a task completed swiftly, but Nehemiah 13:6 says he returned to Persia after a twelve-year stint as governor. (That was quite a sabbatical from his job as wine taster for the king!) [Dates in the Book of Nehemiah]

The new villain in Nehemiah 13:4-14 is Eliashib, the high priest, and the old villain is Tobiah, whom Nehemiah earlier had castigated as an "Ammonite." (Tobiah had appeared in Nehemiah 2, 4, 6, and 7 both as an official and also as a co-conspirator with Sanballat.) In v. 7 the high priest Eliashib is ascribed administrative oversight of the temple. Acting in that capacity, he allowed Tobiah to stay in a room in the temple housing area. The room he chose was one where the priests could store grain, wine, and oil brought and given to the sanctuary by worshipers. Clearly, the room was considered sacred enough to store sacrifices there, and Tobiah was no priest, regardless of whether he really was an Ammonite or that term was just a slur. The layman Nehemiah was outraged since he thought Tobiah was not qualified to sleep where he did. Writing in the first person singular (v. 6), the author has Nehemiah inform the reader that he was not in Jerusalem when that permission was granted, but in Persia. Upon his return to Jerusalem, he discovered what had happened. Taking matters into his own hands, Nehemiah

---

Dates in the Book of Nehemiah

As in the book of Ezra so also in the book of Nehemiah, one of the redactional motifs is the marking of time. Six date markers appear in Nehemiah, namely in Nehemiah 1:1, 2:1, 6:15, 7:73b, 9:1, and 13:6.

Text	Date	Event
1:1	9th month (Chislev) of 19th year of Artaxerxes, 446(?)*	Hanani arrives in Susa
2:1	1st month (Nisan) of 20th year, 445	Nehemiah departs for Jerusalem
6:15	6th month (Elul) of 20th year, 445	Repairs on wall finished
7:73b	7th month (Tishri) of 20th year, 445	Reading of the Law in Jerusalem
9:1	7th month, (Tishri) of 20th year, 445 (implied)	Separation of "Israel" from others
13:6	Month omitted, 32nd year of Artaxerxes, 433	Nehemiah returned to Susa

* Neh 1:1 sets its action in twentieth year of Artaxerxes, i.e., 445. Neh 2:1 also sets its action in the twentieth year of Artaxerxes, but Nisan was the first month in the Babylonian year. D. J. A. Clines suggests plausibly a slight slip of the pen and dates Neh 1:1 four months earlier in year 446.

D. J. A. Clines, "An Introduction to and Notes on Nehemiah," in *HarperCollins Study Bible* (ed. Wayne A. Meeks; New York: HarperCollins, 1993) 717, n. on Neh 1:1.

Nehemiah Cleanses the Temple

167.

Nehemias hace sacar todos los muebles de Tobias de la habitacion que ocupaba en los atrios del Templo.

Phelipe Scio de San Miguel. "Nehemiah Cleanses the Temple," *The Latin Vulgate Bible.* 1794–1797. (Credit: Pitts Theological Library)

Nehemiah cleanses the room in the Temple that was used to house Tobiah's furniture and belongings so that the room may be used once again as a storage place for grain offerings and tithes.

threw out the possessions of Tobiah, had the room cleaned, and had the temple storage places returned to their proper use as storage places—for grain offerings and frankincense.

In the process, Nehemiah discovered that the portion of the offerings for the Levites and the temple singers had not been stored in the temple to pay those groups, so they had returned to their own fields to farm them for their complete living. Nehemiah berated the "officials" for neglecting their duty toward the Levites, called the latter back to the temple, and reinstalled them in service there. What perhaps surfaces here is tension between the priests and the Levites over the perquisites for their services. If so, Nehemiah himself appears to side with the Levites, whom he does not seem to hold guiltless for abandoning their assignments. In any case, the people responded by bringing their tithes to the storehouses. Readers would do well in this connection to remember the charge of the fifth-century prophet Malachi: "Bring the full tithe into the storehouse, so that there may be food in my house . . ." (Mal 3:10). Does Nehemiah 13:12 know and employ that verse, applying it to the Levites and not just the priests? The verse closes with the observation that "all Yehud" brought the tithe. While that phrase clearly meant to include all returnees, it might not have been used with that restrictive meaning. In any case, it is a concluding generalization.

Nehemiah appointed as treasurers the priest Shelemiah, the Levite Pedaiah, and the scribe Zadok. Presumably Shelemiah and Pedaiah represented their groups to receive and distribute the offerings, and the scribe Zadok kept the records, the three assisted by

Hanan ben Zaccur ben Mattaniah. Their duty was to see to the prescribed distribution of the offerings. The situation seems to have been quite stressful to Nehemiah, who cried out to God to remember him for his work in this trying context and to reward him (materially? spiritually?) for his work in settling the issue and bringing a temple crisis to a successful conclusion. Joachim Schaper sees a Persian value and objective at work in these verses: "The committee served both the need for a just collection and distribution of tithes *and* the Achaemenid interest in efficient collection and administration of imperial taxes. It thus ensured a smooth running of temple affairs and contributed to the fiscal administration of the Persian Empire."[4] Perhaps so, but v. 13 says nothing about Persian taxes. It speaks only about an efficient system of collecting offerings.

Example 2—Sabbath Observance Reformed, 13:15-22

The second episode, 13:15-32, is dated simply: "in those days." It was precipitated by Nehemiah's observation that people were violating Sabbath laws. Contra the fourth of the Ten Commandments (Exod 20:8-11), people were working on the Sabbath: treading wine presses, harvesting grain (contra Exod 34:21), and making their animals work (contra Exod 23:12). Presumably, these violations are only illustrative examples, and not an exhaustive list. People were also engaged in the retail selling of food. Out-of-towners from Tyre on the seacoast also brought fish and other merchandise to sell.[5] For Nehemiah, these practices represented a serious threat to the spiritual welfare of the people. He disputed with the "nobles of Yehud" (presumably local officials not receptive to Nehemiah's strictures), and he attempted to prohibit such action by ordering the guards to close the gates at sundown, i.e., to lock down the city on Friday at sundown when Sabbath began and not allow them to reopen until Sunday morning.[6] Not surprisingly since profits were concerned, his mandate did not go unchallenged.

Example 3—Mixed Marriages Condemned, 13:23-27

In 13:23-27 the book returns to a familiar theme, namely mixed marriages. Various earlier passages in Ezra-Nehemiah had dealt with this issue. Specifically, Ezra 9–10 showed the necessity of purging members of the original company of returnees who had removed themselves from the "true" community by marrying local Judean women. Nehemiah 7:5-73a showed the continued viability of that community, guaranteed now by the reconstruction of the wall around the city. Verses 1-3 reported the separation of the

Ammonites and Moabites from the people of Israel. Now vv. 23-27 describes one final ethnic purging of the community by Nehemiah.[7]

They describe a situation typical not just for the aftermath of a series of wars and of displacement, but of human society in many times and places. Jews (descendants of Abraham, even returnees; see Ezra 9–10) had married non-Jews. Yes, and that was nothing new. Nor had it always been forbidden. Nor was it necessarily bad, as the story of Ruth, the ancestress of King David (how more Judean could one be?) proves. Israel's founding monarch, the man after God's own heart, the father of the king who built the temple, had descended from a Moabitess—one of the groups whose presence in the temple Nehemiah so detested. Nehemiah's description of his actions seems to be intended as a boast about his rectitude. Nehemiah excluded wives from (the Philistine city of) Ashdod, Ammon, and Moab, identifiable because they did not speak the language of Yehud. "I contended with them and cursed them and beat some of them and pulled out their hair; and I made them take an oath in the name of God" not to marry or allow their children to marry non-returnees or their descendants (vv. 25-26). [Pulling the Hair/Plucking the Beard] Why not, and for how many generations? Does not his action consist simply of class and other kinds of prejudice (pre-judging)? Are all methods and actions permissible in the defense of the faith? Or must admission to God's household be wide open, and must the conditions be the same for everyone?[8] The author of Isaiah 56:1-8 thought the answer to that question was affirmative.

If this last line of thinking in rebuttal seems extraneous to Nehemiah's situation, one must admit that it is. But so is the

Boaz and Ruth

Charles Lock Eastlake (1793–1865). *Boaz and Ruth*. c. 1853. Oil on canvas. Shipley Art Gallery, Gateshead, Tyne & Wear, UK. (Credit: © Tyne & Wear Archives & Museums/Bridgeman Images)

modern view that if a character in the Bible (or a person today) thinks or says he is acting in God's will, or at least was not condemned for such action, then that makes it so. Who, however, could defend the sexual misconduct and the robbing and killing by Samson as moral? The book of Judges portrays his action simply as revenge, in the pursuit of which he implored God's help. Indeed, the Bible portrays its heroes (except Jesus) as sinners who mix up the good and the bad. Readers are left to think and judge for themselves and act with discrimination.

Next, v. 26 turns to biblical texts in support of Nehemiah's position, citing the example of Solomon who sinned by marrying foreign wives. Readers will note that Solomon is not blamed for polygamy per se, but for marrying foreign wives who did not worship God. First Kings 11:1-13 reports that they tempted him to sin. Does, however, the source of his temptation negate the guilt of his sin? Foreign wives or no, did Solomon not choose to sin? Readers should not absolve Solomon. Nehemiah, therefore, may be accused of cherry picking his issue. Many modern pagans would have more trouble with Solomon's polygamy than with the fact that some of his wives did not worship God. (Gen 2:24 stands at variance with the practice of polygamy too. See [Polygamy and Other Sexual Variations in the Hebrew Bible].) Should believers read Solomon's marital immorality less negatively? No. What Nehemiah goes on to say about God and Solomon, moreover, is pure gospel. That old sinner Solomon was beloved by his

Pulling the Hair/Plucking the Beard

In Neh 13:25 the hero says he pulled out or plucked the hair of men he accused of misconduct. Michael Heltzer addresses Isa 50:6, which speaks of the servant's turning his cheeks to those who pull the hair from his beard, and he notes that Rashi, the great medieval Jewish commentator, calls attention to that text in connection with the verse in Nehemiah. Heltzer also calls attention to a cuneiform text from the fifth year of Darius II, i.e., 420 BCE, which speaks of plucking the hair of the beard as a common feature of ridicule or punishment in the Persian Empire, adding that Artaxerxes himself had ordained that type of punishment.

Michael Heltzer, "The Flogging and Plucking of Beards in the Achaemenid Empire and the Chronology of Nehemiah," *Archaeologische Mitteilungen aus Iran* 28 (1995/6): 305–307.

Phelipe Scio de San Miguel. "Nehemiah Punishes Intermarriage," *The Latin Vulgate Bible*. 1794–1797. (Credit: Pitts Theological Library)

God (despite his sin, not because of it), and God had made him king over all Israel. That glimpse of grace notwithstanding,

Polygamy and Other Sexual Variations in the Hebrew Bible

Despite Gen 2:24 and the clear preference for arranged monogamy in the Hebrew Bible, polygamy and concubinage were known. Abraham took a concubine when he and Sarah could not conceive; Jacob had two wives and two concubines; David took three wives and various concubines; and Solomon took a harem full of both. 1 Kgs 11:3, in fact, says that "among his wives were seven hundred princesses and three hundred concubines," who "turned away his heart" from God. In Judg 19, "a certain Levite" had a concubine who was raped along with the virgin daughter of another man, concubinage being further aggravated by rape. These examples are the best-known cases of variations on marriage, but do not constitute an exhaustive list. Of course, prostitution also was practiced. The Hebrew Bible also frowned on birth control by withdrawal, or spilling one's semen on the ground (Gen 38:9).

Nehemiah pounded the point of exclusivism. As far as he was concerned, marriage with non-returnees amounted to treachery against God, i.e., betrayal of God's intentions to limit worshipers in Jerusalem to the returnees.

Example 4—Priesthood and Temple Purified and Offerings Enabled, 13:28-31

The last four verses constitute not only the fourth example of Nehemiah's reforms but also the conclusion to the book. One of the priests in the temple was the son of Jehoiada, but also the son-in-law of Sanballat the Horonite, another of Nehemiah's opponents. Clearly, Nehemiah did not control who did and who did not become priests or whom the priests married. That process was handled internally by priests, whether Nehemiah the governor approved or not, and they were not as convinced as (Ezra and) Nehemiah that non-returnees could not serve. They had their own lines of descent and their own means of selection/elimination. The issue of legitimacy and primacy appeared elsewhere in the post-exilic community in the form of Aaronic versus other priests. Attempting to trace that struggle is a study in and of itself. This volume is focused solely on Ezra-Nehemiah.

The villain from Nehemiah's perspective again was Eliashib, the high priest and the son-in-law of Sanballat. Nehemiah's aims were limited first to eliminating anything foreign and second to making provisions for the temple: priests, animals, times of observances, and the like. The outcome of the struggles in Nehemiah's time is left open, as is the final outcome of everyone's efforts and life. The book of Nehemiah ends with its hero's prayer: "Remember me, O God, for my good," i.e., for the good things he had done. That is the prayer of a man who has tried hard to be faithful to God. Nehemiah had done what he could; he had stood for what he thought was right—even if this author finds his zeal sometimes to have been wrongly directed. He entrusted himself and the outcome of his efforts to God. Will the reader of this commentary allow Nehemiah's own words be the final evaluation of his career?

CONNECTIONS

1. When people perceive other people as their enemies, almost anything will suffice as an excuse to justify animosity toward them. Nehemiah 13:1 offers a perfect example. It appeals to Deuteronomy 23:3-6, which bars Ammonites and Moabites from "the assembly of the LORD." S. D. McBride identifies this assembly as "the covenant community functioning as a restricted religious, military, and political association."[9] Although McBride wrote those words as a description of Israel as conceived in Deuteronomy, it fits perfectly the community of the post-exilic returnees as conceived in Ezra-Nehemiah. Both Deuteronomy and Ezra-Nehemiah perceive the people of God narrowly and defensively, perhaps with justification. Still, God is not boxed in by peoples' fears, and perfect love casts out fear. (See 1 John 4:18.) Readers of this volume may understand and sympathize with Nehemiah's fears, but those readers should not assume that God was the God only of Nehemiah and other returnees or that they and they alone were the only ones in Yehud who loved and worshiped God.

Suspicion of others can separate and make enemies of people who largely agree with one another and who might benefit from mutual trust and cooperation. Tiny Yehud held a small population that *might* have benefitted from cooperation and trust. Instead, distrust and exclusivism divided the community as various groups vied with others over such power and perks as the Persians permitted locals. Even together they could have posed no viable threat to the hegemony of Persia, but divided they squandered resources and energy vying with one another and thus helped to consolidate Persian control! To be sure, Ezra-Nehemiah portrays those differences as religious, but to this rank outsider living thousands of years later, the differences look more like petty ambitions than moral or theological obstacles. Of course, this writer is not a member of that community but a practicing, Baptist-type Christian who thinks modern Christians should be careful about excluding other children of God from their communities on theological, racial, or socioeconomic grounds, which appear to be among the main bases of divisions within the church as a whole and denominations more particularly.

2. Nehemiah was an able and efficient administrator, and he took especially good care of the temple and offerings given to it for its services, upkeep, and employees. This text seems to show several keys to the proper management of gifts. His appointees represented competing interests or claims upon the gifts and seem to have

worked efficiently. It is always admirable to manage carefully the property and gifts brought to places of worship. The temptation now as in ancient Israel, however, can be to subvert gifts from their intended good functions to something more selfish or even sinister. It might be a good idea for prospective (or active!) ministers to take a course in small business accounting and to insist that all church business be open and above board, not to mention audited by someone. It might also be a good idea for those prospective ministers to take a course in ethics.

3. Work like that described in Nehemiah 13:15-16 is typical for all societies. In a perfect world, all people could rest, worship, and renew themselves on their holy days. Modern life does not allow everyone to do so, however. Emergency workers, pastors and church professionals, and workers in factories like steel mills (whose blast furnaces must run twenty-four hours a day, seven days a week if they operate at all), make it impossible for everyone to take off Sundays or the day appropriate to other religions. When stores are open on Sundays, for example, Sunday may even become a major shopping day. That being so, American Christians live in a context where they might and some others must work on Sunday. What can they do? One possibility is simply to be sure that they set aside regular periods for rest and worship some

Sunday Rest
The hands at the right of the painting, perhaps folded in prayer, indicate deliberate stillness. Larsson's painting suggests a type of quiet and tranquility that is often impossible for us today.

Carl Larsson (1853–1919). *Sunday Rest.* Watercolor on paper. (Credit: © Nationalmuseum, Stockholm, Sweden/Bridgeman Images)

other day. Another is to find a church that worships Saturday or Sunday night. American Jews and Muslims have even more trouble than Christians because it is even more difficult for them to rest and worship on Saturday or Friday.

4. Ethnic discrimination is discrimination, i.e., the act of distinguishing and valuing/devaluing persons on the basis of categories rather than individual worth or merit. It takes many forms, including racial, sexual, national, cultural, and economic as well as

ethnic. It is not simply a matter of valuing; all thinking people must value, must choose, between or even among options. Rather, discrimination often is a matter of valuing concerning matters over which individuals have no control (e.g., race or gender) or that are irrelevant to the issue. Nehemiah might well object to calling his actions "discrimination," but it is difficult to see what else to call it. He valued and privileged returnees, regardless of the actions, intentions, or beliefs of his opponents. Readers need to remember that Judeans who had never been in exile had the same basic claim to Jerusalem and the temple as did the returnees. What they did not have was the backing of the Persian government, but might does not make right.

So it is in modern times as well. The Bible speaks of the common origin of humanity, and at its best the Bible proclaims God's love for all humanity. As noted several times in the commentary, the so-called Third Isaiah thought the new temple in Jerusalem was for all peoples. The New Testament clearly teaches that "God so loved the world that God gave God's only begotten Son to redeem the world." Moreover, the Great Commission commands Christians to "go . . . and make disciples of all nations, baptizing them in the name of the Father and of the Son and of the Holy Spirit, and teaching them to obey everything that [Jesus] commanded them."

Exclusivism and privilege such as claimed by Nehemiah may be understandable on the part of people struggling to live before God in a hostile world, but they are not to be defended, accepted as God's will for people, or practiced by God's people. That is true even although Nehemiah was God's instrument for his time. Like all of God's human instruments, he was fallible.

NOTES

1. So also D. J. A. Clines, "Notes on Nehemiah" in *The HarperCollins Study Bible* (New York: HarperCollins, 1989) 733.

2. In the opening comments to Neh 11:1–12:43, the possibility was raised that that whole passage belonged to Nehemiah's second ministry. Those verses are not usually treated that way, but—aside from Neh 11:27-43—they do not discuss activities of Nehemiah, and vv. 27-43 supply no date for the dedication ceremony. The issue cannot be settled conclusively.

3. Ibid., 733.

4. Joachim Schafer, "The Temple Treasury Committee in the Times of Nehemiah and Ezra," *VT* 47 (1997): 200–206, here 206.

5. Benjamin J. Noonan ("Did Nehemiah Own Tyrian Goods? Trade between Judea and Phoenicia during the Achaemenid Period," *JBL* 130 [2011]: 281–98) raises the issue of whether Phoenicians had established a trade colony in Jerusalem, finding the idea plausible. In any case, the text presents Phoenicians as active in the city's commercial life at an early time.

6. Jeffrey H. Tigay, "*Lifnê Haššabbāṭ* and *ʾAḥar Haššabbāt*—'On the Day before the Sabbath' and 'On the day after the Sabbath' (Nehemiah XIII 19), *VT* 23 (1973): 362–65.

7. For a discussion of these verses, see Lester L. Grabbe, "The Triumph of the Pious or the Failure of the Xenophobes? The Ezra-Nehemiah Reforms and their Nachgeschichte," *Jewish Local Patriotism and Self-Identification in the Graeco-Roman Period* (ed. Siân Jones and Sarah Pierce; JSPSup 31; Sheffield: Sheffield Academic Press, 1998) 50–65, conclusion on p. 64.

8. H. G. M. Williamson (*Ezra, Nehemiah* [WBC 16; Nashville: Thomas Nelson, 1985] 398) notes with dissent that this verse is sometimes used to try to show that Nehemiah flourished earlier than Ezra and that Ezra had not yet undertaken his reform. Instead it appears that it is one more place in which Ezra's reform and that of Nehemiah too were of concern only to returnees who deemed themselves the ones to run the temple and ancient Yehud.

9. S. Dean McBride, notes on Deuteronomy in *The HarperCollins Study Bible* (ed. Wayne A. Meeks; New York: HarperCollins, 1989) 303.

BIBLIOGRAPHY

I. Commentaries

Batten, Loring W. *A Critical and Exegetical Commentary on the Books of Ezra and Nehemiah*. International Critical Commentary, 1913.

Blenkinsopp, Joseph. *Ezra-Nehemiah*. Old Testament Library. Philadelphia: Westminster, 1988.

Boda, Mark J. *1–2 Chronicles. Cornerstone Biblical Commentary*. Carol Stream IL: Tyndale House, 2010.

Bowman, R. A. "Ezra and Nehemiah." *The Interpreter's Bible*. Volume 3. New York, Nashville: Abingdon, 1954. 549–819.

Clines, D. J. A. *Ezra, Nehemiah, Esther*. New Century Bible. Grand Rapids MI: Eerdmans; London: Marshall, Morgan & Scott, 1984.

Coggins, R. J. *The Books of Ezra and Nehemiah*. Cambridge: Cambridge University Press, 1976.

Conti, Marco. *Ancient Christian Commentary on Scripture. Old Testament V. 1–2 Kings, 1–2 Chronicles, Ezra, Nehemiah, Esther*. Downers Grove IL: InterVarsity Press, 2008.

Davies, Gordon F. *Ezra & Nehemiah*. Berit Olam. Collegeville MN: Liturgical Press, 1999.

Emslie, W. A. L. "The First and Second Books of Chronicles." *The Interpreter's Bible*, edited by G. A. Buttrick. New York, Nashville: Abingdon, 1954.

Fensham, F. Charles. *The Books of Ezra and Nehemiah*. The New International Commentary on the Old Testament. Grand Rapids MI: Eerdmans, 1982.

Francisco, Clyde T. "1–2 Chronicles." *The Broadman Bible Commentary*. Volume 3. Nashville: Broadman, 1970.

Hamrick, Emmett Willard. "Ezra-Nehemiah." *The Broadman Bible Commentary*. Volume 3. Nashville: Broadman, 1970. 422–506.

Hill, Andrew E. *1 & 2 Chronicles*. New Application Commentary. Grand Rapids MI: Zondervan, 2003.

Japhet, Sara. *I & II Chronicles*. Old Testament Library. Louisville: Westminster/John Knox, 1993.

Klein, Ralph W. "The Books of Ezra & Nehemiah." *The New Interpreter's Bible Commentary*. Volume 4. Nashville: Abingdon, 1999. 661–851.

Knoppers, Gary N. *1 Chronicles 1–9*. Anchor Bible 12. New York, London, Toronto, Sydney, Auckland: Doubleday, 2003,

———. *1 Chronicles 10–29*. Anchor Bible 12A. New York, London, Toronto, Sydney, Auckland: Doubleday, 2004.

Levering, Matthew. *Ezra & Nehemiah*. Brazos Theological Commentary on the Bible. Grand Rapids MI: Brazos, 2007.

Mason, Rex. *Preaching the Tradition*. Cambridge, New York, Port Chester, Melbourne, Sydney: Cambridge University Press, 1990.

Myers, Jacob M. *Ezra-Nehemiah*. Anchor Bible 14. 2 volumes. Garden City NY: Doubleday, 1965.

Noss, Philip A., and Kenneth J. Thomas. *A Handbook on Ezra and Nehemiah*. UBS Handbook Series. New York: United Bible Societies, 2005.

Slotki, Judah. *Daniel • Ezra • Nehemiah*. Soncino Books of the Bible. London, New York: Soncino Press, 1985.

Sweeney, Marvin A. *TANAK; A Theological and Critical Introduction to the Jewish Bible*. Minneapolis: Fortress, 2012.

Williamson, H. G. M. *Ezra, Nehemiah*. Word Biblical Commentary. Nashville: Thomas Nelson, 1985.

Wijk-Bos, Johanna W. H. van. *Ezra, Nehemiah, and Esther*. Westminster Bible Companion. Louisville: Westminster John Knox, 1998.

II. Additional Works

Ackroyd, Peter R. *Exile and Restoration*. Old Testament Library. Philadelphia: Westminster, 1968.

Albertz, Rainer. *A History of Israelite Religion in the Old Testament Period. II. From the Exile to the Maccabees*. Translated by John Bowden. Old Testament Library. Louisville: Westminster John Knox, 1994.

———. *Die Exilszeit. 6. Jahrhundert v. Chr.* Biblische Enzyklopädie 7. Berlin, Cologne: Kohlhammer, 2001.

Becker, Joachim. *Der Ich-Bericht des Nehemiabuchs als chronistische Gestaltung*. Forschung zur Bible 87; Würtburg: Echhter Verlag, 1998.

Berquist, Jon L. *Judaism in Persia's Shadow. A Social and Historical Approach*. Minneapolis: Fortress, 1995.

Blenkinsopp, Joseph. *Judaism: The First Phase. The Place of Ezra and Nehemiah in the Origins of Judaism*. Grand Rapids MI: Eerdmans, 2009.

Boda, Mark J., and Paul L. Redditt, editors. *Unity and Disunity in Ezra-Nehemiah; Redaction, Rhetoric, and Reader*. Hebrew Bible Monographs 17. Sheffield: Sheffield Phoenix Press, 2008.

Bromiley, Geoffrey, editor. *The International Standard Bible Encyclopedia*. 4 volumes. Grand Rapids MI: Eerdmans, 1979–1988.

Brown, Francis, S. R. Driver, and Charles A. Briggs. *Hebrew and English Lexicon*. Peabody MA: Hendrickson, 1979.

Carter, Charles E. *The Emergence of Yehud in the Persian Period: A Social and Demographic Study*. Journal for the Study of the Old Testament Supplement Series 294. Sheffield: Sheffield Academic Press, 1999.

Davies, Philip R. *On the Origins of Judaism*. London, Oakville: Equinox, 2011.

Eskenazi, Tamara Cohn. *In an Age of Prose*. Society of Biblical Literature Monograph Series 36. Atlanta: Scholars Press, 1988.

Freedman, David Noel, editor. *The Anchor Bible Dictionary*. 6 volumes. New York, London, Toronto, Sydney, Auckland: Doubleday, 1992.

Frei, Peter, and Klaus Koch. *Reicshidee and Reichsorganisation in Perserreich*. Second edition. Orbis Biblicus et Orientalis 55. Freiburg: Universitätsverlag Freiburg, 1996.

Fried, Lisbeth S., editor. *Was I Esdras First? An Investigation into the Priority and Nature of 1 Esdras.* Society of Biblical Literature Ancient Israel and Its Literature 7. Atlanta: Society of Biblical Literature, 2011.

Gerstenberger, Erhard S. *Israel in the Persian Period; The Fifth and Fourth Centuries B.C.E.* Translated by Siegfried S. Schatzmann. Biblical Encyclopedia 8. Atlanta: Society of Biblical Literature, 2011.

Grabbe, Lester L. *Ezra-Nehemiah.* Old Testament Readings. London and New York: Routlege, 1998.

Hoglund, Kenneth G. *Achaemenid Imperial Administration in Syria-Palestine and the Missions of Ezra and Nehemiah.* Society of Biblical Literature Dissertation Series 125. Atlanta: Scholars Press, 1992.

Kalimi, Isaac. *An Ancient Israelite Historian; Studies in the Chronicler, His Time, Place and Writing.* Studia Semitica Neerlanica. Assen: Kononklijke Van Gorcum, 2005.

———, editor. *New Perspectives on Ezra-Nehemiah; History and Historiography. Text, Literature, and Interpretation.* Winona Lake IN: Eisenbrauns, 2012.

Lipschits, Oded, Gary N. Knoppers, and Rainer Albertz, editors. *Judah and the Judeans in the Fourth Century B.C.E.* Winona Lake IN.: Eisenbrauns, 2007.

———, and Manfred Oeming, editors. *Judah and the Judean in the Persian Period.* Winona Lake IN: Eisenbrauns, 2006.

———, Gary N. Knoppers, and Rainer Albertz, editors. *Judah and the Judeans in the Fourth Century B.C.E.* Winona Lake IN.: Eisenbrauns, 2007.

Pritchard, James B., editor. *The Ancient Near East: An Anthology of Texts and Pictures.* Princeton and Oxford: Princeton University Press, 2011.

Sakenfeld, Katherine Doob, editor. *The New Interpreter's Dictionary of the Bible.* Nashville: Abingdon, 2006–2009.

Smith-Christopher, Daniel L. *A Biblical Theology of Exile.* Overtures to Biblical Theology. Minneapolis: Fortress, 2002.

Sweeney, Marvin A. *Tanak: A Theological and Critical Introduction to the Jewish Bible.* Minneapolis: Fortress, 2012.

Woude, A. S. van der. The *World of the Old Testament.* Translated by Sierd Woudstra. Grand Rapids MI: Eerdmans, 1989.

INDEX OF MODERN AUTHORS

INDEX OF SCRIPTURES

INDEX OF SIDEBARS AND ILLUSTRATIONS

INDEX OF TOPICS

Made in the USA
Monee, IL
18 September 2023

42952388R00212